THE GARDEN BOOK

THE GARDEN BOOK

Phaidon Press Limited
Regent's Wharf
All Saints Street
London N1 9PA

First published 2000
© 2000 Phaidon Press Limited

ISBN 0 7148 3985 X

A CIP catalogue record for this book is available from the British Library

Printed in China

LIST OF ABBREVIATIONS

ARG = Argentina
ASL = Australia
AUS = Austria
BAH = Bahamas
BAR = Barbados
BEL = Belgium
BR = Brazil
CAN = Canada
CH = Chile
CHN = China
CI = Canary Islands
COL = Colombia
CR = Costa Rica
CRO = Croatia
CU = Cuba
CZ = Czechoslovakia
DK = Denmark
EC = Ecuador
EG = Egypt
FIN = Finland
FR = France
GER = Germany
GR = Greece
HUN = Hungary
IN = India
IR = Iran (formerly Persia)
IRE = Ireland
IS = Israel
IT = Italy
JAP = Japan
KOR = Korea
LAO = Laos
MAR = Martinique
MEX = Mexico
MOR = Morocco
NL = Netherlands
NOR = Norway
NZ = New Zealand
POL = Poland
POR = Portugal
ROM = Romania
RUS = Russia
SA = South Africa
SL = Sri Lanka
SP = Spain
S VIET = South Vietnam
SW = Switzerland
SWE = Sweden
TRK = Turkey
UG = Uganda
UK = United Kingdom
UKR = Ukraine
USA = United States of America

THE GARDEN BOOK is a comprehensive illustrated survey of 500 of the world's most influential garden makers – designers, patrons and owners – and their gardens. The selection gives an unrivalled overview of the world's gardens and landscapes, from ancient times to the present day. Garden design is a large-scale, time-consuming artform, with relatively few celebrated *auteurs* – such as Capability Brown, Kobori Enshu, Gertrude Jekyll and André le Nôtre. **THE GARDEN BOOK** brings these and many lesser-known but highly deserving garden makers to wider attention. It ranges over centuries and across continents, to reflect times and places when garden innovation and creativity were at their height: Ancient China and Japan; Renaissance Italy; seventeenth-century France and Holland; eighteenth-century Britain; and the USA in the twentieth century. Each entry is illustrated by a sublime setpiece view of the designer's finest garden and arranged in A–Z order, with an accompanying commentary to place both garden and maker in stylistic and historical context. **THE GARDEN BOOK** helps us to discover the rich artistic inheritance of this ever-changing artform.

The 500 Designers page 4 Glossary of garden terms and styles page 504 Directory of gardens page 506

Aalto Alvar

Villa Mairea

Inscribed in a simple forest clearing, an asymmetrical pool recalls the contours of a lake. The timber screen of the porch on the villa reflects the rhythms of the tree trunks in the forest. This stunning design, which is simultaneously organic and modern, is extended inside the villa with, for example, the irregular staircase balustrade which echoes the view out on to the forest. The design of the Villa Mairea and its garden refers to the metaphorical opposition between artificial and natural forms, as well as to the energy that originates from their union. Much admired since its completion in 1941, the Villa Mairea constitutes a link between the national Finnish Romantic tradition and the Rational-Constructivist Movement of the early twentieth century, to which the architect and designer Alvar Aalto was committed. Apart from his numerous furniture designs, Aalto realized over 200 buildings in his lifetime which makes him the second most productive architect of the twentieth century, after Frank Lloyd Wright.

☛ **Asplund, Church, Scarpa, F L Wright**

Alvar Aalto. b Kuortane (FIN), 1898. **d** Helsinki (FIN), 1976. **Villa Mairea**, Noormarkku (FIN), 1938–41.

Abd al-Rahman III Caliph of Cordoba Madinat al-Zahra

Built high above Cordoba, the palace city of Madinat al-Zahra draws its distinctive design from two primary sources of inspiration – the Cordoban Umayyad tradition of building garden estates, and the sophistication of the garden palaces brought by the Muslim rulers of Spain from the Abbasid courts of Samarra, Iraq. Madinat al-Zahra was built on a series of levels. Only three

gardens are evident: the Prince's Garden, the Upper Garden and the Lower Garden. Water channels, four-part parterres and paved walkways with axially aligned square pools typify the symmetry and contained intimacy of the Islamic garden tradition found at this site. Madinat al-Zahra served as the model for all subsequent Islamic royal palaces and capital cities in Spain, especially in the

region of Al-Andalus (southern Spain). All the important garden palaces of this area – including the Alhambra – were rebuilt on elevated sites which yield spectacular vistas over irrigated landscapes and productive farm lands.

☛   Allah, Moorish Governors, Muhammad V, Nazarite

Abd al-Rahman III (Caliph of Cordoba). Active c930s. **Madinat al-Zahra (Medina Azahara)**, Cordoba (SP), c936.

Aberconway 2nd Baron Bodnant

The Pin Mill, built c1740 as a summerhouse, was moved from Woodchester in Gloucestershire and reconstructed on the Canal Terrace in 1938. This was the last of the twentieth-century improvements made by Henry Duncan McClaren, later 2nd Baron Aberconway. His other major additions, made from 1904–14, include the five Italianate terraces in front of the house. These are a reflection of the enormous influence of Italian Renaissance design on the gardens of Edwardian Britain. At Bodnant the site was perfect, and the terraces have spectacular views out over the River Conway to Snowdon in the distance. The gardens were originally conceived in 1875 by Henry Pochin MP, with help from the designer Edward Milner. One of their greatest triumphs was the Dell, a wild, informal valley garden down which cascades the River Hiraethlyn. The garden is also significant as a recipient of early introductions from plant hunters such as Ernest Wilson, Frank Kingdon-Ward and George Forrest.

☛ Barry, Colchester, Rochford, Savill, Sitwell

6

Henry Duncan McClaren, 2nd Baron Aberconway. b Denbigh (UK), 1879. d (UK), 1953. **Bodnant**, Gwynedd (UK), 1904–14.

Acton Arthur

La Pietra

A remarkable collection of antique statues enliven the succession of balustrades, terraces, shaded groves, fountains and pools of this refined garden. Though Baroque in style, La Pietra's garden was laid out between 1908 and 1910 by Henri Duchêne for Arthur Acton, a leading light in the set of learned and rich English men and women who colonized the Florentine hills and surrounding Tuscan countryside at the end of the nineteenth century. Acton's learning and deep love of Italian aesthetics inspired him to recreate this ideal garden, loosely basing his scheme on plans of the original seventeenth-century gardens for La Pietra, created by Cardinal Capponi (who was also responsible for La Gamberaia). Unfortunately these had been lost to the irresistible fashion of the landscape garden which swept through Europe in the nineteenth century. In this instance a great wrong committed in the name of the English garden was put right by an Englishman's efforts.

☛ **Capponi, Harrild, Peto, Sitwell**

Arthur Acton. Active end nineteenth century. **La Pietra**, Florence, Tuscany (IT), 1908–10.

Aislabie John

Studley Royal

A garden composition of abstract beauty, the early eighteenth-century water garden at Studley Royal consists of a lake, a canal and a series of formal ponds that ornament the floor of the steep-sided Skell Valley in Yorkshire. Small garden buildings, including a banqueting house by Colen Campbell, adorn the valley sides, creating a variety of vistas. Unlike other early landscape gardens, the natural topography at Studley Royal takes precedence over the designer's architectural impulse, heralding the Picturesque Movement later in the century. The climax of the garden, reached via a ride along one edge of the valley, is the surprise view from Anne Boleyn's Seat towards the ruins of medieval Fountains Abbey. Recent restoration by the National Trust has reinstated a sense of the variety of episodic effects created by John Aislabie to manipulate visitors' emotions.

☛ W Aislabie, Bridgeman, Cane, Jencks, Kent

John Aislabie. b nr York (UK), 1670. d (UK), 1741. **Studley Royal**, North Yorkshire (UK), 1693–1741.

Aislabie William

Hackfall

The romantic tower of Mowbray Castle peeps above the treeline in the wooded landscape garden at Hackfall, created in the mid-eighteenth century by local landowner and MP William Aislabie, who had assisted his father in creating the formal water garden at nearby Studley Royal. The atmospheric, wooded gorge that descends steeply to the cascading River Ure was originally purchased for its agricultural potential, but William Aislabie instead made it into a landscape garden ornamented with some forty built features. Narrow paths lead to seats and structures such as Fisher's Pavilion (named after Aislabie's head gardener) with dramatic views up and down the river. Overlooking the scene and boasting dramatic views is Mowbray Point, a terraced banqueting house. From the late eighteenth century Hackfall Wood became a popular destination for Picturesque tourists, including William Wordsworth and J M W Turner, but most of the garden buildings are now derelict.

☛ J Aislabie, Gilpin, Knight, Wordsworth

William Aislabie. b (UK), 1700. d (UK), 1781. Hackfall, North Yorkshire (UK), 1749–67.

Akbar Emperor

Fatehpur Sikri

The main courtyard and huge quartered tank of Emperor Akbar's palace at Fatehpur Sikri near the River Jumna, not far from Agra, was designed in 1571 by the emperor himself. Thousands of stonemasons and workmen were employed from around the realm, resulting in a fusion of rich Hindu and Indian decorative styles with grand architectural elements reminiscent of Persian architecture. Some of the most advanced water systems of the Mughal period were installed. Aqueducts were ingeniously incorporated in walls and paving. This is an innovative reworking of the classic *chahar-bagh*, and the earliest form of island retreat. The palace buildings are laced together by a series of terraces and pavilions, and pools are scattered across a broad area, creating a series of wide vistas within the complex. The overall effect is of an airy, warm and elegantly open-planned garden palace – a dramatic contrast to the intimacy and secrecy of a high-walled Persian courtyard garden.

☛ Ineni, Jahangir, Musgrave, Sangram Singh, Sennacherib

Emperor Akbar. Reigned 1556–1605 (IN). **Fatehpur Sikri**, nr Agra (IN), 1571.

Albert & Isabella Archduke & Archduchess Mariemont

When Jan Bruegel painted this picture of the garden at Mariemont around 1608 it was in the second of the many forms that it took over the centuries. The Archduke Albert and his wife Isabella, daughter of Philip II of Spain, had arrived to govern The Netherlands in 1598 and it was their influence that determined its Spanish style. They were responsible for the garden until it was abandoned in 1633 when Isabella died. Mariemont, or Mary's Mount, was originally named after Mary of Hungary, the widowed sister of Emperor Charles V. She laid out extensive terraced gardens in the Italian style and planted them with French roses in the middle of the sixteenth century. After Mary's death the garden had lain abandoned until the arrival of Albert and Isabella. In 1668 Louis XIV of France appropriated the neglected estate. Nearly one hundred years later, in 1756, Charles of Lorraine rebuilt the castle and transformed the gardens in the French classical style. However, none of these gardens, or the castle, survived the French Revolution.

☞ Arenberg, Balat, Joséphine, Ligne, Philip II

Archduke Albert & Archduchess Isabella. Reigned (NL), 1598–1621. **Mariemont**, Hainaut (BEL), painted by Jan Bruegel, c1608.

Aldington Peter

Turn End

At Peter Aldington's own house at Turn End he has realized a happy transition from house to garden via this enclosed courtyard with its pool and gnarled Robinia pseudoacacia. The fact that the three houses and their gardens at the Turn End development were designed as a piece by the same architect, and that this was considered revolutionary even in the 1960s, is symptomatic of the classic division between the landscape and architectural professions. Peter Aldington is an accomplished and imaginative gardener as well as a Modernist architect. The half-acre grounds are packed with incident and feature several separate areas, including a daisy garden and a formal box courtyard planted with different brightly coloured annuals each year. A variety of mature shrubs and trees provides a setting for sculptures. A gravelled area called No-Mans is intensively gardened, with herbaceous perennials, grasses, troughs of alpines and pans of houseleeks.

☛ Crowe, Jellicoe, Nordfjell, Tunnard

Peter Aldington. b Preston, Lancashire (UK), 1933. **Turn End**, Haddenham, Buckinghamshire (UK), 1964.

Allah

Qur'anic Description of Paradise

Illustrated in this vision of Paradise as a quartered garden, or *chahar-bagh*, is a design form that is found in virtually all the gardens of Islam. The ethereal functions and distinctive designs of the Islamic garden and courtyard derive from two primary sources of inspiration – the ancient Persian garden tradition and, on a higher plane, the reward promised to the Faithful. Other elements seen in this painting remind us of the myth of the Garden of Eden: a walled space (or *pairi-daeza*, in ancient Persian) containing the Fountain of Life at its centre, ever-fruitful trees symbolizing the Tree of Life, flowering plants and four unstalling rivers. All these elements are linked to the imagery of ancient Mesopotamia. With time, these Paradise elements became universal to all Semitic myth. The Qur'anic description of the Garden of Allah includes a series of dark green enclosures planted with date palms and all kinds of fruit; it is crossed by rivers of sweet milk, honey and wine, with a central fountain gushing with water.

☛ Almohad, Judeo-Christian God, Muhammad V, Nazarite

13

Allah. Qur'anic Description of Paradise, as depicted in *A Vision of Paradise and The Deeds of Ali (cousin and son-in-law of the prophet Muhammed) and His Companions*, Persia, miniature painting, 1686.

Allason Thomas & Abraham Robert   Alton Towers

A conifer collection provides the backdrop to the pristine gravel paths, which contrast with the manicured lawn and ostentatious display of bedding. Laid out from 1814, and cluttered with many diverse features, including a two-tiered megalith, a three-storeyed cast-iron prospect tower, and a Swiss cottage for a blind harper, this romantic valley site became infamous as the early nineteenth century's most inharmonious garden. Abraham added a series of exotic conservatories and in the late 1820s John Claudius Loudon, the leading garden writer of the day, commented that the garden was 'the work of a morbid imagination joined to the command of unlimited resources'. Perhaps Allason's greatest influence was to force early Victorian garden designers to think about the congruity of features in the landscape. In the 1840s Alexander Forsyth, the head gardener, planted the conifers and rhododendrons, which introduced a degree of harmony by removing the sharp contrasts between the features.

☞ **Barron, Barry, Lainé, Loudon, Tyers**

14

Thomas Allason. b 1790. **d** 1852. **Robert Abraham. b** 1773. **d** 1850. **Alton Towers**, Staffordshire (UK), 1814.

Allen Ralph

Prior Park

The view from the house down to the Palladian bridge and the lake is the triumph of Prior Park. The house at Prior Park was designed for Ralph Allen by John Wood the Elder in 1735. The pastoral simplicity of the undulating greensward, with livestock grazing, evokes a Virgilian idyll that combines well with the classical mansion. Allen kept the built ornamentation in this landscape to a minimum, given the singular drama of the main vista, which sets a miniature Elysium against panoramic views over Bath. He devised a simple circular walk starting at the house terrace and skirting the lake. Nearer the house is a wilderness area, possibly created with first-hand advice from Alexander Pope, with a rococo sham bridge and Mrs Allen's grotto. It is thought that Capability Brown may have advised Allen on the transformation of the original park into the fine English landscape that we see today.

☞ Brown, Grenville-Temple, Kent, Monet, Pope

Ralph Allen. b Bath (UK), c1694. d Prior Park, Bath (UK), 1764. **Prior Park**, Bath (UK), 1734–64.

Almohad Empire   Menara Gardens

The Menara gardens and pavilions are enchanting reminders of the exquisite garden palaces of the Alhambra and Generalife in Granada. During the twelfth and thirteenth centuries, under the rule of the Almohad Empire (1130–1269), the Islamic arts and culture of Andalusian Spain spread to the cities of North Africa. Built just outside Marrakesh, with the Atlas mountains in the distance, Menara was a large agricultural country estate, or *agdal*, for the élite. Such gardens were primarily built for pleasure, but vegetables and flowers were planted to supply the royal household, and the extensive fruit orchards – mainly date-palm and olive – provided income as well. Overlooking a vast manmade lake, or water tank, this blush-pink garden pavilion was a pleasure retreat for the Saadien Dynasty. The tank provided water for the fields and was also used by members of the court for swimming and boating.

☞ Asaf Khan IV, Majorelle, Muhammad V, Nazarite, Sangram Singh

16

Almohad Empire. 1130–1269. **Menara Gardens**, Marrakesh (MOR), twelfth century.

Ando Tadao

Garden of Fine Arts

Lying on the base of a long pool, Monet's *Water-lilies* shimmer under a shallow layer of clear water. All around, the concrete lines of the walls, large panes of glass and sheets of flowing water carve up the sky and delineate the space. Further on are more reproductions of some of art history's most revered masterpieces (Leonardo's *Last Supper*, Seurat's *La Grande Jatte* and so on) providing sources of colour and texture in this dramatic open-air structure of concrete and water. Highly durable, these life-size reproductions are photographs transposed and fired on to ceramic panels. Tadao Ando is one of the most influential architects of the late twentieth century. In this garden he has applied the architectural theories that are so beautifully expressed in his churches and temples. Ando is a self-taught, widely travelled figure with a highly independent attitude to building. Zen philosophy and traditional Japanese architecture inform his constant concern with landscape and the elements, enabling him to describe the essential void and stillness.

☞ Barragán, Halprin, Libeskind, Suzuki, F L Wright

Tadao Ando. b Osaka (JAP), 1941. **Garden of Fine Arts**, Kyoto (JAP), 1994.

André Edouard

La Roseraie du Val-de-Marne

The climbing roses trained over this trellis arbour are among more than 3,000 varieties to be seen growing in this garden in the French town L'Haÿ-les-Roses (renamed in 1910 by its townsfolk after the garden itself). In 1892, Jules Gravereaux commissioned the landscape architect Edouard André to design the 1.7 hectares (4 acres) with beds, trellises, walls, arbours and underground walkways, to provide a garden for wild and rare shrub roses – notably specimens saved from the rose gardens of the Empress Joséphine at Malmaison. André is also well known for his work at other gardens around the world, including Sefton Park in Liverpool, and for redesigning the gardens of the Villa Borghese in Rome. He was also a scholar, and wrote *L'Art des jardins: Traité générale de la composition des parcs et jardins* (1879), about the classification and principles of garden design.

☛ **Barillet-Deschamps, Forestier, Joséphine, G S Thomas**

Edouard André. b Bourges (FR), 1840. d 1911. **La Roseraie du Val-de-Marne**, L'Haÿ-les-Roses, nr Paris (FR), 1892.

Anhalt-Dessau Leopold Friedrich Franz von   Schloss Wörlitz

This classic view of the Temple of Venus (1794), taken from the Wolf Bridge at Wörlitz, was completely overgrown by *Rhododendron ponticum* by the end of the Communist years in East Germany. Wörlitz is the single-most important landscape garden in central Europe – breath-takingly beautiful and blessed with an apparently endless number of delightful features. Prince Franz travelled widely in England, sometimes taking as many as three gardeners with him. He frequently drew inspiration from gardens such as Stourhead, Stowe and Claremont. Indeed, this temple was built in imitation of Colen Campbell's Temple of Venus at Hall Barn. Prince Franz sought to both beautify the landscape and to improve his estates. Wörlitz extends to about 120 hectares (296 acres), of which some 80 hectares (198 acres) are lakes and agricultural areas which have been worked into the parkland. But his entire principality, some 40 km long, was designed as one continuous landscape – stunningly beautiful even 200 years later.

☞   Bridgeman, Grenville-Temple, Hoare, Pückler-Muskau

Leopold Friedrich Franz von Anhalt-Dessau. b (GER), 1740. **d** (GER), 1817. **Schloss Wörlitz**, Halle (GER), 1765–1817.

Arakawa & Gins

Site of Reversible Destinies

In a vast oval bowl that sits in the landscape like a geological accident, a world of small hills, bizarre constructions and wonky paths on uneven ground awaits the visitor. The Site of Reversible Destinies in Kyoto is meant to overturn one's perceptions and destabilize physically and conceptually – only to eventually 'open a new horizon'. Here, as in a traditional Japanese stroll garden, on each turn one will encounter a new vista: ranges of half-sunken kitchen units colliding with upturned sofas, flat staircases or tiled roofs on the floor. Japanese-born conceptual artist Shusaku Arakawa, now based in New York with his American partner, writer and artist Madeleine Gins, has been given the opportunity to take the concept of deconstruction on to a new plane. Using the traditional garden device of the labyrinth in a series of physical encounters, they add a textual layer with a set of 'Directions for Use' in a leaflet distributed to each visitor.

☞ Chand Saini, Hamilton Finlay, Hideyoshi, Miró, Tschumi

Arakawa & Gins. Shushaku Arakawa. b Nagoya (JAP), 1936. **Madeline Gins. b** New York, NY (USA), 1941. **Site of Reversible Destinies**, Kyoto (JAP), 1995.

Arenberg Antoine d'

Château d'Enghien

In 1606 Charles d'Arenberg acquired Enghien from Henry IV of France. Antoine, the sixth of his twelve sons, became a Capuchin monk and took the title of Père Charles. It was he who began the work of laying out a vast, complex park of compartments at Enghien. The garden was designed largely by Père Charles and his nephew Philippe-Francois, 1st Duke of Arenberg. Enghien was described by Mademoiselle de Montpensier in 1650 as the most beautiful garden in the world. Engravings by Romeyn de Hooghe show parterres with four *cabinets*, a parterre of flowers with orange trees, a maze and an amphitheatre. The triumphal arch, the Slave Gate, is still there today and the Pavillon Chinois and the Pavillon aux Toiles are newly restored. An L-shaped canal and two lakes, one the Etang du Miroir, remain, overlooked by some good statues. In the woodland is the moated Pavillon des Sept Etoiles, at the centre of seven radiating rides each bordered by a different species of tree.

☞ Bingley, Cockerell, Le Nôtre

21

Antoine d'Arenberg (Pére Charles). **b** Brussels (BEL), 1593. **d** 1669. **Château d'Enghien**, Enghien (BEL), 1606–.

Armstrong Lord   Cragside

Looking up the stream through an informal, picturesque landscape, the woodland provides a dramatic setting for the imposing house designed by Norman Shaw. Lord Armstrong, the creator of the garden, took his inspiration from the *Himalayan Journals*. Published by the plant hunter Sir Joseph Hooker in 1852, the book contains romantic descriptions of the wild, rugged scenery of the then Kingdom of Sikkim. On a naturally dramatic hillside setting, Armstrong embarked on a recreation of a part of a Himalayan valley in Britain, and by the 1890s he had planted 'several hundred thousands' of rhododendrons. Such imitation of nature was part of the late-Victorian movement away from the formality of bedding schemes and ornate terraces towards a much more natural form of gardening, often called 'wild gardening'. This approach, as promoted by William Robinson, took full advantage of the hardy-but-exotic plants that were being brought back by the plant hunters from across the world.

☞ Cook, Rhodes, Robinson, Savill

William George, Lord Armstrong. b Newcastle (UK), 1810. **d** (UK), 1900. **Cragside**, Northumberland (UK), c1890s.

Asaf Khan IV

Nishat Bagh

True to its name, this 'garden of gladness' is the most playful and fanciful of the Mughal gardens in India. Breathtakingly set within a landscape of awesome beauty, Nishat Bagh lies at the base of the blue, rocky mountainsides between Shalimar and the city of Srinigar and on the shores of Lake Dal. This non-royal garden, built by Jahangir's brother-in-law, was originally composed of twelve terraces, each one symbolizing a sign of the zodiac. Feeding the cascades is a wide canal running the length of the garden. As the garden has a far steeper ascent than any other Mughal garden, the features have a more dramatic and lively effect: the water cascades faster, the sizes of the chutes are greater. This garden is much louder and visually ostentatious – a radical move away from the subtle and sublime tranquility of most other Mughal garden settings. The site is superb – and a crowning jewel of the Kashmir.

☛ Akbar, Almohad, Gustafson, Jahangir, Nazarite, Sangram Singh

Asaf Khan IV. d (IN), 1641. **Nishat Bagh**, Kashmir (IN), 1625.

Ashikaga Takauji

Tenryu-ji

Framed by the veranda, this perfectly still autumn glade is like a Chinese landscape painting of the Sung era. The repeated horizontals of pond, islands, bridge and waterfall are specifically designed to evoke the spatial depth of a painted landscape in the Sung style. Indeed, Tenryu-ji's affiliations with Chinese visual arts are so strong that some scholars suggest that it may have been

designed by a Chinese hand. Tenryu-ji was commissioned by the first Ashikaga shogun, Takauji, who had forced Emperor Gosaga into exile. He was inspired by the influential state priest and Zen master Muso Kokushi, who suggested that the only way to appease the spirit of the old Emperor, who had died in exile, was to establish a Zen temple and garden in the grounds of the Imperial Palace.

Already abbot of nearby Saiho-ji, which he had designed and built, Muso Kokushi became master of Tenryu-ji, though it is unlikely he had anything to do with its design.

☛ **Ashikaga Yoshimasa, Ashikaga Yoshimitsu, Kokushi**

Ashikaga Takauji. b 1305. **d** 1358. **Tenryu-ji**, Kyoto (JAP), 1249–1388.

Ashikaga Yoshimasa   Ginkaku-ji (Silver Pavilion)

It is not known whether the name of this magnificent edifice reflects a wish that was never realized or whether the edifice was at one time actually silver-plated. This palace was converted into a Zen temple after Yoshimasa's death. Modelled on the old Saiho-ji garden, the Silver Pavilion gardens are also divided between a mossy hillside garden and a lower pond. This small expanse of water has an intricate shoreline and a scattering of islands and peninsulas. One of the main features of the hillside garden is a 3 m (10 ft) waterfall called 'Spring in which the Moon Washes'. Like his grandfather Yoshimitsu, builder of the Golden Pavilion, Yoshimasa – the eighth Ashikaga shogun – retired early from government, hoping to give himself entirely to the practice of the arts he loved: literature, garden-making and the tea ceremony, of which he was an early advocate. But he had to contend with years of civil war which greatly slowed the building of the Silver Pavilion complex.

☛ Ashikaga Takauji, Ashikaga Yoshimitsu, Kokushi, Soami

Ashikaga Yoshimasa. b (JAP), 1435. d (JAP), 1490. Ginkaku-ji (Silver Pavilion), Kyoto (JAP), 1473.

Ashikaga Yoshimitsu

Kinkaku-ji (The Golden Pavilion)

Bathed in a golden haze, the magnificent pavilion looks out on to a tranquil lake divided by a peninsula. In the near part is a busy archipelago of 'islands' made up of huge distinctive rocks – mostly individual gifts from vassals, a common practice at the end of the fourteenth century. The outer part of the lake is virtually empty, which creates a great impression of space and distance. It was extensively used for boating and the garden is to a certain extent designed to be viewed from the water. The third Ashikaga shogun, Yoshimitsu, unlike his ancestors, was a refined and spiritual man. A sincere devotee of Zen Buddhism, then a new religion, he retired early from the burdens of government and moved to his new estate in 1394. In 1408 Yoshimitsu invited Emperor Gokomatsu to stay at the Golden Pavilion. The magnificence of this visit became the stuff of legend. At Yoshimitsu's death the estate was converted into a Buddhist temple, which it remains to this day.

☛ Ashikaga Takauji, Ashikaga Yoshimasa

Ashikaga Yoshimitsu. b (JAP), 1358. **d** (JAP), 1408. **Kinkaku-ji (The Golden Pavilion)**, Kyoto (JAP), established 1220.

26

Asplund Gunnar

Woodland Cemetery

Hidden away in dense woodland, a modest chapel awaits the mourners. The surrounding spruces are over twice its height and they are echoed in the twelve simple concrete columns of the ante-room. Further on, the landscape dramatically opens into a vast expanse of grass sweeping towards an artificial hill on which stands a monumental cross. This deliberately biblical landscape is completed by a modernistic temple-like hall and by the Faith, Hope and Charity chapels. A profound sense of balance and peace emanates from Asplund's landscaped complex at the Stockholm cemetery. Here the geometric framework of Modernism blends happily with the intrinsic values of the landscape. Asplund is widely recognized as one of the few architects of the early twentieth century to have achieved this synthesis. At that time garden-makers and the first ecologists tended to reject modern architecture, while modern architects shunned the models of the traditional home and garden.

☞ Aalto, Brongniart, Le Corbusier, Scarpa, F L Wright

Gunnar Asplund. b Stockholm (SWE), 1885. **d** Stockholm (SWE), 1940. **Woodland Cemetery**, Enskede, Stockholm (SWE), 1935–40.

Assurbanipal King   Nineveh Palace

This relief captures the courtly pursuits of King Assurbanipal as he reclines in his garden palace at Nineveh. Date palms, pine trees and pomegranates line this garden terrace, and trellised overhead we see heavily laden grape vines. Clearly, this is a palace room outdoors. Here, the royal lovers celebrate victory, and feast and drink from bejewelled vessels. This is an earthly paradise filled with song and vibrant colour – where musicians entertain, birds enliven the boughs above and lush green plantings soothe the eye. Two garden traditions were developed during this period: the enclosed terraced gardens within a palace complex, such as we see here; and the expansive walled royal garden parks used primarily for the hunt. Watercourses and channels quartering the gardens and lavish open-air pavilions are key components of these gardens of the ancient Near East. This relief gives us a vivid picture of how gardens were used and enjoyed, yet also shows us how perfectly the designers crafted their sacred recreational spaces.

☛ **Allah, Babur, Ineni, Khosrow II Parvis, Sennacherib, Thutmosis**

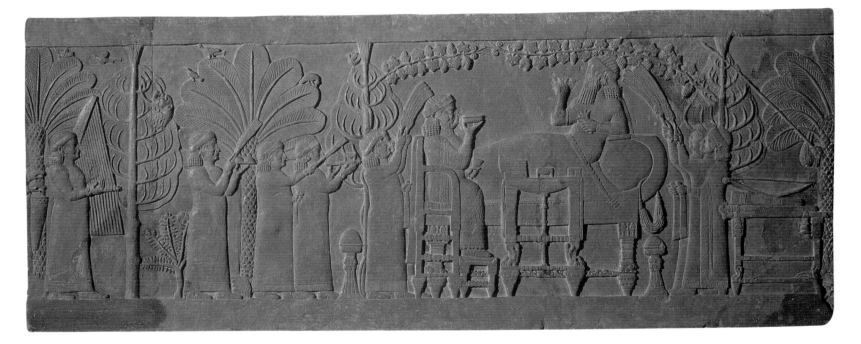

28

King Assurbanipal. Active c7th century BC. **Nineveh Palace**, Nineveh, Persia (IR), depicted in *Banquet Under the Arbor*, Frieze on palace walls, c7th century BC.

Atabak Qaracheh Governor of Shiraz   Bagh-e Takht

This spectacular Persian garden follows the natural slope of the Baba-Kuhi Mountain. It was built for Qaracheh, governor of Shiraz, to the north-west of the city and was probably a country retreat. A fortified wall surrounds it, adding an air of power and austerity to the site. Seven planted terraces cascade down to the foot of the rocky hillside. The site is crowned with the palace on the top terrace, while a large artificial boating lake extends across the whole of the lower terrace. The garden was built on the site of a natural spring, with sufficient water pressure to maintain water-jets and fill elaborate watercourses and basins on every terrace. These shallow stone-lined basins and pools form intricate interlacing patterns spanning the length of each terrace – dazzling octagons, star-shapes and cusped or lotus-edged foliate designs. The symmetry and detail of these garden features are stunning. The gardens had fallen into ruins by the twentieth century and have now been converted into local housing.

☞   Babur, Fath Ali Shah, Jahangir, Shah Jahan

Atabak Qaracheh, Governor of Shiraz. Reigned eleventh century (IR). **Bagh-e Takht** (IR), eleventh century.

Augustus the Strong King of Saxony   Schloss Gross-Sedlitz

This panoramic vista is just one of a series of huge Baroque compositions which surround the palace and lead away to distant views across the Elbe Valley and the Sandstein Hills. Most of the garden was made by King Augustus the Strong of Saxony after he acquired the estate in 1723. Though perhaps best known for having sired no less than 365 illegitimate children, Augustus was also a compulsive garden-maker: he founded the gardens at Pillnitz on the River Elber, and greatly expanded the already famous gardens at Dresden and Moritzburg. His work at Gross-Sedlitz includes everything within this view: the Lower Orangery, the pot-lined pool and the magnificent semicircular parterre known as the Stille Musik, whose name derives from the statues of musician-cherubs on either side of the staircase in the foreground, which are by M D Pöppelmann.

☛ Bouché, Esterházy, Rinaldi, Tessin

King Augustus the Strong of Saxony. **b** Dresden (GER), 1670. **d** (GER), 1733. **Schloss Gross-Sedlitz**, Dresden (GER), 1723.

Babur Emperor Mahomet   Ram Bagh

A succession of fountains line the Ram Bagh, originally the Aram Bagh or Garden of Rest, which was first designed by Emperor Mahomet Babur, founder of the Mughal dynasty. It is the earliest Mughal garden to survive in recognizable form, and it directly inspired all North Indian and Kashmiri gardens that followed. Babur drew from central Asian and Persian garden-design traditions, and first introduced the four-part garden, or *chahar-bagh*, layout to India. As Babur wished, the site is orderly and symmetrical, dominated by the watercourse, with paved walkways, and pavilions on raised platforms for garden viewing. Babur's garden was an open-air garden palace, where he held public audience, composed music and poetry, planned military campaigns, wrote his memoirs, and entertained friends. In essence, he conducted both his public and private life within his garden compound.

☞ Jahangir, Nazarite, Sangram Singh, Shah Jahan

Emperor Mahomet Babur (1st Mogul Emperor). Reigned 1508–30. **Ram Bagh**, Agra (IN), 1750.

Bac Ferdinand

Les Colombières

Rich colours enhance Les Colombières, Ferdinand Bac's masterpiece on the steep, wooded hillside outside Menton. Painter, garden designer and author of *Villas et jardins méditerranéens* and *Les Colombières, ses jardins et ses décors*, Bac designed several notable gardens on the French Riviera, including the Villa Croisset at Grasse and the Villa Fiorentina at St-Jean-Cap-Ferrat. He worked with Mediterranean flora – rosemary, lavender, pine and blue echiums – combined with the natural stone of the area. He also used brilliantly coloured ceramics to wonderful effect. A deep terracotta colour was used for some of the temples, balustrades and viewpoints, which went particularly well with the deep green of the cypress trees. Les Colombières is a garden of exploration.

Paths meander up and down the hillside, and the visitor is frequently delighted with an unexpected *trompe-l'oeil* design in vivid tiles, a beautifully framed view of the Mediterranean, or a classical, symbolic area, such as the Philosopher's Stair, or Homer's Garden.

☛ **Gildemeister, Hanbury, Johnston, B Rothschild**

32

Ferdinand Bac. **b** Stuttgart (GER), 1859. **d** Compiègne (FR), 1952. **Les Colombières**, Menton (FR), c1925.

Bacciocchi Elisa   Villa Reale

Complete with footlights, pit, seating and even terracotta actors, the green theatre at the Villa Reale, planted in 1652, sets the tone for this whimsical Baroque garden. Leading from it are a succession of rooms, each meant to hold a surprise. A water theatre in a semicircular shell-encrusted grotto, a beautifully proportioned, balustraded pool adorned with lemon trees and swans and a two-storey grotto of Pan. This precious, late seventeenth-century ensemble is only a nucleus standing in a large, romantic park, created by Napoleon's formidable sister, Elisa Bacciocchi. Elisa's ambitions were realized when her brother crowned himself King of Italy and then made her Princess of Lucca and Piombino. She promptly coerced the Orsetti family into selling her their villa at Marlia. Then she annexed neighbouring properties and created a park with huge vistas, a lake, grotto and specimen trees. She planned to do away with the remaining seventeenth-century garden and was only prevented from doing so by Napoleon's downfall in 1814.

☞ Borghese, Capponi, Fontana, Walska

Elisa Bacciocchi, née Bonaparte. **b** Ajaccio (IT), 1777. **d** nr Trieste (IT), 1820. **Villa Reale**, Lucca (IT), established 1651, extended late eighteenth century.

Baden-Durlach Carl Wilhelm von   Karlsruhe

Nothing so illustrates the self-aggrandizement of the eighteenth-century German princes as this bird's-eye view of the new city of Karlsruhe, built by the Protestant margrave Carl Wilhelm von Baden-Durlach in 1715. The formal gardens, at the bottom of the picture, occupy one third of the site; their nine avenues represent the nine muses. The woodland garden behind the palace and the city beyond the gardens' circular boundary all give glory and honour to their founding prince. Right at the centre of no less than twenty-seven radiating avenues is the palace of Carl Wilhelm. Like the town, the castle was built on a strictly geometrical star design. The function of Carl Wilhelm's Schlossgarten was to rival his Catholic cousin's palace and garden at Mannheim. It was, above all, a place where the margrave could enjoy himself, in the company of his many mistresses: the translation of Karlsruhe is 'Carl's rest'.

☞ Bingley, Bowes-Lyon, Le Nôtre, Switzer

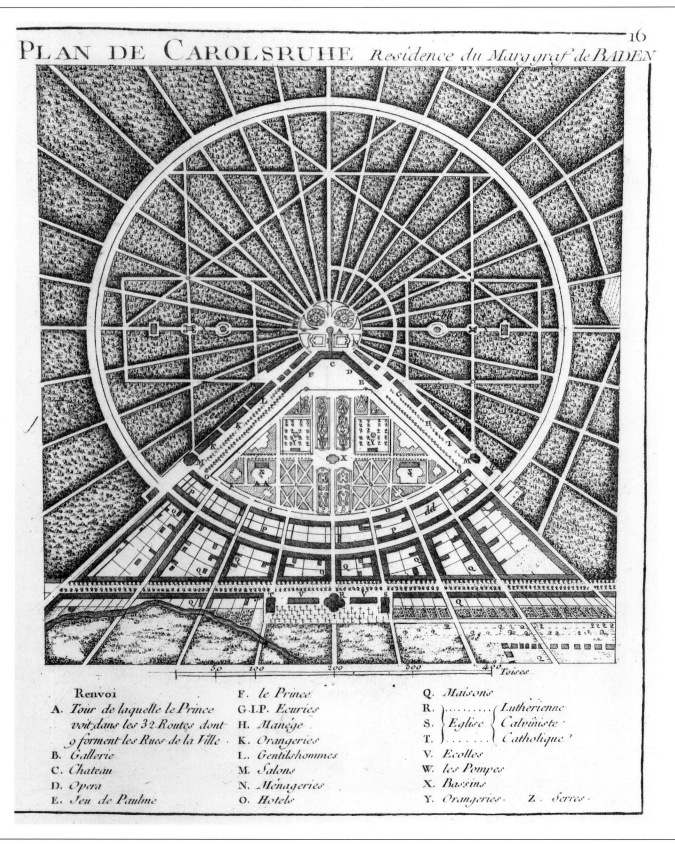

PLAN DE CAROLSRUHE *Residence du Marggraf de BADEN*

16

Renvoi

A. *Tour de laquelle le Prince voit dans les 32 Routes dont 9 forment les Rues de la Ville.*
B. *Gallerie*
C. *Chateau*
D. *Opera*
E. *Jeu de Paulme*
F. *le Prince*
G.I.P. *Ecuries*
H. *Manége*
K. *Orangeries*
L. *Gentilshommes*
M. *Salons*
N. *Ménageries*
O. *Hotels*
Q. *Maisons*
R. } .... *Lutherienne*
S. } *Eglise* { *Calviniste*
T. } .... { *Catholique*
V. *Ecolles*
W. *les Pompes*
X. *Bassins*
Y. *Orangeries*   Z. *Serres*

Carl Wilhelm von Baden-Durlach. b Durlach (GER), 1679. **d** Karlsruhe (GER), 1738. **Karlsruhe**, Karlsruhe (GER), 1715.

34

Bai Jodh

Amber Palace Lake Garden

The Amber Palace was the lakeside home of Jodh Bai, the Rajput princess who was one of the wives of Akbar, the third Mughal emperor. In the garden, water from the lake below was raised by twelve rehants to the highest of the three levels. It then cascaded down, crossing the decorative niches and channels which divide the terraces. The highest terrace contains a *chahar-bagh*-style garden divided by a wide water channel with a central foliated octagonal water basin, very similar to that of Babur's Lotus Garden and quintessentially Mughal in design. The innovations found in this garden are the use of complicated geometric star patterns and hexagrams, designs that are repeatedly found in Hindu iconography. In essence, the Lake Garden at Amber is a Hindu adaptation of a Mughal design – a fusion of Indo-Islamic garden art. Viewed from the palace above, it seems natural that the stone divisions would have originally been planted with flowers and meant to provide a colourful view from above – a spectacular three-tiered garden carpet.

☛ Akbar, Babur, Borromeo, Sangram Singh, Suraj Mal

Jodh Bai. Niece of Akbar, active (IN), seventeenth century. **Amber Palace Lake Garden**, Jaipur (IN), seventeenth century.

Baillie Scott M Hugh 48 Storey's Way

The clipped yews, ornamental path and simple fence and gate have an Old English country-cottage feel to them, while the steeply pitched tile roof and white walls of the house are characteristic of the Arts-and-Crafts cottage vernacular architecture practised by Baillie Scott during the first decades of the twentieth century. At that time he was working as an independent architect on the Hampstead Garden Suburb project. Baillie Scott was of the opinion that house and garden should be designed as a united entity, as he explained in his 1906 book *Houses and Gardens*: 'It is not a case of first designing a house and then laying out its immediate surroundings as a garden bearing a certain relation to it, for house and garden are here the product of a single initial idea which comprehends the whole.' In his approach to garden design he acknowledged the great influence of Gertrude Jekyll – even though her garden at Munstead Wood predated the Lutyens-designed house by a number of years.

☛ **Barnsley, Greene & Greene, Jekyll, Lutyens, Mawson, Parsons**

M Hugh Baillie Scott. b Ramsgate, Kent (UK), 1865. **d** Broughton, Sussex (UK), 1945. **48 Storey's Way**, Cambridge (UK), 1912–13.

Balat Auguste

Serres de Laeken

The circular winter garden designed by Auguste Balat in 1876 is the finest of all the glasshouses that make up the 2 hectares (5 acres) of the Serres de Laeken at the Royal Palace outside Brussels. The three-tiered dome, 57 m (170 ft) in diameter is, like the other houses, constructed of glass and iron decorated with flowing designs of curves and circles and painted a soft green. The individual houses, with the collections of palms, ferns, camellias, orchids and medinillas in huge glazed pots, are linked by glazed corridors over a mile long and lined with climbing geraniums and trained fuchsias. There was an orangery and a round hothouse containing a precious *Victoria amazonica* water-lily in existence at Laeken before Leopold II came to the Belgian throne in 1865.

However, it was Leopold's enthusiasm for tropical plants and the vast fortune he made from his investments in the Congo that allowed the Royal Greenhouses to grow to the extent they did.

☞ Burton & Turner, Dupont, Fowler, Paxton

Auguste Balat. b Gochenée (BEL), 1818. **d** Axeller, Brussels (BEL), 1895. **Serres de Laeken**, Brussels (BEL), 1876.

Bannochie Iris

Andromeda Gardens

The Andromeda Gardens in Barbados are home to the biggest range of indigenous and exotic tropical plants in the West Indies containing a wealth of palms, ferns, heliconia, hibiscus, bougainvillea, begonias, cacti and orchids. Andromeda, the goddess of Greek myth, was chained to a rock, just as these gardens cling to the rocky cliffs of Barbados' eastern shore. Iris Bannochie, the local horticulturalist whose family had owned the land for 200 years, began planting on the unpromising rocky area in 1954. She used the natural areas of the terrain to best effect, in particular the stream, which has provided a series of clear pools and waterfalls. When Bannochie came to live in the house here in 1964, work began in earnest to build up the diversity of the plants through visiting other nearby islands and requesting help from other botanists from all over the world. Bannochie opened her garden to the public and donated her beloved Andromeda to the Barbados National Trust on her death in 1988.

☞ **Raffles, Sanchez & Maddux, Thwaites**

38

Iris Bannochie. d (BAR), 1988. **Andromeda Gardens**, St Joseph (BAR), 1954–88.

Barillet-Deschamps Jean-Pierre   Buttes Chaumont

This rocky mound lies in the public park of Buttes Chaumont, one of the most exciting parks in Paris. It was created in an area of disused quarries, which had long been used as rubbish dumps and even, between 1864 and 1869, for public hangings. One of these mounds was dramatized by digging a lake around the bottom of it and building a replica of the Temple of the Sibyl on top.

Another mound became an island and is reached by a footbridge. A waterfall crashes down from a height of 30 m (96 ft) inside a cave. Winding paths allow visitors to walk around the lake and enjoy the changing views of the park as well as the view over Paris from its steep, grassy slopes. The romantic idiom is typical of the work of Jean-Pierre Barillet-Deschamps who, as chief gardener, assisted

Baron Haussmann and J-C-A Alphand in remodelling parts of central Paris from 1860. All three were involved in the creation of Buttes Chaumont.

☞ André, Bélanger & Blaikie, Brongniart, Clément & Provost, Paxton

Jean-Pierre Barillet-Deschamps. **b** Indre-et-Loire (FR), 1824. **d** (FR), 1875. **Buttes Chaumont**, Paris (FR), c1870s.

Barlow Pamela

Rustenberg Farm Gardens

Situated in a small valley at the base of the craggy Simonsberg Mountain range, the Rustenberg estate and gardens are breathtakingly beautiful. It is a working dairy and fruit farm with a productive vineyard. The garden is very picturesque, with its long rolling lawns, verdant wild-looking herbaceous borders filled with many native plants, clumps of mature trees and statuesque cypresses punctuating the landscape. The landscape architect and garden designer Pamela Barlow has successfully and artfully integrated vistas of the natural countryside surrounding the estate with more cultivated planting styles reminiscent of the classical English landscape to create a refreshingly new South African ranch-gardenscape. The integration of native plants with traditional, British-derived herbaceous planting scheme is typical of the best of South African gardening.

☞ Bannochie, Lady Phillips, Rhodes, Tyrwhitt, Walling

Pamela Barlow. **Rustenberg Farm Gardens**, Stellenbosch (SA).

Barnsley Ernest

Rodmarton Manor

In spring, daffodils provide a link between the series of rooms that make up the garden at Rodmarton Manor and the farmland beyond. The architect Ernest Barnsley designed the house and garden from 1909, but predeceased their completion. In both house and garden, Barnsley used natural materials in a traditional way and employed local craftsmen. This approach reflected the ethos of the Arts and Crafts Movement, which was epitomized in the Cotswolds. It was a style that he had originally learnt during his training in the offices of John Dando Sedding. Barnsley became a member of a Cotswolds community of artisans, gardeners, writers and artists that respected such traditional values and made the area their home – notable others included Johnston at Hidcote and Morris at Kelmscott.

However, the garden is also a tribute to Sedding's approach to garden design, which was essentially 'Old English', a style that used tall yew hedges, topiary, ornaments such as sundials and beds filled with a profuse display of traditional hardy perennials.

☞ **Baillie Scott, Blomfield, Harrild, Johnston, Mawson, Morris**

41

Ernest Barnsley. b (UK), 1863. **d** (UK), 1926. **Rodmarton Manor**, Gloucestershire (UK), 1909.

Baron Ash Graham

Packwood House

According to a popular myth, this collection of topiaried yews represents the Sermon on the Mount, with Christ on top of the spiral mound, the Apostles on the nearby terraces, and below, represented by a variety of shapes and sizes, the masses. Topiary was a popular form of ornamentation in the sixteenth and seventeenth centuries, and Packwood may be a rare surviving example of an English Renaissance garden, complete with mount, gazebo, terracing, orchard and courtyard. However, these clipped yews are of dubious antiquity. They were probably planted in the 1850s as part of the nineteenth-century 'improvements', which included new flower borders and the planting of evergreens. When Baron Ash inherited the property and extended the house in the 1930s, he also restored the garden, but he left the yews and indeed he may well have encouraged the myth about the history of the topiary. He certainly added a 'Charles II parterre' (removed early in World War II) and a sunken garden. The garden was donated to the National Trust in 1941.

☛ **Barnsley, Boy, Franco, Pinsent**

Graham Baron Ash. Packwood House, Warwickshire (UK), 1930s.

Barragán Luis   San Cristobal

Under the sweltering Mexican sun, the flat expanses of vivid reds, pinks and ochres connect with the deep blues of the water and sky. Rigorous and engaging, this carving of the space at the San Cristobal ranch creates a serene and uplifting mental space. One of the most influential architects of the twentieth century, Luis Barragán called himself primarily a landscape architect. A deeply spiritual man, he remained close to his Mexican roots, working and living there most of his life. He drew the foundation of his art from vernacular Mexican architecture but he also integrated the work of French designer Ferdinand Bac and of Le Corbusier. But most of his enduring 'lessons' came from chance encounters. He recalls a particular epiphany in Granada: 'Having walked through the darkened Alhambra I suddenly emerged into the serene, silent and solitary Patio of the Myrtles. I had the feeling that it enclosed what a perfect garden no matter its size should enclose: nothing less than the entire universe.'

☞ Bac, Burle Marx, Le Corbusier, Muhammad V, Yturbe

Luis Barragán. b Guadalajara (MEX), 1902. **d** Mexico City (MEX), 1988. **San Cristobal**, Egerstrom Residence and Stables, Los Clubes, Mexico City (MEX), 1968.

Barron William

Elvaston Castle

This painting by E Adveno Brooke, dated 1856, shows 'Mon Plaisir', Barron's reconstruction of a seventeenth-century garden plan by the French designer Daniel Marot. Inside the enclosing yew hedge wound covered walks with 'windows' cut into the walls, while within the garden the central feature was a large monkey puzzle tree, a recent reintroduction from Chile by William Lobb.

Around it were symmetrically arranged niches of clipped yew with hedge-lined paths leading to the entrances. The garden was begun in 1830, when the Earl of Harrington, who had shocked society by living openly with his mistress, retired to Elvaston to live as a recluse with his new wife. Barron spent five years preparing the site, and developing techniques for successfully transplanting

huge trees great distances. Dominated by conifers, Barron created the formal gardens in a series of compartments, which also included the Moorish inspired 'Alhambra' garden.

☛ Blandy, Johnston, Lennox-Boyd, Sackville-West, Verey

44

William Barron. b (UK), 1800. **d** (UK), 1891. **Elvaston Castle**, Derbyshire (UK), 1830–5, illustration from book entitled *The Gardens of England* by E Adveno Brooke, published 1857.

Barry Sir Charles

Harewood House

This view represents one of the best examples of an early Victorian garden: you are standing on the steps of Harewood House, looking over Sir Charles Barry's formal garden, towards Capability Brown's lake and landscape below. It was quite the fashion in the mid-nineteenth century to insert a formal garden between the house and the 'natural' landscape of the previous century. The terraced formal gardens would be laid out on the Italian model – Italianate rather than Italian – and richly planted with colourful bedding. Barry was one of the leading exponents of this change of fashion, although he is better known for building the Gothic-styled Houses of Parliament in Westminster. Many formal gardens were abandoned in the mid-twentieth century, but Harewood was restored in the 1990s: the outlines of the formal beds are exactly as Barry designed them, though the statue in the centre of the pool is modern.

☛ Barron, Lainé, Nesfield, Sitwell

Sir Charles Barry. b London (UK), 1795. d London (UK), 1860. Harewood House, nr Leeds, West Yorkshire (UK), 1844.

Bartram John

Bartram's Garden

The beds behind Bartram's house are the 'common flower garden' – a collection of medicinal, vegetable and herb beds. However, these plants are only a small part of the vast collection gathered together by Bartram and displayed within his 10.8-hectare (27-acre garden). Bartram, a Quaker farmer who began his garden in 1728, was the first person to gather together a thorough collection of native North American plants. But the garden is augmented with many species sent to him from other colonies, the West Indies and from botanists world wide. In 1729 he established his own nursery nearby, from which he supplied plants to George Washington at Mount Vernon and Thomas Jefferson at Monticello. In 1736 Bartram became a plant hunter, and over the next thirty years he made a series of expeditions to gather new species of North American flora. He is credited with introducing c200 species into cultivation, many of which he dispatched to England. In 1765 Bartram was appointed King's Botanist with an annual salary of £50.

☞ Jefferson, Shurcliff, van Riebeeck, Washington

John Bartram. **b** Philadelphia, PA (USA), 1699. **d** Philadelphia, PA (USA), 1777. **Bartram's Garden**, Philadelphia, PA (USA), 1728.

Bateman James & Cooke Edward

Biddulph Grange

A glorious display of foliage is framed by one of the many buildings that grace this garden while, in the distance, another archway beckons you on. In 1849, Cooke, an artist turned garden designer, visited Bateman and over the next decade or so the pair contrived a garden made up of a series of rooms, each home to a different collection of plants. The presence of a pinetum and an arboretum testify to the influence of Chatsworth and Elvaston. The garden rooms were inspired by different aspects of garden history, with names such as 'China', 'the Cheshire Cottage' and 'the Egyptian Court'. They are graced by an array of stylized garden buildings. One of the finest attributes of Biddulph's design is the way in which the separate rooms are ingeniously linked by a series of effects that constantly surprise and amuse. Together with Elvaston, Biddulph's design was an example of what could be achieved in a garden without the need for distant vistas, and both gardens were influential in moulding suburban villa gardens.

☞ Barron, Cockerell, Paxton, Vanbrugh

James Bateman. b Redivals, nr Bury, Lancashire (UK), 1811. d Worthing, Sussex (UK), 1897. **Edward Cooke**. b London (UK), 1811. d (UK), 1880. **Biddulph Grange**, Staffordshire (UK), 1842–71.

Bawa Geoffrey

Lunuganga

This serene lakescape is part of the garden made by Sri Lankan architect Geoffrey Bawa at his country house since 1950. He uses an exotic plant palette to create verdant garden episodes. The design of the house is distinguished by the effortless interplay of indoor and outdoor spaces – small outdoor courtyards and passageways alternate with interior spaces. Bawa, who has designed many buildings throughout Indonesia, including the Sri Lankan Parliament building, 1977–80, describes his design philosophy: 'A building can only be understood by moving around and through it and by experiencing the modulation and the spaces – from the outside into verandahs, then rooms, passages, courtyards – the view from these spaces into others and to the landscape beyond – from outside the building, back through rooms, inner rooms and courts. Equally important, the play of light in both garden and inner room – from a shaded inner space to the celebration of light in a courtyard. To achieve the possibility of enjoyment and pleasure is a necessity'.

☞ Barlow, Rhodes, Tyrwhitt

48

Geoffrey Bawa. b Colombo (SL), 1919. Lunuganga, nr Bentota (SL), 1950.

Beaumont Guillaume Levens Hall

The parterre at Levens Hall is celebrated for its magnificent collection of topiaried yews clipped into an amazing array of shapes. The park and garden, which were influenced by the formal French tradition, were laid out by Beaumont between 1689 and 1712 for Colonel Graham, who had been Privy Purse and Keeper of the Buckhounds to James II before the king fled the country in 1688. Beaumont planted great beech and yew hedges to divide the garden into five 'quarters'. These were the orchard, bowling green, soft-fruit garde, the 'mellion-ground' with hot beds and heated frames, and the box-edged parterres with their formal beds and topiary, which are now much larger than would have originally been intended. It is not known whether the designs are based on originals or are entirely the innovations of Alexander Forbes, head gardener from 1810–62, who restored much of the garden and added the golden yew topiary. Beaumont's plan of the gardens is also notable for its very early ha-ha and great bastion.

☛ **Barron, Le Nôtre, Monasterio de San Lorenzo, Wirtz**

49

Guillaume Beaumont. b (FR), 1650. **d** Cumbria (UK), 1729. **Levens Hall**, Cumbria (UK), 1689–1712.

Beck Marion & Walter & Collins Lester   Innisfree

Somewhere in the extraordinary landscape of Innisfree, a stream meanders gently amidst soft slopes covered in careful plantings. Single rocks selected and placed as natural masterpieces stand in still ponds. For Innisfree's 80 hectares (200 acres), Walter Beck originally designed a series of landscapes inspired by his own Chinese painting and his knowledge of the eighteenth-century painter, designer and poet Wang Wei. Noticing that in these scroll paintings the landscapes were contained in what amounted to a cup shape, he used natural elements in the landscape to frame each 'cup'. He and his wife Marion worked for thirty years on perfecting the gardens at the family estate. When they later met the designer Lester Collins they found him so sympathetic that they asked him to link these different 'cup' elements into a perfect whole. Using an ancient Japanese handbook, Collins created a world where the viewer seamlessly strolls from one perfect composition to another.

☞ Hosogawa, Jencks, Sørensen, Wilkie

50

Marion Beck. b Saginaw, MI (USA), 1876. **d** Millbrook, NY (USA), 1960. **Walter Beck. b** Dayton, OH (USA), 1864. **d** Millbrook, NY (USA), 1954. **Lester Collins. b** Moorestown, NJ (USA), 1914. **d** Millbrook, NY (USA), 1993.

Innisfree, Millbrook, NY (USA), 1930.

De Belder Family Kalmthout

Charles van Geert first established his nursery at Kalmthout in 1856. Antoine Kort extended the nursery when he bought it after van Geert's death but he was forced to close it after World War I. It was not until 1952 that the derelict site was acquired by Georges and Robert de Belder. In 1954 Robert's wife Jelena Kovacic, an agriculturist, joined them and together the trio transformed the abandoned nursery into an arboretum. Van Geert had planted many fine conifers, including an avenue, which is still the backbone of the garden. The arboretum itself was never designed but evolved. A series of informal island beds are separated by wide, mown grass paths. Each bed is a subtle grouping of trees, shrubs and perennial plants with contrasts of colour, texture and form.

There are collections of wych-hazels, flowering cherries, magnolias, rhododendrons and, in late summer, richly coloured Japanese maples.

☛ Cabot, Holford, Mackenzie, Thwaites, Vilmorin

53

Georges de Belder. Robert de Belder. Jelena Kovacic de Belder. Active Kalmthout (BEL), from 1952. **Kalmthout**, nr Antwerp (BEL), 1952.

Bigelow Jacob

Mount Auburn Cemetery

Such was the impact of Mount Auburn Cemetery that the young were brought there to acquire proper ambitions and learn from the exemplary lives of buried notables. According to the American *Cyclopaedia of Useful Knowledge* (1835) the cemetery, built in 1831 on 72 acres four miles west of Boston, was 'celebrated as the most interesting object of the kind in our country'. It is credited as the first large-scale designed landscape open to the public in America and inspired the public parks and designed suburbs of the nineteenth century. Jacob Bigelow, a gifted Boston physician and botanist, promoted the concept of a 'rural cemetery', a place beyond the city limits 'composed of family burial lots, separated and interspersed with trees, shrubs and flowers in a wood or landscape garden'. Mount Auburn Cemetery celebrates his vision as effectively now as in its heyday.

☛ Asplund, Beckford, Brongniart, Downing & Vaux, Eaton

Jacob Bigelow. b Sudbury, MA (USA), 1786. **d** Boston, MA (USA), 1879. **Mount Auburn Cemetery**, Boston, MA (USA), 1831.

Bijhouwer Jan

Kröller-Müller Sculpture Park

Dancing with its own reflection, a white sculpture by Hungarian artist Marta Pan floats on a small pond. This 1960 special commission was created by the artist as 'a meeting point between sky and water', taking into account the surrounding lawns, trees and paths. Placed with equal precision, dozens of other sculptures are dotted around the Otterlo park of the Kröller-Müller Museum.

The idea of siting modern sculptures outdoors was present right from the beginning, in the 1930s, when the enterprising and wealthy Kröller-Müller couple created their museum. When it opened to the public in 1961, Otterlo was one of the very first sculpture parks. F D Hammacher, director of the museum, had by then commissioned the renowned landscape architect Jan

Bijhouwer to design a landscape with open places and secluded spots, lawns and pools. These areas were then 'curated' as in any art gallery. In the 1970s a wild woodland was added where artists were invited to place their work.

☛ Brancusi, Hepworth, Jellicoe, Miró, Moore, Saint-Phalle

55

Jan Bijhouwer. b (NL), 1794. **d** (NL), 1898. **Kröller-Müller Sculpture Park**, Otterlo, nr Amsterdam (NL), 1961.

Bingley Robert Benson, Lord   Bramham Park

The Gothic Temple at Bramham Park is an exquisite garden building seen in context, perfectly scaled and at ease in its setting. The garden was created by Robert Benson in the French formal style of Le Nôtre, with *allées* of high beech hedges, a series of formal pools linked by a cascade and a T-shaped canal. It was later embellished by Benson's descendants. The Gothic Temple was added in 1750 by Harriet Benson, Lord Bingley's daughter, based on a pattern-book design in Batty Langley's *Gothic Architecture* (1742). This is an exhilarating, spacious garden of wide open spaces and long, narrow vistas, ornamented with obelisks, ponds and a variety of temples that command wide views. It is a unique and successful fusion of French formal and English landscape features, with perhaps a touch of the Italian Renaissance in the formal set-pieces, too: an example of the panache and confidence in English garden-making in the early eighteenth century.

☞ Allen, Bowes Lyon, Le Nôtre, Vanbrugh

Robert Benson (1st Lord Bingley). b Wrenthorpe, Yorkshire (UK), 1676. d 1731. **Bramham Park**, Yorkshire (UK), 1699–1731.

Blanc Patrick

Mur Végétal

Growing on a near vertical wall, an attractive group of plants thrives as if in a perennial border. At first glance, the Mur Végétal is a mystery. It is as beautiful as a natural cliff covered in flowers and vegetation. A small pool below – home to a few goldfish – collects continuously trickling water. The wall itself consists of a fine wire mesh stretched on a metal structure which is covered in a thick layer of felt. With no earth involved here, the vegetation is 'planted' in pockets of the felt fabric. It germinates and grows thanks only to the presence of water. Despite its highly attractive appearance, this was a significant scientific experiment undertaken by the French agronomist Patrick Blanc at the annual garden festival of Chaumont-sur-Loire in 1994. It has now become a permanent installation there and the technique is being perfected, finding practical applications in various French cities.

☞ Carvallo, La Quintinie, Latz, Vogue

Patrick Blanc. b Paris (FR), 1956. **Mur Végétal**, Chaumont-sur-Loire (FR), 1994.

Blandy Family

Quinta do Palheiro Ferreiro

Occasional small formal gardens have been created within the great garden of Quinta do Palheiro Ferreiro, Madeira, made by successive generations of the Blandy family since 1885. Overall, however, the garden is an example of the wild style introduced by William Robinson. This was an attempt to simulate the Garden of Eden by growing as rich a collection of plants as possible in such a way that one would think they had grown together naturally. The apparent artlessness of this garden style belies the careful thought employed in its realization. The particular character of Palheiro Ferreiro's Eden is imparted by the great number of plants native to the Southern Hemisphere growing in this Northern Hemisphere garden. For centuries, the island of Madeira, located on the old trade routes between Europe, Asia, Africa and the Americas, has been a repository of exotic plants intercepted from passing mariners, missionaries and botanists.

☛ Barron, Jekyll, Robinson, Rochford, Thijsse, Verey

Blandy Family. Active Madeira (POR) since 1885. **Quinto do Palheiro Ferreiro**, Madeira (POR), 1885.

Blomfield Sir Reginald   Mellerstain

This bird's-eye perspective of the gardens perfectly demonstrates how Blomfield, a distinguished architect and author of *The Formal Garden*, was influenced by the formality of the English Renaissance and, at Mellerstain, the work of Le Nôtre at Versailles. This grandiose scheme was not fully implemented, but the garden's architectural shape, structure and materials are typical of Blomfield's work, where plants were used only as decorative accessories. Blomfield saw the garden as a setting for the house and therefore part of the architect's remit, and this brought him into conflict with many horticulturists, notably William Robinson, who saw garden design as a role for the gardener. These polar views, held by two vociferous men, sparked the late nineteenth-century 'Battle of Styles', which was waged between the formalists and naturalists to decide the future direction of garden design. The resolution of the 'Battle' was the new English Arts-and-Crafts garden of Gertrude Jekyll and Sir Edwin Lutyens.

☞ **Barnsley, Jekyll, Le Nôtre, Lutyens, Robinson**

Sir Reginald Blomfield. b Bow, Devon (UK), 1856. **d** London (UK), 1944. **Mellerstain**, nr Gordon, Berwickshire (UK).

Bomarzo Orsini, Duke of   Sacro Bosco, Bomarzo

Emerging from the deep woods, the gaping mouth of a giant stone head is at once hideous and strangely enticing – an episode among many others in the surreal pageant of mythical beasts, mysterious figures and bizarre architectures hewn straight out of the rock which constitutes the Sacred Grove of Bomarzo. One of the most captivating and enigmatic gardens in Italy, it reflects the complex personality of its creator, Prince 'Vicino' Orsini, who retired from the Roman court and settled in Bomarzo in 1557. Making no attempt to tame the wilderness of the valley below his family castle, he used it to create a very personal symbolic and metaphysical itinerary. In this he was turning his back on contemporary garden philosophy, opposing both the refinement of a Villa Lante and the arrogance of a Villa d'Este. After Orsini's death, silence and neglect fell on Bomarzo for three centuries. It was rediscovered in 1949 by another eccentric character, the surrealist painter Salvador Dalí, whose interest brought the park back into the public eye.

☞ Borromeo, Goldsworthy, Monteiro & Manini

Prince Pier Francesco 'Vicino' Orsini (Duke of Bomarzo). b (IT), 1513. d Bomarzo (IT), 1584. **Sacro Bosco, Bomarzo**, Lazio (IT), 1557–.

Borghese Cardinal Scipione   Villa Borghese

Scipione Borghese was the nephew of Pope Paul V, who completed the building of St Peter's in Rome. He was a man of great power and wealth and in 1605 he started to buy land on the Pincian Hill in order to lay out a garden. Girolamo Rainaldi designed the formal gardens and Bernini provided many of the sculptures. John Evelyn remarked in 1644 that it 'abounded with all sorts of the most delicious fruit, and Exotique simples: Fountaines of sundry inventions, Groves and small Rivulets of water'. Almost everything was swept away when a fashionable Scottish landscape painter, Jacob Moore, was employed in 1787 to 'extend it to double the Size and ... to plant Trees in Groups in a Picturesque manner which they were not acquainted with such as weeping willows etc'. Now it is a huge public park offering every imaginable attraction, including Rome's zoo and the annual international horse show.

☞ Fontana, Mansi, Mozzoni, Palladio, Raphael

Cardinal Scipione Borghese. b Rome (IT), 1576. d Rome (IT), 1633. Villa Borghese, Rome (IT), 1605–.

Borromeo Count Carlo III Isola Bella

For drama, there are few garden sights that compare with the approach by boat to the extraordinary Baroque extravaganza that is Isola Bella, on Lake Maggiore in northern Italy. Count Carlo Borromeo III instigated the work in 1632, employing Angelo Crivelli to create a summer palace and gardens on what had been a barren island. His son, Vitaliano IV, continued the work, employing Carlo Fontana as architect. The garden was finished during the 1690s, although the palace complex has since been in an almost continuous state of development. The centrepiece of the garden is a series of five terraces topped by stone obelisks and statues, which make the island appear from a distance to be some sort of fantastical ship. Each terrace contains fruit trees and flowers; the lowest is a formal parterre of box and bright flowers. Behind the terraces, on the palace side, is a central courtyard with a water theatre, topped with a jumping unicorn and ornamented with decorative niches. Evergreens – principally clipped box – form the basis of the planting.

☞ Bai, Fontana, Garzoni, Rochford

Count Carlo Borromeo III. b (IT), 1600s. **d** (IT), 1680s. **Isola Bella**, Lake Maggiore (IT), c1630–70.

Bosworth William Welles   Kykuit

Neo-classical colonnades, fountains and formal plantings set the tone for the gardens of the grand American estate of Kykuit in the Hudson Valley. They were modelled on the European Renaissance gardens in a style that has become known as American Renaissance. In that spirit, the Oceanus fountain, along with the gigantic allegories of the Nile, Euphrates and Ganges, has been remodelled to include the nearby Hudson. The renaissance celebrated here is the one the USA owed to great industrialists and philanthropists like the owner of Kykuit, John D Rockefeller. The landscape architect W W Bosworth, a protégé of Frederick Law Olmsted, was brought on board in 1913 to design these extensive gardens early on in a career which would later include landscaping for Stanford University, MIT and Arlington. After World War II, Bosworth established himself near Paris in order to supervise a number of historical restorations sponsored by Rockefeller money.

☛ Hearst, Hosack, Johnson, Ligorio, Olmsted, Vanderbilt

William Welles Bosworth. b Marietta, OH (USA), 1868. d Vaucresson (FR), 1966. Kykuit, Pocantico Hills, NY (USA), 1913.

Bouché Karl

Pillnitz

This brightly coloured, formal garden at Schloss Pillnitz was the work of Karl Bouché in the 1870s: in high summer the parterres are richly planted with roses and bedding plants. Over the years, many designers – notably Karl Bouché – have contributed to the evolution of this remarkable garden at the summer residence of the kings of Saxony. The most famous was Matthäus Daniel

Pöppelmann, who laid out the first formal garden in the 1720s: it lies between the oldest part to survive, the Chinese-Baroque *Wasserpalais* or Waterside Palace, and the River Elbe, along which the king arrived in the royal barge from Dresden. The palace in this illustration is the *Neuespalais* or New Palace, built in 1826 to connect the *Wasserpalais* to the *Bergpalais* or Hillside Palace. Elsewhere in the

garden are a nineteenth-century pinetum; a chestnut avenue; the famous, enclosed *Heckengärten* or Pleasure Gardens; an English pavilion in the 'English' garden; a huge palm house; and, at the highest point of the garden, a Chinese pavilion.

☞ **Baden-Durlach, Carl-Theodor, Wilhelm, Wilhelmina**

64

Karl Bouché. b 1850. **d** 1933. **Pillnitz**, nr Dresden (GER), c1870.

Bowes-Lyon Sir David   St Paul's Waldenbury

The Classical statue provides a focal point at the end of this beech-lined *allée* or avenue, one of three that converge at an acute angle outside the northern facade of the house to form a *patte d'oie*, a shape that suggests a goose's foot. The garden, the restoration of which was commenced in 1932 by Sir David Bowes-Lyon, was begun in 1725 under the guidance of Edward Gilbert, when contemporary opinion was in favour of loosening the bonds of formality. Flying in the face of the new fashion for 'landskip' gardening, Gilbert filled the spaces between the *allées* with a formal woodland of winding walks and 'incidents' such as fountains and statuary. In so doing he created what is arguably the best surviving English park laid out in the early eighteenth century in the style of Le Nôtre at Versailles. St Paul's Waldenbury was the birthplace of Elizabeth Bowes-Lyon, the Queen Mother.

☞ Bingley, Jellicoe, Le Nôtre, Manning

Sir David Bowes-Lyon. b (UK), 1902. d Birkhall (UK), 1961. St Paul's Waldenbury, Hertfordshire (UK), 1725 (restored 1932).

Bowles Edward Augustus Myddelton House

A pergola, that most Edwardian of features, is underplanted with part of the enormous and eclectic collection of plants that E A Bowles gathered in his 2-hectare (4.8-acre) garden from 1895. Bowles was a leading plantsman of the late nineteenth and early twentieth centuries, and one of a breed of enthusiastic and talented amateurs who helped push forward the science of horticulture and also wrote of their experiences. His was a highly individual garden, filled with compartments linked together in a somewhat incoherent way, but boasting many and varied plant species. Enlivened with seasonal bulbs, the Alpine Meadow was surmounted by the famous Rock Garden. Great swathes of irises flanked one bank of the river, while the Stone Garden boasted a fossilized tree, and the Lunatic Asylum consisted of a collection of botanical oddities. Bowles is possibly best remembered for the charming trilogy of books that describe *My Garden in Summer*, *My Garden in Autumn* and *My Garden in Winter*, which were published in 1914.

☛ **Crisp, Fish, Johnston, Verey**

Edward Augustus Bowles. b (UK), 1865. **d** (UK), 1954. **Myddelton House**, Enfield, Middlesex (UK), 1895.

Boy Adolf

Wilanów

The upper terrace at Wilanów is a highly ordered area of cone-shaped yews, box-edged flowerbeds and tulips. The first garden was formally laid out in the late seventeenth century by Adolf Boy round the palace built by Augustyn Locci for King John III Sobieski. The upper terrace, influenced by contemporary Italian gardens, had box parterres, gilded mythological statues, stone vases, fountains and summerhouses, as well as a symmetrically planted orchard. In the late eighteenth century, Szymon Bogumil Zug extended the formal gardens, and it was probably Zug who also planned the landscape park, with winding paths and a cascade, which dates from this time. Romantic early nineteenth-century additions included a Chinese summerhouse, a Roman bridge, a sarcophagus and a now-ruined triumphal arch. The garden and park, devastated during World War II, were restored by Gerard Ciolek to reflect the earliest garden and later changes.

☞ Barron, Pinsent, I Thomas, Zug

Adolf Boy. Active (POL), seventeenth century. **Wilanów**, Warsaw (POL), c1680s–90s.

Boyceau Jacques

Jardins Luxembourg

This famous view of the Jardins Luxembourg, by Perelle, shows the gardens as they looked in the 1640s. It was at this time that they so impressed the visiting essayist John Evelyn, who commented, 'the Parterr is of box, so rarely designd and accurately kept cut, that the mbrodery makes a stupendious effect to the Lodging which front it'. The garden was made for the Italian Queen Marie (de Medici),

widow of Henry IV of France and regent for her son Louis XIII. The designer of the garden was probably Boyceau, the queen's garden advisor, whose *Traité du jardinage* (published posthumously in 1638) was one of the first French books on garden design. The Luxembourg gardens are sunken and were originally surrounded by pots and statues. The design is square, with a semicircular apse

to provide a focal point at the far side. The *parterres de broderie* in box that Evelyn so admired were among the first in France.

☛ **S Caus, Du Cerceau, Gallard, Le Bas, Le Blond, Ligne, Pembroke**

68

Veuë et Perspectiue du Parterre du Palais d'Orleans.

Perelle sculp.

Jacques Boyceau (Jacques de la Barauderie Boyceau). b Saintonge (FR), c1562. **d** Paris (FR), c1633. **Jardins Luxembourg**, Paris (FR), 1612.

Bradley-Hole Christopher   Chelsea Flower Show Garden

This 'Virgilian Garden' comprised sleek rendered walls, stainless steel, glass panels, contemporary furniture and a bold axis along the whole length of the plot. Quotations from the Georgics were inscribed on stone plaques, a device borrowed from Ian Hamilton Finlay's Little Sparta. London's annual Chelsea Flower Show is not known as a fount of design innovation, but Christopher Bradley-Hole's winning show garden in 1997, sponsored by the *Daily Telegraph*, marked a stylistic turning point – away from the pastiche of Arts and Crafts which had reigned supreme for decades. Bradley-Hole is an uncompromising Modernist. The planting utilized a pared-down but effective palette of striking specimens: tall irises and drumstick alliums provided dramatic purple notes above an underplanting of grasses. Bradley-Hole's example has led to a vogue for Classical-contemporary show gardens at Chelsea, although the judging panel's need for horticultural sophistication still mitigates against many contemporary design approaches.

☞ Hamilton Finlay, Latz, Le Corbusier, Mies van der Rohe, Ruys

Christopher Bradley-Hole. b Sussex (UK), 1955. **Chelsea Flower Show Garden**, London (UK), 1997.

Bramante Donato

Belvedere Court

Bramante's revolutionary design for Pope Julius II linked the Vatican Palace with the old Villa Belvedere, creating three garden spaces joined by monumental ramps and stairs and a strong central axis. The two loggias along each side lose storeys to cope with the awkwardly rising ground. Begun c1505 and finished after Bramante's death, the Belvedere admirably fulfilled its brief to link the Palace to the Villa, and to provide a setting for the pope's collection of antique sculptures and a vast stage for theatre and pageantry. Bramante's great innovation was to subvert the tradition of enclosure in late-medieval gardens and to introduce the drama of perspective. His design, in which outdoor space is treated as architectural space, represented an entirely new way of thinking about the garden landscape and it dominated European traditions for more than two centuries. Unfortunately, this garden no longer exists. In 1585 a new wing added to the Vatican library was built across it; later, the museum was extended into it.

☞ Palladio, Raphael, Sulla

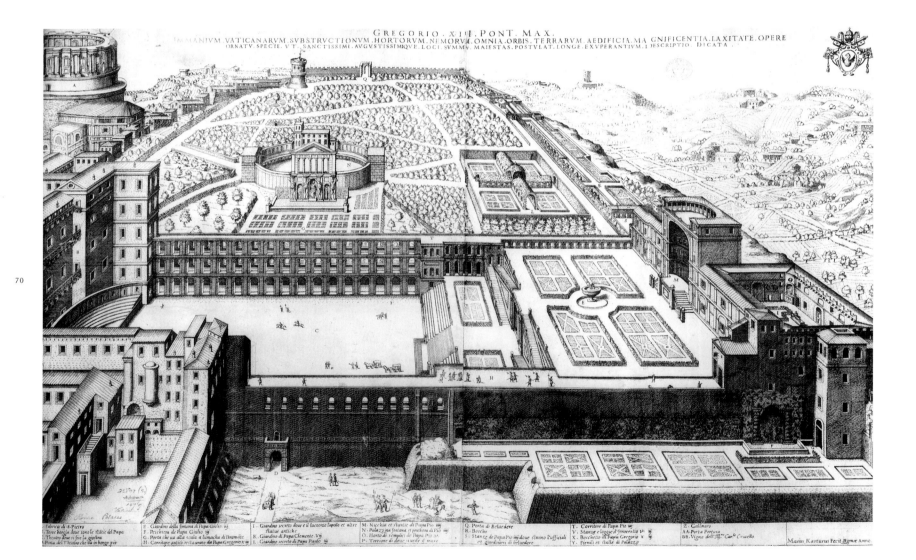

Donato Bramante. b Monte Andruvaldo, nr Urbino (IT), 1444. **d** Rome (IT), 1514. **Belvedere Court**, The Vatican, Rome (IT), c1505.

Brancusi Constantin   Tirgu Jiu Sculpture Park

In a vast wooded park designed for meditation and remembrance *The Table of Silence*, a circular limestone slab surrounded by twelve seats, sits as if suspended in time. Further down the central *allée*, *The Gate of Kiss* and *The Endless Column* complete this remarkable ensemble of sculptures. Constantin Brancusi designed both park and sculptures, creating a highly spiritual environment reminiscent of ancient stone alignments. A pioneer of abstraction, he was one of the first modern sculptors to be interested in the relationship between his art and the environment, suggesting the idea of an ever-changing work of art following the viewers' perspective. Commissioned by the Bulgarian State, Tirgu Jiu was built in 1938. Its site is close to Brancusi's native home in Romanice, although he had not lived there since 1903, when he crossed the whole of Europe on foot to reach Paris.

☞ Hamilton Finlay, Hepworth, Heron, Miró, Moore

Constantin Brancusi. b Hobitza (BUL), 1876. d Paris (FR), 1957. **Tirgu Jiu**, nr Hobitza (BUL), 1938.

Brandt G N

Tivoli Gardens

The Tivoli Gardens in the centre of Copenhagen are synonymous with the idea of urban recreation, and much of the planting has always been informal, to chime with the romantic layout of the landscape and the surprise effect created by the principal, zigzag path. Informal herbaceous planting within a large-scale landscape typifies the work of G N Brandt. He created the parterre garden at

Tivoli – elliptical beds interspersed with fountains in wooden tubs (a wartime austerity measure). Brandt appropriated the ideas of Lutyens and Jekyll – the softening of architectural formality with subtle planting schemes – and incorporated wildflowers and strips of unmown grass in otherwise formal designs. He was a leading proponent of an ecological approach to horticulture, and

steadfastly maintained he was a gardener rather than a designer. His style represented a confident mix of formal and informal approaches, as in his June Garden at Swastika, where formal flowerbeds give way to randomly spaced trees.

☞ Jekyll, Loudon, Lutyens, Sangram Singh, Stanislas II, Tyers

G N Brandt. b 1878. d 1945. **Tivoli Gardens**, Copenhagen (DK), 1943.

Bridgeman Charles Claremont Landscape Garden

A cedar of Lebanon casts its shadow across Bridgeman's great turf amphitheatre that tilts its eight circular terraces (four concave, four convex) like a giant saucer, following the classical example. Cut into rising ground above the lake (then a formal round pond), the amphitheatre was created c1725 for its landscape drama rather than real theatre. It also gave fine views across the valley. Once owned by architect Sir John Vanbrugh, Claremont's successive developments tell the story of the English landscape garden. William Kent loosened the reins of Bridgeman's formal landscape, adding a cascade (now a grotto) and ruffling the pond into a more 'natural' lake. Capability Brown built a new house and hid the amphitheatre under trees. Planted with rhododendrons and exotics, the gardens later became a favourite retreat for Queen Victoria. Bridgeman was appointed gardener to George II and Queen Caroline. His work heralded the new landscape style, but regrettably few of his gardens survive.

☞ Goethe, Grenville-Temple, Hoare, Kent, Piper

Charles Bridgeman. d London (UK), 1738. **Claremont Landscape Garden**, Esher, Surrey (UK), 1715.

Brongniart Alexandre Theodore   Père-Lachaise

An intensely dramatic and romantic landscape, the cemetery of the Père-Lachaise is not, as it might appear, a remote and tranquil burial place. It sees a constant stream of visitors, each looking for their particular favourites, from Chopin to Jim Morrison, Proust to Oscar Wilde, or just strolling to 'see who's there'. When Alexandre Brongniart, designer of the Paris stock exchange, was commissioned in 1804 to create a new burial ground for the capital, he landscaped the top of this beautifully situated hill overlooking the whole of Paris with a cypress-lined central *allée* off which an infinite number of paths diverge. For its time this was a completely new style of cemetery, but it soon became a reference for European cemetery designers. To 'promote' the site the remains of celebrities such as Molar and Beaumarchais were moved there by the municipality. Soon the Père-Lachaise became a fashionable and sought-after place of rest, despite escalating prices.

☞ **Asplund, Bigelow, Eaton, Scarpa**

Alexandre Theodore Brongniart. b Paris (FR), 1739. **d** Paris (FR), 1813. **Père-Lachaise**, Paris (FR), 1804.

Brookes John   Denmans

This is the home of garden designer John Brookes, whose book *Room Outside* (1969) popularized the now-familiar concept of outdoor living and 'patio gardening'. The 14-hectare (3.5-acre) garden at Denmans lies on stony, alkaline soil close to England's south coast. It was begun by the late Joyce Robinson, who arrived in 1946 and subsequently laid out a 'dry river' of gravel, running in sinuous curves down a gentle slope, planted with silver birch trees and Mediterranean-type plants. Mrs Robinson's innovative gravel garden was inspired by a visit she had made to the Greek island of Delos in the late 1960s. When John Brookes arrived in 1980 he continued the theme of planting in a stony landscape and also made a fragrant, informal herb garden within the former walled kitchen garden. Now in its maturity, this garden shows a relaxed style, at ease with itself, since its most attractive plants are allowed to self-sow, with pleasing informality.

☛ Aldington, Chatto, Gildemeister, Pearson, Toll

John Brookes. b (UK), 1933. **Denmans**, West Sussex (UK), 1980.

Brown Capability

Blenheim Palace

The apparently natural features at Blenheim – the lake, undulating sward and clumps of trees – are all manmade, part of the design of Capability Brown, who held a monopoly over English landscape design during the mid- to late-eighteenth century. Brown's genius was in adapting a successful formula, based on a romantic idea of pastoral England, and having the confidence to shape it to fit different places and different patrons. Brown assessed the 'capabilities' of each situation, hence his nickname. While it is true that he demolished many formal gardens (notably those of London and Wise) in favour of pastureland right up to the house, Brown was not averse to retaining formal elements where appropriate. However, he had no interest in the symbolic and literary preoccupations of his predecessors: there are no hidden meanings in his work. It is partly the simplicity of his work which makes it attractive.

☛ Emes, Grenville-Temple, Kent, Repton, Vanbrugh

Capability Brown (Lancelot 'Capability' Brown). b Northumberland (UK), 1716. d London (UK), 1783. **Blenheim Palace**, Woodstock (UK), 1764–74.

Bullant Jean

Château de Chantilly

Bullant is often credited with the famous gardens at Chantilly, seen here in a print from the 1680s. In fact, nothing remains today of his work except the château he built in the 1550s for Duke Anne de Montmorency, the constable of France. The château stood on an island, surrounded by the water of the medieval moat. It had a loggia opening on to a small parterre garden. The garden we see today is largely the ingenious work of the royal gardener André Le Nôtre, who built on Bullant's original conception. It was laid out for the Prince de Condé in the 1660s, with help from a water engineer, Jacques de Manse, and a battery of architects, sculptors, botanists and horticulturists. But it was the waterworks which most impressed the prince's contemporaries: the course of the River Nonette was diverted to create spectacular reflective terraces. The largest of the two water terraces is 1800 m (1,962 yards) long and 80 m (87 yards) wide.

☛ J Aislabie, Dashwood, Le Nôtre, Philip II

Jean Bullant. b Amiens (FR), c1515. d Ecouen (FR), 1578. **Château de Chantilly**, nth of Paris (FR), 1550s, *Château of Chantilly*, gouache, unknown French artist, c17th century.

Buontalenti Bernardo   Villa Pratolino

Surveying a moody lotus pond, this Herculean giant by the Mannerist sculptor Giambologna stands in the now-derelict park of Pratolino, once hailed as the most remarkable of the Medici villas. Here, around 1569, the stage designer and architect Buontalenti created labyrinthine paths on the densely wooded hillside. It was a dramatic itinerary punctuated by cascades, automata, fountains, grottoes and monuments designed by the most famous artists and architects of the time for Grand Duke Francesco I de' Medici. Although it is now being restored, Pratolino's history is a sad tale of destruction. It will be hard to repair the damage done first in the eighteenth century when the garden was turned into hunting grounds, then in the Napoleonic era and finally in the nineteenth century when all was made into an 'English' park. It is a wonder that with only a few elements left Pratolino still has such strong evocative powers.

☞ **Bomarzo, I Caus, Garzoni, Mardel, Orsini, Vignola**

78

Bernardo Buontalenti. **b** Florence (IT), 1536. **d** Florence (IT), 1608. **Villa Pratolino**, now Parco Demidoff, nr Florence (IT), c1569–81.

Burle Marx Roberto   Fernandez Residence

Generous swathes of hemerocalis and coleus interweave near the shore of a lake, while bright pink rhododendrons lead the eye into the extraordinary mountainous landscape. Through his masterful sense of balance, bold use of curves and brilliant plantings, Roberto Burle Marx transformed this already beautiful valley estate in the Orgaos mountains of Brazil into a landscape of tranquility and peace. Long hailed as 'the true inventor of the modern garden', Burle Marx certainly innovated greatly when, on his return to Brazil after studying in Germany, he began combining large drifts of plants, arranged in curvaceous bio-morphic borders, with the geometric patterns of modernistic architecture. A true artist when working with the bright Brazilian flora, he was also a master of pure design, as his famous wave-like mosaic walkways in Copacabana testify. Burle Marx always remained close to his Brazilian roots and he realized his most important designs, including many ground-breaking collaborations with Le Corbusier and Niemeyer.

☞ **Barragán, Bye, Le Corbusier, Pepper, Silva**

Roberto Burle Marx. b São Paulo (BR), 1909. **d** nr Rio de Janeiro (BR), 1994. **Fernandez Residence**, Correias (BR), 1948, restored 1988.

Burley Griffin Walter   Australian Botanical Garden

The American architect and landscape designer Walter Burley Griffin won a competition to design the new federal capital Canberra in 1912 and through his plans ensured that Australia's native flora would be a significant feature of the city. Although it took fifty years until the botanic gardens were officially opened in 1970, the ambitious scale of Burley Griffin's designs meant that in the intervening years no succeeding politician could easily suppress them. The original idea, fashionable at the time, to build a Continental arboretum with specimens from similar climates around the world was dropped in favour of concentrating solely on native Australian flora and using devices such as the Rain Forest Gully to transform an arid area into a humid rainforest environment through use of time-switch controlled sprays. Work to preserve threatened or rare species is ongoing, with about half of the total 90 hectares (222 acres) on the lower slopes of the Black Mountain awaiting development. The Gardens currently host 90,000 plants representing 5,000 species.

☛ Dow, Raven, Rhodes, Thays, Wilton & Cockayne, F L Wright

Walter Burley Griffin. b Maywood, IL (USA), 1876. **d** Lucknow (IN), 1937. **Australian Botanical Garden**, Canberra (ASL), planned 1912, opened 1970.

Burlington Lord

Chiswick House

John Rocque's 1736 map highlights the irregular winding paths, strong axial layout and natural areas favoured by Lord Burlington following his Grand Tour, as characteristic of ancient classical gardens. In contrast to the Baroque formality of earlier gardens, Chiswick House, modelled on Palladio's Villa, was set in grounds landscaped by Charles Bridgeman and William Kent and was at the forefront of fashionable taste. Its features included a river, grotto cascade, hedged exedra with statues (said to be from Hadrian's Villa), banqueting house and pool with an obelisk, some shown in the vignettes bordering the map. Dominant is the *patte d'oie*, with clipped hedges, each of the three vistas culminating in a classical garden building. Burlington's ideas on the natural style of gardening were immortalized by Alexander Pope in the poem *Epistle to Lord Burlington* (1734), which praised his pioneering work, and advised designers to 'consult the genius of the place'.

☞ **Hadrian, Kent, Palladio, Pope, Switzer, Vanbrugh**

81

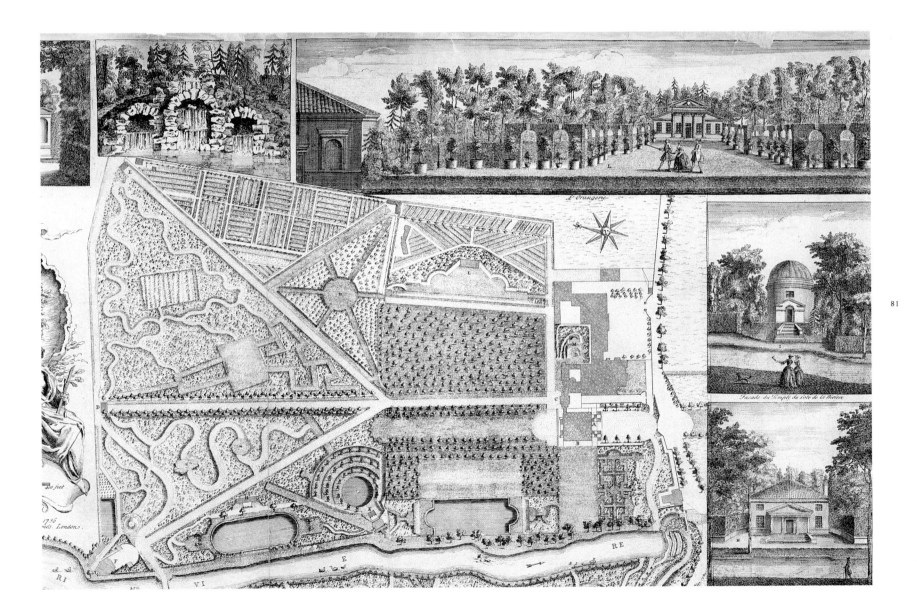

Richard Boyle (3rd Earl of Burlington). b London (UK), 1695. d London (UK), 1753. **Chiswick House**, London (UK), 1725, engraving by John Roque, 1736.

Burnett Frances Hodgson   The Secret Garden (Great Maytham Hall)

Who has not been enchanted by Frances Hodgson Burnett's classic children's story, *The Secret Garden*, written in 1911? Few realize that fictional Misselthwaite Manor was based on Great Maytham Hall in Kent where Burnett lived as a tenant a century ago. It was rebuilt in 1910 with architecture by Sir Edwin Lutyens. The beautiful eighteenth-century walled garden was then a tangled mess. But it inspired Burnett to write her memorable story after she had returned to America. Visitors wonder, 'Will the garden be as Mary and Dickon secretly transformed it, unbeknown to Mary's reclusive uncle - Archibald Craven?' That is all part of mysterious anticipation. Now lovingly restored, visitors today may even spot a descendant of the famous robin, still singing in the tree on the fringe of the Secret Garden! Also the author of *Little Lord Fauntleroy*, 1886, Burnett emigrated to the States at the end of the American Civil War.

☛ Lutyens, Potter

Frances Eliza Hodgson Burnett. **b** Manchester (UK), 1849. **d** Washington, DC (USA), 1924. **Great Maytham Hall**, Kent (UK), eighteenth century.

Burton Decimus & Turner Richard   Kew Palm House

The spectacular Palm House, 120 m (384 ft) long, 30 m (96 ft) wide and 20 m (64 ft) tall, was commissioned by the first official Director of Kew, Sir William Hooker, and built between 1844 and 1848 as a home for the many different tender palms that were being brought back from all corners of the empire. Initially the plants were displayed in pots on step shelves, and it was not until the 1860s that the bed system was adopted. The original plans for the Palm House, submitted by the innovative engineer and iron founder Richard Turner, were modified by Burton, who had recently worked with Paxton and who 'de-ornamentalized' Turner's Gothic plans. The combination of Turner's technical skill and Burton's simplification resulted in the building's curvilinear pattern. With its domes, semicircular apses and barrel-vaulted galleries, the structure was not only functional, but also attractive to look at, and the style found favour in many new gardens. However, cast iron rusts and in 1985 a £5 million restoration was undertaken.

☞ Balat, Dupont, Fowler, Grimshaw, Paxton

Decimus Burton. b London (UK), 1800. d London (UK), 1881. Richard Turner. b Dublin (IRE), c1798. d 1881. Kew Palm House, Kew, London (UK), 1844–8.

Bushell Thomas

Enstone

Reached through a watery curtain, this underground cave hung with stalactites displays Thomas Bushell's marvellous hydraulic effects that were accompanied by artificial thunder, lightning, rain, hail, drum-beats, bird-song, lights, rainbows and sounds of the dead arising. One-time page and secretary to philosopher-statesman Sir Francis Bacon, Bushell came to Enstone in the 1620s, living in a small house where he draped his study in black like a melancholy hermitage. In his upper garden were walks, groves, flower gardens and water jokes, or *giochi d'acqua*, which were added to after his death. Fame came briefly when he was twice visited by Charles I, but he left Enstone at the start of the Civil War and never returned. The 'Enstone Marvels' linked back to Hero of Alexandria (1st century AD) and the water toys and jokes of European gardens, such as the Italian Villa d'Este and the Austrian Schloss Hellbrunn.

☛ **I Caus, S Caus, Ligorio, Robins**

Thomas Bushell. b Worcestershire (UK), 1594. **d** London (UK), 1674. **Enstone**, Oxfordshire (UK), 1620s.

Bye A E

Leitzsch Residence

On a woodland site near Ridgefield, Connecticut, A E Bye worked his subtle magic, merging and entwining art and nature. The balconies and docks of the house have been built to extend into the surrounding landscape. Vistas have been cut through the woods, pushing the view out into the distance and establishing the garden in a larger setting. Bye likes to juxtapose nature and humanity, bringing the woods right up to the windows of the house. He does not believe in introducing exotic species that would disturb the natural ecology of a site and pose problems of cultivation and maintenance. It worries him to think that the natural character of the local environment might disappear because native species are being replaced by plants from other parts of the world. Bye is also well known for his fieldscapes: undulating turf reminiscent of ancient earthworks.

☛ Gildemeister, Hall, Manrique, Pearson, Rothschild

A E Bye (Arthur Edwin Bye). b PA (USA), 1919. **Leitzsch Residence**, Western Connecticut (USA), mid-late 1970s.

Cabot Frank  Les Quatre Vents

The Chinese Moon Bridge is a copy of a bridge in Seven Star Park in Kweilin. When the water is still, the reflection completes a perfect circle. Les Quatre Vents, in Quebec, overlooks the St Lawrence estuary. The original garden, planned with a strong axis looking west from the terraces of the house, along the Tapis Vert to the Laurentian Mountains, was laid out early in the nineteenth century for the Cabot family. Today the site is much larger, having been expanded by the present owner, Frank Cabot. This is a stylish garden full of atmosphere and revealing a passion for plants. There are almost thirty different areas, each with a strong character of its own but never at the expense of overall unity. Clipped cedars are much used to link areas with their rich velvet greenness.

Indigenous North American ground covers like Cornus canadensis, Maianthemum canadense and pretty yellow Clintonia borealis flower beside ferns in the quiet woodland, while huge-leaved gunneras, petasites and rheums revel in waterside positions.

☛ Holford, Thwaites, Van Geert, Veitch, Vilmorin

Frank Cabot. b New York, NY (USA), 1925. Les Quatre Vents, Quebec (CAN), established nineteenth century.

Caetani Family   Ninfa

The crumbling buildings and stone bridges of the town of Ninfa are a dreamlike setting for a garden. The medieval town near Rome was deserted for 600 years until the twentieth century, when three generations of the Caetani family created a magical garden amongst the ruins. In 1922 the English-born Duchess of Sermoneta planted the roses which still cascade over trees and ruins, scrambling to enormous heights. Her son, Prince Gelasio, planted the ilexes, cypresses, black walnuts and *Magnolia grandiflora* which, now mature, give the garden its air of timelessness. After the prince's death his brother Roffredo and his American wife Marguerite lived at Ninfa for twenty-five years, adding collections of flowering trees and creating more streams to criss-cross the garden. They were followed by Lelia Caetani, an artist, and her husband Hubert Howard, who added more magnolias, *Paulownia fargesii* and began an arboretum outside the walls. Today, the garden is cared for by a charitable foundation.

☛   **W Aislabie, Gilpin, Knight, Messel**

Caetani Family. Active (IT), twentieth century. **Ninfa**, nr Latina (IT), 1922–77.

Cameron Charles   Pavlovsk

The Temple of Friendship, a domed rotunda with Doric columns, no windows and a single oak door, was the first of the buildings designed at Pavlovsk by the Scottish architect Charles Cameron for the Grand Duke Paul, later Paul I, and his wife Maris Fedorovna. Cameron also designed the palace, the formal gardens around it and other buildings in the park, mainly Classical but including a thatched dairy and a charcoal-burner's hut, both apparently simple rustic structures but with elegantly appointed interiors. His landscaping along the banks of the River Slavyanks is English in style, but, on the large flat tract of land known as the White Birches, Pietro Gonzago, primarily a theatre designer, created an idealized north Russian landscape of meadow and forest. The Empress Maris Fedorovna, a keen gardener and knowledgeable plantswoman, also contributed to the development of the park. This temple inspired many similar buildings in Russian parks.

☛ Catherine II, Guerniero, Palladio, Peter II

Charles Cameron. **b** London (UK), c1743. **d** St Petersburg (RUS), 1811. **Pavlovsk**, sth of St Petersburg (RUS), mid-eighteenth century.

Cane Percy

Dartington Hall

In the Tiltyard at Dartington Hall in Devon, terraced grass banks, a broad York stone stairway and clipped yew hedges combine in a poetic interplay of geometric forms, sharply defined by sunlight and shadow, and contrasting dramatically with the surrounding trees. It is one of the world's most distinctive garden landscapes, located in one of Britain's most magical gardens. Grandeur – as seen in the Tiltyard – is combined with the intimacy of quiet woodland walks, a secluded meadow and a rustic gardener's cottage. Dating back to the fourteenth century, Dartington Hall was built for Richard II's half-brother John Holand. The present garden is largely the work of Percy Cane, a prolific designer whose clients included Haile Selassie. Cane was commissioned by Dorothy and William Elmhirst, who acquired the estate in 1925 and founded the experimental College of Arts. He followed two other consultants used by the Elmhirsts – the American Beatrix Farrand and Harry Avray Tipping.

☞ Farrand, Hall, Jencks, Sørensen, Wilkie

Percy Cane. b Bocking Mill, Essex (UK), 1881. **d** 1976. **Dartington Hall**, nr Totnes, Devon (UK), 1945-.

Cao Andy

Glass Garden

Impressionistic swathes of colour are blended together with great subtlety and finesse in Andy Cao's Glass Garden at Echo Park, LA. The white mounds half submerged in a blue-lined pool are evocations of the roadside salt mounds Cao remembers from his childhood in Vietnam, and other aspects of the garden – such as the tufts of the grass *Stipa tenuissima* (redolent of lemon grass) – are also evocations of his native country. Cao started using glass as a material in 1994, after picking up a batch of tumbled table-glass shards from a local recycling depot. He began experimenting with its potential and found that it could be put to many uses in garden design. The glass, which is safe to walk on barefoot, also acts as a mulch as it suppresses weeds and slows the evaporation of water. Cao is now receiving commissions for more glass-garden designs and has created installations for hotels in the Los Angeles and Las Vegas areas. In 1999 British garden designers began to experiment with glass, but none have yet demonstrated Cao's skill with the material.

☛ I Greene, Schwartz, Shigemori, Sitta, Smyth

Andy Cao. b Tay-Ninh (S VIET), 1965. Glass Garden, Los Angeles, CA (USA), 1998.

Capponi Family

Villa Gamberaia

The staircases and walls of this small, secret garden are decorated with rustic stonework and encrusted with mosaics. Busts, obelisks and terracotta urns adorn the balustrade leading to the upper level of terraces, where a lemon garden and a *bosco* open on to magnificent views. These are the only areas to have remained unchanged since the seventeenth century, when two generations of the Capponi family improved and redesigned La Gamberaia. On the lower level the most famous feature of the garden is an immaculate parterre bordered by yews and narrow paths which leads to a theatrically curved wall of cypress. Here shallow pools and fountains have replaced the traditional Renaissance plantings of herbs and roses. This modern reworking of the front of the garden – in a style that is still respectful of Alberti's principles – was undertaken at the beginning of the twentieth century by the reclusive Bulgarian Princess Ghycka, then the owner of Gamberaia.

☛ Borromeo, Buontalenti, Michelozzi, Mozzoni

Capponi Family. Active (IT), eighteenth century. **Villa Gamberaia**, Florence (IT), 1717–.

Cardasis Dean

Plastic Garden

Coloured plexiglass panels create a remarkable formal division in this now-vanished but widely noted garden design. The idea for a plastic garden sprang from Cardasis's view that the vinyl-sided suburban house, part of a new development, looked like a plastic toy simply thrown onto the landscape. Red and yellow plastic panels form the perimeter to a gravelled outdoor room, while blue panels are used to roof part of the decked area adjoining the house. A sense of enclosure is created through the planting of native trees at the edges of the garden, designed to enmesh eventually with the mature forest beyond, cut back by the developers. The garden was relatively cheap to make and was designed as a low-maintenance space with the safety and inspiration of children's play in mind. Dean Cardasis is a professor in landscape architecture and also a practicing designer.

☞ Cao, Cooper, Delaney, Guevrékian, Mallet-Stevens, Schwartz

92

Dean Cardasis. b 1949. **Plastic Garden**, Northampton, MA (USA), 1995.

Carl-Theodor Elector of the Palatinate Schloss Schwetzingen

There is no better place to enjoy the transition from Baroque to Landscape styles of gardening than Schwetzingen, the summer residence of the elector Carl-Theodor of the Palatinate who laid out its garden over more than forty years. His first features were pure Baroque, designed by the French architect Nicolas de Pigage: a circular parterre enclosed by curving pergolas of trelliswork. Next came such features as the ravishing Temple of Apollo, the Bath House, the dramatic Fountain of the Birds and a Chinese bridge. Friedrich Ludwig von Sckell redesigned the outer areas of the garden in the English Landscape style in 1776 – the rectangular pool at the end became an irregularly shaped lake – but de Pigage returned to design the Temple of Mercury and the Turkish mosque in 1785. Schwetzingen is no less compelling today: it is a place of exceptional beauty. Emperor Joseph II travelled incognito from Austria to see its gardens. Voltaire declared that his dying wish was to revisit this 'earthly paradise'.

☛ Baden-Durlach, Friedrich I, Friedrich II, Wilhelm, Wilhelmina

Elector Carl-Theodor of the Palatinate. b 1724. d 1799. Schloss Schwetzingen, Rheinland-Pfalz (GER), 1776–85.

Carmontelle Louis Carrogis de Parc Monceau

This pyramid is one of many architectural set-pieces and fragments that lie strewn around the Parc Monceau in Paris. They were designed to bring together 'all times and all places' in a natural landscape. Tombs, broken columns, an obelisk and an antique colonnade enclosing one end of a *naumachie* and ancient arches were all erected by Carmontelle for the Duc de Chartres, later Duc d'Orleans, known as Philippe-Egalite, in 1769. Louis Carrogis de Carmontelle was a dramatist, illustrator and garden designer and in his published folio *Views of the Jardin de Monceau* he commented, 'Let us introduce into our gardens the shifting scenes of the opera'. He wanted to transform a Picturesque garden into an illusory landscape. The operatic result, disdained by many commentators, today seems rather attractive, even though the Picturesque landscape element is barely noticeable. An equally intriguing cascade and grotto were added after 1860 by Alphand, Barillet-Deschamps and Davioud as part of the re-designing of Paris.

☛ Barillet-Deschamps, Chambers, Pückler-Muskau, Tschumi

94

Louis Carrogis de Carmontelle. b Paris (FR), 1717. d Paris (FR), 1806. Parc Monceau, Paris (FR), 1773.

Carter George

Silverstone Farm

A gate sculpted from gardening tools helps to frame a flint obelisk topped by a gilded finial; the other sides of the frame are formed by a hornbeam *allée*. Perfectly composed, rich with meaning and slightly surreal, this is one of many arresting tableaux in George Carter's Norfolk garden. In this 0.8-hectare (2-acre) plot, acquired in 1990, Carter has skilfully woven together historical influences to create a garden that is uncompromisingly formal yet distinctly modern in its mood, scale and materials. It includes a curved wall of hornbeam based on an eighteenth-century exedra, a Dutch Mannerist duckhouse and a variety of obelisks and sculptures in muted paint colours that blend with the cool green background. This is not a flower garden – most of the plants are trimmed or trained. Carter is practised at 'creating a *mis-en-scène* out of nothing' – balls and obelisks are cast from concrete and statues are cut from plywood. He changes the elements frequently, like stage sets, and illuminates features at night with footlights.

☛ Cane, Johnston, Lennox-Boyd, Shenstone, Strong & Oman

George Carter. b Rotherham, Yorkshire (UK), 1948. **Silverstone Farm**, North Elmham, Norfolk (UK), 1990–.

Caruncho Fernando   Wheat Garden

Inscribed into this Spanish landscape, following the grid of orange groves and plough marks, this garden shows a high degree of formality, albeit expressed in a contemporary fashion. Although it never attempts to mimic an ancient pattern, it could have been there since time immemorial, belonging to an undiscovered civilization. Fernando Caruncho is undoubtedly heir to the Spanish garden tradition, which is rooted in the Moorish style and the Alhambra at Granada. He is also a great admirer of such gardens as Vaux-le-Vicomte near Paris and the Boboli in Florence. But his particular brand of formality runs deep; it is not a simple design tool but a fundamental belief, inspired by his philosophical studies, notably of the ancient Greeks. The sense of order and balance, of permanence and history, is achieved by bringing together Caruncho's own aesthetic heritage and the history of the landscape. He is particularly interested in the science of irrigation and ancient agricultural patterns.

☛ Hall, Le Nôtre, Muhammad V, Tribolo, Wirtz

96

Fernando Caruncho (Fernando Caruncho Torga). b c1962. **Wheat Garden**, Palma de Mallorca (SP).

Carvallo Dr Joachim   Villandry

The apogee of the formal French ornamental kitchen garden, or potager, can be found at the gardens of Villandry, created in the early twentieth century by Dr Joachim Carvallo. When he acquired the sixteenth-century, Loire-region château, Dr Carvallo was faced with an eighteenth-century *jardin anglaise* (landscape garden), and he set about making a series of formal parterre terraces to complement the house. The ground slopes gently to the north and at the lowest level Dr Carvallo made the centrepiece of the garden: the formal potager, which is still immaculately maintained. Nine differently patterned box-edged squares contain a wide variety of vegetables, grown for their appearance as well as for their taste. Villandry led the cult for ornamental vegetables – notably purple and green cabbages, ruby chard and coloured lettuce – that was at its height in the 1980s and 1990s. Indeed, the ornamental purple cabbage, perhaps romantically frosted, has become an iconic image.

☛ Blanc, Duchêne, B Rothschild, Shurcliff, Vogue

97

Dr Joachim Carvallo. b Don Benito (SP), 1869. **d** Paris (FR), 1936. **Villandry**, nr Tours, Indre-et-Loire (FR), 1906–24.

Catherine II Tsarina of Russia   Ekaterininsky Park at Tsarskoye Selo

The Palladian Bridge is one of several features in Catherine's park which were inspired by features at Stowe, thanks to her passionate enthusiasm for English landscape parks. While some of the formal gardens with which Benjamin F Rastrelli had surrounded his impressive palace for the Empress Elizabeth were retained, John Bush was persuaded to leave his Hackney nursery and to reshape a large part of the palace grounds for Catherine after the English fashion. Among the designers of the many park buildings in various exotic styles was the Scottish architect Charles Cameron, who was responsible for the Chinese village and the pyramid mausoleum for the tsarina's Italian greyhounds. A Turkish pavilion, the Turkish Cascade and the later Turkish Bath all celebrated victories over the Turks. The Sliding Hill, one of the world's first rollercoasters, fell out of favour and was dismantled after Catherine narrowly avoided a nasty accident.

☛   **Allen, Brown, Cameron, Grenville-Temple, Peter II**

Catherine II, Tsarina of Russia (Catherine the Great). b Stettin (POL), 1729. **d** St Petersburg (RUS), 1796. **Ekaterininsky Park at Tsarskoye Selo**, sth of St Petersburg (RUS).

Caus Isaac de

Woburn Abbey

This highly ornate grotto is a unique survival of Isaac de Caus' idiosyncratic work. It was constructed in the basement of the abbey for Lucy Harrington, wife of the 3rd Earl of Bedford, and since it bears his arms, it must have been created prior to his death in 1627. Isaac, like his elder brother Salomon, was a French hydraulic engineer, architect, garden designer and builder of automata. He was greatly influenced by the gardens of the Italian Renaissance, particularly that of Pratolino. With its walls covered in imitation coral formations and manmade rock, its vaulted ceiling decorated with arabesques in shells, and the classical imagery of the frieze that depicts sea gods drawn in shell chariots and *putti* riding on dolphins, Woburn's grotto is a testament to the magical world of the late Renaissance Mannerist style. It also demonstrates how far and wide the impact of the Renaissance was felt, and its survival provides an insight into just how ornate the grotto at Wilton (on which Isaac advised) would have been.

☛ Buontalenti, S Caus, Francini, Isham, Lane, Pulham

Isaac de Caus. b Dieppe (FR), 1590. **d** (UK), after 1655. **Woburn Abbey**, Bedfordshire (UK), 1630s.

Caus Salomon de

Hortus Palatinus

This painting by J Fouquières shows all the intricate details of Salomon de Caus' finest garden. Elizabeth Stuart, daughter of James I of England and wife of the Elector Palatine, Frederick V, summoned de Caus (her former drawing-master) to Heidelberg in 1613. By 1618 the garden was complete. De Caus, a French engineer and garden designer who had spent three years in Italy, created a garden that was strongly influenced by the Renaissance gardens that he had seen there. The site was composed of five superimposed, narrow terraces. Each terrace was divided using hedges and pergolas and the garden contained typical Renaissance features such as a maze, statuary, a gazebo, topiary, parterres and, most importantly, grottoes, waterworks and musical automata, for which he also composed the music. All that remains of de Caus' garden today are the inappropriately planted terraces and a forlorn statue of Father Rhine and even this is an epoxy resin copy.

☞ Buontalenti, Bushell, I Caus, Francini, Ligorio, Robins

Salomon de Caus. b (FR), 1576. **d** Paris (FR), 1626. **Hortus Palatinus**, Heidelberg (GER), 1613–18, as depicted by J Fouquières, 1620.

Chambers William   Kew Gardens

Across the lake, between the Temples of Victory and Arethusa, William Chambers' ten-storey pagoda rises 49 m (163 ft) against the sky, a testimony to his venture into chinoiserie at a period when Chinese style was the prevailing taste in Europe. In 1757 Princess Augusta commissioned Chambers to lay out her garden at Kew, earlier developed as a landscape garden by Capability Brown.

Chambers disliked the blandness of Brown's smooth lawns and lakes, preferring gardens that displayed variety – 'the pleasing, the terrible and the surprising'. He filled the garden with more than twenty temples, an aviary, menagerie, mosque, Palladian bridge and the largest hothouse of the time, the Great Stove, illustrated in *Plans of the Gardens and Buildings at Kew* (1763). During this period a

small botanic garden was also formed. This garden expanded to become the Royal Botanic Gardens, Kew, with Chambers' pagoda remaining as a reminder of its early history.

☛   **Friedrich II, Hardtmuth, Hoare, Qian Long**

101

William Chambers. b Gothenburg (SWE), 1723. **d** London (UK), 1796. **Kew Gardens**, Kew, Richmond, Surrey (UK), 1757, *A View of the Lake and Island at Kew*, Paul Sandby after William Marlowe, 1763.

Chand Saini Nek
Rock Garden, Chandigarh

Frozen in the rigidity of their steel armature, coated with tightly packed rags, crowds of statues and herds of animals populate the clearings, waterfalls and temples of the Rock Garden at Chandigarh, one of the world's most poignant and spectacular visionary environments. As is often the case with extraordinary places, their genesis is equally remarkable. In the 1950s, Nek Chand Saini was a civil servant employed on the huge building site which was the new city of Chandigarh – an extraordinary project designed by Le Corbusier. But Chand had a dream. Collecting stones and waste material from the tons of rubble from the twenty villages razed to make way for the new city, he secretly started designing his dream kingdom in a clearing behind his state-owned dwelling. Support for Chand's great work grew so strong that the authorities were compelled to offer men and means to allow Chand to complete his dream. Now covering 20 hectares (50 acres), it receives over 5,000 visitors a day.

☛ Arakawa & Gins, Cheval, I Hicks, Le Corbusier, Saint-Phalle

102

Nek Chand Saini. b (IN), 1924. **Rock Garden**, Chandigarh (IN), 1950s–.

Chatto Beth

Gravel Garden

It is still possible to create a spectacular display of plants, even when the growing medium is nothing but 60 cm (2 ft) of gravel and sand overlaying clay. The Gravel Garden, which was once the car park for Beth Chatto's garden, was made in 1991. Its inspiration was a dried-up river bed in New Zealand, where a wide range of plants thrived on the inhospitable banks. The garden is an extension of the concept of working with nature. By taking the decision never to water or feed the garden, to let the plants live or die on their own ability to withstand her conditions, Mrs Chatto experienced the sad deaths of unsuitable plants and the joy when others thrived. But 'survival of the fittest' is only half of the experiment. The other half has been the careful crafting of the plant associations in order to create a display of flowers, form and foliage that looks stunning year round and remains relatively low maintenance.

☞ Brookes, Jarman, Kingsbury, Lloyd, Oudolf

Beth Chatto. b (UK), 1923. **Gravel Garden**, nr Chelmsford, Essex (UK), 1991.

Cheval Joseph Ferdinand   Le Palais Ideal

Defying any notion of integrated design, the Palais Ideal is haphazardly made up of colonnades and balustrades, staircases and grottoes, fountains and sculptures. This intense and fantastical environment, which combines mythical bestiaries, far-reaching mythologies and multiple religious references, was built between 1879 and 1912, the work of Joseph Ferdinand Cheval, a country postman with no qualifications except limitless imagination and energy. Bored not only by his job but also with his vegetable allotment, Cheval began collecting oddly shaped pebbles and stones while on walks in the countryside. Remarking on the beauty of some of these shapes, he decided, 'If nature can be such a sculptor, I can be a builder and an architect'. He integrated the objects in 'embellishments' to his plot – a rill here, a fountain or a grotto there – using cement, then a new material, which fascinated him. His grand composition eventually took over neighbouring plots. Cheval's original plantings are now being restored.

☞ Arakawa & Gins, Chand Saini, I Hicks, James, Saint-Phalle

Joseph Ferdinand Cheval (Facteur Cheval). b 1836. d Hauterives (FR), 1924. **Le Palais Ideal**, Hauterives (FR), 1879–1912.

Child Susan

Grande Isle Pathway

Zigzagging through beech and birch woodland towards a meadow, a raised wooden boardwalk path ends as abruptly as it begins. Elsewhere on this huge 32.3-hectare (80-acre) site overlooking Lake Champlain in Vermont, stairs, viewing platforms, a rustic pavilion and other raised pathways are used to draw attention to the special character of the landscape. With this minimal intervention by Susan Child, the lake's shore, the woodlands, the lowlands and the meadows are left undisturbed. It is the visitor's perception that changes and becomes heightened. The walker is encouraged to explore his own feelings as well as the landscape: standing to contemplate the view on a platform, walking quickly but carefully (poison ivy abounds) between the sections of boardwalk, sitting in meditation in the pavilion. With her practice based in Boston, Child has produced some of her finer works in New England, undoubtedly inspired by the landscape. Her most famous work, however, is the landscaping of the South Cove in Manhattan's Battery Park.

☛ Dow, Goldsworthy, Hall, Ruys, Schaal, Suzuki

Susan Child. b 1928. **Grande Isle Pathway** Grande Isle, VT (USA), 1995.

Church Thomas El Novillero

This free-form pool designed by Thomas Church was inspired by the beautiful curved shores of the bay and the work of Alvar Aalto. It became an icon of twentieth-century landscape design. When it was built, its biomorphic shape was revolutionary. The image of this pool transformed the way swimming pools were designed, firstly in California and then across the States over the next thirty years. Church was commissioned to design the pool and the surrounding terraces shaded by evergreen holm oaks at the northern end of San Francisco Bay by Mr and Mrs Donnell, who built a house on the site in the 1950s. The property is still owned by the Donnell family today. Through his work, and his book *Gardens are for People*, Church encouraged the wider public to visualize a real use of space based on a twentieth-century modern design aesthetic. Church also mastered the deck design for small gardens.

☞ Aalto, Eckbo, Halprin, Kiley, Moore, Rose

Thomas Church. b Boston, MA (USA), 1902. **d** San Francisco, CA (USA), 1978. **El Novillero,** Sonoma, CA (USA), c1950s.

Clément Gilles & Provost Alain Parc André Citroën

A series of rectangular ramped lawns of varying widths give a slightly lopsided symmetry to this vista at Parc André Citroën in Paris. The scattering of informally planted Versailles tubs adds another playful twist to classic design tradition. On the former site of the Citroën car works, the celebrated French landscape designers Gilles Clément and Alain Provost have created a public space of dazzling inventiveness. The various themed areas include Black, White and Blue Gardens, Six Sense Gardens, and a plaza where children run through random water jets. Although it deliberately echoes the formal layout of other great Parisian parks, Parc André Citroën makes a distinctly contemporary appeal to mind, body and spirit, as well as complementing the surrounding modern architecture. Provost is responsible for the Great Lawn to the right of the photograph, while Clément – who famously hates lawns – is behind the Garden of Movement, a meadow where plants move in the breeze.

☞ Gustafson, Lassus, Pepper, Tschumi, Walker

Gilles Clément. b (FR), 1943. Alain Provost. Parc André Citroën, Paris (FR), 1988–92.

Clerk Sir John

Penicuik

The landscape at Penicuik is an example of an amateur designer taking a lead from prevailing fashions, but adding great individuality. Sir John was a central political and artistic figure in Edinburgh at the turn of the eighteenth century, and both facets of his life were played out at Penicuik. From 1700 onwards he spent his Exchequer stipend creating a poetic landscape. Early work was carried out to a planting plan by William Adair, penned in the 1690s. Shelter-belts enclosed regular fields and blocks of woodland. Avenues were planted and existing streams were lined with trees to create serpentine walks. Over three decades Sir John experimented with various types of landscape design. Perhaps taking his lead from the writings of Stephen Switzer, he created a sort of *ferme ornée*, with ornamental walks, terraces, a summerhouse and a grotto representing the cave of the Cumaean Sibyl, with all its associated 'horrific' imagery.

☛ J Aislabie, Hamilton, Shenstone, Southcote, Switzer

Sir John Clerk. b Edinburgh (UK), 1679. d Penicuik, Midlothian (UK), 1755. **Penicuik**, Midlothian (UK), 1720s.

Clusius Carolus   Leiden Botanical Garden

This small gazebo creates a focal point at the centre of the restored Botanical Garden in Leiden. In his later years Charles de l'Ecluse, known as Clusius, the first scientific botanist in Europe, was in charge of the Hortus Academicus at Leiden University. The sixteenth-century botanic garden is now just a small part of Leiden's *Hortus Botanicus*. Small rectangular beds laid out around the gazebo are edged with bricks and separated by paths of crushed white shells. Old-fashioned beehives stand in one corner. In the beds are ranks of those early tulips and other small bulbs which Clusius introduced to The Netherlands. While he had been prefect of the Imperial Gardens in Vienna, Clusius had acquired tulip bulbs and seeds from the imperial ambassador at the Turkish court in Constantinople. His descriptions of the numerous varieties of tulip, especially their habit of 'breaking', or becoming variegated, eventually led to 'Tulipomania' and the Dutch bulb industry.

☞ Balat, Chambers, Moroni, Sloane, van Riebeeck

Carolus Clusius (Charles de L'Ecluse). b (NL), 1526. **d** (NL), 1609. **Leiden Botanical Garden**, Leiden, South Holland (NL), 1594.

Cockerell Samuel Pepys   Sezincote

Drawing heavily on Indian architecture for their inspiration, the house and garden buildings at Sezincote were designed for Sir Charles Cockerell by his brother Samuel Pepys Cockerell in 1805. Sir Charles had spent time in India and Samuel took for his inspiration Thomas and William Daniell's sketches, published in 1788 as *Select Views of India*. Repton designed the landscape garden, and probably advised Samuel as to which of Daniell's sketches would be most appropriate to adapt. Sezincote shows perfectly how Indian architecture could be anglicized to become a peculiar blend of Indian and Palladian styles. The garden is an equally odd amalgam, with Indian ornamentation – Brahmin bulls, a Hindu temple and serpents entwined around a pole – a Repton landscape and, in front of the curving conservatory, an Islamic *chahar bagh*. Today, Sezincote is also celebrated for the quality and variety of its planting.

☞ Bateman & Cooke, Chambers, Nash, Repton, G S Thomas

Samuel Pepys Cockerell. **b** Somerset (UK), 1753. **d** London (UK), 1827. **Sezincote**, Gloucestershire (UK), 1805.

Colchester Manyard — Westbury Court

Bordered by a hedge, the long canal reflects the tall, slim, and elegant summerhouse or gazebo, the dominant feature in this compact garden built between 1694 and 1705. The building's architecture and the surrounding garden reflect a strong Dutch influence. The hedges are topped with 'Dutch topiary', a style in which different evergreens are grown through the top of the yew hedge and clipped into geometric shapes, here cones and balls. Colchester covered the garden walls with many different types of fruit tree, and filled the parterre garden with thousands of bulbs imported from Holland. This intimate and intricately planted style had become popular when William and Mary ascended the English throne in 1689, and wars with France ensured that the grandiose French style fell from fashion. Manyard's nephew, also Manyard, continued to develop the garden in the same vein between 1715 and 1756, although by this time it was completely at odds with the prevailing trend, the English landscape garden.

☞ Huygens, London, Marot & Roman, van Campen, William III, Wise

Manyard Colchester. d 1715. Westbury Court, Gloucestershire (UK), 1694–1705.

Colvin Brenda

Little Peacocks

Little Peacocks was Brenda Colvin's private garden. The planting is naturalistic but diverse, and the range of spring flowers and foliage creates a perfect foil to the lovely Cotswold house. As the seasons change, so does the display, and the selection of species and their arrangement amply demonstrates Colvin's wide plant knowledge and planting design skills. Such talents were also put to use in other, larger-scale garden schemes, notably the Riverside Garden at Buscot Park and the replanting of Sutton Courtenay, both in Oxfordshire. Brenda Colvin was a founder member of the Landscape Institute (formed in 1929 under the name British Association of Garden Architects) and author of one of the first standard texts of the new profession – *Land and Landscape* (1947).

In her professional capacity as a landscape architect, she was responsible for several urban design projects. Among them was the military town of Aldershot, Hampshire, as well as power stations, land reclamation sites and reservoirs.

☛ Crowe, Fish, Gibberd, Jellicoe

Brenda Colvin. b Simla (IN), 1897. **d** Filkins, Gloucestershire (UK), 1981. **Little Peacocks**, Filkins, Gloucestershire (UK), 1955–81.

Cook William Douglas

Pukeiti Rhododendron Garden

From the members' clubhouse at Pukeiti the lawns can be glimpsed flowing into and through the collection of 1,000 rhododendron species and 300 hybrids. Cook was a visionary of New Zealand conservation and gardening. The twin aims of his 'project for posterity', begun around 1937, were to conserve the several hundred hectares of virgin or regenerating natural forest on this North Island farm and create a garden in which a comprehensive Northern Hemisphere plant collection would act as a genetic resource for the reintroduction of plant families endangered or extinct in the wild. In 1951 he bought Pukeiti, and his twin aims coincided. He pioneered the controlled regeneration of the native bush, as well as making a garden for a rhododendron collection which is now the most important in the Southern Hemisphere. Pukeiti was developed and maintained with the assistance of a voluntary trust of paying members – a method used frequently to maintain large gardens today.

☞ Armstrong, Middleton, Savill, Walska

William Douglas Cook. b New Plymouth (NZ), 1884. d Gisborne (NZ), 1967. **Pukeiti Rhododendron Garden**, New Plymouth, Taranoki (NZ), 1951.

Cooper Paul

Golders Green Garden

A projection of Roy Lichtenstein's iconic Pop Art piece *Wham!* enlivens the night-time ambience of a small North London garden. The garden's owners intended to use the garden mainly at night, so Paul Cooper incorporated smooth white panels into his design to provide the potential for constantly changing visuals in this enclosed space. Architectural and textile designs are particularly effective projections. Metal balustrades section off small areas of the decked terrace, and a selection of shrubs grown for their foliage effects (hebes, bamboos, euphorbias) are confined to raised planters. A stainless steel cascade – cleverly lit – adds to the nocturnal drama. Cooper is an iconoclastic figure in contemporary garden design, well known for showcasing outrageous ideas, such as floating planters or mid-air hanging baskets, at Chelsea Flower Show. On one occasion he was censured for incorporating erotic drawings in his design.

☛ Cardasis, Delaney, Jellicoe, Le Corbusier, Schwartz, Smyth

Paul Cooper. b Manchester (UK), 1949. **Golders Green Garden**, London (UK), 1998.

Copeland Pamela & Lighty Richard   Mount Cuba Residence

Dappled woodland light falls on candelabra primula and native American phlox. Mount Cuba's garden addresses one of the great questions of contemporary gardening – the relationship between conservation and gardening. Pamela Copeland was awakened to the need to conserve land for wild flowers by the steady depletion of the Delaware wildlands. During the 1960s, she acquired a meadow and woodland adjacent to her garden and the new area was developed with the advice and supervision of Dr Richard Lighty. Its planting is limited mainly to the native plants of the Piedmont mountain chain which runs north-south through the Delaware region. Only occasionally are exotic plants used to enliven the garden visually. Using approximately 300 native plant species, the garden is planted not only for conservation but also for aesthetic effect, which changes annually as controlled self-seeding of the wild flowers is encouraged.

☞   Jensen, Oehme & Van Sweden, Robinson, Toll, Walling

Pamela Copeland. b 1906. **Dr Richard Lighty. b** 1933. **Mount Cuba Residence**, DEL (USA), 1960s.

Cox Madison

Show Case House

Terracotta pots of foxgloves are playfully arranged on a chequerboard of gravel in this Manhattan rooftop garden, the strong framework echoing the grid of the city below. This is a town garden *par excellence*. The garden is not designed to be used, and the very graphic layout is all for show – Madison Cox prefers his gardens to have a sharp structure. Clear definition and strict organization are, in his eyes, the best way to achieve a peaceful environment. Though he is a keen plantsman, Cox puts little emphasis on plants, preferring to use a relatively narrow repertory of evergreen shrubs, vines and trees to soften and dress his strong structures. Having chosen to train in France, this New Yorker established himself in Paris, where he designed elegant town gardens for private *hotels particuliers* and public spaces like the Franco-American Museum. He eventually returned to his bustling home town to create rooftop oases.

☞ Delaney, Hancock, Herman, Hosack

Madison Cox. b Washington, DC (USA), 1958. **Show Case House**, New York, NY (USA), 1990s.

Crisp Sir Frank

Friar Park

This rock garden with the celebrated (or notorious) 'Mini Matterhorn', is considered the most complex and important of the nineteenth century. In the 1890s, Blackhouse made the rockworks for the main Alpine landscape; Pulham (inventor of the popular Victorian reconstituted *trompe l'oeil* rocks, 'Pulhamite') created the waterfall and the rocky banks around the lake. The Matterhorn recreation itself was the work of Sir Frank Crisp's own gardener, Knowles. Crisp was an expert on alpines and some 2,500 species were grown among the rocks. William Robinson said that it was the best 'natural' stone rock garden that he had ever seen – he particularly liked the bright colours of the little colonies or carpets of alpines. Inside the 'Mini Matterhorn' was the 'ice grotto' copied from the cave in the Glacier du Geant at Chamonix, but with stalactites of real blue ice at the right time of year.

☞ I Caus, S Caus, Gildemeister, Isham, Lane, Pulham

Sir Frank Crisp. Active (UK), late nineteenth century. **Friar Park**, Henley on Thames, Oxfordshire (UK), 1890s.

Crowe Sylvia

Wexham Springs

The concrete blocks used for this textured wall contrast with the smooth-cast concrete floor, steps and sculptural water basin, the whole blending with the more natural materials of water-washed cobbles and plant matter. Dame Sylvia, a contemporary of Sir Geoffrey Jellicoe and Brenda Colvin, was mainly occupied by large-scale commissions such as the layout of new towns, nuclear power stations, forestry plantations, reservoirs and the routing of the National Grid. Her landscape designs reflected loyalty to Brown and Repton, yet she never lost the connection between the garden and its role, as she observed in *Garden Design*, her *magnum opus* published in 1958: 'Men in every age have felt the need to reconcile themselves with their surroundings, and have created gardens to satisfy their ideals and inspirations.' This ethos is evident in all her gardens. This garden was modern in style, created for a new-town setting. Others, such as Sutton Courtenay, have a more 'country cottage' feel to them.

☞ **Colvin, Gibberd, Halprin, Jellicoe, Le Corbusier, Tunnard**

Dame Sylvia Crowe. b Banbury, Oxfordshire (UK), 1901. **d** 1998. **Wexham Springs**, Wexham Springs (UK), 1969.

Cyrus the Great Pasargadae Palace

Only ruins of the ancient garden palace complex at Pasargadae remain – dry and lifeless on the plain of Mashhad-e Morghab. Backed by a range of mountains and overlooking the broad sweep of a once-fertile plateau crossed by the waters of the River Pulvar, this site was ideal for a royal compound. Pictured here is the monumental gatehouse which led to the main palace via an avenue of cypresses, pomegranates, sour cherry and fragrant grasses. A bridge led on to the reception palace, which was surrounded by loggias overlooking the gardens. Another avenue led to the main palace and royal garden which was flanked by pavilions. Pasargadae was the first monumental palace and garden to be built of stone in Persia – previously mud brick and wood were used.

Most importantly, the elaborate water features that typify the Persian garden were developed at this site, for under Cyrus the Great the revolutionary hydraulics system called the *qanat* was invented.

☛ Abd al-Rahman II, Assurbanipal, Darius the Great, Ineni, Thutmosis

Cyrus the Great. Reigned Persia (IR), c557–530 BC. **d** 529 BC. **Pasargadae Palace**, Persia (IR), c557–530 BC.

Czartoryska Izabelle   Lancut

This gloriette or eyecatcher, takes the form of a semicircle of classical Corinthian columns and an entablature of festooned bucranial decoration. It stands on a rise in the garden laid out in the early years of the nineteenth century at Lancut. This is one of four landscape parks in Poland commissioned by the great patron Duchess Izabelle Czartoryska. Lancut is a combination of classical and historical elements. Originally the château was surrounded by a star-shaped fortified moat. The duchess reduced the fortifications, leaving the moat as a ha-ha to gain views into the park which was landscaped in an eighteenth-century manner, with groups of trees and classical buildings as focal points. Inspired by a visit to Rome, she had the conservatory walls painted by the decorator to Tsar Paul I as a *trompe l'oeil* Italian loggia, with sunlit views through vine leaves of classical ruins: the duchess' antidote to the cold Polish winter. She was also the author in Polish of the standard work on English landscape gardens, *Various Thoughts on the Creation of Gardens*, published in 1805.

☛ Brown, Palladio, Radziwill, Vanbrugh, Zug

Izabelle Czartoryska. b Warsaw (POL), 1746. d Wysoch, nr Jaroslaw (POL), 1835. Lancut, Rzeszow (POL), early nineteenth century.

Darius the Great
Apadana Palace

Following in the footsteps of Cyrus the Great, Darius designed Apadana, his garden palace, at Persepolis, transforming a barren landscape into a watered paradise (*pairi-daeza*) and mirroring the Persian images of Eden. He integrated architectural and design styles from all the nations that the Persian Empire had conquered and absorbed – India, Egypt and Libya, Greece and as far south as Ethiopia. Here in the soaring royal halls, on pillars and garden walls, we see bas-reliefs and carvings of lotus blossoms, sacred pine trees and other decorations reminiscent of Babylonia, Greece and Egypt. There is evidence that Darius planted rows of pine trees on the broad esplanade at the foot of the lower terrace, echoing these elegant wall carvings. Like Pasargadae, the Apadana Palace had rooms surrounded by vast colonnades, and the throne rooms overlooked reflecting pools, trees and walled green spaces. The stairway pictured here led to the first of three immense terraces.

☞ **Assurbanipal, Cyrus the Great, Ineni, Thutmosis**

Darius the Great. Reigned 521–486 BC, Persia (IR). **Apadana Palace**, Persepolis, Persia (IR), founded c515 BC.

Darwin Charles

Downe House

This woodland walk, which Darwin called his 'sand-walk' or 'thinking path', leads from the house to an orchard. Here lay the laboratory and the greenhouses in which Darwin made his plant studies, particularly of orchids and carnivorous plants. The 7 hectares of landscaped grounds that surround Down House, in which Darwin lived from 1842–82, were places in which he could relax, be with his family and recover from his psychosomatic illness. They were also key to much of the research that underpinned his writings. Other garden features include, adjacent to the house, a small flower garden laid out around a sundial by Emma Wedgewood, Darwin's wife (and cousin), and a shrubbery. One of Darwin's eccentricities was that many of the trees were planted on individual mounds of earth. Darwin's confidant throughout the preparation of *On the Origin of Species* was Sir Joseph Hooker, the second director of Kew and the plant hunter who introduced twenty-eight new rhododendron species from the Himalayas.

☞ **Clusius, Manning, Moroni, Ruskin, Wordsworth**

122

Charles Darwin. b Shrewsbury (UK), 1809. **d** Downe, Kent (UK), 1882. **Downe House**, Kent (UK), 1842–82.

Dashwood Sir Francis West Wycombe Park

Viewed across a rippling lake, the timelessly classical Doric columns of West Wycombe's east portico belie the colourful history of its principal creator: the mercurial 2nd baronet, practical joker, occasional scholar, failed Chancellor of the Exchequer and member of the notorious Hell-Fire Club in the mid-eighteenth century. After a series of Grand Tours to Europe and Asia Minor,

Dashwood began his formally informal rococo landscape from c1735, linking set-piece temples with straight avenues and serpentine walks. He reputedly shaped his lake into the form of a woman's body and kept a small fleet for mock sea battles. A Temple of Venus suggestively placed on a mound has since been rebuilt to designs by architect Quinlan Terry. During the 1770s, a

pupil of Capability Brown smoothed the landscape into the 'English' style; a generation later, Humphry Repton removed 'some useless and unmeaning buildings'. But park and flamboyantly Italianate house remain Dashwood's very personal creation.

☞ Burlington, Grenville-Temple, Hoare, Medinacelli, Walpole

123

Sir Francis Dashwood. b 1708. **d** West Wycombe, Bucks (UK), 1781. **West Wycombe Park**, West Wycombe, Buckinghamshire (UK), c1735.

Delaney Topher

Bank of America

On the rooftop of a San Francisco corporation, colourful windsocks behave like giant plants swaying in the wind. Brightly painted concrete surfaces and rough blocks of stone delineate this paradoxical and whimsical garden. Inspired by both contemporary conceptual art and by other landscape architects of the new formalist tradition, such as Luis Barragán, Topher Delaney is one of America's most inventive designers. She often likes to refer to what she calls every individual's 'personal narrative'. For one client in California who had just been through a relationship break-up, she imagined a 'Garden of Divorce', using as a main feature the shattered pieces of a stone table, a gift from the estranged partner. In the mid-1990s Delaney focused her attention on gardens for hospital and medical facilities, investigating and finding applications for the healing powers of the garden. In this she was following her own 'personal narrative': her struggle with cancer and subsequent treatment.

☛ Barragán, Chand Saini, Cox, Hancock, Schwartz

124

Topher Delaney. b 1948. **Bank of America**, San Francisco, CA (USA), 1997.

Dow Herbert

The Dow Gardens

The lacquer-effect fretwork of a Chinese-influenced ornamental bridge stands out dramatically against the snow, in the 3.5-hectare (8-acre) Dow Gardens, inland from the coast at Saginaw Bay, Michigan. The gardens, sited on a flat sandy plateau were the creation of Herbert Dow, founder of the Dow Chemical Company. When he started laying out the gardens in 1899, Dow, who had a keen interest in agriculture and architectural design, followed one basic tenet, which he summed up: 'never reveal the garden's whole beauty at first glance'. This led Dow to create a garden landscape that entertains and engages the visitor by revealing its many secrets in a range of experiences, each enlivened by a wide variety of plants. The Chinese bridge in this woodland compartment also draws inspiration from the contemporary American architectural details introduced by Frank Lloyd Wright and the Chicago School. The gardens now cover 110 acres and contain 1700 varieties of trees, shrubs and flowers, including an extensive collection of All American roses.

☛ **Beck & Collins, Forestier, Hornel, Shipman, F L Wright**

Herbert Dow. d MI (USA), 1930. **The Dow Gardens**, Midland, MI (USA), 1899.

Downing Andrew Jackson & Vaux Calvert   The Capitol

This view of the Capitol, Washington, DC, is one of the most potent symbols of the US Government. Andrew Jackson Downing and Calvert Vaux created the formal landscape between the Capitol and Capitol Hill modelled on the town plan for Versailles. They also designed the Smithsonian Institution and the White House, and, had Downing not drowned at a tragically young age in a steamboat accident, it might have been Downing and Vaux, instead of Frederick Law Olmsted, who designed Central Park. Downing had persuaded Vaux, an English architect, to visit the USA, and after Downing's death he went on to become Olmsted's partner. Downing had edited *The Horticulturist* for the last eight years of his life, using the magazine to promote the creation of public parks in America and to advocate recreational uses for rural cemeteries, encouraging the 'tasteful and harmonious embellishments of these sites by art'. He was also an exponent of the simple, natural and permanent landscape.

☞ Bigelow, Eaton, Le Nôtre, Loudon, Olmsted

Andrew Jackson Downing. b Newburgh, NY (USA), 1815. d nr Youleers, NY (USA), 1852. **Calvert Vaux.** b London (UK), 1824. d Brooklyn, NY (USA), 1895. **The Capitol**, Washington, DC (USA), 1851.

Dubsky Emanuel

Lysice

A monumental Doric colonnade was constructed by Emanuel Dubsky in about 1853 as a covered promenade around the garden at Lysice. The models for the design were the *peristyle* or colonnade-surrounded gardens of ancient Rome. Later, his growing interest in the Czech National Revival led to his abandonment of the neo-classical style and his construction on top of the colonnade of a gallery in a style derived from that of traditional Czech wooden structures. Lysice thus combines one of the principal neo-classical gardens in central Europe with an important garden of the Czech Arts and Crafts Movement. This is an extremely unusual – perhaps unique – hybrid. The garden also boasts much traditional carpet-bedding in which dwarf foliage and succulent plants are grown in geometric patterns and scissored over during the growing season to maintain a low carpet-like effect.

☞ Bosworth, Lutyens, Sitwell, Tibernitus

Emanuel Dubsky. b (CZ), 1806. **d** (CZ), 1881. **Lysice,** nth of Brno (CZ), 1833.

Du Cerceau Jacques Androuet Verneuil

In harmony with the architecture of the château, the garden develops in a succession of squares and rectangles. The lower part is encircled by a canal reminiscent of the old moat of this once medieval castle, but here is a decorative feature. Symmetrical orchards, formal vegetable gardens and ornamental vineyards were an integral part of the garden. The ornate parterres were designed in low clipped bushes of lavender, thyme or marjoram. Commissioned by the Boullainvillier family, Du Cerceau worked on the garden and the castle from 1570. His son and grandson, both renowned architects in their own right, continued the work. This engraving, made by du Cerceau himself, is all that is left of the garden of the Château of Verneuil. Along with fifty other engravings it is part of his famous *Les Plus Excellents Bastiments de France* (1576–9), a precious source book for destroyed landmarks of the French Renaissance.

☛ L'Orme, Mercogliano, Poitiers

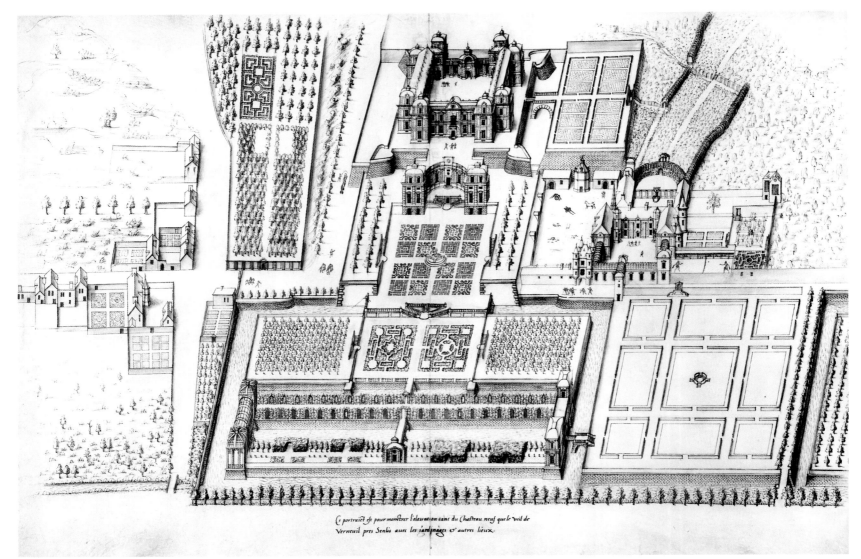

128

Jacques Ier (or François I) Androuet du Cerceau. b Paris (FR), 1510. **d** Annecy (FR), 1585. **Verneuil** (FR), 1570.

Duchêne Achille

Blenheim Palace Parterre

A succession of stone-lined pools carve an intricate pattern into the parterre of scrolling clipped box. Punctuated by great stone balls and the vertical sprays of the fountains, this 'water parterre' lies on the west front of Blenheim Palace, descending towards the lake. Like the adjacent Italian garden, and despite its Baroque feel, it was commissioned by the 9th Duke of Marlborough and created in the late 1920s by Achille Duchêne. The duke wanted to recapture some of the formality lost to Capability Brown's radical 1764 landscaping, so he commissioned Duchêne to restore the north forecourt and to replant a long avenue of elms that led up to it. Duchêne worked on the site of Henry Wise's sixteenth-century formal garden, but his designs were original. A talented designer in his own right, he is most famous for his important restorations at Courances and Vaux-le-Vicomte, and also for his unlikely enthusiasm for Modernism. Achille learned the trade from his father, Henri, and father and son worked together until 1902.

☛ Brown, Gallard, Hardouin-Mansart, Legrain, Wise

Achille Duchêne. b (FR), 1866. **d** 1947. **Blenheim Palace**, Woodstock, Oxfordshire (UK), 1920s.

Duncombe Thomas Rievaulx Terrace

The view from Thomas Duncombe's Rievaulx Terrace is constantly changing – 'a moving variation' Arthur Young called it in 1770. Duncombe laid out the long, spacious terrace near the top of the steep hillside in the 1750s: it curves for more than 1 km (½ mile) between a domed Ionic cupola and a pedimented Tuscan temple; both are banqueting houses. As you walk along the terrace, the views open and shut, so that sometimes the romantic Gothic ruins of the Cistercian Rievaulx Abbey far below are framed by woodland rides and sometimes they disappear altogether. By the time you reach the end, the views of Rievaulx have changed your perception completely. Crucial to Duncombe's scheme is the contrast between the classical landscape and the sublime decay of the ancient abbey.

The terrace represents an important landmark in the history of the English landscape movement, foreshadowing the rise of the Picturesque and renewed antiquarian interest in medieval architecture.

☛ J Aislabie, Gilpin, Kent, Knight

Thomas Duncombe (Thomas Brown, succeeded Sir Charles Duncombe, 1711). d (UK), 1799. **Rievaulx Terrace**, Yorkshire (UK), 1758.

Dunmore Lord

The Pineapple at Dunmore Park

This 15-m (48-ft) high pineapple was built for Lord Dunmore in 1761 to create a focal point in his walled garden. Pineapples had been grown in Scotland since the early eighteenth century and it is likely that they were cultivated at Dunmore Park. This may be the explanation for Lord Dunmore's whimsical commission. Below the pineapple shoots sits the banqueting hall, and on the south side of the folly are two levels of terraces containing an old orchard full of apple trees. In the original execution, glasshouses and a vegetable garden framed the folly, but both are long gone. The top of the pineapple sits above a circular drum with seven ogee arched windows, matching the door to the terrace on the north side. The pineapple and surrounding land have been owned by the National Trust of Scotland since 1974 and are open to the public. The pineapple itself can be short-let through the Landmark Trust.

☛ Chambers, Lenné, Monville, Smit

Lord Dunmore. b 1730. **d** Dunmore (UK), 1809. **The Pineapple at Dunmore Park**, Stirlingshire (UK), 1761.

Dupont Pierre S   Longwood

This greenhouse is the main feature at Longwood. It covers 1.4 hectares (3.3 acres) and is divided into sections according to climatic conditions. One area has palm trees growing to 60 ft with other sub-tropical plants around it reflected in pools. Immediately next door is an area with a lawn, temperate trees and flowerbeds where plants are changed on a monthly basis so that visitors always see the flowers at their peak. In 1906 Pierre S Dupont bought the 400 hectares (960 acres) of the Peirce Estate, which date from 1798. The gardens at Longwood were created over a thirty year period and every second year a new garden was created: A *vista à la Versailles*; an outdoor theatre seating 2,100 visitors; an Italian water garden; a fountain garden, almost as large as the fountains designed by Le Nôtre at Versailles. Longwood lacks a cohesive design, but as a rich man's toy, it is spectacular – and perhaps the most visited garden in America.

☞ **Balat, Burton & Turner, Fowler, Grimshaw, Paxton**

Pierre S Dupont. b Wilmington, DE (USA), 1870. **d** Wilmington, DE (USA), 1954. **Longwood**, Philadelphia, PA (USA), 1907–30s.

Duquette Tony

Dawnridge

A shrine to *objets trouvé*, Tony Duquette, designer to the stars, created his own oriental *Xanadu*. Located in a ravine, Dawnridge is filled with carvings from Indonesia, pagodas and small pavilions, set against jungle-like foliage and giant eucalypti. Inspired by his travels in Indochina, Thailand and Indonesia, Duquette mixed diverse elements in a kaleidoscopic experience, using the general layout of an Indonesian village. After beginning his career creating shop-front and window displays, Duquette became a legendary maverick designer – of movie sets, private interiors and theatrical costumes. His clients included J Paul Getty, the Duchess of Windsor and David O Selznick, for whom he designed the sets for *Ziegfield Follies*. Sadly, the garden was destroyed by a fire that consumed his opulent Baroque oriental extravaganza in its entirety.

☛ Bawa, Hearst, James, Jungles, Mizner, Washington Smith

Tony Duquette. b 1914. **d** Beverly Hills, CA (USA), 1999. **Dawnridge**, Beverly Hills, CA (USA), 1950s–.

Eaton Dr Hubert

Forest Lawn Memorial Park

Tombstones are set among flush graves and markers to create a relaxed layout of lawns, clumps of trees, informal paths and drives. Dr Hubert Eaton was the founder of the Forest Lawns Cemeteries company in California. He was inspired by the promotion of private garden cemeteries in the USA in the 1840s by Andrew Jackson Downing. Downing said that 'the great attraction of these cemeteries is not in the fact that they are burial places ... all these might be realized in a burial ground planted with straight lines of willows and sombre avenues of evergreens ... [but] in the natural beauty of the sites, and in the tasteful and harmonious embellishment of these sites by art'. He had possibly been inspired by the work of Dr Jacob Bigelow at Mount Auburn Cemetery in the 1820s. Eaton, in his own words, wanted to fill the parkland 'with towering trees, sweeping lawns, splashing fountains, singing birds' and to make the cemetery a place for the community.

☛ Asplund, Bigelow, Brongniart, Downing & Vaux, Scarpa

134

Dr Hubert Eaton. b 1881. **d** 1966. **Forest Lawn Memorial Park**, Glendale, CA (USA), c1910.

Eckbo Garrett

Alcoa Forecast Garden

An arrangement of vertical and horizontal panels in tinted aluminium creates an intriguing inside–outdoor transition from the house to a luxuriant garden, planted with sub-tropical plants. The Aluminum Forecast House was a 1959 experiment by Alcoa Aluminum to explore the use of their products in garden designs. Eckbo used his own house in Laurel Canyon, Los Angeles, for the experiment. Eckbo was a major influence on landscape architecture throughout his long career, engaging with social and technological innovations in his own work and in collaboration with some of the most important architects of the time. He studied at Harvard with James Rose and Dan Kiley, and all were influenced by Walter Gropius. Early in his career, Eckbo participated in social and agricultural experiments during the New Deal. His *Landscape for Living* and *The Landscape We See*, along with his teaching at Berkeley, helped revolutionize modern American landscape architecture.

☞ Church, Kiley, Neutra, Rose, Steele

Garrett Eckbo. **b** Cooperstown, NY (USA), 1910. **d** Oakland, CA (USA), 2000. **Alcoa Forecast Garden**, Laurel Canyon, Los Angeles (CA), 1959.

Egerton 3rd Baron
Tatton Park Japanese Garden

A spectacular autumnal foliage display sets off the thatched teahouse in the Japanese Garden which, created from 1910 by Japanese gardeners brought in for this very purpose, also contained lanterns, stepping-stone bridges, lakes and a Mount Fuji. This up-to-the-minute addition was in keeping with Tatton's past, which had seen Humphry Repton (in 1791) and Sir Joseph Paxton (in 1856)

add to the garden at the height of their careers. It was the opening up of Japan to the West and the arrival of new and exotic plants in the 1860s that sparked the recurring fad for Japanese gardens. This coincided with the publication of several books describing Japan's gardens, and displays at various international exhibitions. The natural-looking yet contrived style of Japanese gardens represented

a call to abandon the Italianate style or garish bedding schemes in favour of a more natural approach. Other famous Japanese gardens were created at Shipley Glen (1880s), Gunnersbury Park (1900), Fanhams Hall (1901) and Cottered (1905–26).

☞ Bateman, Hornel, Paxton, Repton

3rd Baron Egerton. b (UK), 1845. **d** (UK), 1920. **Tatton Park Japanese Garden**, Knutsford, Cheshire (UK), 1910.

Egerton-Warburton R E   Arley Hall

The perfect sward path leading to the classical seat is flanked on either side by a wide herbaceous border backed by a tall yew hedge. The richly planted borders could be mistaken for late nineteenth-century creations, but in fact they date from the 1840s and are one of the earliest examples of a 'mixed border'. In keeping with the vogue of the time, Egerton-Warburton not only planted the borders in a deliberately anti-Picturesque style that clearly displayed the hand of man, but he also drew inspiration from historic gardens, in this case the enclosed seventeenth-century herb gardens of Parkinson, Culpeper and Gerard. Although the borders at Arley are an early example, they demonstrate that, contrary to popular myth, the hardy herbaceous perennial did not become extinct when the craze for tender annual and bedding schemes took hold, nor did Gertrude Jekyll 'invent' the herbaceous border. Indeed, from the 1850s onwards these 'old-fashioned' plants acquired romantic poetic associations.

☛ Barron, Farrand, Johnston, Jekyll

R E Egerton-Warburton. b (UK), 1804. d (UK), 1891. Arley Hall, Cheshire (UK), 1840s.

Eldem Sedad

Kiraç Villa

Sedad Eldem combined in his gardens an uncompromising Modernism – as exemplified in this columned garden space – with traditional Turkish architectural and sculptural forms. Perhaps the greatest Turkish architect of the twentieth century, Eldem arranged the gardens or settings for many of his buildings, most notably in the villas he designed along the shores of the Bosphorus. His aim was to create a specifically Turkish style of architecture and garden design for the twentieth century. His most significant contribution to garden design is his book *Turk Bahceleri* (1976), an exhaustive survey, through paintings, photographs and measured drawings, of the gardens of the Ottoman Empire. It contains painstaking surveys of many gardens that are now lost, and it is the most important single resource for the study of one the world's great garden heritages.

☛ Bosworth, Gibberd, Kiley, Pearson & Cheal

138

Sedad Eldem (Sedad Hakki Eldem). b Istanbul (TRK), 1908. d Istanbul (TRK), 1988. **Kiraç Villa**, Tarabya (TRK), 1965–6.

Emes William   Erddig

The formal, walled garden created by John Meller on the east front of the house survives almost intact. Built between 1718 and 1733, it replaced the earlier garden, now marked by double avenues of pleached limes on each side of the rectangular lawns. Following contemporary fashion, Meller's garden was aligned on the main axis of the house, a broad gravel walk leading to a long central canal with views across the countryside. The park is enclosed by intricate wrought-iron gates (originally at the west entrance and re-erected here in 1971). In 1767, with less formal tastes in vogue, landscape gardener William Emes 'improved' the park in the style of Capability Brown. His work, which is reflected in much of the existing layout, included lavish tree planting, informal woodland walks and a unique waterfall feature, known as the Cup and Saucer. In terms of business, Emes came a poor second to Brown as a landscape designer in mid eighteenth-century England.

☞   **Brown, Goethe, Repton**

William Emes. b 1730. **d** 1803. **Erddig**, nr Wrexham, North Wales (UK), 1767.

Emma Queen

Lawai Kai (Allerton Gardens)

A distinctive, wavy edged rill of original design is one of the European-inspired features at *Lawai Kai*. Kaua'i is known as 'The Garden Isle' of the Hawaiian island chain. It is no wonder that Queen Emma chose to build her garden estate in this most beautiful setting. She named her garden retreat *Lawai Kai* ('Garden by the Sea' in the Hawaiian language) and carefully introduced ornamental specimens into the natural landscape. The cascading bougainvillea vine and the Moreton Bay fig tree were among her most striking introductions. Between 1938 and 1989, Robert and John Gregg Allerton, who were avid plant collectors themselves, brought more plants to the garden from around the globe. They also added design features such as water channels, cascades, pools and waterfalls, latticed pavilions and modern European sculpture. The overall effect is eclectic in design and dazzling in its botanical diversity – it is a series of imaginative gardens that compliment and enliven the natural landscape of this Pacific paradise.

☛ Hancock, Nazarite, Rhodes, Vignola

Queen Emma. b Honolulu, HI (USA), 1836. **d** Honolulu, HI (USA), 1885. **Lawai Kai (Allerton Gardens)**, Kaua'i, HI (USA), founded c1875.

140

Enshu Kobori

Nanzen-ji

With most of the garden given over to an empty expanse of finely raked white gravel, the careful arrangement of large rocks and shrubs is confined to the eastern corner, accentuating the impression of space. Chosen for their natural beauty rather than being imbued with abstract or symbolic meaning, as in earlier dry gardens, these rocks and the mounds of clipped azaleas form a magnificent naturalistic composition. Laid out in the late seventeenth century by Kobori Enshu, this important Zen temple garden belongs to the Ryoan-ji tradition. Originally from the military class, Kobori was a friend of Prince Toshihito and a renowned tea master and founder of the Enshu school of *cha-no-yu*. Enshu designed many important gardens, but his influence was so great that he has been credited with most of the gardens of that era, including the famous Katsura – for which he probably only gave friendly advice – and the Imperial Palace at Kyoto, during the Keicho era.

☛ **Hideyoshi, Mandokora, Pan En, Toshihito**

141

Kobori Enshu. b Nagahami (JAP), 1579. **d** Fushimi (JAP), 1647. **Nanzen-ji**, Kyoto (JAP), established 1337.

Esterházy Prince Miklós — Esterháza

Scrollwork parterres and fountains adorn the formal entrance courtyard at Esterháza in Hungary, built in the mid-eighteenth century to rival Versailles. The long ranges on either side of the main palace facade are curved to allow carriages to draw up at speed. Prince Miklós Esterházy embellished the gardens from 1756 until his death in 1790, commissioning a variety of ornamental buildings, temples and fountains, including a Chinese pavilion and a fireworks arena. He held sumptuous summer parties in the gardens, and there are many contemporary accounts of the wonders of the place. The wider estate was traversed by formal *allées*, with an octagonal boar-hunting ground at the eastern perimeter. Visitors would be transported through the estate in specially designed, extra-large carriages. However, just twenty-five years after the Prince's death the house and gardens were in a neglected state, no longer used by the family. Serious damage was inflicted in World War II, but the garden and what remains of the house have been restored.

☛ Catherine II, Fischer von Erlach, Hardouin-Mansart, Le Nôtre

Prince Miklós Esterházy. b Vienna (AUS), 1714. **d** Vienna (AUS), 1790. **Esterháza**, Fertöd (HUN), 1756–90.

Fairhaven Huttleston Broughton, 1st Baron

Anglesey Abbey

The Temple Lawn, a circle of ten Corinthian columns of Portland stone surrounding Bernini's *David* and enclosed by a yew hedge, was created in 1953 to commemorate the coronation of Queen Elizabeth II. The classical theme demonstrates that, despite many new concepts promulgated since Edwardian times, the Italian Renaissance continued to exert a strong influence on twentieth-century garden design. Anglesey is one of the few gardens that was actively developed in the post-war years when soaring taxes crippled many landowners. The garden was begun in 1930 and pre-war creations included a series of smaller, densely planted garden compartments near the house. Beyond, echoing the Renaissance concept of axes and the grandeur of the seventeenth-century formal landscape, is the most striking feature, the 17-m (54-ft) wide Great Avenue, planted in 1937 to commemorate the coronation of King George VI. The garden is celebrated today for its planting, notably snowdrops and dahlias.

☛ Bingley, Gibberd, Hamilton Finlay, Jellicoe, Peto

Huttleston Broughton (1st Baron Fairhaven). b (UK), 1896. d (UK), 1966. **Anglesey Abbey**, Cambridgeshire (UK), 1926–.

Farrand Beatrix

Dumbarton Oaks

Informal groupings of perennials and annuals are contained within a grid of paths and yew hedges. A single yew quietly terminates the main vista and a curvaceous, hip-roofed gazebo peeps out of the adjacent Cutting Garden. The border planting may have changed since the gardens were created (1921–47) but Dumbarton Oaks, in Washington, DC, remains one of the great twentieth-century American gardens. Beatrix Farrand had a love of French and Italian Renaissance gardens; she also admired contemporary English designers such as Jekyll, Lutyens and Mawson. Her great achievement was to combine these influences with a small palette of native American plants to create a garden that embodied the best of European design but had a strong connection to the surrounding landscape. The 20-hectare (50-acre) plot is divided into terraces and enclosures, with formal areas and loggias near the house and a more relaxed mood further away.

☞ Cane, Jekyll, Johnston, Mawson

Beatrix Jones Farrand. b New York, NY (USA), 1872. d 1959. **Dumbarton Oaks**, Georgetown, Washington, DC (USA), 1921–47.

Fath Ali Shah

Golestan Palace

Set within the Qasr-e Qajar in the Royal Quarter of Tehran, the Golestan garden typifies palatial garden styles of the late Qajar period of the late nineteenth century. A broad central avenue – as well as cascading watercourses – lead down three terraces from the palace to the main garden and the pavilion below. Such dramatic terracing and opulent water features were standard Qajar design elements. The Golestan Palace summer bathing pool, known as 'The Crown of the Kingdom', sat within an octagonal pleasure pavilion. Arched portals, or *ivans*, spanned each of its sides. The waters of a central fountain danced within the white marble bathing pool designed for the women of the Shah's extensive harem. The pavilion was two stories high and the women's quarters were on the upper floors. A marble slide was used by the women to reach the waters below. The Shah is said to have taken his midday repose in these upper chambers, in order to view the bathing beauties. Balance and symmetry resonate throughout this whole garden complex.

☛ Atabek Qaracheh, Babur, Nazarite, Sangram Singh, Shah Jahan

Fath Ali Shah. Reigned (IR), 1797–1843. **Golestan Palace**, Tehran (IR), built early nineteenth century.

Fischer von Erlach Johann Bernhardt Schönbrunn

This painting by Bernardo Bellotto shows how an eighteenth-century Austrian royal garden was designed, with wide paths and extensive spaces to accommodate a large crowd of courtiers. Created in emulation of Versailles, Schönbrunn exhibits an unusual unity of design. This is because the palace, park and garden were all designed by one man: J B Fischer von Erlach.

Fischer von Erlach brought exceptional intimacy to the garden by planting groves of trees close to the palace. These groves were laid out to make comfortable areas of shade where people might promenade, even in the heat of the day. The ambience beneath the trees is quite distinct from the open splendour of the garden's parterres. Fischer's book *Entwurf einer historischen Architektur* (1721),

with illustrations in many exotic styles, had considerable influence on garden architecture throughout Europe.

☛ Gallard, Hardouin-Mansart, Le Nôtre, Tessin the Younger

146

Johann Bernhardt Fischer von Erlach. **b** Graz (AUS), 1656. **d** Vienna (AUS), 1723. **Schönbrunn**, Vienna (AUS), as depicted by Bernardo Bellotto, c1758–61.

Fish Margery

East Lambrook Manor

Although this ebullient display of country cottage flowers – the perfect foil to the manor house – appears old fashioned, it was actually developed during the 1950s. Margery Fish's particular passion was country cottage herbaceous perennials, which she used to great effect, creating a planting style that was informal, simple and sensible, while keeping her beds filled with a great diversity of interesting plants, both common and unusual. Her approach epitomized the ideal post-war country cottage garden, an idyll attainable by weekend gardeners. Through her writings she helped make perennials fashionable once again, and inspired many other weekend gardeners to follow her naturalistic use of them. She was also instrumental in popularizing the concept of using carpets of weed-smothering species – ground cover – as a form of labour-saving gardening, and was never averse to leaving a weed in situ if it added to the overall planting scheme.

☛ Bowles, Colvin, Jekyll, Lorimer, Robinson, Roper, Sackville-West

Margery Fish. b 1892. **d** 1969. **East Lambrook Manor**, Somerset (UK), 1937.

Fontana Carlo — Villa Cetinale

Few Baroque garden features dominate the countryside so completely as the main axis at Villa Cetinale. This is the view as you descend Fontana's grand double staircase from the *piano nobile* of the house itself – 'an unusually protracted vista' the American Rose Nicholls called it in 1929. It runs through the statued gateway (crowned with imperial busts) and along a wide grass path, flanked with dark Italian cypresses, then through another gateway and up a rough staircase cut from the hillside and cleared of gnarled ilexes until it reaches the Romitorio at the summit of the Sienese contado. It will take you at least half an hour to arrive at the top, from which you will see that the axis runs right through the house, past formal gardens decked with lemon trees in pots and down through another ilex wood to the valley below – a distance of 5 km (3 miles). The garden at Cetinale, built for Cardinal Flavio Chigi, is Fontana's masterpiece, and it is still extremely well-maintained.

☛ **Bacciocchi, Beckford, Borghese, Dubsky, Duncombe, Mardel, Nasoni**

148

Carlo Fontana. b nr Como (IT), 1638. **d** Rome (IT), 1714. **Villa Cetinale**, Siena, Tuscany (IT), 1713.

Forestier J C N

Rose Garden, Bagatelle

On the west side of Paris, in the Bois de Boulogne, is one of the so-called *Jardins Anglais*, designed by Thomas Blaikie and F J Bélanger for the Comte d'Artois in 1775. The garden is made up of many sections, but the best known is J C N Forestier's rose garden. A circular classical pavilion stands on a higher level, with steps leading down to the comparatively formal garden of roses. They grow in geometrically shaped beds surrounded by a clipped box hedge. They are mainly old-fashioned French roses, which would have been widely available to designers in the latter part of the nineteenth century. Conically shaped yews are included in the formal design to give it height. Some of the climbing roses are on ropes or columnar-shaped climbing frames. Beyond the rose garden are a lake bordered by rocks, a winding river with cascades and an extensive vegetable garden with a high yew hedge at either end. There is also a park-like area with expansive lawns where there are occasional exhibitions of contemporary sculpture.

☛ André, Bélanger & Blaikie, Joséphine, Mallet-Stevens

J C N Forestier. b 1861. d 1930. **Rose Garden, Bagatelle**, Bois de Boulogne, Paris (FR), 1905.

Förster Karl

Förster Residence

The use of sturdy perennial plants, ornamental grasses and ferns was promoted by Förster, the father of contemporary German landscape design. He advocated their use in loose, informal arrangements, rather than the more formally arranged English-style herbaceous border. During his long life, Förster introduced more than 650 new plant varieties into cultivation for use as part of his new planting approach. He wrote twenty-seven books and employed in his nursery and design studio many of the succeeding generation of German garden designers. His own garden at Bornim near Potsdam, which he began in 1910, features a remarkable sunken garden and a rockery. It remains a place of pilgrimage for many contemporary garden designers, and Förster's legacy can be seen in the naturalistic plants of many of Germany's public parks. His daughter is supervising the restoration of the garden.

☞ Brandt, Chatto, Jensen, Oudolf, Robinson

Karl Förster. b Berlin-Westend (GER), 1874. d Bornim, nr Potsdam (GER), 1970. **Förster Residence**, Bornim, nr Potsdam (GER), 1910.

Fowler Charles

Syon House

The spectacular glass dome rises from the centre of the Great Conservatory, built in the 1820s by Charles Fowler to house the plant collection of the 3rd Duke of Northumberland, continuing the botanical tradition of previous owners. The 20-m (64-ft) high dome is supported by twelve cast-iron columns and flanked by two side wings and corner pavilions enclosing a formal lawn in a semicircle, a design characteristic of the transition from Baroque orangery to nineteenth-century conservatory. Set in a Thames landscape garden, designed by Capability Brown in the eighteenth century, the Great Conservatory was at the cutting edge of contemporary technology, pre-dating Paxton's Great Stove at Chatsworth House. Still a young architect when commissioned, Fowler was already well known for projects such as Covent Garden Market and was co-founder of the Institute of British Architects. He also designed the formal flower garden on the south side of the building.

☞ Balat, Burton & Turner, Dupont, Paxton

Charles Fowler. b Devon (UK), 1792. **d** Great Marlow, Bucks (UK), 1867. **Syon House**, Syon Park, Brentford (UK), 1820s.

Francini Tomasso & Alessandro   St Germain-en-Laye

In the reign of Henri IV of France, the royal palace of St Germain-en-Laye could boast the grandest Italian garden in the kingdom. Spread over six stately terraces which stretched down to the River Seine, the design was completely symmetrical and, as this illustration shows, centred on the palace itself. St Germain-en-Laye was built in the 1550s for Henri II by Philibert de l'Orme. In the 1600s, the Francini brothers, hydraulic engineers in the service of the Medici family, added a series of grottoes and automata, half hidden in the arcading of the terraces. Sir Roy Strong describes their achievements thus: 'There were grottos of Neptune, Orpheus and of the Dragon (all mythological allegories celebrating Henri IV), but the most astounding was the Grotte des Flambeaux. In this, the visitor was subjected to a series of transformation scenes ... the sun rose, a storm followed and then subsided to reveal a view of the palace with the royal family strolling in front of it and the Dauphin descending from the clouds in a chariot supported by angels.'

☛ Bramante, I Caus, S Caus, Du Cerceau, L'Orme, Vignola

Tomasso Francini. b 1571. **d** 1651. **Alessandro Francini. b** unknown. **d** 1648. **St Germain-en-Laye**, Paris (FR), c1550s.

Franco Guerrero Jose Maria Azuel Tulcan Gardens

Some of the most elaborate topiary in the world has been produced by an untrained genius in Tulcan, a small Andean city in Ecuador. In the early 1940s, Franco Guerrero began to clip hedges of Arizona cypress, *Cupressus arizonica*, located in the town cemetery, into a variety of geometric, anthropomorphic and zoomorphic forms. Arranged in avenues along the cemetery's walks or outdoor garden 'rooms' are myriads of clipped shapes. There are truncated cones, pyramids, obelisks and arches and bas-reliefs of architectural mouldings as well as human, animal and bird-like forms. There are also portraits of heroes drawn from South American, Oriental and Egyptian mythology. The inspiration for the incised modelling of these forms can be traced to the stone-carving style of the pre-Colombian cultures of Ecuador. The art of twentieth-century topiary has reached an apogee in this remote South American town.

☞ Baron Ash, Lennox-Boyd, Monasterio de San Lorenzo, Verey

Jose Maria Azuel Franco Guerrero. **b** Tulcan (EC), 1907. **d** Tulcan (EC), 1985. **Tulcan Gardens**, Tulcan (EC), 1940s.

Fraser James

Castle Coole

This view across the Lough Coole shows how beautifully the neo-classical mansion which James Wyatt built for the 1st Earl of Belmore sits in its landscaped park. The park was originally designed by William King in the 1780s in the fashionable naturalistic style. Three generations later, the 3rd Earl of Belmore consulted the Irish landscape gardener James Fraser, a latter-day devotee of the picturesque, who had been described by John Claudius Loudon as 'an excellent botanist and gardener, as well as a man of general information'. Fraser had advised three substantial Irish noblemen on how to increase the picturesque effects on their estates and how to make their landscapes more dramatic: the Earl of Arran in Co. Wexford, the Earl of Dunraven in Co. Limerick and the Earl of Shannon in Co. Cork. It seems, however, that Fraser was so impressed by the park at Castle Coole that he limited his recommendations to the management of the woodlands.

☞ Allen, Brown, Emes, Hamilton, Loudon

154

James Fraser. b 1793. d 1863. **Castle Coole**, Fermanagh (IRE), early nineteenth century.

Frederick Hendrik Prince   Honselaarsdijk

The entrance avenue to Prince Frederick Hendrik's monumental garden at Honselaarsdijk culminated in a semicircular piazza enclosed by trees and water, depicted at the bottom of this etching of 1683. Honselaarsdijk was one of the earliest Dutch classical gardens based on mathematical principles, and was richly decorated with statues, fountains, parterres and trelliswork. It was laid out in strict divisions and sub-divisions around a dominant central axis which united the moated house and garden. Prince Frederick Hendrik of Orange, Stadholder and grandfather of William III, laid out Honselaarsdijk in the 1630s. The gardens were further embellished by William of Orange in the 1670s. Waterworks were renewed, statues and an orangery with a collection of exotic plants were added. It was to Honselaarsdijk, conveniently situated on the Orange polder, a crossing point to England, that William III invited the English ambassador to discuss his plan to marry Mary Stuart.

☛ Colchester, Marot & Roman, Van Campen, William III

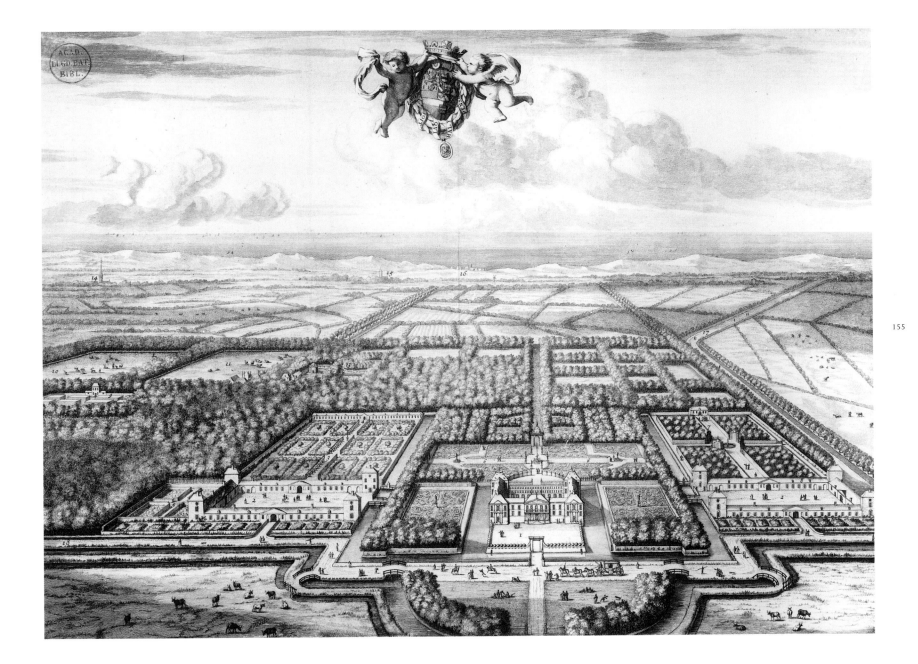

155

Frederick Hendrik (Prince of Orange, Stadholder of the Dutch Republic). b Delft (NL), 1584. d 1647. Honselaarsdijk, Zuid-Holland (NL), 1630–70.

Friedrich I **Grand Duke of Baden** Insel Mainau

The fine display of spring bulbs pictured here is typical of the high quality of horticulture to be found at Mainau. This view shows the arboretum on the upper slopes, while the Italianate gardens which Grand Duke Friedrich I of Baden laid out on Mainau Island in 1871 sum up all the yearnings of the north Europeans for the sun and light of Italy. Terraces surround the Baroque palace which was built in 1740 at the eastern end of the island, with splendid views across Lake Constance. Friedrich inherited the 45-hectare (108-acre) island in 1853 and planted a sumptuous collection of record-breaking conifers. The rose garden is surrounded by a pergola of climbing roses on three sides, while the fourth is the balustraded garden of the palace itself. Mainau is Europe's most popular garden. Over two million tourists visit it every year: the hard work and resources of eighty gardeners go into maintaining this Mediterranean island paradise north of the Alps.

☞ **Barry, Borromeo, Boy, Seinsheim**

156

Grand Duke Friedrich I von Baden. b 1826. **d** 1907. **Insel Mainau**, Baden (SW), 1871.

Friedrich II King of Prussia   Sanssouci

The Chinese teahouse at Sanssouci is quite unlike any garden building anywhere else in the world: the swirling lines of the roof and the gilded umbrella which acts as a finial owe nothing to other examples of fashionable eighteenth-century chinoiserie. Nevertheless, the Chinese teahouse is a wonderful mix of east and west – a European fantasy of imperial Peking, where life-sized figures with oriental features play musical instruments that would not be out of place in Frederick the Great's own court at Sanssouci. Frederick built the palace as an escape from the cares of the world: hence its name, 'Sanssouci'. The gardens that he began have since developed into a large and beautiful complex of formal and informal features, given cohesion by beautiful landscaping by Peter Joseph Lenné. Thus the Chinese teahouse itself sits not in an eighteenth-century Baroque garden, but in the embrace of a romantic nineteenth-century landscape.

☞ Chambers, Girard, Goethe, Lenné

Friedrich II, King of Prussia (Frederick the Great). b Berlin (GER), 1712. d Sanssouci (GER), 1786. **Sanssouci**, Potsdam (GER), 1744–70.

Frigimelica Girolamo — Villa Pisani

This view of the formal woodland at Villa Pisani reveals the garden's current state of elegant decrepitude. The only trace of Girolamo Frigimelica's striking Baroque layout lies in the glint of still water in the glade beyond. It is the axis of a water parterre which was installed when his extensive *parterres de broderies* were ripped out in 1911. Frigimelica was the architect of a villa that was never actually built. Alvise Pisani, his patron, was elected Doge of Venice in 1735, the year in which Frigimelica laid out the gardens in the French style. The parterres were accompanied by a complex geometrical system of *allées* which led the eye along formal woodland walks out into the countryside beyond – at that time, a novel element of garden design in Italy. The woodland, too, has suffered from neglect: the hedges which enclosed the walks have long since disappeared and random plantings have interrupted many of the views.

☞ Fontana, Fronteira, Mansi, Oliviera

158

Girolamo Frigimelica. **b** (IT), 1653. **d** (IT), 1732. **Villa Pisani**, nr Padua (IT), 1735–56.

Fronteira Marquis of   Palacio dos Marquises de Fronteira

Caerulean blue tiles line the upper part of the Kings' Gallery, while deeper blue and white tilework tells the story of the dashing knights of the Fronteira line. Originally the hunting palace of the 1st Marquis of Fronteira, the current palace and its gardens were completed in 1712. The 2nd Marquis of Fronteira, Dom Fernao Mascarenhas, is credited with the planning of the gardens. The King's Gallery forms the dramatic back wall of a highly decorated water tank, a characteristic feature of Portuguese gardens. The Gallery, set with niches lined with copper-toned, three-dimensional pine cones and acorns, housing busts of the kings of Portugal, provides the perfect vantage point from which to view the balustraded water tank and well-manicured parterre garden that lies in front of the palace. In the upper level of the palace grounds there are smaller parterre gardens, other water features and the Chapel Walk, lined with tiles in a combination of Portuguese and Italian styles. Colourful pelargoniums highlight the typically tiled, raised beds.

☞ Mardel, Mozzoni, Nasoni, Oliveira & Robillon

Marquis of Fronteira. b 1655. **d** 1729. **Palacio dos Marquises de Fronteira**, Lisbon (POR), 1712.

Gallard Claude

Château de Courances

Beyond a terrace of perfectly balanced parterres, a belt of magnificent ancient trees encircles a still *mirroir d'eau*. The park of the Château de Courances is one of the highest expressions of the golden age of French gardens. Here, the overwhelming impression is of great purity and clarity. Beautifully maintained *allées* and huge stone-lined pools lead to tree-lined canals which open on to wide vistas – some emphasized by optical illusions. When he bought Courances in 1622, Claude Gallard, counsellor and secretary to the king, immediately called in Le Nôtre to help him develop his vision. Together they evolved this perfect canvas, proving that French formality could be even more seductive when developed on a smaller, more human scale. Over time, the park suffered neglect and misled 'embellishments' until 1912, when Achille Duchêne, the renowned designer specializing in grand restorations, was brought in by the new owner of Courances, the Ganay family, to restore the garden to its former glory.

☛ Duchêne, Emes, Hardouin-Mansart, Le Nôtre, Ligne

Claude Gallard. Active (FR), seventeenth century. **Château de Courances**, Île de France (FR), 1622.

Garzoni Romano

Villa Garzoni

Three monumental flights of stairs form the heart of this highly theatrical Baroque garden. At their base two large, round pools are surrounded by massive topiary art, formed in the shapes of animals and birds, and the bright plantings of the parterre. Climbing up the steep hill, the balustraded staircase is decorated with mosaics, *rocaille*, coloured bricks and monumental statues. Off the second level a path leads to a secluded green theatre and on to an intricate maze by way of the bizarre covered bridge which links villa and gardens. Halfway up, a *giochi d'aqua* once trapped the unsuspecting visitor in a grotto by means of a series of automated jets of water. Romano Garzoni completed this notable Baroque garden in 1756 with the help of local architect Ottavio Diodati. He was determined to radically transform the once austere medieval seat of his ancestors into a site of pleasure designed both to amaze and amuse.

☛ **Borghese, Borromeo, Frigimelica, Gaudí, Ligorio**

Romano Garzoni. **b** Tuscany (IT). **d** Collodi, Tuscany (IT), 1787. **Villa Garzoni**, Collodi, Tuscany (IT), 1756.

Gaudí Antonio

Parc Guëll

The apparently endless, irregularly snaking mosaic bench in Gaudí's Parc Guëll, Barcelona (1900–14), doubles as a perimeter wall that encircles the large, flat main terrace at the heart of the park. Gaudí's patron Eusebio Guëll had asked him to create a garden city of houses and allotments, on 20 hectares (50 acres) of steeply sloping barren land. The residential development generated little interest, however, so Gaudí concentrated instead on creating the city's second largest park. On entering, visitors are faced with a monumental staircase that leads up to the main terrace. On the way they pass the columned hall – a forest of hollow Doric columns that support the main terrace and are integral to Gaudí's ingenious irrigation system. Here, as elsewhere, there is extensive abstract mosaic decoration made from broken tiles and *faience*, some of it realized spontaneously by local artisans. Gaudí created a tropical parkland of pine woods and palm avenues. Parc Guëll is Gaudí's only large-scale landscape.

☛ Goldsworthy, James, Jungles, Loudon, Morris, Paxton

Antonio Gaudí. **b** Rens, nr Tarragona (SP), 1852. **d** Barcelona (SP), 1926. **Parc Guëll**, Barcelona (SP), 1900–14.

Gehry Frank

Schnabel House

A path of Californian sandstone leads past a seemingly haphazard grouping of metallic shapes, which form the office, to the series of boxes that make up the living area. This is architect Frank Gehry's essay in suburban deconstructivism, in which the components of a house are taken apart and rearranged to make a sculpture garden in which to live. The house was built between 1987–9 in the wealthy Brentwood district of California, with landscaping by Nancy Goslee Power. The separation of living spaces produced a variety of outdoor areas, thus extending the perceived size of the 250 x 100 foot plot. The largely drought-tolerant plants are cleverly used in conjunction with the architecture. For example, the radially branching palms, phormiums and cordylines make a striking counterpoint to the angular buildings, while the olive grove adds a softening, rural feel to the harsh modern setting. In a lengthy career, Gehry has constantly pushed forward the boundaries of architecture, most famously in the Guggenheim Museum in Bilbao.

☞ Greene, Libeskind, Martino, Smyth

Frank Owen Gehry. b Toronto (CAN), 1929. **Schnabel House**, Brentwood, CA (USA), 1987–9.

Geuze Adriaan

VSB Bank

An elegant footbridge spans the breadth of this linear garden, where long blocks of low box hedges alternate with bands of red stone chippings. Stretching out along the curve of the painted metal bridge, a wooden bench invites quiet contemplation of this corporate garden, created in 1995 by the Dutch designer Adriaan Geuze, a leading light of the West 8 landscape group. He

has worked on projects ranging from huge dammed areas on the North Sea to Schiphol airport. Describing himself as a functionalist and a 'hyperrealist', Geuze doesn't believe in creating idealistic and supposedly soothing green spaces at this time in our history. He believes in taking full account of contemporary realities, such as increased speed or restricted space, and using the

materials that constitute our environment – such as steel, asphalt or concrete. This positive reclamation of the environment is evolved from constant confrontation with the intensely man-altered landscape of his native Holland.

☞ Allen, Child, Dow, Hornel, Monet

Adriaan Geuze. b (NL), 1960. VSB Bank, Utrecht (NL), 1995.

Gibberd Sir Frederick

The Gibberd Garden

In this twentieth-century garden of surprises, massive columns in Portland stone and marshalled Coade-stone urns rise from a wild planting of acanthus. Improbably, the statuary came from Coutts Bank in London's Strand, incorporated by the master-planner of Harlow New Town into his eclectic sculpture garden. Gibberd moved here in 1956, inheriting a soaring avenue of limes, a gazebo and a formal pool. Over the years (and without a formal plan) he developed a series of interlocking walled spaces near the house and intimate garden enclosures for his growing collection of sculptures, most of which were modern, as well as play features for his grandchildren. 'I consulted the genius of the place,' he said, 'and then exercised some intuition, without which no art exists.' Within an essentially informal English garden of 2.8 hectares (7 acres), Gibberd introduced an architect's masterly manipulation of space, adding drama to each of his sculptures. After several years of quiet neglect, the garden is now being restored by the Gibberd Garden Trust.

☛ Acton, Anhalt-Dessau, Cameron, Hepworth

165

Sir Frederick Gibberd. b Coventry (UK), 1908. d Harlow (UK), 1984. **The Gibberd Garden**, Harlow, Essex (UK), 1956.

Gildemeister Heidi   Majorca Garden

On a dramatic rockscape in arid conditions, Heidi Gildemeister has created over twenty years one of the finest Mediterranean gardens, filled with thriving maquis plants, such as cistus, rosemary, santolina, olive trees, helichrysum, sages and other aromatic herbs. The plants are placed for sculptural effect to create a constantly changing perspective. Gildemeister's technique, however, is as notable as her artistry, because in this unforgiving landscape she has championed what she terms 'waterwise gardening' – conserving this precious resource by use of a non-watering policy, relying instead on the winter rainfall alone, keeping the moisture in the soil by a rigorous mulching regime. Gildemeister, who has also gardened in South America, also advises choosing only plants suitable to the climate, and making the best use of natural shelter from burning wind and sun.

☞ Blandy, Manrique, Page, Sventenius, Tyrwhitt, de Vesian

Heidi Gildemeister. **Majorca Garden** (SP), 1980s.

Gill Irving

Laughlin House

In southern California, during the first three decades of the twentieth century, Irving Gill pioneered low-cost Modernist house design, with an unusual emphasis on the importance of the outdoor areas to the overall effect. In developments in San Diego and Santa Monica, he created clusters of flat-roofed, white concrete houses. By setting the entrance porches at different distances from the street and placing the porches off-centre, he lent each house its own individuality. Gill understood he was making homes, and the shrubs and flowers he included on his preliminary drawings became reality, as here at the Laughlin House, Los Angeles, where the pure white walls are softened with windowboxes and potted plants and trees. Gill's use of pergolas and courtyards in his designs – the rear of the Laughlin House was ornamented with vine-covered pergolas – highlights the affinity between white-walled Modernism and the traditional adobe of the Hispanic tradition.

☞ **Church, Loos, Mizner, Neutra, Washington Smith, F L Wright**

Irving Gill. b Syracuse, NY (USA), 1870. **d** Lakeside, CA (USA), 1936. **Laughlin House**, Los Angeles, CA (USA), 1907–8.

Gilpin William Sawrey   Scotney Castle

From the balustraded terrace, a sweeping view across the autumnal landscape towards the romantic ruins of a turreted castle looks breath-takingly natural. Though the castle is real, the view is entirely manipulated as a last glorious essay in Picturesque gardening by William Sawrey Gilpin, called in by owner Edward Hussey in 1836 to advise on the siting of a new house (by architect Anthony Salvin). Gilpin's advice demonstrated his painter's eye: build the new house high on a bastion and incorporate the old as ruins into the view, obeying the principles of landscape composition with foreground, middle-ground and distance. A protégé of Picturesque theorist Sir Uvedale Price, Gilpin came to landscape gardening late (aged fifty-eight) after his career as a painter faltered. He had helped his famous uncle, the Reverend William Gilpin, with illustrations for his Picturesque tour of the River Wye, sparking a whole new sensibility that looked for pictures in the wild landscape.

☛ W Aislabie, Armstrong, Johnes, Knight, Rochford

William Sawrey Gilpin. b 1762. d Sedbergh, Yorkshire (UK), 1843. Scotney Castle, Lamberhurst, Tunbridge Wells, Kent (UK), 1836.

Girard Dominique

Nymphenburg

The entrance court of the Palace of Nymphenburg rises up at the end of a long straight canal which runs back down into the centre of Munich. Seen from the end of the tree-lined avenues on either side of the canal, the gardens set off the sprawling palace itself. The architecture, water and parterres are held together by strict adherence to geometrical propriety. The Elector Maximilian-Emanuel of Bavaria engaged Dominique Girard, a pupil of Le Nôtre, to lay out these gardens in the early eighteenth century: the ideas expressed in this contemporary view are repeated, on a much grander scale, in the main gardens on the far side of the palace. Maximilian-Emanuel greatly admired the impressive gardens of Versailles – as did every German prince. The same desire for grandeur may be seen at Ludwigsburg in Baden and Herrenhausen in Hanover – and, indeed, at Maximilian-Emanuel's palace at nearby Schleissheim, where Girard also worked.

☛ Bullant, Le Nôtre, Sophia, Zuccalli

Dominique Girard. Fl 1715. d Munich, Bavaria (GER), 1738. **Nymphenburg**, Munich, Bavaria (GER), early eighteenth century.

Girardin Marquis de   Ermenonville

As in a carefully composed painting, a grove of poplars stands vigil around a simple tomb in the middle of a peaceful lake. This shrine was meant as the resting place for the philosopher Jean-Jacques Rousseau, who died in 1762 while staying at Ermenonville as a guest of the Marquis de Girardin, one of his most fervent followers. Rousseau believed that the teachings of Nature and of simple folk were the only antidote to the evils of civilization. Girardin, a wealthy and enlightened aristocrat, who also admired Voltaire and Newton, was the author of a treaty, *On the Composition of Landscape*. He nevertheless invited the renowned designer and landscape painter Hubert Robert to work alongside him at Ermenonville, which he intended as an ideal and philosophical landscape. He had travelled to England and greatly admired Shenstone's Leasowes. Although Ermenonville has a distinctly English feel, it is far from the uninspired imitations of the *jardins à l'anglaise* which were to follow.

☛ Pearson, Pückler-Muskau, Robert, Shenstone

René-Louis (Marquis de Girardin). b Paris (FR), 1735. d Vernoillet (FR), 1808. Ermenonville, nr Meaux (FR), from 1766.

Goethe Johann Wolfgang von Park an der Ilm

This view across the Park an der Ilm captures two of Johann Wolfgang von Goethe's many interests: horticulture and landscaping. The house is his Gartenhaus, where he lived during the first six years of his stay at Weimar and which later served as his summer residence. Its garden is planted with the old-fashioned roses and herbaceous plants to which he referred in his writings and studies. Goethe was a serious botanist and developed an evolutionary theory based on the idea of the *Urpflanz*, or ideal plant. Around the Gartenhaus is the spacious Park an der Ilm, Goethe's greatest essay in landscaping, in whose creation he was encouraged and assisted by his patron Duke Karl August of Saxe-Weimar. The 50-hectare (120-acre) park is laid out as an arcadian ideal and fills the long, flat river valley of the Ilm. Goethe designed and planted it out in the landscape style in 1777–8. More than two centuries later, his classic plantings radiate peace and beauty.

☛ Hamilton Finlay, Pückler-Muskau, Repton, Wordsworth

Johann Wolfgang von Goethe. b Frankfurt-am-Main (GER), 1749. d Weimar (GER), 1832. **Park an der Ilm**, Weimar (GER), 1777–8.

Goldney Thomas

Goldney Hall Grotto

A river god stares implacably into the gloom from within the grotto at Goldney Hall in the centre of Bristol. He is lit naturally from above and water cascades from his urn into the dark pool before him. Thomas Goldney was a merchant with major shipping interests – and a whimsical streak. From a tower in his modest landscaped garden, he could look down at the port activity – at the ships which brought him small additional cargoes of shells, coral and minerals, which he then used to decorate the grotto. The underground chamber consists of one large room, informally divided into three by two rows of columns. The architectural details – doors, windows, arches – are Gothic, but the rough stone and tufa used for the ceiling lend it a wild appeal. Large conches, fossils, quartzes (Bristol diamonds) and other minerals encrust the walls and columns, while the river god and a lioness recline in niches. The only note of formality is the floor, a handsome tessellation of multicolured Coalbrookdale quarry tiles.

☞ S Caus, Francini, Isham, Lane

172

Thomas Goldney. **b** Bristol (UK), 1696. **d** 1768. **Goldney Hall Grotto**, Bristol (UK), 1737–64.

Goldsworthy Andy　'Taking a Wall for a Walk'

This structure in Grizedale Forest is a snaking serpentine wall. It was made by Andy Goldsworthy, an artist and sculptor well known for creating either temporary or permanent outdoor structures from natural materials that he has collected locally. These might be leaves, the branches of trees, pebbles or snow. At Grizedale Forest – the 17.5-sq-km (7-sq-mile) plantation forest and leisure park in England's Lake District – he has drawn inspiration from the local vernacular of dry stone walling. This serpentine section, built by a team of skilled wallers, weaves like a sidewinder rattlesnake through the larches and firs for around 137 m (150 yards). It has embraced, rather than flattened, any trees in its path. The forest itself contains a network of old stone walls, dating from when the area was open pasture. Goldsworthy, who relishes the functional nature of stone walls, manipulated the traditional straight-lined wall 'to articulate a changing relationship between people and place'.

☛　Child, I Hicks, Latz, Smit

Andy Goldsworthy. b (UK), 1956. **'Taking a Wall for a Walk'**, Grizedale Forest, Cumbria (UK), 1990.

Gomizunoö Emperor   Shugaku-in

Beyond the tranquil waters, the harmonious outlines of the vegetation and lake lead the eye to the distant mountains beyond the city of Kyoto. As seen from the pavilion, poetically named 'Cloud Touching Arbor', which towers above the vast estate of Shugaku-in, this carefully composed view is the most flamboyant example of *shakkei*, the Japanese garden technique of 'borrowing' a determined piece of landscape. In previous gardens, *shakkei* had been used in subtle and effective ways to frame or serve as a background for dry landscape gardens. But here, used with assurance and audacity, it becomes the principal feature of the garden. Emperor Gomizunoö, creator of Shugaku-in, was indeed a confident man and this made for a difficult relationship with the shoguns. He eventually abdicated before he reached forty and spent most of his remaining life at Shugaku-in. Gomizunoö, a nephew of Prince Toshihito, was equally drawn to the arts and practice of Zen Buddhism.

☞ **Gyokuen, Kokushi, Toshihito, Wang Xian Chen**

174

Emperor Gomizunoö. b Kyoto (JAP), 1596. d Kyoto (JAP), 1680. **Shugaku-in**, nr Kyoto (JAP), 1655–9.

Greene & Greene

The Gamble House

The garden at the rear of the Gamble House is one of the little advertised features of this masterpiece of American Arts and Crafts. The Japanese design sensibility so skilfully employed in the house's interior is continued into this small terrace garden, which was designed by the Greenes at the same time as the house. The terrace gives on to the dining room and is overlooked by the spacious master bedroom balcony, which was intended, like all the balconies, as a health-giving sleeping area. Ventilation was a key aspect of the Greenes' design, since several of the Gamble family members suffered from asthma, and the indoor–outdoor design creed is partly a result of that fact. Originally a tall tree stood where the ivy hummock is today, making a delightful shady area. The Greenes also incorporated wide and deep windowboxes into their balcony designs, and continued the Japanese theme by planting camellias throughout the garden.

☞ **Church, Greene, Hornel, Lutyens, Morris, Mawson, Rose**

Charles Sumner Greene. b Brighton, OH (USA), 1868. **d** Carmel, CA (USA), 1957. **Henry Mather Greene. b** Brighton, OH (USA), 1870. **d** Pasadena, CA (USA), 1954. **The Gamble House**, Pasadena, CA (USA), 1908.

Greene Isabelle   The Valentine House

Spiky agaves, grasses, aloes and yuccas punctuate a patchwork of low-growing succulent plants in a garden designed to be viewed as much from above as from within. Isabelle Greene responded to the Modernist pueblo house by softening the hard edges with bougainvillea and espaliered figs. The view from the first-floor terrace was inspired by views of agricultural land from the air, and the areas with succulents (among them green cerastium, blue kleinia, reddish sedum, pink kalanchoe) are designed to resemble field patterns. The terraces are formed by terracotta-coloured concrete cast in cedarwood moulds. From the bottom of the garden looking back to the house, their horizontal alignment creates a sense of foreshortened distance, another deliberate effect. Isabelle Greene has had a garden-design practice in California since the early 1960s, and she has received most of her commissioned work from within the state.

☞ Gildemeister, Greene & Greene, Hertrich, Oehme & Van Sweden

Isabelle Greene. b 1934. **The Valentine House**, Santa Barbara, CA (USA), 1985.

Grenville-Temple Richard Stowe Landscape Gardens

The Corinthian Arch on the great South Vista draws the eye across the Octagon Lake to the horizon. The 18-m (60-ft) high triumphal arch, which is inhabited, was designed in 1765 for Richard Grenville-Temple (Earl Temple) to complement the new, broader view from the house which had been created by well-placed clumps of trees and the reconstruction of Vanbrugh's Lake Pavilions at a greater distance apart. Throughout the eighteenth century the Temple family employed leading designers such as Bridgeman, Kent and Brown to create an idealized classical landscape, including over thirty temples and monuments (many celebrating liberal political beliefs). Their style reflected the contemporary obsession with the buildings of ancient Rome and Greece. Three successive generations of the family – Viscount Cobham, Earl Temple and the Marquess of Buckingham – were influential in transforming the formal seventeenth-century terraces into a naturalistic garden, taken as the model of the English landscape garden throughout the world.

☞ Bridgeman, Brown, Hoare, Kent, Vanbrugh

Richard Grenville-Temple (Earl Temple). b Stowe (UK), 1711. **d** Stowe (UK), 1779. **Stowe Landscape Gardens**, Buckinghamshire (UK), c1680.

Grimshaw Nicholas & Partners   Eden Project

These biomes are the focal point of a visitor attraction and educational project built in a disused china clay pit in Cornwall. The 14-hectare (34.5-acre) bowl-shaped site is 60 m (192 ft) deep with steep, south-facing walls that catch the sun. The biomes are giant conservatories, manufactured with the latest technology and materials and designed to be as energy efficient as possible. Inside

them, two of the world's climate zones have been recreated: the humid tropics (rainforests and Oceania) and the warm temperate regions (the Mediterranean, South African Cape and California). The biomes are alive with plants native to these regions to create a natural and sustainable eco-system. Another, roofless, biome is the temperate zone, and the planting reflects the huge range of

native British and exotic plants that thrive in the mild climate of Cornwall.

☞ **Balat, Burton & Turner, Dupont, Paxton, Smit**

Nicholas Grimshaw. b (UK), 1941. **Eden Project**, Cornwall (UK), Phase 1, 2000, Phase 2, 2001.

Guangdong Gardeners of Chinese Garden of Friendship

The Chinese Garden of Friendship is an oasis of calm amid the bustle and skyscrapers of Darling Harbour in Sydney. It was especially designed by expert landscape architects from Guangdong Province and is the largest and most elaborate Chinese garden outside China. It seems even larger than it is, for there are many levels linked by steep narrow paths leading to pavilions or viewpoints overlooking cascades. The central Lake of Brightness contains symbolic rocks – dragon, tortoise, phoenix and unicorn – and, like the lake at Stourhead or Capability Brown's stretches of water, seems to have no end. From wherever you view it, the water disappears around another pebbled outcrop. The garden is densely furnished with pavilions and galleries, a reading room and music room, a delightful teahouse, tumbling waterfalls and a fine array of Chinese plants. Although it is often filled with visitors, a sense of harmony and stillness pervades it.

☛ Bateman & Cooke, Brown, Hoare, Song Zenhuang, Tien Mu

Gardeners of Guangdong. Active late twentieth century. **Chinese Garden of Friendship**, Darling Harbour, Sydney (ASL), 1988.

Guedes Manoel Pedro Quinta da Aveleda

The Fountain of the Four Sisters or Four Seasons consists of a central pillar adorned with the faces of the sisters, or seasons, and four scalloped bowls. It is encircled by a necklace of delicate bedding plants in summer and bright bulbs in spring. The main driveway to the Guedes family home, lined with azaleas, sweeps around the fountain. The gardens, model farm and Arts-and-Crafts buildings were the work of Manoel Pedro Guedes, a late nineteenth-century scion of the family. The garden is noted for its rare trees and the azaleas, camellias and other flowering shrubs that create a dazzling understorey to the woodland planting. Among the whimsical architectural features in the garden are a thatched duckhouse and rustic cottages, some owing their origins to illustrations in *Rustic Adornments for Homes of Taste* by Shirley Hibberd, published in 1857.

☞ **Blandy, Lainé, Lotti, Nesfield, Veitch**

Manoel Pedro Guedes. Active twentieth century. **Quinta da Aveleda**, Lisbon (POR).

Guerniero Gianfrancesco Wilhelmshöhe

The formal gardens at Wilhelmshöhe are enormous. Their focal point is a colossal statue of Hercules on top of a pyramid – the tiniest of specks on the skyline at the right-hand side of this beautiful early nineteenth-century painting. The landscaped park extends to nearly 1,000 hectares (2,400 acres) and there is a difference in altitude of 288 m (920 ft) between the highest and lowest points. The origins of the garden are Italian, for it was to Italy and, in particular, to the architect Gianfrancesco Guerniero, that Landgrave Karl of Hesse turned when he commissioned the formal garden in 1699. Little is known of Guerniero, but his brief was to put into effect the ideas which Landgrave Karl had imbibed from his Grand Tour of Italy and especially from his visits to Villa Aldobrandini at Frascati. A dramatic cascade runs down the steep mountain behind Wilhelmshöhe, through pools and grottoes set amid rocky outcrops and sublime spruces. Hercules, now the symbol of the city of Kassel, surveys it all from his Olympian pedestal.

☞ Maderno, Vanbrugh

Gianfrancesco Guerniero. b (IT). Active end of seventeenth century. **Wilhelmshöhe**, Kassel (GER), 1699–1700, depicted by Johann Erdmann Hummel, c1875.

Guevrékian Gabriel Villa Noailles

The only survivor, albeit rebuilt, of the French Modernist garden movement of the 1920s and 30s, the Cubist garden at the Villa Noailles was commissioned by Vicomte and Vicomtesse de Noailles after they had seen Guevrékian's show garden at the 1925 Paris Exposition. The garden is an abstract, geometric composition with a dynamic forward thrust, a complement to the Modernist house by Robert Mallet-Stevens. Guevrékian's original design specified tulips at the point of the triangle and in alternate squares of the interlocking geometric design. Orange trees were planted where the box balls now are and an automated abstract sculpture was a focus at the garden's apex. The garden works as a still-life tableau viewed from above, and also as a three-dimensional space where multiple viewpoints are gradually discovered, rather than revealed in a single glance, as in a Cubist painting. In the same year, Guevrékian designed a garden of terraced Modernist compartments at the Villa Heim in Neuilly, but such commissions were rare.

☛ Legrain, Lurçat, Mallet-Stevens, Steele, Tunnard, Vera

182

Gabriel Guevrékian. b Istanbul (TRK), 1900. d Antibes (FR), 1970. **Villa Noailles**, Hyères (FR), 1927.

Gustafson Kathryn

Terrasson

A formal Modernist cascade flanked by fountain jets provides the centrepiece for Kathryn Gustafson's water garden at Terrasson. It is part of a large-scale design for a public park overlooking and enveloping the historic village of Terrasson in the Dordogne region of France. London- and Paris-based Gustafson is a leading exponent of large-scale landscape work. She demonstrates a confident creativity in three dimensions that is partly the result of her decision to work out ideas with sculptural clay models, rather than with paper alone. The park at Terrasson is called 'Fragments of a Garden History' and is intended to provide snapshots of different types of garden. For example, the 'Ephemeral Tracing' garden is a full-size historical plan of a formal garden painted on grass, and 'History Boxed' comprises nine abstract topiaries. Gustafson's other work includes the interior of Sir Norman Foster's glasshouse at the National Botanic Garden of Wales.

☛ Asaf Khan IV, Geuze, Haag, B Rothschild, Schwartz

183

Kathryn Gustafson. Terrasson, Dordogne (FR), 1995.

Gyokuen

Entsu-ji

Below the crisp, clipped hedge, lies an arrangement of stones and moss dictated only by rhythm; above the hedge runs a line of treetops and the magnificent spectacle of the mountain. These horizontals are further accentuated and framed by the decking and the roof of the veranda. The only uprights are the pillars of the temple and the tall trunks of the Japanese cedars. Entsu-ji is considered one of the best examples of the *shakkei* technique. Here it is Mount Hiei, Kyoto's highest hill, 6 km (4 miles) away, which is 'borrowed' or 'captured'. It becomes an integral part of the garden because the middle ground is abolished by the hedge. Originally a large horizontal boulder lay just underneath the view of the mountain, and this must have reinforced the link. Emperor Gomizunoö had already mastered the *shakkei* technique at his large estate of Shugaku-in when he commissioned this small contemplative garden from the monk Gyokuen in c1670. It is probable that the retired emperor was involved in the concept of this design.

☞ **Gomizunoö, Enshu, Toshihito**

Gyokuen. Active (JAP), seventeenth century. **Entsu-ji**, Kyoto (JAP), c1670.

Haag Richard

Bloedel Reserve

A paragon of equanimity and simplicity, this reflective pool captures the surrounding forest and sky in its perfectly still waters. But such a powerful effect of artlessness can only be achieved through skilled design. In the Bloedel Reserve the natural environment is celebrated and jealously protected. Other features include an orchid walk designed by Thomas Church and a dry Zen garden. The clients, Mr and Mrs Prentice Bloedel, as keen on oriental philosophies as on conservation, sought designers who would make minimal interventions and would be versed in the art of ancient oriental gardens. Richard Haag fitted this bill. Very conscious of the 'the bigger picture' and of our modest place in the universe, he favours a sober formality which involves minimalistic but decisive intervention. To study more closely the reverence and subtlety of the garden tradition which best expressed his beliefs, he spent a year in Kyoto on a Fulbright grant.

☛ Child, Church, D Hicks, Jellicoe, Shigemori, Suzuki

Richard Haag.b Louisville, KY (USA), 1923. **Bloedel Reserve**, Bainbridge Island, WA (USA), 1979–84.

Hadrian Emperor

Villa Adriana

The elegant colonnade and 118-m- (128-yard-) long canal known as *canopa* are an imaginary recreation of the famous canal, punctuated by delightful gardens, which led from Alexandria to Canope – a sight which greatly impressed Hadrian on his travels. Likewise, other elements in the extensive grounds of the villa were meant as reminders of landmarks seen throughout the Roman world or as personal statements by this exceptional emperor, passionate about art and architecture. He is thought to have designed the villa himself between AD 118 and 134, displaying extraordinary skill in spatial composition and a rare instinct for the exploitation of the natural environment. Here, the perfect articulation and flow of buildings and garden spaces results in a surprisingly intimate and inspiring experience that one does not expect from Roman architecture. Hadrian adored this villa and was often criticized by the Senate for spending too much time there, especially after the death of his young favourite Antinoüs, when he became even more reclusive.

☛ Akbar, Babur, Ligorio, Plato, Pliny the Younger, Tibernitus

Emperor Hadrian. **b** Italica (SP), 76 AD. **d** Rome (IT), 138 AD. **Villa Adriana**, Tivoli (IT), 118–138 AD.

Hall Janis

Waterland

The undulating landforms of this northwestern Connecticut site provide a multitude of experiences. From one berm to another and over the dips and into valleys between, sweeping views and a sense of tranquility is established, a feeling of looking out to sea. The designer Janis Hall removed tumbledown barn buildings, trees and collapsed stone walls in order to uncover, as she describes, 'the character of the surrounding countryside, where, due to ancient glacial forms, naturally dramatic wave-like land forms are found'. Janis Hall is an environmental artist and architect, who worked alongside Isamu Noguchi and has collaborated in partnership with A E Bye from 1984. She is concerned with the interface between art and nature – 'I want to make places that resound with the natural forces present'– and her site-specific sculptural use of form effects constantly changing patterns of light and shadow.

☞ Bye, Jencks, Noguchi, Sørensen, Wilkie

Janis Hall (Janis Helen Hall). b IL (USA), 1952. **Waterland**, Northwestern Connecticut (USA), 1987.

Halprin Lawrence

McIntyre Garden

This Modernist garden contrasts solid, non-organic forms with the essence of nature: its sounds, smells and textures. Loosely based on traditional Spanish patio design – running water in geometric channels, enclosure and an emphasis on a limited number of trees and plants – the garden is low-maintenance and its layout encourages curiosity. Low walls screen water features which can be heard but not seen until another route through the garden is followed. In this way, movement through the space is encouraged, echoing the movement of the water. Halprin began his career as an apprentice in the office of Thomas Church in 1945, and was his assistant at El Novillero. The McIntyre Garden was Halprin's first large-scale commission and many of its ideas were to be incorporated, on an even larger scale, for major waterfalls, plazas and parks in some of his high-profile projects, such as the Franklin Delano Roosevelt memorial in Washington and Lovejoy Plaza, in Portland.

☛ Barragán, Church, Crowe, Le Corbusier, Legrain, Tunnard

Lawrence Halprin. b New York, NY (USA), 1916. **McIntyre Garden**, Bay Area, CA (USA), 1960.

Hamilton Charles

Painshill

Illusion, atmosphere and poetry combine in this tiny Gothic temple (both eyecatcher and viewpoint), mirrored in the still waters of Painshill's artificial lake. From 1738 until his near-bankruptcy in 1773, Hamilton transformed his 80 hectares of barren heath into an earthly paradise, entirely separate from his modest house. One of the eighteenth century's great amateur landscapers, Hamilton manipulated scenes like a painter and theatre designer, introducing many new conifers and shrubs from North America and planting for mood: colourful flowers for the Temple of Bacchus, gloomy yews for the mausoleum. Ever the showman, he hired a duplicitous 'hermit' for his hermitage and instructed his gardener to switch on the waterworks when visitors entered his magical rockwork-and-crystal grotto. His garden's fame was celebrated in sketches by William Gilpin and on Catherine the Great's Wedgwood dinner service. Something of his spirit has driven Painshill's painstaking restoration.

☞ I Aislabie, Catherine II, Gilpin, Hoare, Kent, Lane, Monville, Robins

The Honourable Charles Hamilton. **b** 1704. **d** 1786. **Painshill**, Cobham, Surrey (UK), 1738–73.

Hamilton Finlay Ian Little Sparta

A quotation from the French revolutionary Saint Just is a highlight of the literary garden created in Scotland by the 'concrete poet' Ian Hamilton Finlay. Since 1966 Hamilton Finlay has adorned the garden with buildings, statues and inscribed stone tablets with deep classical resonances. The emblems and maxims of the leading thinkers of the French Revolution, who championed ancient Roman virtues, as well as Rousseau and his philosophy of the simple pastoral life, are repeated in features that adorn the mown paths, woodland glades and open vistas. The garden is implicitly a critique of contemporary cultural values. Since 1978 Finlay has been involved in a tax dispute with the local authority and the garden has been mobilized as if for artistic war, with hand grenades and battleships now enriching its decoration. The dispute also led to the renaming of the garden, which was originally called Stonypath. Finlay has contributed inscribed stones for gardens and parks all over Europe.

☞ Burlington, Gibberd, Jarman, Shenstone, Strong & Oman

Ian Hamilton Finlay. b Nassau (BAH), 1925. Little Sparta, Lanarkshire (UK), 1966–.

Hanbury Sir Thomas La Mortola

Cascading majestically 100 m (300 ft) down the hillside in a series of terraces to the Mediterranean, this paradise garden, full of exotic and unusual species, covers 45 hectares (108 acres). In 1867 Sir Thomas fell in love with the naturally terraced hillside with its olives, citrus, cypresses and vines. He bought the site and developed an experimental garden, growing whatever would thrive on the site. In this he enlisted the help of his brother Daniel, a proficient pharmacologist and botanist. The gardens quickly became known for the unity between the pools, fountains, belvederes and steps, and the natural landscape, as well as for the richness of the extraordinary plant collection. Species from as far apart as Central and South America, South Africa and Australasia thrive alongside plants native to the Mediterranean region. Following the death of Cecil, Sir Thomas' son, in 1937, the garden fell into decay until 1983 when it became property of Genoa University, which has carried out an ambitious restoration project.

☞ **Acton, Gildemeister, Johnston, Page, Pinsent**

Sir Thomas Hanbury. b (UK), 1832. **d** 1907. **La Mortola**, nr Ventimiglia (IT), 1867.

Hancock Ralph

Derry & Toms Roof-garden

Strolling through the Court of Fountains, the sound of running water, the exotic Chusan palms, whitewashed buildings and colourful glazed tiles recall the Moorish gardens of southern Spain. Built in a 0.6-hectare (1.5-acre) walled garden 30 m (100 ft) above street level, this Spanish garden is part of the lavish rooftop resort above a Kensington department store. Despite the shallow soil, it also features an English woodland garden with over one hundred species of trees, a stream, a bridge, a number of flamingos and a Tudor court with arches said to come from an unknown country house. The garden, constructed between 1936 and 1938 at a cost of £25,000, was conceived by Trevor Bowen and designed by landscape architect Ralph Hancock, designer of the rooftop gardens of the Rockefeller Center, New York. Surviving bomb damage during the 1940s, the garden later succumbed to the ravages of Dutch Elm disease, but is now restored and regularly open to the public and used for private parties.

☛ Cox, Delaney, Hosack, Muhammad V, Tortella, Vignola

192

Ralph Hancock. b 1893. **d** 1950. **Derry & Toms Roof-garden**, London (UK), 1936–8.

Hardouin-Mansart Jules   Marly

All the diplomacy of the courtier-architect can be seen at work in Hardouin-Mansart's design for Louis XIV's retreat at Marly: extremely grand but still positively intimate compared with neighbouring Versailles. Here the king held private parties, as Marly was invisible from the road. The king's house is central, with a long prospect beyond, and twelve smaller guest pavilions face each other on rising ground across a formal, terraced garden dominated by sheets of water. Dense woodland with *bosquets* near the king's house provided romantic contrast, and further diversion could be had at the Riviére, a grand cascade, and on the Roulette, an early rollercoaster. Hardouin-Mansart worked closely with Le Nôtre here and at other châteaux, notably Versailles, and attribution of particular features is often difficult to apportion between them.

☞   **Fischer von Erlach, Gallard, Le Nôtre, Ligne**

Jules Hardouin-Mansart. b 1645. **d** 1708. **Marly** (FR), 1679–86.

Hardtmuth Joseph Lednice

An Ottoman-style minaret is romantically reflected in the reed-fringed lake of one of Europe's great landscape parks. Lakes and watercourses covering 34 hectares (84 acres) were created from the marshland of this 27-hectare (667-acre) estate. There are fifteen artificial islands in the lake, which provide homes for a variety of rare waterbirds. The park was built to replace the original, formal garden at the end of the eighteenth century. It is adorned with an agglomeration of follies and pavilions of a grandeur rarely equalled in central Europe. The minaret of 1797 was designed by Joseph Hardtmuth in a style known as *à la Turc*, one of many exotic architectural styles used in the design of Lednice's park buildings to entertain and instruct visitors. A curvilinear conservatory and a suite of nineteenth-century formal gardens complete a park and garden complex which vividly demonstrates the varied tastes of successive generations of the Liechtenstein family.

☛　**Chambers, Mehmed II, Nash**

Joseph Hardtmuth. b 1762. **d** 1807. **Lednice**, sth of Brno (CZ), c1797–1807.

Hargreaves George   Villa Zapu

High above the Napa Valley, on a densely wooded ridge, a post-modern lookout tower stands in front of a long pool. At its base, wide bands of grasses spiral and unfurl in a wave-like pattern across the site. Consisting of two distinct, native, drought-tolerant grasses, these zigzagging bands echo the pattern of the vineyards winding across the valleys below. This is one of George Hargreaves' rare designs for a private residence. He and his San Francisco-based firm are more usually involved with large developments such as the 2000 Sydney Olympics Plazas or the Louisville Waterfront Park. For Hargreaves, most landscapes today have such a long and complex history that they can never again be 'natural'. His aim when intervening on a site is to re-establish connections by integrating all aspects of any given environment. The Villa Zapu is exemplary of this philosophy as it combines and translates the natural, agricultural, historical and cultural environment of the Napa Valley into an aesthetic model.

☛ Caruncho, Church, Jellicoe, Wirtz

George Hargreaves. b Atlanta, GA (USA), 1952. **Villa Zapu**, Napa Valley, CA (USA), 1984.

Harrild Frederick

Castle Tor

Extraordinary hooped stone arches lend a sense of occasion to the steps that lead steeply down by the side of a modest white stucco villa and into the main garden at Castle Tor above Torquay, on the 'English Riviera'. Fred Harrild was a pupil of Lutyens who had subsequently established his own flourishing practice, and the garden has the dignity and elegance of Lutyens' work. However, its grandeur is out of all proportion to the house: terraces formed by towering limestone retaining walls – complete with medieval detailing – dwarf the visitor. The steepness of the site meant that a large amount of stone was used, and the softening effect of plants does not counterbalance the architecture. The first terrace is taken up by a long, narrow pool flanked by a Tuscan colonnade; the lower terrace features an exquisitely crafted medieval gatehouse, complete with working portcullis. It is the grandeur and quality of the stonework that is the chief pleasure here.

☞ **Barnsley, Lutyens, Mawson, A Parsons**

Frederick Harrild. **b** 1883. **d** 1960s. **Castle Tor**, Torquay (UK), 1922–.

Harrison Newton & Helen Mayer   Future Garden

The rooftop of the Bonn Art and Exhibitions Centre hosts a wild meadow interspersed with blue conical towers. The meadow, which forms a 'representational sculpture, a continuously changing, living, colour field' was transplanted from the hilly region of the Eifel where it was threatened by a housing development. A dry meadow, a wet meadow and a stone meadow were added to it by the ecological artists Helen Mayer Harrison and Newton Harrison in 1996. With this installation they wanted to evoke the healing powers of the European meadow, which they consider the most successful collaborative venture between humans and the rest of the eco-system. Having shaped our environment over the centuries, the meadow habitat is now endangered by monoculture, overgrazing and overcutting. The Harrisons have worked all over the world to draw attention to the planet's most painful ecological wounds.

☞ Libeskind, Linden, Oudolf, M Rothschild, Tschumi

Helen Mayer Harrison. b New York, NY (USA), 1929. **Newton Harrison**. b New York, NY (USA), 1932. **Future Garden**, Bonn Kunstmuseum, Bonn (GER), 1996.

Hay William

Nooroo

This picture gives a glimpse of the dense summer plantings and an aged wisteria in full bloom at Nooroo. Between 1875 and 1880, the slopes of Mt Wilson, in the Blue Mountains just West of Sydney, were developed as summer home retreats. Here William Hay designed and built the Nooroo (Aboriginal for 'Shady Place') garden estate in 1880. The rich soil of the area allowed Hay to work with a wide variety of indigenous plants as well as introductions from around the world. He developed several outdoor spaces with lawns and terraces surrounding the house. In 1917, the Valder family bought the estate and doubled the garden in size to reach its current 2 hectares (4.9 acres). The garden is divided into fifteen primary sections. Different levels are linked by simple stone stairs almost obscured by the dense plantings. Colourful vistas are found at almost every turn, and the range of plantings is extensive, ranging from Japanese wisteria, azaleas, camellias, magnolias, maples, oaks, to daffodil and bluebell fields but to name a few.

☛ **Burley Griffin, Cook, Phillips, Verey**

William Hay. Active Blue Mountains (ASL), end of nineteenth century to 1917. **Nooroo**, Mt Wilson, NSW (ASL), 1880.

Hearst William Randolph — Hearst Castle

The Neptune Pool is perhaps the most spectacular feature of the quite extraordinary house and gardens at Hearst Castle, which Randolph Hearst himself – the model for *Citizen Kane* – named 'La Cuesta Encantada' ('The Enchanted Hill'). It is dominated by this Graeco-Roman temple and framed by Italian cypresses. The pool is fully integrated with the gardens: Hearst's architect Julia Morgan, one of the first women to practise architecture in the USA, was a twentieth-century proponent of the Italianate style. The scale is impressive: the drive is 8 km (4.8 miles) long and rises to 500 m (1,640 ft); the estate is over 100,000 hectares (240,000 acres); in its heyday, the bedding schemes required 700,000 annual plants every year; there are over 2,000 cultivars of trees and shrubs grown in nurseries on the estate. The castle itself is a temple to Mammon, yet it has a certain decadent splendour.

☛ Duquette, Gibberd, Mizner, Peto, Vanderbilt

William Randolph Hearst. b San Francisco, CA (USA), 1863. **d** San Simeon, CA (USA), 1951. **Hearst Castle**, San Simeon, CA (USA), 1922–47.

Heinrich of Prussia Prince   Schloss Rheinsberg

The evening light falls on one of the many statues at Rheinsberg, a large garden which was entirely developed during the period of transition between the Baroque and landscape styles. It was begun in 1736 by Friedrich II, while Crown Prince of Prussia, and became the precursor of Sanssouci, but most of the garden is the work of Friedrich's younger brother Prince Heinrich, to whom he gave the estate in 1744. The structure is Baroque, with a long and all-important transverse axis parallel to the side of the lake around which the estate extends: along this axis are the Salon (the central building of a former orangery) and statues of the four seasons. Nearby are an outdoor theatre dating from 1758, a memorial to Prince Heinrich's brother Prince August-Wilhelm (father of Friedrich II's successor, Friedrich-Wilhelm II) and a pyramid where Prince Heinrich himself is buried. But all around this Baroque structure, with its rococo ornaments, is a harmonious English-style landscape.

☞ Friedrich II, Frigimelica, Hardouin-Mansard, Le Nôtre

Prince Heinrich of Prussia (Friedrich Heinrich Ludwig of Prussia). b Berlin (GER), 1726. d Rheinsberg (GER), 1802. **Schloss Rheinsberg**, Brandenburg (GER), 1744.

Hepworth **Barbara**   Barbara Hepworth Sculpture Garden

Positioned exactly how and where she wanted it, and taking full advantage of changing shadows and surrounding planting, this sculpture is one of a collection of Hepworth's works that transforms the small garden adjacent to her Trewyn Studios into an outside gallery. Studying the sculptures in the way that Hepworth wished them to be seen provides an extra insight into the works themselves and the philosophy behind her art. Hepworth was convinced that: 'Full sculptural expression is spatial – it is a three-dimensional realization of the idea, either by mass or spatial construction ... There must be a perfect unity between the idea, the substance, and the dimension ... The idea ... actually is the giving of life and vitality to material ... Vitality is not a physical, organic attribute ... it is spiritual inner life.' This can be seen in the sculptures themselves, but since it is an ethos that applies equally to garden design, the overall experience is greater than the sum of the individual parts.

☛ **Gibberd, Heron, Jellicoe, Miró, Moore, Sventenius**

Dame Barbara Hepworth. **b** Wakefield, Yorkshire (UK), 1903. **d** St Ives, Cornwall (UK), 1975. **Barbara Hepworth Sculpture Garden**, Barnoon Hill, St Ives, Cornwall (UK), c1939–75.

Herman Ron

Ellison Residence

A three-dimensional chequerboard of black riverwash stones and mind-your-own-business moss (*Soleirolia soleirolii*), overshadowed by bamboos planted in dwarf mondo grass, distinguishes the courtyard at the Ellison Residence. Ron Herman's design for the central courtyard, which can be seen from several rooms inside William Wurster's 1961 Modernist house overlooking San Francisco Bay, was inspired by gardens in Kyoto. While Japanese gardens provide much of the inspiration for Herman's style, his work is no simple pastiche. Elsewhere at the Ellison Residence he has introduced a sleek, brimful rectangular pool, abutted at a right angle by a wall made of opaque, textured blocks of glass overlaid with shiny steel bars. This construction owes something to the later work of the artist Piet Mondrian. The use of barriers – the glass screen, dividing walls, bamboos – helps create a sense of surprise in a relatively small space. Herman's work represents a fusion of Californian Modernism and Japanese Zen precepts.

👉 Enshu, Gyokuen, Jungles, Lutsko, Sitta, Soami

202

Ron Herman. b Los Angeles, CA (USA), 1941. **Ellison Residence**, San Francisco, CA (USA), 1997.

Heron Patrick

Eagles' Nest

A simple stone feature is the keystone and summit of artist Patrick Heron's Cornish garden. Massive granite outcroppings, their outlines rounded and roughly smoothed by Atlantic storms, loom over the azalea-covered hillside. A path winds down under pines, bent to the winds, through a green domestic shelf of farmland, to an invisible rocky shore, hundreds of feet below. Eagles' Nest is set amongst the mossed and lichened stones of Zennor, at the land's western edge in Cornwall. Heron lived and worked here from the spring of 1956, his work immediately taking on a new spirit and new forms under the influence of the place and its moods. From this moorland eyrie, Heron has watched the infinite variegations of light and colour, of sea and sky that have shaped his painting.

In his last years, Heron became more preoccupied with his garden and his collection of azaleas, regarding it as a work of art in its own right.

☞ Hepworth, Jellicoe, Monet, Wordsworth

Patrick Heron. b Leeds (UK), 1920. **d** Cornwall (UK), 1999. **Eagles' Nest**, Zennor, Cornwall (UK), 1956–99.

Hertrich William

Desert Garden, Huntington Library

The Desert Garden at the Huntington Library is the biggest such garden in the world – 4.8 hectares (12 acres) of cacti and succulents laid out in a beautiful, fluid design which encourages you to walk further and to explore more. Taken with the enormous number of plants grown under glass, it can also claim to be the world's largest collection, where over two-thirds of all known cacti and succulents are cultivated. The Desert Garden was the work of the garden's supervisor Dr William Hertrich, who worked for the railway magnate Henry Huntington from 1905 to 1949 and persuaded his employer in about 1920 to undertake this project. The plants are grouped geographically, but planted for their ornamental effect so strikingly that it is sometimes difficult to decide where to turn next.

Nor were cacti and succulents Hertrich's only interest at the property, which was originally known as 'San Marino Ranch': the famous Japanese Garden and the Rose Garden are each the largest of their kind in southern California.

☛ Cao, Farrand, I Greene, Martino, Otruba, Walska

204

William Hertrich. b unknown. d 1961. **Desert Garden, Huntington Library**, Los Angeles, CA (USA), 1920.

Hicks David

The Grove

In the centre of the garden around David Hicks' house is this large reflecting pool surrounded by a stone coping. It is enclosed by a wall of clipped chestnuts which open out to a chestnut avenue leading to the open landscape beyond. In the distance, approximately a quarter of a mile away, is an obelisk placed as an eye-catcher. Its complete enclosure by hedges means that visitors remain unaware of the pool, the climax of the design, until they are drawn along the path to its edge. There are few flowers in the garden as Hicks allowed only pots of annuals on either side of the front door. As a garden created in less than ten years, it is a remarkable achievement by a formalist designer who understood the relationship between space, scale and surprise. Hicks developed a highly successful international practice, creating elegant garden designs that reflected the formal English tradition.

☛ Aldington, Bingley, Bowes-Lyon, Haag, Jellicoe, Page

David Hicks. b London (UK), 1929. d 1999. **The Grove**, Britwell Salome, Oxfordshire (UK).

Hicks Ivan — The Garden in Mind

A spring coiled around a head of David begins a series of echoing spiral shapes flanked by ghostly floating ornaments. Further back, paulownia trees formed into hands grasp rusting antique gardening tools. When you enter this walled, former kitchen garden at Stansted Park in Hampshire, reality dissolves. Its designer Ivan Hicks worked for ten years as head gardener to Edward James, the eccentric patron of Dalí and Magritte. Blending this formative experience with fragments from myth and literature, Hicks made a garden that is dreamlike in the most literal sense – seemingly irrational, it is full of hidden meanings. Within a layout based on the ancient metaphor of the World Tree, he designed symbolic rooms, paths and mounds and surreal installations. Plants are trimmed, shaped or fused to make living artworks and arches. Since the late 1990s, Hicks has been working on The Enchanted Forest at Groombridge Place, Sussex.

☞ Chand Saini, Gibberd, Hamilton Finlay, James, Saint-Phalle

Ivan Hicks. b Donnington Castle, Derbyshire (UK), 1944. **The Garden in Mind**, Stansted Park, Rowlands Castle, Hampshire (UK), 1991.

Hideyoshi Toyotomi Sambo-in

This large-scale pond garden of the Momoyama era was designed to be enjoyed while walking. It is organized around a large lake and closed off by a three-tiered waterfall. Exquisite tea pavilions are skilfully hidden away in small gardens of their own and come as a total surprise. This famous garden was first established in April 1598 when Prince Hideyoshi decided to throw an extravagant cherry blossom party lasting several days. The site of the old Sambo-in temple was hastily embellished for the occasion but the landscaping, which started shortly after, was to last more than twenty years. Over 700 remarkable stones were transported from the nearby Juraku-dai or other well-known gardens and arranged by 300 soldiers under the supervision of Yoshiro Kentei, a riverbank man with a feeling for stones. Hideyoshi was a peasant's son who rose to power beneath the shadow of shogun Nobunaga. Great displays of power and wealth were part of his iron rule and the gardens at Sambo-in, delightful as they seem, were also an effective political tool.

☛ Gyokuen, Kokushi, Shigemori, Soami

Toyotomi Hideyoshi. **b** Edo, now Tokyo (JAP), 1536. **d** Edo, now Tokyo (JAP), 1618. **Sambo-in**, Fushimi, nr Kyoto (JAP), 1598.

Hildebrandt Johann Lukas von   Belvedere Palace

A stone sphinx guards the entrance to this garden, which was designed to link two Viennese palaces, the Upper Belvedere (1732), from which this view was taken, and the Lower Belvedere (1716) in the distance. The garden was conceived to reflect the glory of the military commander Prince Eugene of Savoy, who saved Austria (and the rest of Europe) from the Ottoman army in 1683. In the Upper Belvedere he gave great receptions for as many as 6,000 guests, so this part of the garden is correspondingly grand in scale. He lived from day to day in the Lower Belvedere, its garden being more intimate in design. Hildebrandt, the Austrian architect, was assisted in the garden's design by a French pupil of Le Nôtre, François Girard, one of many pupils who disseminated the French Baroque style of garden design throughout Europe in the seventeenth and eighteenth centuries.

☞ **Girard, Le Nôtre, Marot & Roman**

Johann Lukas von Hildebrandt. b Genoa (IT), 1668. **d** Vienna (AUS), 1745. **Belvedere Palace**, Vienna (AUS), 1716–23.

Hill Sir Rowland & Sir Richard   Hawkstone Park

This is one of several deep ravines cut out of the rocky landscape at Hawkstone in Shropshire. In order to understand its context, it helps to know that these gloomy chasms are accompanied by dizzying pinnacles, soaring sandstone rocks and ornamental follies which fill a huge estate, once more than 300 hectares (700 acres) in extent. It is the contrasts which make this landscape unique: the mosses, ferns and dampness of these dark gullies turn suddenly into dramatic cliffs, tunnels, crags and bridges, while the peaks of the precipitous outcrops offer views across thirteen counties. These effects are deliberate – an essential element of the Picturesque movement of which Hawkstone is one of the best examples: it sought to create contrasts of emotion in the natural landscape. Sir Rowland Hill began the landscaping in the 1750s, but most of what remains was initiated by his bachelor elder son Sir Richard, and completed by his grandson, another Sir Rowland Hill, best known for inventing the postage stamp.

☞ Bomarzo, Johnes, Knight, Laborde, Pulham, Wilhelmina

Sir Rowland Hill. d 1783. Sir Richard Hill. b 1733. d 1809. Hawkstone Park, Shropshire (UK), c1748.

Hirschfeld C C L

Prater Park

This painting by Yohenn Ziepler (after a drawing by Lorenz Yanscha) shows the Volksgarten at Prater Park, designed in the late eighteenth century by the Danish architect C C L Hirschfeld. The Volksgarten was an evolution of the public promenade, an open space made accessible for the public to enjoy 'pleasure strolling' (an early example being the Tiergarten, Berlin of 1649). Within the Volksgarten, which was designed to incorporate views out to the surrounding countryside, all social classes mixed together to enjoy the beauties of nature within an urban setting. According to Hirschfeld, what differentiated the Volksgarten from a public promenade was the inclusion of buildings and statuary, which tell the story of the nation's architecture and heroes. Hirschfeld laid down his theories on public park design in his epic five-volume work *Theorie der Gartenkunst* ('Theory of Garden Art', Leipzig, 1779–85). Hirschfeld popularized this style in Scandinavia as well as Austria.

☞ **Brown, Kent, Tyers**

C C L Hirshfeld. b 1742. **d** 1792. **Prater Park**, Vienna (AUS), late eighteenth century.

Hoare Henry

Stourhead

The Pantheon, a domed rotunda symbolizing the classical ideal, is glimpsed across a lake, lending a magical aspect to the surrounding landscape. The scene could be from an old master painting, but was the creation of Henry Hoare at Stourhead, his estate in Wiltshire. After the death of his second wife in 1743, Hoare threw himself into the job of improving Stourhead in the most fashionable manner. A large lake was created from a series of ponds formed by the River Stour. Hoare then commissioned Henry Flitcroft to add a sequence of exceptionally fine buildings to its perimeter, punctuating a circular walk. Temples to Flora and Apollo are well placed and there is a delightful recessed grotto under the lip of the edge of the lake. The scion of a great London banking family, Hoare was closely connected with several early protagonists of the English landscape school, notably Lord Burlington, Alexander Pope and William Kent, as well as his West Country neighbour, Coplestone Warre Bampfylde of Hestercombe.

☞ **Bingley, Bridgeman, Kent, Piper, Pope**

Henry Hoare II. b London (UK), 1705. **d** London (UK), 1785. **Stourhead**, Wiltshire (UK), c1743.

Holford Robert

Westonbirt Arboretum

The Acer Glade is a sight to wonder at, with its collection of Japanese maples glowing at the peak of their spectacular autumnal foliage display. The arboretum was begun in 1829 when Captain Robert Holford laid out the bones of his grand scheme, a series of radiating rides linked together by informal paths and glades, on his father's estate. It became his life's work; Holford even commissioned plant hunters to bring back new and rare species from abroad. The famous Acer Glade and Colour Circle were planted between 1850–75. Robert's son, George, continued to develop the arboretum, as did Lord Morley (George's nephew) who inherited the estate in 1926. However, five years after his death in 1956, Westonbirt passed to the Crown in lieu of death duties and thence to the Forestry Commission, which has restored, consolidated and maintained this wonderful collection. Today, gathered together within the 242-hectare (600-acre) site are over 18,000 trees.

☞ de Belder, Cabot, Friedrich I, Veitch, Vilmorin

212

Captain Robert Holford. b 1808. **d** London (UK), 1892. **Westonbirt Arboretum**, Gloucestershire (UK), 1829.

Hornel Edward Atkinson

Broughton House

A hint of oriental garden bridge betrays the artistic influences at work at Scottish artist Edward Atkinson Hornel's coastal garden, by the Dee estuary. Hornel, one of the 'Glasgow Boys' painters in the 1890s, travelled to Japan in 1893 and his experiences there informed both his painting and his gardening. His original scheme was essentially a romantic cottage garden filled with curios such as monolithic stones and sculptural fragments, as well as features with a vaguely oriental flavour, including the pool with boulder stepping stones. Hornel's interest in Japan can be seen as part of Britain's long-held fascination with that country, especially potent in the late nineteenth century. Recently the garden has been augmented with features such as the oriental handrail and imitation bonsai. Japanese cherries, anemones, ferns, bamboos, cornus and fatsia add to the sense that this is a garden where the oriental impulse has long beat strongly.

☛ Bateman & Cooke, Gominzunoö, Guangdong, Monet

213

Edward Atkinson Hornel. b 1863. d 1933. **Broughton House**, Kirkcudbright (UK), 1901–33.

Hosack David

Rockefeller Center Roof Gardens

A thousand office windows look onto what must be the most dramatic roof garden in the world, atop the Rockefeller Center on 5th Avenue in New York. There are in fact four gardens in a row, identical to this one, incorporated into the Rockefeller Center's design. Ralph Hancock installed the gardens in 1933, apparently in line with the wishes of one Dr David Hosack, the botanist owner-founder of the Elgin Botanical Gardens that had occupied the site on which the Center is built, who envisaged a Hanging Gardens of Babylon for New York. The design is a kind of international formal, a mixture of Italian, French and English influences, with clipped pyramid yews, box hedges, a square pool and compartments for flowers. Since the gardens were part of the building's original design, there is a 2 ft depth of soil throughout. A good place from which to view the Rockefeller Gardens is the seventh-floor café in Saks, 5th Avenue.

☞ Athelhampton, Bosworth, Boy, Cox, Delaney, Hancock, Sennacherib

Dr David Hosack. b 1769. d 1835. **Rockefeller Center Roof Gardens**, New York, NY (USA), 1933.

Hosogawa Tadayoshi Joju-en Park

This garden tricks the viewer's sense of scale. The grassy mounds and a miniature representation of Mount Fuji are assembled around a circular pond that masquerades as a large lake. To further the illusion of travelling through a picturesque landscape, this artificial site uses the natural lay of the land and incorporates elements of the landscape beyond. Tadayoshi Hosogawa, the Daiymo Lord of the Higo Province, designed the 6 hectares (15 acres) of grounds around his private villa as a 'strolling garden', typical of the late Edo period. These pleasure gardens were experienced as one walked along a circuitous route, encountering remarkable sights reminiscent of poems, songs or actual famous places. Incorporating hills and ponds, bridges and islands, the stroll gardens can be related to pilgrimage circuits or penitential walks, though their intention is purely secular. They echo the Daiymo nobles' new-found love for the landscape which they saw from their carriages on their forced twice-yearly journeys to Edo (today's Tokyo).

☞ **Gomizunoö, Jencks, Kokushi, Toshihito**

215

Tadayoshi Hosogawa. Active (JAP), late Edo period, early nineteenth century.. **Joju-en Park**, Kamamoto, Higo (JAP), late Edo period, early nineteenth century.

Huygens Constantijn Hofwijck

These plans and drawings of Hofwijck were made to accompany a poem about the house and garden by its owner, Constantijn Huygens, poet, statesman and secretary to the Princes of Orange. Huygens designed his *villa suburbana*, on the outskirts of The Hague, following the principles of Vitruvius, who stated that the proportions of the human body were a microcosm of cosmic laws.

The house was his head, the forecourt his upper body, the road which cut across the estate – even in those days – was his waist and the rest of the garden was his lower body. It was an expression of both classical and Calvinist ideals. Today the pretty moated house with *trompe-l'oeil* panels on the exterior walls is a museum to Huygens. What remains of the garden is a simple layout of

ornamental canals and avenues of beech and red oaks squeezed between a motorway, railway line, canal and trading estate.

☛ Bowes-Lyon, Colchester, Post, Van Campen

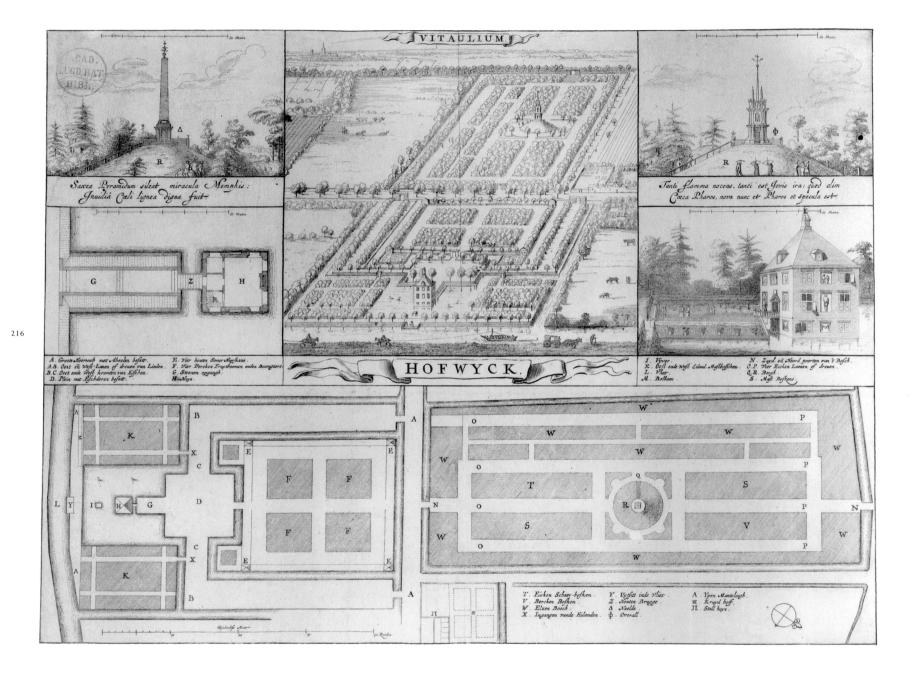

Constantijn Huygens. b The Hague (NL), 1596. **d** The Hague (NL), 1687. **Hofwijck**, Voorburg, The Hague (NL), 1639–42.

Ineni

Queen Hatshepsut's Funerary Temple

A magnificent vista was created here by the architect Ineni at Dier el-Bahari in Egypt through the use of the great sweep of the cliffs as the backdrop to the temple complex. Although it is hard to imagine this arid and sandswept site as a lush garden setting, there is evidence that it was once elegantly planted and watered. Extensive porticos open on to broad sandstone terraces that were once planted with fragrant trees. The brightly painted relief carvings on the loggia walls give an indication of the plantings and layout of the garden. Queen Hatshepsut was the first ruler in documented history to send out plant hunters. They brought back incense trees from the Land of Punt. Archaeological evidence shows that a mixed grove of trees covered much of the lower terrace. Rows of sycamore-fig, palms and tamarisk trees lined the ramparts leading to the temple above. This grove covered an area the size of an Olympic swimming pool. Inspiration for the design was drawn from the myth of the grave mound of the god Osiris.

☛ Akbar, Cyrus the Great, Darius the Great, Jahangir, Musgrave

Ineni. Active (EG), c1450s BC. **Queen Hatshepsut's Funerary Temple**, Dier el-Bahari (EG), c1458 BC.

Irwin Robert

Lower Central Garden, J Paul Getty Museum

The tiered circles of the Getty Museum garden in Los Angeles are pictured here. 'Play it as it lays' is the philosophy that informs Robert Irwin's work as a garden designer and sculptor. At the Getty he has enclosed and masked the view of Greater Los Angeles from the hilltop site. In this way the view, when it is eventually revealed, creates an even greater impact. As a preparation and a contrast to the view, Irwin has used tiers of diverse planting: trees, evergreen grasses, a wonderful range of scented plants and the splendid labyrinth of clipped azaleas seeming to float on the pool. Most of the plants Irwin has chosen are highly sculptural, even in winter. Irwin had the following words carved for the garden's 1998 completion into a large stone at the bottom of the serpentine watercourse above the image here, and they are an accurate reflection of the triumph of this garden:
'Ever Present, Never Twice the Same
Ever Changing, Never Less Than Whole'.

☞ Gehry, Hamilton Finlay, Wilkie

Robert Irwin. b Long Beach, CA (USA), 1928. **Lower Central Garden, J Paul Getty Museum**, Brentwood, Los Angeles, CA (USA), 1997.

Isham Sir Charles

Lamport Hall

This rockery was begun in 1848, when it received acclaim for its daring use of 'deep recesses, bold protrusions, mounds as if fallen from ruins', its wide range of carpeting and climbing plants, and its dwarf trees – many of them kept small by root-pruning. Isham's obsession with things small took a new direction in 1881 when an etching was published that showed a tiny toy monkey swinging from one of the trees at Lamport Hall. This was just the beginning of the invasion. By the 1890s, the rockery was home to a swarm of small clay figures of continental origin – gnomes! This was the first recorded appearance of gnomes used as garden ornaments – the first batch were reportedly imported from Germany as table decorations – *gnomen figuren*. These particular gnomes were set up to represent a group of striking miners, probably a reflection of the 1894 miners' strike. Isham, like his friend Sir Arthur Conan Doyle, was an ardent spiritualist and truly believed in fairies at the bottom of the garden. Just one of Isham's original gnomes has survived.

☞ **Crisp, Lane, Pulham, Robins, Robert**

Sir Charles Isham. Active (UK), nineteenth century. **Lamport Hall**, Northamptonshire (UK), 1848.

Jahangir

Shalamar Bagh

Shalamar Bagh, built just outside of the fortress city of Lahore, was Shah Jahan's magnificent *serai*, or country estate and guest house. The walled garden is divided into three terraces, each 3 m (10 ft) above the other. The upper and lower sections are *chahar bagh*-style parterres divided by water channels and paved walks. The central section pictured here is a three-part water garden. Water flows from the upper terrace down an intricately inlayed marble waterchute, or *chaddar*, to a pool which surrounds this central terrace pavilion. This tank was originally lined with 150 fountains which misted the water terrace. Connecting the central terrace to the lower terrace is a *sawan bhadun*, or sunken room. Three interior walls of water cascade around the room, the fourth side is an open marble walkway. Behind these curtains of water are marble walls pierced with small niches in which colourful flowers and candles were placed – a breath-taking spectacle by night.

☛ Akbar, Allah, Shah Jahan

Jahangir. b (IN), 1605. **d** (IN), 1627. **Shalamar Bagh**, Lahore (IN), 1641.

Jakobsen Preben

Foresters House

A sharply defined, angular edge between path and grass sets off the exuberant planting for shape and colour in this 46-m- (150-ft-) long Cotswold garden. The movement of the path encourages the eye to linger on the planting scheme. Danish-born designer Preben Jakobsen began his career in the nursery trade in Europe and trained at Kew before returning to Denmark to study landscape architecture. There he absorbed the principles of Modernism, but retained an unusually sensitive eye for planting. In this garden, the horizontal and vertical axes are emphasized not only by built features such as a pergola and a pond at the far end of the garden, but by the shapes of the trees: the horizontal tiers of *Cornus controversa*, for example, against the verticals of slender silver birches. Jakobsen's skill on a domestic scale can also be seen in his work on the Span housing estates in the 1960s.

☛ Aalto, Le Corbusier, Sørensen, F L Wright

221

Preben Jakobsen. b (DK), 1934. **Foresters House**, Wiltshire (UK), 1983–.

James Edward

Las Pozas

Elaborate colonnades, convoluted staircases to nowhere, flamboyant fountains and whimsical bridges span the acres of this most extraordinary estate called Las Pozas. This surreal concrete jungle within the Mexican jungle was built between 1949 and 1979 by Edward James – a character even more fantastic than the vision he gave life to. Born in England to wealthy Anglo-American parents, he became involved with the most creative personalities of his time. He married (and divorced) the dancer Tilly Losh, published Betjeman, sponsored Dylan Thomas, posed for Magritte, collected Picasso, commissioned Stravinsky and confided in Sigmund Freud. His most enduring kinship, however, was with the Surrealists. Discovering the Mexican jungle in 1944, he bought acres of land in the semi- tropical forest. Helped by a young Mexican, Plutarco Gastelum, he engulfed a fortune by employing an army of masons to build his startling vision out of concrete. Even concrete has a finite life, though, and Las Pozas is slowly deteriorating back to the jungle.

☞ Cheval, I Hicks, Saint Phalle, Smit

Edward James. b London (UK), 1907. d Xilitla (MEX), 1984. **Las Pozas**, nr Xilitla (MEX), 1949–79.

222

Jarman Derek

Prospect Cottage

Derek Jarman's unique, totemic sculptures, made of pebbles and flotsam, and his exuberant and unlikely plantings surround a small, wooden, fisherman's cottage on an exposed pebble beach in Kent, in the shadow of the Dungeness B nuclear power station. The garden rapidly became (and still is) a cult destination, inspiring many imitations, most of them poor. 'I invest my stones with the power of Avebury,' Jarman wrote. 'I have read all the mystical books about leylines and circles – I built the circles with this behind my mind.' In the unearthly and beautiful landscape of Dungeness, Jarman's sculptures of driftwood, rusted metal and weathered stones took on a magical quality. The success of his gardening was equally arresting, with bright poppies, marigolds, irises and dog roses thriving next to the less surprising sea kale, santolina and cotton lavender. The garden survives.

☞ Chatto, Hamilton Finlay, I Hicks, James, Smit

223

Derek Jarman. b London (UK), 1942. d London (UK), 1994. **Prospect Cottage**, Dungeness, Kent (UK), 1986–94.

Jefferson Thomas   Monticello

Thomas Jefferson's reputation as an experimental gardener is well illustrated by this picture of his kitchen garden, where rows of many different vegetables are lined out and grown on. The belvedere looks out over vast orchards of American apples, mainly cultivars grown from seed. The design owes much to Jefferson's years as the American Minister to the Court of Louis XIV of France.

During this time he also toured English gardens to study landscape gardening and horticultural skills. All this contributed to the excellence of Monticello's design, setting and management. Its flower garden is one of the few examples to have survived intact from the early nineteenth century: its main feature is a long sinuous walk around the edge of a large lawn, with ornamental

plantings on either side. Jefferson was committed to growing flowering plants and shrubs that were native to America. Monticello is beautifully maintained as a monument to his ingenuity and breadth of interests.

☛ Bosworth, Palladio, Vanderbilt, Washington

Thomas Jefferson. b Shadwell, VA (USA), 1743. **d** Monticello, VA (USA), 1826. **Monticello**, nr Charlottesburg, VA (USA), 1768–1809.

Jekyll Gertrude Munstead Wood

Crammed full of herbaceous plants, this border looks artless, and yet it is all due to the designer's skill. Jekyll's planting schemes, while profuse and ebullient, were also carefully orchestrated and controlled to achieve exactly the effect she wanted. This photograph was taken during Jekyll's lifetime. As a painter she had spent time in Paris with the Impressionists, but when her eyesight began to fail she dedicated herself to gardening. Jekyll moved into Munstead Wood, a house designed by the architect Sir Edwin Lutyens in 1897. The 6 hectares (15 acres) of garden were a laboratory in which she experimented with her plant associations and honed her skill of using painterly colour theory in the garden. Jekyll literally used plants as paints and made garden pictures within her borders. Hers was a completely innovative approach to planting, and her partnership with Lutyens created a new English garden style in the Arts-and-Crafts vernacular.

☛ Egerton-Warburton, Lutyens, Mallet, Philips, M Rothschild

225

Gertrude Jekyll. **b** London (UK), 1842. **d** Surrey (UK), 1932. **Munstead Wood**, Godalming, Surrey (UK), 1897.

Jellicoe Sir Geoffrey Sutton Place

A much-enlarged version of a relief sculpture by Ben Nicolson, surrounded by yew hedges and prefaced by a rectangular pond, is the endpiece of Geoffrey Jellicoe's major (albeit unfinished) work, the garden at Sutton Place commissioned by Stanley Seeger in 1980. Jellicoe's intention was to make a Modernist garden of distinct features that were intended to be visited in a specific order.

The programme is based on man's passage through life, from birth to death, and is informed by Jellicoe's preoccupation with the philosophy of Carl Jung. Birth is represented by a huge lake in the shape of a foetus; death and beyond by the Nicolson wall. Surviving features at Sutton Place include a Surrealist walk – a homage to Magritte, with huge urns that create an optical illusion

– and the Paradise Garden, a delightful space of meandering paths, fountains and rose arbours. Jellicoe was an architect who turned to landscape after a tour of Italian Baroque gardens in the 1920s.

☛ Bowes-Lyon, Hepworth, Jekyll, Miró, Moore

Sir Geoffrey Jellicoe. b London (UK), 1900. d London (UK), 1996. Sutton Place, Surrey (UK), 1980–6.

Jencks Charles

Garden of Cosmic Speculation

This sinuous 120-m- (400-ft-) long terraced earthwork, twisting away from two crescent ponds, here viewed from the top of a snail mound, is the highlight of Charles Jencks' Garden of Cosmic Speculation, created in Scotland in the 1990s. Jencks is a passionate advocate of the latest theories about the universe and its history, and several areas of his garden are designed as visual metaphors for scientific theories. The twisting earthwork, for instance, is the most dramatic expression of a fractal – the irregular curves produced by repeated subdivision in mathematics. Its form (but not its meaning) was inspired by the early experiments of Maggie Keswick, Jencks' late wife, into the *feng shui* principle of laying bare the 'bones of the earth'. Similar ideas occur in other parts of the garden: Jencks has made an unconventional potager called the Physics Garden, comprising six large metal sculptures that represent the double-helix structure of DNA, surrounded by a 'cell wall' of low box and swirling bands of lettuces.

☛ Enshu, Hall, Kokushi, Qian Long, Sørensen

Charles Jencks. b Baltimore (USA), 1945. **Garden of Cosmic Speculation**, Portrack (UK), 1991.

Jensen Jens

Lincoln Memorial Garden

This quiet glade of spring-flowering trees set in a public park is the epitome of Jensen's style as a landscape architect and designer. The garden became a living memorial to Abraham Lincoln, most illustrious son of Illinois, and Jensen – an émigré from Denmark – waived his fee when he worked on the project from 1936–49. Because many of the species he wanted were unavailable commercially, Illinois school children and garden clubs collected acorns, seeds and wild plants from woodland areas before they were cleared. Volunteers planted thousands of acorns, hundreds of saplings and all the wild plants into the series of open spaces between the wood that Jensen had designed. He was best known for his plantings of indigenous species and he evolved the Prairie Style of landscape and garden design which was sympathetic to the contemporary Midwest school of architecture, Prairie School, led by the great Frank Lloyd Wright, with whom Jensen collaborated on some projects.

☞ **Brookes, Oehme & Van Sweden, Oudolf, Robinson, F L Wright**

228

Jens Jensen. b Dybbøl (DK), 1860. **d** Ellison Bay, WI (USA), 1951. **Lincoln Memorial Garden**, Springfield, IL (USA), 1936–49.

Johnes Thomas

Hafod

The River Ystwyth crashes down through a narrow, rocky gorge, flanked by the gnarled forms of trees and traversed by a fragile wooden bridge, making a very dramatic scene. Johnes, who inherited the Hafod estate in 1783, was an advocate of the Picturesque style of landscape design. At Hafod, he created a series of rides and walks to take advantage of the cascades, streams and gorges, and the dramatic views out over the natural landscape. He was also a keen horticulturist and, as well as creating one of the earliest rock gardens, he had John Nash build him a large conservatory in 1793. He also planted over two million trees between 1795 and 1801, in order to 'improve' the landscape. Eventually, the money spent on improvements outstripped the estate's income. Much of Johnes' paradise fell into decay but, using a series of paintings and visitors' descriptions, the gardens have recently been restored to something of their former glory.

☞ W Aislabie, Gilpin, Hamilton, Knight, Laborde, Nash

229

Thomas Johnes. b (UK), 1748. d (UK), 1816. **Hafod**, Dyfed, Wales (UK), 1783.

Johnson Philip

MOMA Courtyard Sculpture Garden

The courtyard of the Museum of Modern Art in New York is more than a display space for modern sculpture; the works seem to 'live' there very happily and there is a sense, when entering this garden, of coming into the sculptures' very own space. A simple design of canals, stone perimeters and walkways, together with sober plantings, creates an impression of space and balance, while providing the necessary seclusion. At the time of this commission, in 1953, Philip Johnson was a trustee of the museum and the director of the architecture department. His design for the courtyard was inspired by Mies van der Rohe, whom he very much admired. Having initially studied philosophy at Harvard, Johnson suddenly changed direction in his thirties after reading the writings of Mies, Le Corbusier and Walter Gropius. Johnson's International Style (as it came to be known) and, in particular, his daring skyscrapers left their mark on many North American city skylines. In 1984 he stunned the world with the AT&T building in New York.

☞ Hadrian, Le Corbusier, Libeskind, Mies van der Rohe, Noguchi

Philip Johnson. **b** New London, OH (USA), 1906. **MOMA Courtyard Sculpture Garden**, New York, NY (USA), 1953.

Johnston Lawrence

Hidcote Manor

The twin pavilions are set on either side of a grassy path bordered by pleached hornbeams at Hidcote, a hugely influential English garden created by Captain Lawrence Johnston, an American. Johnston inherited the manor and its garden from his mother. The strong design is defined by high hedges of yew, holly and beech, which act as the walls of a variety of different garden rooms. All the rooms are off to one side of this main vista, which ascends towards the two pavilions, with their tiled interiors. The confident handling of space and scale within these enclosures, and the sophistication, originality and elegance of the planting – as here in the red border – have made Hidcote into one of the most influential gardens of the twentieth century, most often mentioned in tandem with Vita Sackville-West's celebrated garden at Sissinghurst. Surprise vistas are a strong feature at Hidcote, and there is a superb bog garden.

☞ **Barnsley, Lindsay, Peto, Robeson & Gray, Sackville-West**

Lawrence Johnston. b (USA), 1871. d Gloucestershire (UK), 1957. **Hidcote Manor**, Gloucestershire (UK), c1902–48.

Jones Inigo

Arundel House

The English architect Inigo Jones remodelled Arundel House and grounds between 1615 and 1625, providing a gallery wing, which gave onto a walled garden laid out with gates. This appears in the background of this portrait of the Countess of Arundel. His introduction of formal gateways between different gardens was an innovation and his adoption of the garden gate as the boundary between tamed and untamed nature was a distinctive contribution to garden architecture. The novelty of Jones' design also lay in its richly textured rustication and the purity of its classical detail as in the courtyard and garden gates. His unaffected style can be seen in the simple arch visible at the far end of the garden. Topped with coping and ball finials, it is set into the full-height flanking walls surrounding the garden. Jones's fantastical stage-set designs, often Italianate in inspiration, were an important influence on contemporary garden design.

☛ Kent, Landsberg, Lumley, More, Palladio

Inigo Jones. b London (UK), 1573 d London (UK), 1652. **Arundel House**, The Strand, London (UK), 1615–25, as depicted in *Alathea, Countess of Arundel and Surrey*, Daniel Mytens, c1618.

Joséphine Empress of France Malmaison

An elegant serpentine lake, carefully situated between clumps of trees, invites guests to take their ease in the open air. This watercolour conveys some of the relaxed charm of Malmaison, the romantic garden with Picturesque overtones created by Napoleon's wife, the Empress Joséphine, from the 1780s onwards: 'My garden is the prettiest in the world. It is more popular than my drawing room.'

This more relaxed garden style, so different from the aggressive formality of nearby Versailles, headquarters of the Sun King and his Bourbon successors, reflects the romantic spirit of liberation associated with the First Empire (1804–14), and with the writings of Rousseau. It is also directly linked with the English landscape school. Joséphine's garden, widely celebrated at the time, has now largely disappeared, but the name of Malmaison will forever be associated with roses. Pierre-Joseph Redouté used the collection as the basis for his famous series of rose portraits. The Malmaison rose is a highly scented, double-flowered type that is still widely grown.

☛ Bélanger & Blaikie, Girardin, Le Nôtre, Robert

233

Joséphine, Empress of France (born Marie Josèphe Tascher de la Pagerie). b (MAR), 1763. d Malmaison (FR), 1814. **Malmaison**, Hauts-de-Seine (FR), 1780–1814.

Judeo-Christian God Garden of Eden

'When the Lord God made earth and heaven, there was neither shrub nor plant growing wild upon the earth, because the Lord God had sent no rain ...; nor was there any man to till the ground ... Then the Lord God planted a garden in Eden away to the east, and there he put the man whom he had formed. The Lord God made trees spring from the ground, all trees pleasant to look at and good for food; and in the middle of the garden he set the tree of life and the tree of the knowledge of good and evil ... The Lord God took the man and put him in the garden of Eden to till it and care for it.' (Genesis 2) Unlike the Islamic tradition, the biblical Eden has had little influence (medieval Mary Gardens excepted) on specific elements of garden design – most Western gardens have been designed for pleasure or to celebrate temporal power. However, the idea of the garden as a retreat from cares and as a morally edified space has deep resonances in Western culture.

☞ Allah, Sennacherib

Judeo-Christian God. Garden of Eden, from the book of Genesis, in the Old Testament. 'The Fall from Grace', an illustration by Monte del Fora (1448–1529), in a choir book, *Monte Senario Folio II*.

Jungles Raymond

Jungles/Yates Residence

Huge tropical leaves, mosaic decoration, moving water, comfortable outdoor living areas – all elements that typify the style of Florida-based designer Raymond Jungles, who has built a flourishing private practice in the Miami area. Jungles' wife, Debra Lynn Yates, creates the mosaics while Jungles concentrates on the plantings of dramatic foliage – different palms, bamboos,

ferns, cycads, bananas – and colourful dramatic flowers, including orchids, bromeliads, oleanders, bougainvillea, strelitzia, crinum lilies and hibiscus. Jungles's use of massed plantings to create swathes of ground colour is derived from the work of Brazilian Roberto Burle Marx, whom he greatly admires. In this, his own garden, Jungles has striven to create an overgrown appearance,

inspired by the South American rainforest. Yates describes Miami as the place 'where the US meets the Third World, more than anywhere else in America'.

☛ Burle Marx, Cao, Gaudí, Hargreaves, Herman, Jarman, Watson

Raymond Jungles. **b** 1956. **Jungles/Yates Residence**, Coconut Grove, FL (USA), 1988.

Kang Xi Emperor   River Summer Palace

The moonlit pavilion reflected in the lake is one of hundreds of constructions that were once scattered across this vast park, the largest in China. The exceptionally elegant palace buildings were regularly occupied by emperors and their courts during the summer months. The park was commissioned by the Qing emperor Kang Xi in 1703. Following the contours of the land, a 10-km (6-mile) wall encircles the park. The southern part is made up of a series of lakes dotted with islands and crossed by willow-planted dykes. Various pavilions are strategically placed to offer perfect views across the 'waterscape'. To the north is the Garden of Ten Thousand Trees, once a deer park, on the edge of which stand two imposing pagodas. Kang Xi's grandson the Emperor Qian Long, builder of Yi He Yuan, added to the park and, like his grandfather, celebrated the garden in a famous series of poems and woodcuts.

☞ Beck & Collins, Qian Long, Tien Mu

Emperor Kang Xi. b (CHN), 1661. d (CHN), 1722. **River Summer Palace (Bi Shu Shan Zuang)**, Chengde (CHN), 1703–.

Kebach Karl

Alupka

The gardens of Count Vorontsov's palace at Alupka are dramatically overlooked by the spectacular rock face of Ai Petri beyond. Its magnificent setting is on a narrow coastal strip between the mountains and the Black Sea. The terrace in front of the palace (designed by Edward Blore) overlooks the sea and is embellished with marble fountains, clipped box, flowering plants and three pairs of splendid lions from the Italian workshop of Francesco Bonami. The Countess Vorontsov stands out among the roses. A series of lower terraces lead down to the shore. To the rear of the palace the German gardener Karl Kebach created an outstanding romantic park with winding paths leading through leafy shade past streams, rocks and cascades, followed by a series of open glades surrounded by exceptionally impressive trees – Italian, Mexican and Crimean pines, cedars of Lebanon, planes, chestnuts, sequoias, silver firs and cork oaks. Many of the plants at Alupka were obtained through the Nikitsky Botanic Garden.

☛ Aberconway, Rochford, Savill, Steven

Karl Kebach. b (GER). d (RUS), 1851. Alupka, nr Yalta (RUS), 1830–46.

Kennedy Lewis & George   Drummond Castle

The great rectangular parterre garden uses the diagonals of the St Andrew's cross together with three main walkways. The patterned compartments in between, now filled with bedding plants, were originally planted with herbaceous species, rhododendrons and heathers. This made for a more informal planting that blurred the structure, described in 1837 as 'like an immense Carpet of brilliant Colours'. This was designed by Lewis Kennedy, who worked with his son George at Drummond from 1818 to 1860. There had been a garden at Drummond in the seventeenth century and Kennedy sought to draw his inspiration from the recently 'discovered' history of gardens. However, commentators of the time thought it more an amalgam of Italian, French and Dutch influences than of Scottish ones. Made on an elaborate terrace with flights of steps, which was a great feat of construction, and enlivened with statuary, it was championed by those who sought to promote the Italianate style in the 1850s.

☞ Barry, Beaumont, Sitwell, I Thomas, William III

Lewis Kennedy. b (UK), 1789. d (UK), c1840. George Kennedy. Active (UK), 1820–50s. Drummond Castle, Crieff, Tayside (UK), 1818–60.

Kent William

Rousham

A statue of Pan stares pensively across the frosted octagonal pond towards William Kent's serpentine rill. Mist hides the River Cherwell down below, while Venus (unseen) rises from her cascade further up the vale. Remodelled by Kent in 1738 from a more formal design by Charles Bridgeman, Rousham is one of Britain's best preserved (and best loved) early landscape gardens. Horace Walpole likened it to 'Daphne in little, the sweetest little groves, streams, glades, porticos, cascades and river imaginable'. Rousham's 10 hectares (25 acres) should be viewed by following Kent's intended route around the garden. Scenes open up like stage sets while classical statues and buildings spark poetic associations. With encouragement from his patron, the 3rd Earl of Burlington (met on his Italian travels) and his friend Alexander Pope, Kent is credited with the discovery that 'all nature was a garden'.

☞ **Burlington, Grenville-Temple, Hoare, Pope, Sulla**

William Kent. b Bridlington, Yorkshire (UK), 1685. d London (UK), 1748. **Rousham**, Steeple Aston, Oxfordshire (UK), 1738.

Khosrow II Parviz
Taq-e-Bostan

This fancifully carved simorah, or 'Tree of Life', the mythical source of all the plants in the world and the herbal healer of all maladies, adorns the entrance of Taq-e Bostan's large grotto. Symmetry and balance are beautifully achieved in each tendril, acanthus leaf, exotic fruit and foliate bloom. Built under the Sasanian emperor Khosrow II Parviz (591–628 AD), this historically sacred site is breath-taking.

Two cave-like grottoes – the smaller one was built earlier under Shapur III (383–388 AD) – are set side by side at the base of sheer rocky mountain cliffs overlooking the clear, deep green waters of a spring-fed lake. Drawn by the sanctity of this life-giving lake, many *caravanserais*, or fortified traveller's hostels, were built nearby for centuries. For the ancient Zarathustran or Zoroastrian religion, this tree was a central theme in the description of the sweet-smelling heavenly paradise promised to the faithful – to those believers who sought Light and Truth in life.

☛ **Assurbanipal, Ineni, Thutmosis**

Khosrow II Parviz. b Persia (IR), 591 **d** Persia (IR), 628. **Taq-e Bostan**, nr Kermanshah, Persia (IR), c7th century AD.

Kienast Dieter

Uetliberg Garden

Separating the beautifully composed gardens from a steep wooded slope, a balustrade spells out 'I too was in Arcadia'. The late Swiss garden designer Dieter Kienast inscribed this much-debated quote relating to Virgil's ideal land into the landscape, thereby constructing a distinctive picturesque image for the end of the twentieth century. But this arcadia, defined by a remarkable blend of nature and pure architecture, is to do with an awareness of our contemporary condition. Sometimes considered a 'minimalist' master due to his voluntarily limited palette of plants and his focus on a few architectural elements, Kienast liked to quote the American minimal artist Robert Morris: 'Simplicity of shape does not equate with simplicity of experience.' In particular, Kienast brought new meaning to the notion of edging: borders, paths, terraces, walls, canals and pools intersect with almost transcendent precision. When he died in 1998 Kienast was working on the landscaping of Tate Modern in London with Herzog & de Meuron.

☛ Geuze, Hamilton Finlay, Hargreaves, Wirtz

Dieter Kienast. b Zürich (SW), 1945. d London (UK), 1998. Uetliberg Garden, Zürich (SW), c1980s.

Kiley Dan

J Irwin Miller Residence

Henry Moore's *Seated Woman* reclines gracefully at the end of an immaculate *alleé* of honey locusts (*Gleditsia triacanthos*) planted across the western edge of the house. Completed in 1955, this was Kiley's first coherently modern landscape design, incorporating the 'rich vocabulary of *alleé*, *bosque*, boulevard and *tapis vert*' encountered in post-war Europe, where he had helped to reconstruct Nuremberg's Palace of Justice. Around the house the spaces are ordered and geometric: a redbud grove next to the Moore sculpture interlocks with blocks of apple orchards, lawn, avenued entrance drive and swimming pool, the whole enclosed by staggered arborvitae hedges. To the west, weeping willow clumps and formally planted honey locusts contain a meadow that rolls down to a wooded creek. A master among American landscape architects, Kiley embraced Modernism in the 1930s. After his European epiphany, he strove to build 'landscapes of clarity and infinity', repeating classical elements in a modern composition.

☞ Eckbo, Eldem, Moore, Rose, Saarinen, Tunnard

242

Dan Kiley (Daniel Urban Kiley). b Boston, MA (USA), 1912. J Irwin Miller Residence, Columbus, IA (USA), 1955.

Kingsbury Noël

Cowley Manor

The pink-buff flower spikes of *Macleaya cordata*, crimson globes of *Knautia macedonica* and the arching leaves of the grass *Miscanthus sinensis* 'Silver Feather' are just a few of the plants in the dramatic borders flanking the formal lawn at Cowley Manor. This is the setting for Noël Kingsbury's radical experiment in nature-inspired planting, begun in 1994 when the owners approached him to replant the garden. Further from the house, perennials are massed in great swathes, the result resembling what he describes as 'a cross between a traditional border and a wild flower meadow'. Unlike conventional schemes, these 'open borders' can be walked around and through, creating constantly changing associations of form and colour, and magical lighting effects. Kingsbury is a leading proponent of this 'new perennial' planting style. As with the Continental designers who have influenced him, his approach is both ecologically friendly and low in maintenance.

☛ Egerton-Warburton, Lloyd, Oudolf, Robeson & Gray

Noël Kingsbury. b Reading (UK), 1957. **Cowley Manor**, Cowley, nr Cheltenham, Gloucestershire (UK), 1994.

Knight Richard Payne

Downton Castle

Richard Payne Knight started to lay out this intensely dramatic garden in the 1770s, when Capability Brown was at the height of his influence. So different is the scene from gardens in the mid-century English landscape style that it comes as no surprise to learn that Knight was one of Brown's first and most vociferous critics. Knight was a gentleman-designer who set out his views in *The Landscape*, published in 1794. His garden at Downton was cut out of the thickly wooded valley on either side of the River Teme, and included areas of fairly open parkland, but he was keen to create picturesque effects wherever appropriate and this is well exemplified by the two bridges which he suspended across the river. Knight and other advocates of the Picturesque tried to create a frisson of danger in visitors to their gardens. It was the lack of variety in Brown's landscapes that Knight so deplored: '... wrapt all o'er in everlasting green, [it] makes one dull vapid, smooth and tranquil scene'.

☛ W Aislabie, Gilpin, Hamilton, Hill, Isham, Johnes, Lane, Loudon

Richard Payne Knight. b Hereford (UK), 1751. d London (UK), 1824. **Downton Castle**, Herefordshire (UK), 1770s.

Kokushi Muso   Saiho-ji

More than forty species of moss form the changing green fabric of this mysterious and influential temple garden, also known as the Moss Temple. The lower pond garden contains three main islands and a flotilla of single stones. Further up the hill is a dry garden containing three magnificent stone compositions: the turtle island, a group of stones emerging from a sea of moss, the *zazen-zeki*, a flat-topped meditation stone which seems to float on a ocean of calm and silence, and finally the *kare-taki*, a dry cascade of staggered granite blocks. In complete contrast with the lower garden, the magic here lies in the absence of water; its ghost is felt everywhere but it is never present. Saiho-ji marks the transition between the Heian tradition of gardens, evoking the Pure-Land Buddhist paradise, and the more austere Muromachi dry temple gardens. Though Saiho-ji dates from the twelfth century, it was redesigned in 1334 by Muso Kokushi, an influential Zen abbot.

☞ Ashikaga Yoshimasa, Enshu, Hosogawa, Rikkyu

Muso Kokushi (Muso Soseki). b (JAP), 1275. d (JAP), 1351. **Saiho-ji**, Kyoto (JAP), 1334.

Krieger Johann · Fredensborg Palace Gardens

Fredensborg is Denmark's best preserved Baroque garden. Created by King Frederik IV's preferred landscape architect Johann Kornelius Krieger, the garden was designed to reflect the glory of the palace, with avenues radiating from the building. The parterre built in front of the main facade had royal monograms depicted in the planting schemes. Typically, there were separate functional areas: the ballonplads for ball playing; the meagerioen for exotic animals; the hidseplads used to excite the dogs before the hunts; the kitchen gardens to feed guests and, more unusually, the sneglebakken for breeding edible snails. Changes were made when Nicolas Henri Jardin was invited to develop the gardens on a French model. The most distinctive aspect of his plan is the *tapis vert*, the wide grass carpet surrounded by double avenues. By the mid-nineteenth century parts of the garden had been redesigned in the English Romantic style. In the 1990s Krieger's original avenues were restored, and a new orangery opened in 1995.

☞ Carl-Theodor, Dubsky, Frigimelica

Johann Cornelius Krieger. Active (DK), eighteenth century. **Fredensborg Palace Gardens**, Hillerød, Zealand (DK), 1720–6.

Laborde Marquis de   Méréville

In this arcadian scene, nature and culture enjoy a blissful coexistence. Hubert Robert's marvellous picture is one of a series depicting the famous park of Méréville. Yet it is far more than first a highly accomplished landscape painting. As well as representing an ideal, it also shows a reality. The ideal landscape was born out of the literary and philosophical discussions between Robert and the Marquis de Laborde, his patron and Louis XIV's banker. But the artist also designed the park, indicated the plantings and positioned the follies and bridges. These were then built by the architects J-P Barré and F-J Bélanger. The result is the epitome of the French Picturesque. After Laborde was executed during the Revolution, the celebrated Méréville was almost destroyed. It was not until the end of the nineteenth century that four follies were bought by Henri de Saint-Léon and moved stone by stone to his estate at Jeurre, where they can still be seen today.

☛ Bélanger & Blaikie, Chambers, Girardin, Monville, Robert

Marquis Jean Joseph de Laborde. b (FR), c1724. d Paris (FR), 1794. Méréville (FR), 1793, as depicted by Hubert Robert, *View of the Park of Méréville*, late eighteenth century.

Lainé Elie

Waddesdon Manor

It is hard to believe that this corner of the sumptuous parterre at Waddesdon is a modern reconstruction: no other garden gives a better idea of the opulence, colour and order which characterized Victorian bedding schemes. Over 9,000 scarlet pelargoniums (of the variety *Geranium 'Alex'*) have been incorporated in this scheme. The designer Elie Lainé was responsible for the original concept,

which was laid out on the terrace in front of the French château-style house in the 1870s. Several alterations were made before the end of the nineteenth century and it was then abandoned completely at the outbreak of World War II. Not until 1989 was it possible to remake the parterres according to one of the old designs, for which there was detailed photographic evidence.

The result is seen here. More than any of their other properties, Waddesdon demonstrates the display of riches which characterized the nineteenth-century Rothschilds and their gardens.

☞ Barry, Le Bas, Marot & Roman, Nesfield, Sophia

Elie Lainé. b 1839. d 1898. **Waddesdon Manor**, Buckinghamshire (UK), c1870s.

Landsberg Sylvia   Bayleaf Farmhouse

Looking across the garden to the timber framed recreation of a late-medieval, yeoman homestead, the visitor's senses are intoxicated by the colour and perfume of herbs and flowers. Medieval gardens are most readily imagined as enclosed flower gardens, but many were utilitarian kitchen gardens providing fruit, vegetables and herbs for the family and animals. Sylvia Landsberg, who devised this recreation, drew her inspiration from medieval writing. Most plants at Bayleaf are grown in raised rectangular beds with paths between, enclosed by a wattle fence. The homestead is protected by a small coppice wood and also features an orchard, honeysuckle arbour and delightful grassy bank forming a small, enclosed pleasure garden. Landsberg's research on the medieval garden has led to the creation of a number of other gardens in England, including Queen Eleanor's Garden in Winchester and Brother Cadfael's physic garden at Shrewsbury.

☛ Carvallo, La Quintinie, Shurcliff, Van Riebeeck, Vogue

Sylvia Landsberg. **Bayleaf Farmhouse**, Weald and Downland Museum, Singleton, Chicester, West Sussex (UK), recreated 1990s.

Lane Joseph

Painshill Grotto

The grotto at Painshill is approached across a Chinese bridge and decorated with gypsum, calcite spars and coral. Grottoes are dens and lairs from which the world outside takes on a strange perspective. The Painshill Grotto was executed by Joseph Lane, a fashionable grotto-maker from Tisbury in Wiltshire, but it was probably designed by the garden-maker himself, the Honourable Charles Hamilton. The grotto was accessible by boat, like the smaller example at Stourhead. Hamilton laid out his gardens between 1738 and 1773 with the aim of provoking the greatest variety of moods: other features included a Gothic temple, a ruined abbey and a Turkish tent, but the grotto was always the star attraction. Hamilton was a pioneer of the naturalistic landscape style, and very influential, but never a rich man: he leased Painshill from the Crown and had little to spend (in fact he finally went bankrupt), which makes his achievement all the more remarkable.

☞ **Crisp, Goldney, Hamilton, Hoare, Isham, Pulham**

Joseph Lane. b Tisbury, Wiltshire (UK), 1717. d (UK), 1784. **The Grotto**, Painshill, Surrey (UK), 1760–5.

La Quintinie Jean-Baptiste de   Potager du Roi, Versailles

La Quintinie constructed the new potager, or ornamental vegetable garden, at Versailles between 1677 and 1683. The site on the Rue des Tournelles was originally a marsh. It was filled first with sand from the large lake facing the orangery in the main garden at Versailles, the Pièce d'Eau des Suisse, and then with topsoil and cartloads of manure. Like the rest of Versailles, the Potager du Roi is a triumph of man over Nature. The 8-hectare (19-acre) potager was divided into enclosures which created a series of microclimates, allowing tender plants like melons and figs to be grown. Louis XIV was very fond of figs and in 1687 La Quintinie delivered 4,000 of them to the king's table each day. The centre was a raised, terraced area, against whose walls vines were cultivated. This had a central pool and fountain and was divided into sixteen raised beds. The Potager, now home to the Ecole National Supérieure du Paysage, has recently been restored to its original form.

☞ Blanc, Carvallo, Jefferson, Le Nôtre, Vogue, Washington

251

Jean-Baptiste de La Quintinie. b Chabanais (FR), 1626. d Versailles (FR), 1688. **Potager du Roi**, Versailles, Yvelines (FR), 1677–83.

Larsen Jack Lenor

The Red Garden at the LongHouse

Parallel rows of rough cedar trunks, painted in the blazing red of Japanese Shinto gates and interplanted with scarlet azaleas, contrast with the complementary greens of the grass and higher-level planting to produce a vista of almost shocking intensity. This striking piece of modern garden sculpture is the work of Jack Lenor Larsen, who for over fifty years has been one of the world's leading textile designers. The 'Larsen Look' has evolved to become synonymous with modern sophistication. Construction of the house and garden began in 1986, and at the end of 1991 Larsen established the LongHouse Foundation (later Reserve), which aims to demonstrate a way of living with art and to create landscapes as an art form. The result is a garden of immense vitality and variety, where locally inspired features are combined with references to far-off places, such as an amphitheatre based on ancient Irish ring forts. Found or recycled objects (like the cedar posts) sit alongside commissioned pieces, and old is juxtaposed with new.

☛ **Cao, Child, Duquette, I Hicks, Majorelle**

252

Jack Lenor Larsen. b Seattle, WA (USA), 1927. **The Red Garden at the LongHouse**, East Hampton, Long Island, New York, NY (USA), 1986.

Larsson Carl

Sundborn

In 1888 the painter Carl Larsson's father-in-law gave him and his wife, Karin, Lilla Hyttnäs, a little cottage on the banks of the River Sundborn. Over the ensuing two decades Larsson completed a series of paintings of his home and his family life which remain icons of middle-class domestic bliss in a rural idyll. Larsson and his wife are best known for the simple, light and airy Arts-and-Crafts style they developed for the house's interior decoration, but the wild, romantic garden was an important aspect of their life and is celebrated in many paintings, including this view, entitled The Cottage. A number of Larsson's interior scenes include potted plants or cut flowers, but among the most memorable garden scenes are of joyous family breakfasts in the open air, or events such as the first day of the crayfish season. Larsson applied the familiar notion of the ever-changing garden scene to the house interior: 'A home is not dead but living, and like all living things must obey the laws of nature by constantly changing'.

☞ Aldington, Monet, Morris, Robinson, Ruskin, Wordsworth

Carl Larsson. b Stockholm (SWE), 1853. d Falun (SWE), 1919. Sundborn (SWE), 1888–1919, *The Cottage* by Larsson.

Lassus Bernard — Les Buissons Optiques

In this show garden, the extraordinary combinations of colours, textures and planes were based on careful optical and mathematical observations. They reflect Bernard Lassus' preoccupation with the interplay between imaginary space and what he calls 'real space'. Another important consideration in Lassus' thought processes are the layered references to the various levels of history and culture. Having trained with Fernand Léger, Lassus has long expressed himself through conceptual art. Today he is highly respected as a landscape architect and designer, as well as theoretician and teacher. He has realized such prestigious projects as the Jardins des Retours in Rochefort-sur-Mer and worked on huge portions of the French motorway system. But Lassus has also lost important competitions – the restoration of the Tuileries for example – as he himself likes to point out.

☞ Clément & Provost, Geuze, Hargreaves, Latz, Pepper

254

Latz Peter

Chaumont Mist Installation

Mysterious artificial fog swirls among stone slabs assembled as a twentieth-century *henge* for the International Garden Festival, Château de Chaumont, near Tours, France. Artificial fog began to be used by garden and landscape designers twenty years ago. It is made by water being atomized under high pressure. It was first developed for high-budget public landscape and garden design projects and this is still its prime use. Its time in the private garden has yet to come. The wonderful, mysterious effect blurs landscape elements and boundaries instantly, lending a surreal other-worldliness to the design. Manmade fog has also been used in extremely hot climates for its immediate, but short-term cooling properties. Peter Latz is one of the leading German landscape architects and he masterminded the giant post-industrial people's park in the former Thyssen steel works in the Ruhr at Duisberg.

☞ Blanc, Geuze, Haag, Lassus, Toll

Peter Latz. b (GER), 1939. **Chateau Mist Installation**, Château de Chaumont, nr Tours (FR), early 1990s.

Le Bas Jacques

Château de Brécy

Scrolls of clipped box form a pair of simple *parterres de broderie* on the highest of five terraces, below the walls of the Château de Brécy, a rather misleading title for what was originally a farmhouse. The terraces are laid out across a slope, becoming progressively wider as they ascend. A wide central walkway leads to the top balustraded terrace and a monumental wrought-iron gateway. Through the gateway can be seen a wide vista of green. Lawns and topiary are interspersed with stone statuary and ornaments, in harmony with the ornamented Mannerist stonework of the rather grand farmhouse, which is attributed loosely to François Mansart. The owner of Brécy, Jacques le Bas, was related to the owner of the Château de Balleroy, also designed by Mansart between 1616 and 1636. The origins of *parterres de broderie* such as this are unknown, but they were possibly derived from textile designs.

☞ Hardouin-Mansart, Marot & Roman, Poitiers, Sophia, Wise

256

Le Blond Jean-Baptiste Alexandre   Peterhof

Beneath the Great Cascade sits the fountain-statue of Samson and the Lion at the Palace at Peterhof. From the basins in the Upper Park the water flows under the palace and down the marble steps of the triumphal cascade to the fountain-statue of Samson overcoming the lion – an allegorical celebration of Russia's defeat of the Swedes at the Battle of Poltava, fought on St Samson's Day 1709, and the recovery of her access to the Baltic. The water then flows along a canal, flanked by fountains, to the sea. With its three cascades and more than 150 fountains, including some of the best surviving 'trick' fountains, Peterhof is one of the world's greatest water gardens. While Peter the Great influenced the design, seeking both to emulate and surpass Versailles, Le Blond, a pupil of Le Nôtre, made the most important design contribution during the years 1716–19. He was preceded by J F Braunstein. Niccolo Michetti, Benjamin F Rastrelli and others worked there later.

☛ **Hardouin-Mansart, Le Nôtre, Peter II**

Jean-Baptiste Alexandre Le Blond. **b** Paris (FR), 1679. **d** St Petersburg (RUS), 1719. **Peterhof**, nr St Petersburg (RUS), 1716–19.

Le Corbusier

Villa Savoye

This solarium roof terrace at the Villa Savoye was designed for health-giving nude sunbathing. Le Corbusier regarded the roof or balcony terrace as the proper place for a garden, and practised a non-interventionist approach to the wider landscape. At the Villa Savoye, a limited palette of plants, mainly evergreen shrubs, adorn raised beds in a series of terraces that lead directly on to the interior living areas. The outside is as important a designed space as the inside. Le Corbusier cited the Islamic tradition as an inspiration for the episodic progression here. Distant prospects – in this case, groups of trees – were incorporated into the design by means of formal framing. Le Corbusier designed several such roof terraces, as well as a few gardens on the ground (the Villa Church and the Villa 'Les Terrasses'), where winding paths lead through trees to formal paved areas.

☛ Guevrékian, Mies van der Rohe, Nazarite, Sennacherib, Tunnard

Le Corbusier (Charles-Edouard Jeanneret). b La Chaux-de-Fonds (SW), 1887. d Cap Martin (FR), 1965. Villa Savoye, Poissy (FR), 1929–31.

Legrain Pierre-Emille   Tachard Garden

A formal Modernist *allée* zigzags through the garden made for African art collector Jeanne Tachard. Its cool, ordered dignity, which is nevertheless both asymmetrical and irregular, exemplifies the style of this now-vanished garden. Pierre-Emile Legrain was a leading designer of the 1910s and 1920s, specializing in interiors, furniture and books. This is the only garden he designed. Legrain's scheme was original in its deliberately inconclusive use of irregular geometric forms and changes of level, designed to create varying tones of green and to emphasize the textures of plants. The scheme comprises a series of garden rooms, including an outdoor dining area, in which the impersonal formal style is undercut by playfully off-beat, off-centre motifs. Legrain was unusual among his Modernist contemporaries in his sympathy for and understanding of plants: the Tachard garden included a voluptuous semicircle of red climbing roses that he described as 'a sacrifice to charm'.

☞ Church, Eckbo, Kiley, Mallet-Stevens, Noailles, Rose

Pierre-Emille Legrain. b Levallois-Perret, Hauts-de-Seine (FR), 1889. **d** Paris (FR), 1929. **Tachard Garden**, La Celle-Saont-Cloud (FR), 1924.

Leinster 1st Duke & Duchess of   Carton

Gardeners roll a path as the Duke and Duchess of Leinster embark on their newly created artificial river. Its serpentine shape was a predominant motif of eighteenth-century design, used most notably in the design of The Serpentine lake in London's Hyde Park. The English painter William Hogarth had previously proclaimed the serpentine line to be 'The line of beauty'. The

1st Duke and Duchess of Leinster laid out one of the most important and extensive landscape parks in Ireland. Begun in 1747, the huge project of earth moving, lake creation and planting of over 445 hectares (1,000 acres) was completed by their son in 1837. Among the ornamental pavilions in the park is the 1760s' Shell House, its interior surfaces decorated with patterns formed

with a variety of shells and geological specimens as well as with decorative pine and fir cones. During the 1830s an artificial lake was created and an Italian garden was designed in front of the house.

☞ **Brown, Emes, Goldney, Kent**

James, 1st Duke of Leinster. b Dublin (IRE), 1722. **d** Dublin (IRE), 1773. **Emilia, 1st Duchess of Leinster. b** London (UK), 1731. **d** London (UK), 1814. **Carton**, Co Kildare (IRE), 1747–1837.

Lenné Peter Josef

Pfaueninsel

The enchanted island of Pfaueninsel lies in the Havel Lakes, west of Berlin. It is part of the overall landscaping which Lenné designed for Berlin and Potsdam in the 1820s and 1830s. This strange, white folly of a 'ruined' castle is earlier – built for Friedrich Wilhelm II of Prussia's mistress Gräfin Lichtenau in 1796. The castle is visually linked to palaces and monuments all around the complex of lakes. It was Friedrich Wilhelm III who commissioned Lenné to start landscaping the whole island in 1822 and bring it into harmony with the surrounding lakes. Almost single-handed, Lenné carried the landscape movement in Germany to new heights of compelling beauty long after the English who invented it had moved on to other garden fashions. At Pfaueninsel he looked to the Jardins des Plantes in Paris for inspiration in introducing rare species from all over the world. Lenné's masterpiece is Sanssouci, but Pfaueninsel is the most magical and peaceful landscape in Eastern Germany.

☛ W Aislabie, Friedrich II, Hamilton, Monteiro & Manini

Peter Josef Lenné. b Bonn (GER), 1789. d Potsdam (GER), 1866. **Pfaueninsel**, nr Berlin (GER), 1822.

Lennox-Boyd Arabella   Private Garden

This elegant little garden of clipped box is part of the private garden at Ascott, where Arabella Lennox-Boyd has created a formal design filled with subtly original ideas. Lennox-Boyd's confidence with such formal schemes, and her ability to lift them above mere historical pastiche, is perhaps partly due to her Italian background. The relatively substantial clipped hedges, with low domes within, echo the shape and scale of the central water feature to create a vision of effortless felicity. Elsewhere in the garden Lennox-Boyd demonstrates her skill as a plantswoman in the English mode, although her style is always distinguished by an underlying formal rigour. One of the most effective innovations at Ascott is her use of an uncompromising black as the decorative colour for the built features. Offset by planting, it does not look remotely funereal. In the 1980s and 1990s Lennox-Boyd established herself as Britain's prime society garden designer.

☛   **Acton, Barnsley, Marot & Roman, Page, Pinsent, Trezza, Veitch**

Arabella Lennox-Boyd. Private Garden, Ascott, Wing, Bucks (UK), c1990.

Le Nôtre André

Palace of Versailles

Water, sky, trees, sculpture, massed flowers, turf, topiary, great vistas, horizontal planes, changes of level: André Le Nôtre manipulated these components to create, during a sixty-year career, perhaps the greatest of all large-scale formal landscapes. His masterly manipulation of space can be seen here, at Louis XIV's Versailles, where the visitor reaches the gilded Apollo Basin at the end of the monumental *tapis vert*, and the demesne stretches still further forward beyond the grand canal, apparently to infinity. At Versailles Le Nôtre also worked on a more intimate scale in the *bosquets*, each of which contained a diversion: a water ballroom, a half-buried golden giant, the most elaborate fountains imaginable. Le Nôtre created a number of other château gardens of great spatial felicity – among them Vaux-le-Vicomte, Sceaux and Chantilly – but nothing rivals Versailles for ambition and scale.

☛ Boyceau, Duchêne, Francini, Gallard, Hardouin-Mansart

André Le Nôtre. b Paris (FR), 1613. d Paris (FR), 1700. **Palace of Versailles**, Versailles (FR), 1662–1700.

Libeskind Daniel

E T A Hoffman Garden (The Garden of Exile and Emigration)

Rising up from a sloping ground surface, forty-nine shard-like 6-m (18-ft) pillars are laid out in a square of seven rows of seven pillars. Growing from the top of each pillar are olive branches, symbolic of peace and hope. The Garden of Exile and Emigration is entered via the lower level of the Jewish Museum in Berlin, on one of three axes; the longest, the continuity axis, leads to the steep stairs to the exhibitions of the present-day and the future; the second leads into the Garden of Exile; and the third comes to a dead end at the Holocaust Tower. Daniel Libeskind, the architect, likens the form of the zinc-panelled museum building to a deconstructed Star of David and its shards and voids resonate with sensory and emotive experiences. This concept follows through in the garden, where the sloping cobbled floor disorientates and causes its visitors to stumble. They view their unaccustomed surroundings from the perspective of someone displaced: symbolically and in reality, the path to exile is a difficult one.

☞ Gehry, Guevrékian, Harrison, Johnson

Daniel Libeskind. b Lodz (POL), 1946. **E T A Hoffman Garden (The Garden of Exile and Emigration)**, Berlin (GER), 1999.

Ligne Prince Claude-Lamoral II de   Château de Beloeil

The formal geometry of the French classical garden is seen in all its harmony and on a grand scale at the Château de Beloeil in Belgium. On either side of a vast lake – 450 m (1,500 ft) long with a statue of Neptune at the far end – are a series of enclosures separated by towering hornbeam hedges. The gardens were laid out in the eighteenth century by Prince Claude-Lamoral II de Ligne. The main garden covers an area of 20 hectares (49 acres). The trees to either side of the lake are intersected by *allées* which provide a series of different views and perspectives. Although the design of Beloeil can be attributed to Prince Claude-Lamoral and its execution to Jean-Michel Chevotet, it is his son, the sociable and literary Prince Charles-Joseph de Ligne, whose name appears most frequently in connection with it. His treatise *Un Coup d'Oeil sur Beloeil* records the garden lovingly, an account all the more poignant because the victory of the French at Fleurus in 1794 forced him into exile, never to return.

☞   Arenberg, Gallard, Le Nôtre, Philip V of Spain

Prince Claude-Lamoral II de Ligne. b 1685. **d** 1766. **Château de Boloeil**, nr Leuze (BEL), mid-eighteenth century.

Ligorio Pirro

Villa d'Este

The Terrace of the Hundred Fountains is the best-known feature of the spectacular Renaissance gardens at Villa d'Este. The fountains are arranged in tiers of three: their effect depends upon their scale, their geometry and the element of repetition on every level. The villa was built on a steep hillside for Cardinal Ippólito d'Este, who was a knowledgeable collector and antiquarian with ambitions to the papacy. His architect was the humanist and classical scholar Pirro Ligorio, to whom the Terrace of the Hundred Fountains is usually attributed. Ligorio was a painter, architect and archaeologist who had an immense influence on the garden design of the Renaissance. He established a style of integrated house-and-garden design which remained the cornerstone of Italian architecture for 250 years. These gardens are among the best preserved, and as a result much of our understanding of Renaissance garden design comes from the Villa d'Este.

☛ Bushel, I Caus, Garzoni, Mozzoni, Nazarite

Pirro Ligorio. b Naples (IT), 1513. d Ferrara (IT), 1583. **Villa d'Este**, Tivoli, Lazio (IT), c1560–75.

Linden Ton ter

Tuinen Ton ter Linden

Subtle, shimmering colours is one of the borders in Ton ter Linden's garden. Thirty years ago Ton ter Linden, a painter born and brought up in Amsterdam, bought a farmhouse and a neglected meadow in a quiet, rural part of the Netherlands. He planted windbreaks and internal hedges to baffle the fierce winds that sweep across the flat land and to create the delicate structure of the garden. He fused techniques such as 'selective weeding', used to manage the J P Thijsse Park in Amstelveen, which he knew well, and his love of Impressionist painting to produce a series of garden rooms and borders of extraordinary beauty. Ton ter Linden relies on his knowledge of herbaceous plants, their needs and habits as well as their colours, shapes and textures rather than any paper plan when he gardens. He assembles plants in what seems a spontaneous, almost arbitrary way. The result is nature enhanced, containing both harmony and surprise.

☞ Monet, Pearson, Ruys, Thijsse

Ton ter Linden. **Tuinen Ton ter Linden**, north-east of Meppel (NL), c1980.

Lindsay Norah   Sutton Courtenay

'Without grandeur, but not without formality', Norah Lindsay's own words, written in 1931, capture the essence of the haphazard luxuriance of her timeless garden with its spires of topiary rising above the small clumps of perennials. Yet despite the apparent gay abandon, Lindsay, who was a disciple of and natural successor to Gertrude Jekyll, carefully orchestrated the colour scheme and arrangement of plant form and foliage. However, true to her romantic nature and view that gardening was dramatic theatre, Lindsay allowed the display to be supplemented by self-sown seedlings which succeeded in 'claiming squatter's rights'. Her innate sense of style and good taste won her a list of wealthy clients in the 1920s and 1930s, including the Astors at Cliveden and Lord Lothian at Blickling. She was also a close friend of Lawrence Johnston, creator of Hidcote, and helped him plan his 'jungle of beauty', her natural flamboyance a perfect foil to his inherent shyness.

☞ Beaumont, Farrand, Fish, Jekyll, Johnston, M Rothschild

Norah Lindsay. b (IRE), 1873. d (UK), 1948. Sutton Courtenay, Oxfordshire (UK), c1920s–30s.

Lloyd Christopher

Great Dixter

Christopher Lloyd has become renowned for the iconoclastic planting experiments in his own garden. He has lived at Great Dixter, on the Kent-Sussex border in England, all his life. His father, Nathaniel Lloyd, laid out the garden's simple framework of yew hedges to complement Lutyens' house. Lloyd has retained this rigid structure, but over the past forty years has relied on plants alone for effect. He is unsurpassed as an imaginative and artistic plantsman. His articles, lectures and books (notably *The Well-Tempered Garden*, 1970) have made him one of the world's best-known gardeners, and innovations at Great Dixter – such as the exotic garden which replaced a formal rose garden – have been influential. More than any other contemporary gardener, Lloyd has demonstrated that plantsmanship at its highest level is an art form that stands comparison with any other. Lloyd's ever-changing combinations of form, colour and texture at Great Dixter have made it one of the most notable gardens of the late twentieth century.

☛ Chatto, Kingsbury, Lutyens, A Parsons, Nordfjell, Oudolf

269

Christopher Lloyd. b Great Dixter (UK), 1921. **Great Dixter**, East Sussex (UK), 1950s.

London George

Hanbury Hall

The recently restored sunken parterre garden at Hanbury Hall is a fine example of the Dutch-inspired formal style which dominated English garden design at the end of the seventeenth century. Designed by George London and his partner Henry Wise, the sunken garden proves that this style did not have to be austere or impersonal. The restoration was based on a plan of 1732. A choice of brightly coloured plants such as marigolds, lavender, pinks, stocks, tulips and iris, all of them available in the eighteenth century, create a riotous summer display best viewed from the red-brick Long Gallery which ornaments one raised corner of the quartered parterre. London appears to have worked alone here, and the fruit garden beyond the parterre, with two small trellis pavilions amid apple trees and standard redcurrants and gooseberries in the borders, is a reflection of his horticultural expertise.

☞ Colchester, Marot & Roman, Wise

270

George London. b 1681. d London (UK), 1714. Hanbury Hall, Worcestershire (UK), 1701.

Londonderry 7th Marchioness of   Mount Stewart

The Dodo Terrace, with its cast-concrete representations of both real and fantastic animals, is seen over the richly whimsical planting of the Italianate parterre. One of the most important gardens to have been made during the 1920s, Mount Stewart is really a complex combination of different gardens. These are formal around the house, but become less so as they expand into shrubberies and groves of exotic trees around the informal lake, which was created between 1846 and 1848. The garden views are stopped by a hill above the lake, the location of the family burial ground designed by Lady Londonderry as a simulation of *Tir na nOg*, the Celtic Land of the Eternal Youth. Gertrude Jekyll provided plans for the sunken garden near the house but these were altered in their execution by Lady Londonderry in her own inimitable way. The care lavished on the garden by the National Trust helps to confirm its reputation as one of the most important gardens of the period.

☞   **Acton, Barry, Bowes-Lyon, Pearson & Cheal, Peto, Sitwell, Tilden**

Edith, 7th Marchioness of Londonderry. b (IRE), 1879. **d** (IRE), 1959. **Mount Stewart**, Co Down, Northern Ireland (UK), c1922.

It is not at all obvious from this sketch of a private house and garden why Adolf Loos was considered so outrageous in the early years of the twentieth century. Today it seems clear that the founder of proletarian architecture belonged to the same humanist tradition as the designers of Italian Renaissance gardens. There is the same insistence on line and perspective, purity and economy of

effort. Loos believed that decoration was not only unnecessary, but actually harmful because it appealed to the sensual side of mankind: only the masses of evergreen trees that provided useful shelter were appropriate plantings. These simple gardens may be unsatisfying to the eye of the plant-lover, but Loos considered them conducive to spiritual understanding, which was of much greater

value. Simplicity was better than fussiness: the best modern gardens eliminated all decoration and concentrated on the realities of the soul. Loos's logic was incontestable, although some maintain that the results are unworthy of the name 'garden'.

☛ **Bramante, Gill, Le Corbusier, Mies van der Rohe, Neutra, Nordfjell**

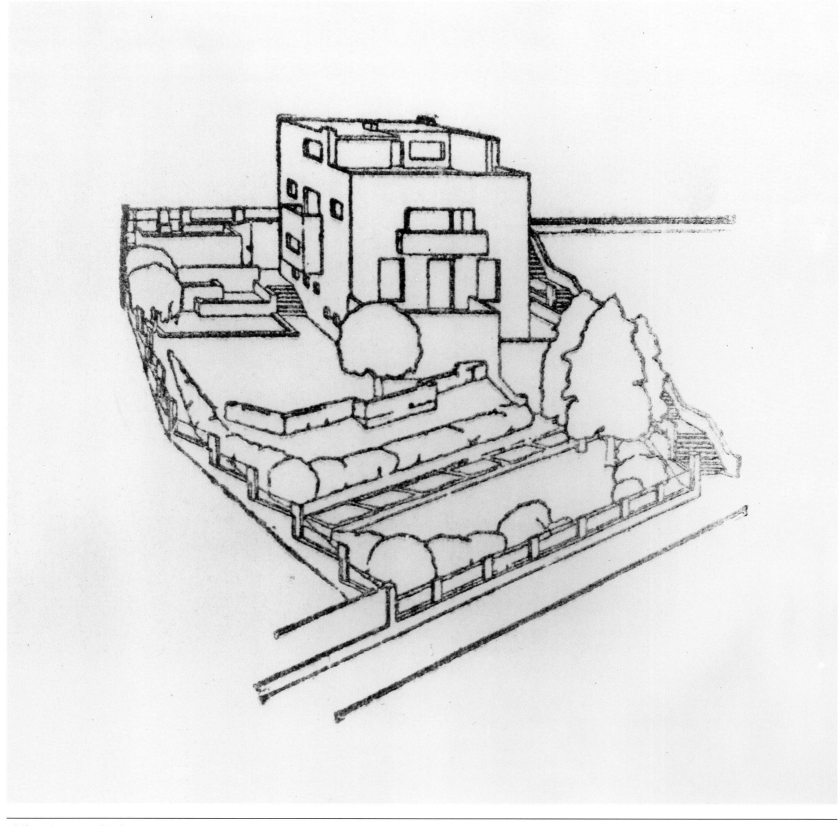

Adolf Loos. b Brno (CZ), 1870. **d** Vienna (AUS), 1933. **Müller House**, Prague (CZ), 1930.

Lorimer Sir Robert Stodart   Kellie Castle

Although 'flowers, fruit and vegetables are all mixed up together', this garden compartment is dominated by twin herbaceous borders, edged with box and arched over with roses. It is one of a number of different compartments, all enclosed within the stone-walled garth (garden space), laid out by Sir Robert for his father. Completed in 1888, the garden is imbued with a seventeenth-century spirit to match the restored castle which, according to the inscription above the door '...having been cleared of crows and owls, has been devoted to honourable repose from labour'. Trained as an architect, Lorimer promoted garden designs based on the pre-Renaissance, formal Scottish pleasure gardens of the seventeenth century, full of large hedges, topiary, viewing pavilions, lawns, grass walks, beds of perennials, and parterres. Although not so outspoken, he was the Scottish equivalent of Sir Reginald Blomfield, champion of the English formal garden. Sir Robert's most famous commission was Earlshall, Fife (1891–4).

☞ Beaumont, Blomfield, Drummond, Egerton-Warburton

273

Sir Robert Stodart Lorimer. b (UK), 1864. **d** (UK), 1929. **Kellie Castle**, Fife (UK), 1888.

L'Orme Philibert de   Château d'Anet

The garden which Philibert de l'Orme designed for Diane de Poitiers, the mistress of Henri II, was famous for its symmetry and its relationship to the house. Symmetry is clearly evident in this print, both in the design of the flower-garden and in the plantings. (It would be pleasing to think that the lady admiring the tulips was Diane de Poitiers herself, but this is actually a later evocation of the garden.) Anet was admired in its day because the house was axially aligned on the main part of l'Orme's garden, an extensive parterre containing a large number of smaller, square and rectangular parterres, surrounded by a stone gallery with a terrace running along the top of it. The garden became widely known after the publication of Du Cerceau's book *Les Plus Excellents Bastiments de France* in 1576, which contained detailed views of almost all the royal and aristocratic gardens of sixteenth-century France.

☛ Du Cerceau, Gallard, Landsberg, More, Poitiers, Serlio

274

Philibert de l'Orme. b Lyon (FR), c1512. **d** Paris (FR), 1570. **Château d'Anet**, Anet (FR), 1548–54.

Lotti Cosimo

Buen Retiro

Lined with statuary of the royalty of the past, the Avenue of the Statues leads from one of the main entrances into Madrid's major park. Originally part of a country estate, the palace and grounds date from the mid-seventeenth century. The gardens were developed from 1628 when Cosimo Lotti arrived from Florence to work on a commission from Philip IV. The palace was destroyed by fire, but remnants of the original garden, such as the great square pond and the large lake, still exist. The island in the lake was used as a venue for open-air entertainments. Once the playground of kings and queens, it became a public park in the mid-nineteenth century. The main carriageway around the park was originally used by the royal family to visit several hermitages that stood within its 121 hectares (300 acres). The hermits were paid an annual allowance. One of the most impressive pieces of statuary in the garden is the *Statue of the Fallen Angel*, reputedly the only statue in the world that represents Lucifer.

☞ **Peter II, Philip II, Philip V, Shenstone**

Cosimo Lotti. b Florence (IT), c1570s. **d** Buen Retiro, Madrid (SP), 1643. **Buen Retiro**, Madrid (SP), 1628.

Loudon John Claudius Derby Arboretum

The importance of this plan lies not so much in its layout as in the fact that it was the first large public park to be designed in Britain. The 4.4-hectare (10.5-acre) site was donated to the people of Derby by the philanthropist Joseph Strutt, and opened in September 1840 as a park. Entry to everyone was free for two days each week (including Sundays) and for a moderate charge at other times.

Having visited public parks and promenades on his travels to Europe, Loudon had come to see them as a as an instrument of social reform, a measure 'for promoting the convenience, the good order, and the instruction of the population'. Derby Arboretum was essentially a collection of trees, following in its layout Loudon's principle of the *gardenesque*. By this method, plants

were positioned to best display their individual attributes and, in contrast with the great naturalistic landscapes of the eighteenth century, the hand of man was clearly visible in their arrangement.

☞ **Olmsted, Paxton, Switzer, Thays**

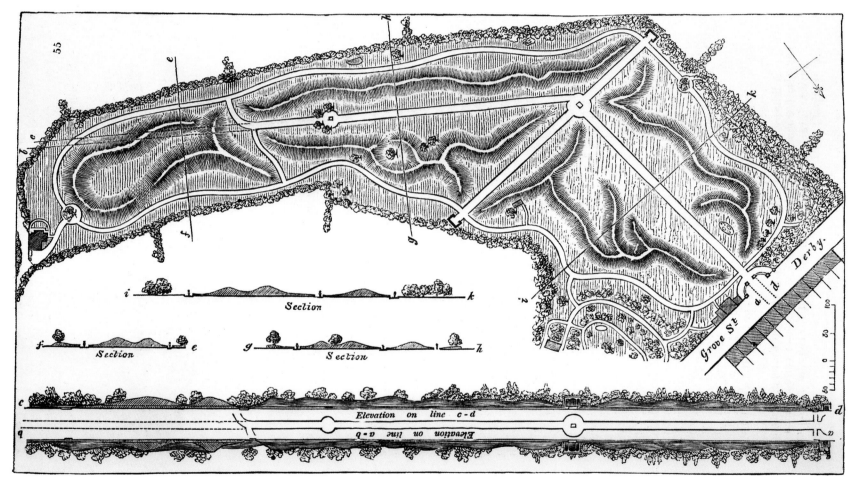

John Claudius Loudon. b (UK), 1783. **d** London (UK), 1843. **Derby Arboretum**, Derby (UK), 1840.

Lumley Lord

Nonsuch Palace

This engraving of 1610, by John Speed, shows the state apartments of the south facade, with their scenes from Classical history and mythology forming a backdrop for the what was undoubtedly the finest part of the grounds, the Privy Garden. This was formally laid out in knots planted with roses, privets and herbs. Marble fountains and a menagerie of animal sculptures on posts were set at intersections of the paths. The great Renaissance palace and gardens of Nonsuch, designed as a hunting lodge for Henry VIII, and remodelled by Lord Lumley from 1579–91, were intended to eclipse even Hampton Court and Whitehall as a monument to his grandeur. Visitors to Nonsuch marvelled at the pleasure gardens surrounding the palace, which included the Privy Garden, an orchard and a kitchen garden. To the west lay the carefully staged Wilderness, with walks leading to the Grove of Diana, the earliest known grotto in England, devoted to the myth of Diana and Actaeon. Sadly, nothing remains of either palace or garden.

☛ **Jones, More, William III, Wise**

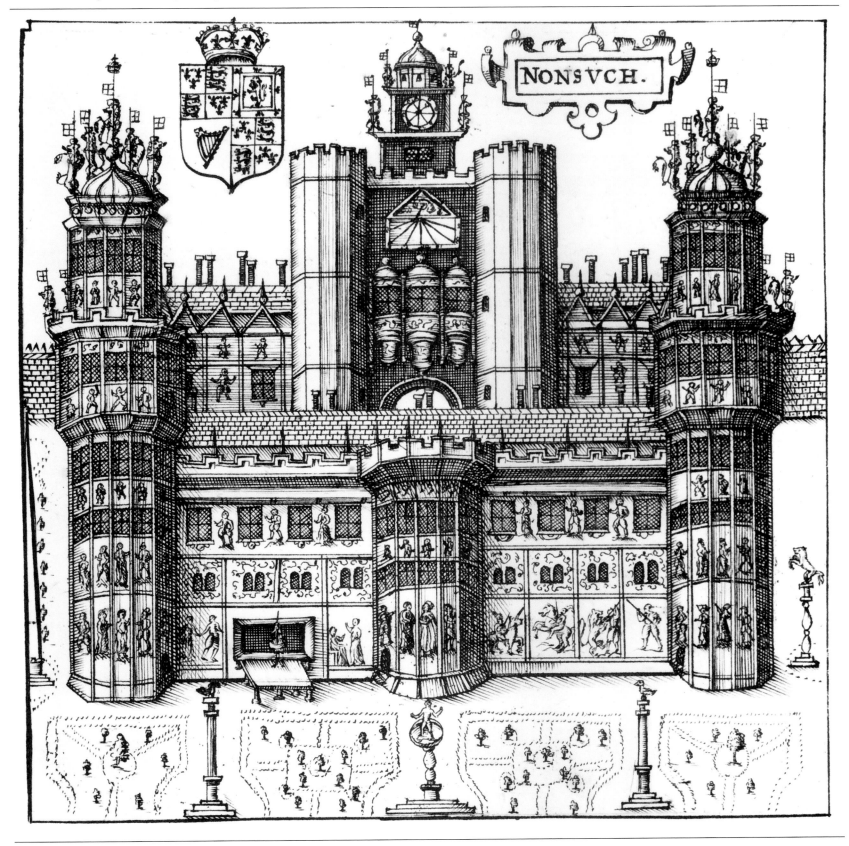

Lord Lumley. Nonsuch Palace and Gardens, nr Cheam, Surrey, 1579–91, engraving by John Speed, 1610.

Lurçat André

Villa Bomsel

This garden at the Villa Bomsel, seen here from the second floor of the house, was one of several doomed attempts in the 1920s and 1930s to create a prototype garden suited to Modernist architecture. André Lurçat's design comprised an irregular geometric parterre of cut turf and flowers, bisected by gravel paths and a water *allée* lined with sword lilies. Lurçat intended the garden to be viewed primarily from above (there is no access from the ground floor) and attempted to unify the house with the garden through the use of materials. As part of this plan, he used slabs of concrete for the water features and benches, and as decorative elements in their own right. Unusually among his Modernist contemporaries, Lurçat demonstrated an interest in horticulture: the light-blue concrete slabs were adorned with climbing roses and espaliered fruit trees line the walls.

☛ Le Corbusier, Legrain, Noailles, Vera, William III

278

André Lurçat. **b** Bruyères, Varges (FR), 1894. **d** Sceaux, Hauts-de-Seine (FR), 1970. **Villa Bomsel**, Versailles (FR), 1926.

Lutsko Ron

Stoney Hill Ranch

From the rough sandstone path with its irregular edges, to the distant blue hills, the eye is lead on through a wealth of visual 'layers'. The geometric pattern of the lawn and the path is eaten away at the edges, indicating a move away from the house's architecture and into the wilderness of the landscape. In the middle ground, the lavender mounds planted in a grid are reminiscent of the native grey and stunted vegetation and also echo the grid patterns which agriculture has etched in the Californian landscape. Further on, a band of stipa grasses proclaim the rhythm and sway of the distant hills. In another area Ron Lutsko has planted swathes of native flowers and encouraged other drought-loving plants to naturalize. Lutsko is passionate about native flora and the natural beauty and diversity of the Californian environment. An advocate of strong modern designs that neither hide nor disguise their intervention, he is heir to the American landscape tradition of Thomas Church and Garrett Eckbo.

☞ Church, Eckbo, Hargreaves, Kiley, M Rothschild, de Vesian

Ron Lutsko. b CA (USA), 1952. **Stoney Hill Ranch**, San Francisco Bay, CA (USA), 1991.

Lutyens Sir Edwin   Folly Farm

Classic elements of the Lutyens style are evident at Folly Farm: formal semicircular steps softened by planting, architectural hedges forming an invitation into the next area of the garden, the Lutyens bench, herringbone brick paving, a red-brick Arts-and-Crafts house topped by tall chimneys. In partnership with Gertrude Jekyll, Lutyens made some seventy gardens that represent the most satisfactory unification of house and garden in twentieth-century garden design. Lutyens would design a series of formal spaces and vistas enhanced by fine architectural detail, and Jekyll complemented and softened the outlines with sophisticated colour planting. Lutyens was particularly skilled with formal water features; Folly Farm boasts an Indian-inspired pool and canal garden. His most ambitious work is the magnificent, Mughal-inspired Viceroy's Garden in New Delhi.

☞ Jekyll, Lloyd, Mallet, Mawson

Sir Edwin Lutyens. b London (UK), 1869. **d** London (UK), 1944. **Folly Farm**, Berkshire (UK), 1912.

MacDonald-Buchanan Family   Cottesbrooke Hall

A long paved walk between borders of delphiniums, catmint and campanulas, leads through low wrought-iron gates hung on pillars surmounted by griffins, giving vistas through onto a wide lawn. This sunny, southern terrace is one of many fine gardens surrounding the house, enhanced by the Macdonald-Buchanans since they came to live here in 1937. An ornamental parterre of clipped yew, added in front of the main entrance, and an adjacent statue walk provide a formal prelude to the house, which merges into a landscaped park such as Repton might have designed, with a long river-like lake spanned by a fine five-arch bridge, dating from 1770. Sir John Langham built Cottesbrooke Hall and laid the park out during the first decade of the eighteenth century. Sylvia Crowe and Geoffrey Jellicoe are among the designers who have worked at Cottesbrooke.

☞ Crowe, Egerton-Warburton, Jellicoe, Repton

Macdonald-Buchanan Family. Active (UK), twentieth century. **Cottesbrooke Hall**, Northamptonshire (UK), 1937.

Mackenzie Osgood   Inverewe

This mix of verdant ferns and exotic erythroniums generates a sub-tropical luxuriance that epitomizes the lushness of this garden, but belies its most unlikely location. On a small, exposed peninsula on the extreme north-west coast of Scotland, Osgood Mackenzie began his 800-hectare (1,976-acre) garden in 1862 with only two dwarf willows. However, once sheltered by the new woodland, Mackenzie discovered that he had created the perfect conditions in which to grow many semi-tender species that thrived in the mild micro-climate caused by the Gulf Stream. The garden was skilfully created to take best advantage of the topography, with winding paths bringing you to various enclosed spaces cut out of the maturing woodland. Mackenzie filled these with an enormous diversity of rare, exotic plants introduced from China, South America, the Antipodes and the Himalayas. Sheltered gardens such as Inverewe and others in Cornwall acted as experimental laboratories testing these new plants.

☞ La Quintinie, Smit, Smith, Tyrwhitt

Osgood Mackenzie. b (UK), 1842. d (UK), 1922. Inverewe, Poolewe, Ross & Cromarty (UK), 1862.

Maderno Carlo

Villa Aldobrandini

Evening sun catches the drama of Aldobrandini's nymphaeum and water theatre, built against the retaining wall between the villa and the steep Frascati hillside. Constructed between 1598 and 1603 for a nephew of Pope Clement VIII, Aldobrandini is resplendently Baroque in its exuberance and the gradual merging of formality into wildness. Though mostly stilled now, piped water welled once from a grotto high up the wooded slopes, then crashed down a succession of cascades towards twin helter-skelter water pillars and a water stairway, re-emerging as a watery skirt around Atlas' globe, just visible below the narrow gap in the trees. The best view, as ever, was from the villa's upper floors. At Aldobrandini, Maderno completed the work begun by architect Giacomo della Porta. Visited by John Evelyn in 1645 (who much admired the water jokes and hydraulics), it became essential viewing on the eighteenth-century Grand Tour and obvious echoes appear in William Kent's cascades at Rousham and Chiswick.

☛ Kent, Ligorio, Mansi, Tribolo

Carlo Maderno. b Copelago (IT), 1556. d Rome (IT), 1629. Villa Aldobrandini, Frascati (IT), 1598–1603.

Majorelle Jacques

La Majorelle

Water, shade and a predominantly green-and-blue colour scheme create a cool, refreshing retreat at La Majorelle, giving welcome respite from the fierce Moroccan sun. Such bold and skilful use of colour betrays the hand of the garden's creator, the French painter Jacques Majorelle, who laid it out in the 1920s in classic Moorish-Spanish style with canals, fountains, *moucharabia* kiosks and dense Rousseauesque planting. The garden is unique among artists' gardens for the intensity of the palette used in both its planting and its architecture: ironwork, windows and pots are bright yellow; doors are apple-green; paths are red, pink or blue; vermillion and fuchsia bougainvillea cover walls and trellis. Running through the garden is the high-key cobalt blue, known as 'Majorelle blue', that both unifies the design and throws the other colours into sharp relief. At the end of the 1960s, the garden was rescued from dereliction by the fashion designer Yves St Laurent and his partner Pierre Bergé.

☞ **Barragán, Gehry, Greene, Manrique, Page, Yturbe**

Jacques Majorelle. b Nancy (FR), 1886. **d** 1962. **La Majorelle**, Marrakesh (MOR), 1920s.

284

Mallet Family

Les Bois des Moutiers

Gunneras, rhododendrons, hydrangeas and other acid-loving plants thrive in the sheltered seaside woodland of the Bois des Moutiers. In contrast with this naturalistic plant paradise, the gardens become increasingly defined as one proceeds up the valley towards the house. There a succession of delightful garden rooms designed by Gertrude Jekyll are carefully articulated and linked by Edwin Luytens' pergolas, steps, summerhouses and gateways. Exemplary of a highly successful partnership between architect, garden designer and patrons, des Moutiers was commissioned in 1898 by Guillaume Mallet, an enlightened banker, and his wife, both of them passionate gardeners. Lutyens, Jekyll and the Mallets were closely associated with each step of the design but the woodland garden was the Mallet family's own personal project, through which they expressed their love of plants. Their descendants continue to maintain and improve this exceptional garden to this day.

☛ Jekyll, Lutyens, Messel, Robinson

Mallet Family. Active Normandy (FR), 1898–present day. **Les Bois des Moutiers**, Normandy (FR), 1898.

Mallet-Stevens Robert   Garden with Concrete Trees

The landscape section of the 1925 Paris Exposition, supervised by J C N Forestier, contained the most avant-garde designs of the century, among the usual homages to tradition or exotic international style. Encouraged to experiment with new materials, Robert Mallet-Stevens championed concrete, creating a series of ornaments and buildings for the Exposition, including this garden with concrete trees. Concrete retaining walls created four raised beds enclosing simple arrangements of planes of grass and sempervivum. Each bed was ornamented with a tall concrete tree made by Jan and Joël Martel, who attached branches (slabs of concrete) to a central concrete trunk. Serious-minded Modernists praised the garden, but there was some hilarity among the press and public, with speculation that the real trees for the garden had died. This showpiece was probably the most uncompromising Modernist garden ever created. As an architect, Mallet-Stevens was responsible for the Villa Noailles at Hyères.

☛ Forestier, Guevrékian, Legrain, Vera

286

Robert Mallet-Stevens. b Paris (FR), 1886. **d** Paris (FR), 1945. **Garden with Concrete Trees**, Paris Exposition (FR), 1925.

Mandokora Kita no   Kodai-ji

In a carefully planned, reflective landscape of hillocks and stream, pines and stones, a covered footbridge leads to the Kaisan-do or founder's hall. Dedicated to the Kodai-ji's founder priest, Sanko Joeki, this beautiful example of Momoyama architecture is in an excellent state of preservation, like most of the pavilions and grounds of this magnificent temple complex. The main temple garden, composed of the trademark pond in the shape of a turtle with an island in the form of a crane, was designed by Kobori Enshu. He was commissioned in 1605 by Kita no Mandokora, the widow of shogun Toyotomi Hideyoshi who became a Buddhist nun after the death of her husband. She died there peacefully at the age of seventy-six. The Kodai-ji also now houses two exquisite tea pavilions, moved here from Fushimi Castle: the Kasa Tei (Umbrella House) and the Shigure Tei (Rain Shower House), thought to have been designed by the great tea master Sen no Rikkyu.

☞ Ashikaga Yoshimasa, Ashikaga Yoshimitsu, Enshu, Sen no Rikkyu

Kita no Mandokora. b (JAP), 1548. **d** (JAP), 1624. **Kodai-ji**, Kyoto (JAP), 1605.

Manning Warren Henry Stan Hywet Hall and Garden

The birch *allée*, which stretches for over 167 m (550 ft), is one of two main axial *allées* of the garden, this one terminating at a fountain and teahouses. Stan Hywet (Old English for Stone Quarry) was laid out between 1911 and 1915 by Warren Manning for Franklin A Seiberling, the co-founder of the Goodyear Tyre company. Manning said of the site in 1911: 'very few of the ... properties that I have examined and made plans for offer within a hundred acres so many and such varied incidents that will give a house estate distinction and interest'. Manning exploited those incidents. The house is framed by high canopy trees with sweeps of lawn beyond, in the manner of an eighteenth-century English estate. Apple trees form an *allée* over the front drive, and the birch *allée* and London plane *allée* run north and south from the house. There is a naturalistic lagoon and several garden rooms, including a Japanese garden and an English garden. The English garden was redesigned by Ellen Biddle Shipman, at Manning's suggestion, in 1928.

☞ Brown, Repton, Shipman, Thwaites, Van Campen, Van Hoey Smith

Warren Henry Manning. b Reading, MA (USA), 1860. **d** (USA), 1938. **Stan Hywet Hall and Garden**, Akron, OH (USA), 1911–15.

Manrique César   Jardín de Cactus

Bulbous cacti and spiky succulents are interspersed randomly against the black volcanic soil. Gentle curving terraces of low rubble walls surround an irregular central arena with interlinking water pools, from the centre of which jut volcanic rocks. The black volcanic geology of Lanzarote bears silent witness to a time before human intervention. César Manrique created a garden in an old quarry that is a fusion of nature, traditional Lanzarote architecture, his own sculptural organic forms, and subtle use of indigenous plants adapted to the arid yet fertile environment. His 'volcanic Baroque' garden is borne from his philosophies of nature and of life. Manrique was a painter and sculptor who studied in Madrid and lived in New York for many years before returning to his native Lanzarote, whose natural beauty he had championed through his work. He said, 'What I take from the scenery of my home is not its architecture but its dramatic feeling, its essence, which is, to my way of thinking, what really matters.'

☛ Gildemeister, Hertrich, Majorelle, Monet, Sventenius, Walska

César Manrique. b Arrecife, Lanzarote (CI), 1919. d Tahíche, Lanzarote (CI), 1992. Jardín de Cactus, Guatiza, Lanzarote (CI), 1990.

Mansi Nicola

Villa Cimbrone

One of the most breath-taking garden terraces ever made can be found at the Villa Cimbrone, where the garden climbs up to the cliff to this viewpoint overlooking the coast at Ravello, near Naples. Visitors transfixed by the view are themselves gazed at by a row of eighteenth-century marble busts of emperors. Lord Grimthorpe bought the dilapidated medieval villa in 1904 and engaged Nicola Mansi to create a romantic, atmospheric garden on the sloping site. Over the next fifteen years Mansi worked to create numerous different areas in the garden, including *allées*, terraces, statuary, a long wisteria-clad pergola and a formal garden with temples and architectural fragments. Lord Grimthorpe died in 1917, two years after the garden was completed. The villa belonged to the family until 1960, when it was sold by Grimthorpe's daughter. Today, the gardens have the highly romantic atmosphere that accompanies gentle decay.

☞ Acton, Garzoni, Mardel, Peto, Pinsent

Nicola Mansi. Active (IT), twentieth century. **Villa Cimbrone**, Ravello (IT), c1910–15.

Mardel Carlos

Palace of the Marques of Pombal

This double staircase lined with blue and white azulejo tilework can be found in the garden built for the Marquis of Pombal, King Jao V's powerful prime minister. A grotto beneath the stairs is lined with gleaming fragments of porcelain reflected in the water of a pool. The architect was Carlos Mardel, a Hungarian. The terracotta tiled roofs and pink walls of the palace are reminiscent of French eighteenth-century architecture. The gardens are formal and studded with fountains set in pebble-mosaic courtyards. Statuary and tilework in blue and yellow predominate. Much of the tilework in the garden is in need of restoration. As in many Portuguese gardens of the eighteenth century, there is a fishing pavilion and water tank. Across the bridge in the park are an ornamental dairy, a silkworm house and a dovecote which can house over a thousand birds.

☞ Gaudí, Fronteira, Medinaceli, Monteiro & Manini, Oliveira & Robillon

Carlos Mardel. Active Lisbon (POR), 1733–63. **Palace of the Marques of Pombal**, Lisbon (POR), c1756.

Marot Daniel & Roman Jacob   Het Loo

The elegant arabesques of the box parterres in the King's Garden at Het Loo, now wonderfully recreated, were the work of Daniel Marot. Marot, a Huguenot, fled from France in 1685 and brought a French Baroque flourish to the gardens and interiors he designed in the Dutch Republic. The parterres *en broderie*, with three shades of gravel in the French manner, are surrounded by *plates-bandes*, narrow borders edged by box, containing the herbaceous plants and bulbs much loved by the Dutch. Jacob Roman began building Het Loo for William of Orange, then the Stadtholder of the republic, in 1686. After William and Mary were crowned king and queen of England in 1689, the house and its grounds were deemed insufficiently 'kingly'. It was then that Daniel Marot was employed at Het Loo along with Jacob Roman who, it is believed, was responsible for the main outlines of the garden, and the sculptor Romeyn de Hooghe – under the direction of Hans Willem Bentinck.

☞ Lainé, Mollet, Nesfield, Sophia, William III

Daniel Marot. b Paris (FR), 1661. d The Hague (NL), 1752. Jacob Roman. b The Hague (NL), 1640. d (NL), 1716. Het Loo, Apeldoorn (NL), 1686.

Martinelli Domenico Buchlovice

Pictured here is a segment of the Baroque garden courtyard at Buchlovice. Garden courts were often used for outdoor theatrical performances and pageants, as was the case with the best-known of all Baroque garden courtyards – that at the Zwinger Palace in Dresden. It is thus appropriate that the courtyard design at Buchlovice is attributed to Domenico Martinelli, who brought his talents as a stage designer here from his native Italy. (The relationship between stage design and garden design in the Baroque period was a close one.) The exuberant design of the Buchlovice court is based on a swirl, as it were, of cupolas, pavilions, gates, statuary and vases arranged around the central fountained space. Part of the court is on a raised level from which spectators might be able to view better a performance taking place on the lower level. Buchlovice also boasts a collection of trees developed by two botanist members of the Berchtold family, Leopold and his brother-in-law, Frederick.

☞ **Augustus the Strong, Bacciocchi, Fontana, Jones, Seinsheim**

293

Domenico Martinelli. b Lucca (IT), 1650. d Lucca (IT), 1718. **Buchlovice**, South Moravia (CZ), late-seventeenth century.

Martino Steve

Douglas Garden

A small house sits in the Arizona desert, surrounded by the sculptural verticals of the scrub-covered hills and the indigenous saguro cactus. Martino is one of the leading landscape architects and designers in the American south-west. He became known during the 1980s and 1990s for his work with architects on the siting of new houses in the context of the desert environment.

He is also respected for his broad and deep knowledge of desert plant subjects and their uses in the landscape. Many of his garden and landscape designs flow seamlessly from the areas around a private house or public building into the surrounding desert. The plants Martino uses are chosen for their innate sculptural qualities. Even though he works primarily in a single region, he is not

unaware of leading designers of the twentieth century; Alvar Aalto being a considerable influence.

☛ Aalto, Barragán, Gildemeister, Greene, Nordfjell

Steve Martino. Douglas Garden, Phoenix, AZ (USA).

Mawson Thomas   Moonhill

This sketch from Mawson's book *The Art and Craft of Garden Making* illustrates his approach to design. The house sits above a series of terraces that provide a setting for the beds and borders, all of them well planted, for Mawson was initially a nurseryman, and a collection of ornaments and topiary. The most Edwardian of features, the rectangular lily pool, graces the lowest level of this area of the garden, which is enclosed by a yew hedge. Although Mawson espoused the Arts-and-Crafts ideals, he was a formalist and his designs were also influenced by medieval and Renaissance gardens, and by the work of Repton and Kemp. Mawson was a prolific garden designer, as well as producing town planning schemes and park designs in Canada, Greece and Australia. He was elected the first President of the Institute of Landscape Architects in 1929. Perhaps the most famous surviving Mawson garden is The Hill in Hampstead, created for Lord Leverhulme which features a monumental pergola.

☞   **Barnsley, Greene & Greene, Lutyens, Morris**

"MOONHILL," CVCKFIELD, SVSSEX; For Walter Lloyd Esq: D. Morley Horder *Archt.* Thomas H. Mawson *Garden Archt.*

Thomas Mawson. b Scorton, Lancashire (UK), 1861. **d** Lancaster (UK), 1933. **Moonhill**, Cuckfield, Sussex (UK), 1920s.

McEarcharn Neil   Villa Taranto

Ever since Goethe trumpeted the charms of Garda – its figs, pears and lemon trees – northern Europeans have been flocking south. The lakes generate a microclimate that reproduces the climate of the Bay of Naples, high rainfall and hot summers followed by mild winters. One European smitten by the botanical beauty of the area was the retired Scottish Captain Neil McEarcharn, who began to plan a garden in 1931 with military precision. The result is a series of formal layouts mixed with successful naturalistic planting and an eclectic collection of plants. Henry Cocker, who was trained at Kew, established the collection of herbaceous plants and bulbs over the 18-hectare (44-acre) gardens, including some peculiarly British gaudy seasonal bedding from tulips and pansies in spring to begonias and geranium in summer. In one particularly felicitous area, much admired by D H Lawrence, a central water channel falls over musical chimes and sweeps of hostas spread into the steep-sided valleys.

☛ Acton, Chambers, Hanbury, Steele, Taverna

296

Neil McEarcharn (Captain Neil Boyd Watson McEarcharn). b (UK), 1884. d (IT), 1964. **Villa Taranto**, Lake Maggiore (IT), 1931–51.

McNab James

The Rock Garden at the Royal Botanic Garden

Some of the rarest alpine plants in the world nestle between jagged outcrops at the Rock Garden of the Royal Botanic Garden, Edinburgh. James McNab created the Rock Garden in 1870, during the great era of plant hunting in Britain. The garden originally consisted of 5,442 planting compartments separated by upright stones. It attracted fierce criticism from the horticultural community – 'the chaotic hideousness', said one critic 'is something to be remembered with shudders ever after' – but was immediately popular with visitors. In 1908, perhaps because of this criticism, it was ripped apart and replaced with more naturalistic rocky outcrops. Recently, there has been a move towards planting by geographical origin and the scree bed and waterfall have been enlarged to this end. There is no grand plan, however. John Main, head of horticulture says, 'It's a bit like the Forth Road Bridge. By the time we finish reconstructing one bit, we have to start elsewhere.'

☛ Crisp, Middleton, Otruba, Pulham, Savill

297

James McNab. b Surrey (UK), 1810. **d** Edinburgh (UK), 1879. **The Rock Garden at the Royal Botanic Garden**, Edinburgh (UK), 1870.

Meath William, 11th Earl of Kilruddery

Low evening light and autumn foliage romanticize strict garden geometry. A French Baroque garden romantically transposed to the rugged landscape of Ireland, Kilruddery exemplifies the wide dissemination of the French garden style in the seventeenth century. (It is known that a gardener called Bonet, thought to be French, entered the service of the 4th Earl of Meath in 1684.) The distinctive feature of the garden's design is its use of twin canals. After substantial hurricane damage in the nineteenth century, the garden was restored by the 11th Earl of Meath, with additions which included a green theatre and much cast-iron, classical-style statuary by famous European manufacturers. During the same period the house was extended with a conservatory designed by William Burn which boasted a curvilinear glass roof. An ornamental dairy by the amateur architect, Sir George Hodson, and new terrace balustrading designed by the prolific Daniel Robertson complemented the new additions.

☞ Bowes-Lyon, Colchester, Johnston, Robert

William, 11th Earl of Meath. b 1841. d 1918. **Kilruddery**, Bray, Co Wicklow (IRE), c1850s.

Medinacelli Family — Pazo de Oca

Stone figures fish from a stone boat designed to appear as if it is afloat on a fishpond at the Pazo de Oca. Many formal gardens are conventional to the point of dullness. The exceptions are those where a special quirk of the designer's mind, as in the theme of Pazo de Oca's garden statuary, or a freak aspect of the garden's site is evident. Also unconventional is the way in which the rectangular geometry of Pazo de Oca's garden is broken by an unexpected angular vista leading the eye over its pair of formal fishponds. Designed in the late eighteenth century under the supervision of the Marques de Camarosa, an exceptional collection of trees was added after 1845 by François Vie, head gardener at Madrid's Palacio Real. Being restored currently by the architect, the Duke of Segorbe, the garden becomes a place of special enchantment in misty or rainy weather, moisture bringing out the true richness of colour in the moss-covered local granite.

☛ Dashwood, Pückler-Muskau, Tortella

Medinacelli Family. Active (SP) eighteenth century. **Pazo de Oca**, Santiago de Compostela (SP), c1790s–1850s.

Mehmed II

Topkapi Palace

Located in a spectacular position on the tip of the Istanbul peninsula and overlooking two seas and two continents, the Topkapi Palace stands on the site of the acropolis of ancient Constantinople. Its gardens incorporate many garden-design traditions, including Persian, Greek, Byzantine, Ottoman and Italianate styles. This is one of the many intimate courtyards within the sultan's private domain. A large pleasure pavilion – or kiosk – overlooks a formally planted courtyard with a central octagonal pool and a tiered marble fountain – representing the celestial fountain of Paradise. Unlike Persian gardens, Turkish gardens were not divided into quarters nor did they have watercourses. Yet, just like the great gardens of Persia and Mughal India, they were typically square or rectangular walled enclosures, often paved with marble slabs, and planted with religiously symbolic trees and plants such as cypresses, date palms and roses.

☞ Almohad, Moorish Governors, Nazarite

Mehmed II. Reigned Constantinople (TRK), 1444–81. **Topkapi Palace**, Istanbul (TRK), begun 1459.

Mercogliano Pacello di Blois

No garden illustrates the origins of the French Renaissance better than Blois: here is a rambling royal palace with a stupendous formal garden in the Italian style, dating from 1500–10. An Italian fountain, two *treillage* rooms, and a two-storey gallery were among its stylistic innovations. Nothing similar had been seen before in France. No attempt was made to integrate the garden with the house – it was essentially a fashionable add-on to the still-medieval castle. This approach was typical of the way the Italian Renaissance was received in northern Europe at the time. The architect of the garden is generally assumed to be Pacello di Mercogliano, a Neapolitan priest whom Charles VIII brought back from his expedition to Italy in 1494–5, where he was overcome by the beauty of contemporary Neapolitan gardens. Di Mercogliano is also credited with the introduction of new plants and methods of cultivation: it is thought that he was responsible for the precious orange and lemon trees in terracotta pots which adorned the gardens in summer.

☛ Du Cerceau, Gallard, L'Orme, Moroni, Poitiers

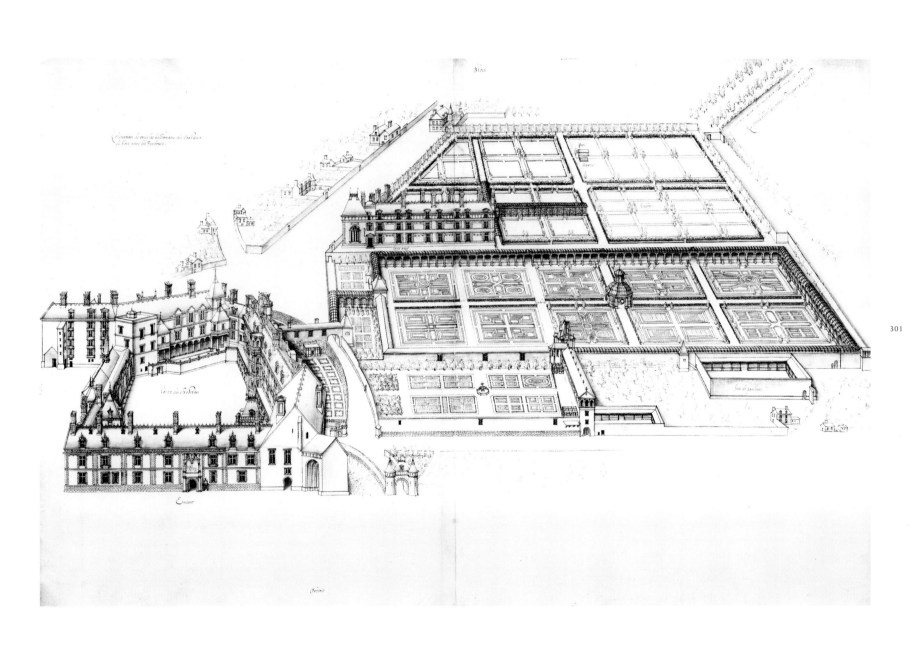

Pacello di Mercogliano. b Naples (IT). d Blois (FR), 1534. **Blois** (FR), 1500–10.

Messel Ludwig & Leonard   Nymans

The burnt-out shell of the house (built in 1928, gutted in 1947) provides a dramatic backdrop to the garden. Ludwig Messel acquired Nymans in 1890 and began the garden, a process continued by his son Leonard and, later, his granddaughter Anne, Countess of Rosse. The garden is renowned for its exceptional collection of plants arranged as a series of episodes. The first garden compartment to be made was the Wall Garden, transformed from an old kitchen garden by the addition of a central fountain flanked by topiary, with spectacular flower borders lining the quartering paths. Other features included an early heather garden, a rose garden and a lime-walk leading to spectacular views out over the Weald. Messel was assisted in his works by his head gardener James Comber, whose son Harold made several plant-hunting expeditions to the Antipodes and South America in order to find botanical treasures with which to enrich the garden further.

☞ Caetani, Johnston, Monville, Rochford, Sackville-West

Ludwig Messel. Active (UK) late nineteenth century. Leonard Messel. Active (UK) early twentieth century. Nymans, Haywards Heath, West Sussex (UK), 1890.

Michelozzi Michelozzo   Villa Medici

The famous Villa Medici at Fiesole has been so often restored and replanted that it is difficult to know what remains of Michelozzi's original concept. The four conical magnolias and the formal parterres are certainly an anachronism: they were planted in 1911 by the English designer Cecil Pinsent for an Anglo-American owner. But the terrace itself has remained basically unchanged since it was first laid out for Cosimo di Medici in 1460. House and garden were conceived as a unit and intended to grow organically out of the surrounding countryside. Michelozzi was a student of Alberti – hence the open view of the steep hillside below the gardens. Alberti was the first scholar to argue that there should exist a unity of style and spirit between a house, its garden and the wider landscape. The steps down from the vine-covered terrace above are modern: this was originally a kitchen garden for fruit and vegetables and, to that extent, detached from the house and its elegant upper terrace.

☞ Acton, Capponi, Garzoni, Mardel

Michelozzo Michelozzi. b Florence (IT), 1396. **d** Florence (IT), 1472. **Villa Medici**, Fiesole, Tuscany (IT), 1460–.

Middleton Sir Arthur   Belsay Hall

Extensive parkland, a series of terraces and a 4.5-m (14.4-ft) arched ha-ha dropping from the Greek-revival house to the tranquil lake are all the work of Sir Arthur's grandfather, Sir Charles. Behind the lake is the deep, picturesque quarry garden that was developed by Sir Arthur on the site created when stone was extracted to build the house. Following the twin Victorian obsessions of novelty and collecting, Sir Arthur filled the quarry garden with many rare and exotic semi-hardy trees and shrubs. In the mid- and late-nineteenth century such novelties were pouring into Britain as a result of expeditions made by the plant hunters, but many required the mild growing conditions found in southern Cornwall or the West Coast of Scotland. The unusually sheltered conditions within the quarry allowed Sir Arthur to make a collection unique in this northern part of Britain. Inside the quarry a high arch and a secret door marked by tangled branches lure the visitor on. Beyond a narrow passage, a view of the ruined manor is revealed.

☞ Aberconway, Gilpin, Mackenzie, Rochford, Savill

Sir Arthur Middleton. b 1838. **d** 1933. **Belsay Hall**, Northumberland (UK), late nineteenth century.

Mies van der Rohe Ludwig   German Pavilion

A nude gestures across the expanse of this shallow marble-lined pool. Built on a 53.6 by 17 m (175 by 56 ft) travertine platform, Mies van der Rohe designed the German Pavilion at the Barcelona International Exhibition of 1929 to have a very minimal structure of cruciform steel columns, with a flat overhanging roof and glass and honey coloured onyx walls. It is the prime twentieth-century example of the seamless integration of exterior and interior spaces – the pool shown is mirrored by an even larger shallow pool lined with pebbles on the entrance side of the pavilion. The glass walls seem to disappear, exemplifying the famous phrase ascribed to Mies, 'less is more'. Mies was the director of the Bauhaus in Germany but emigrated to the USA in 1937. He was one of the most important architects of the twentieth century, responsible for many Modern movement buildings, including the Seagram Building in Chicago and the Farnsworth House in Plano, Illinois.

☛ **Barragán, Le Corbusier, Loos, Lurçat**

Ludwig Mies van der Rohe (Ludwig Mies). b Aachen (GER), 1886. **d** Chicago, IL (USA), 1969. **German Pavilion** (Barcelona Pavilion), Barcelona (SP), 1929, restored 1986.

Miller Carl Ferris

Chollipo Arboretum

On the shores of the Yellow Sea in Korea, the American-born, naturalized Korean, Ferris Miller, began to plant this important arboretum in 1970. Although many plant families are featured, the magnolia family is the focus of the collection since Miller has been much influenced by the contemporary worldwide enthusiasm for these trees, reminiscent of the seventeenth-century mania for tulips. The sensational annual flowering of the magnolias represents the Asian tradition of gardens which focus on the blossoming of one plant family best known through the shakura, the two-week cherry blossom season enjoyed by festive crowds in the parks and gardens of Japan. Another Asian tradition, that of erecting viewing pavilions from which to observe the garden and its blossom, is represented at Chollipo by its collection of traditional Korean dwellings, many of them rescued from demolition in Seoul.

☛ Holford, Smithers, Tyrwhitt

Carl Ferris Miller. b (USA), 1921. **Chollipo Arboretum** (S KOR), 1970.

Milne Oswald

Coleton Fishacre

Terraces built, like the house, from stone quarried in the valley below, provide a strong architectural framework for Coleton Fishacre in Devon, and help to shelter half-hardy exotics such as the elegant, arching wandflower. The terraces give way to an informal garden of wooded slopes, pools and streams, becoming increasingly jungle-like as it descends to the sea. Coleton Fishacre was built between 1923 and 1926 for Rupert D'Oyly Carte, founder-owner of the Savoy Hotel, and his wife Dorothy, who spotted the location from their yacht. The pared down Arts-and-Crafts house was the work of architect Oswald Milne, a former assistant to Edwin Lutyens, whose influence can be seen in the rounded pool on the upper terrace. While Milne was responsible for the formal areas around the house and the Rill Garden, the rest of the garden was created by the D'Oyly Cartes. Taking advantage of the mild, humid coastal climate, they planted a huge range of plants, including thickets of mimosa and a massive tulip tree.

☞ Barnsley, Fish, Harrild, Lutyens, Mawson

Oswald Milne. b 1881. **d** 1967. **Coleton Fishacre**, nr Kingswear, Devon (UK), 1920s.

Monumental ceramics on linked terraces people Joan Miró's Labyrinth, among the pines adjacent to the Maeght Foundation building in the Riviera village of Saint Paul. It is one of very few examples of an artist creating a series of works for a specific outdoor setting. Miró made full-size plywood models of the sculptures in order to experiment with their positioning. Then his collaborator, the ceramicist Josep Artigas, helped him realize the final works. Some of the pieces, such as the marble *L'Oiseau Lunaire*, a bird with a horned head, are recognizable figurative subjects; others, such as *Femme á la chevelure défaite* are abstracts. Miró made eight full-size terracotta models of the largest work, *Le Grand Arc*, before casting it in concrete. At The Labyrinth, Miró fulfilled his ambition to work on a monumental scale in an architectural context. Unusually, the outdoor spaces (by Miró and Alberto Giacometti) and the building were designed simultaneously, to complement each other.

☛ Brancusi, Chand Saini, Hepworth, Monet, Moore, Saint-Phalle

308

Joan Miró. b Barcelona (SP), 1893. **d** Palma de Moyona (SP), 1983. **The Labyrinth**, Maeght Foundation, St Paul (FR), 1963–8.

Mizner Addison

Casa Bienvenita

Inspired by Italian Renaissance gardens, this cellular rose garden was designed by Addison Mizner when he built the villa for the businessman Alfred Dieterich in the 1920s. Mizner was known for his eclectic style and introduced Spanish revival-inspired mansions to the rich and famous of Palm Beach in Florida. For this, his only West Coast mansion, he designed a rose garden, possibly inspired by the rose garden of the Bagatelle or those of Italian Renaissance designers, enclosed with hedges and dotted with statuary. The Casa Bienvenita, typical of his exuberant style, fusing Spanish revival with Moorish, Gothic and Romanesque elements, also has a vegetable garden, teahouse and a cloistered patio and pond, surrounded with palms. The garden was restored in 1979 to Mizner's original designs. Mizner designed many houses in his career but fell out of favour and was bankrupted by a land-development bust in 1927. He stopped practising architecture and spent several years writing his memoirs.

☛ **André, Forestier, Hancock, Suarez, Washington Smith**

Addison Mizner. b Benicia, CA (USA), 1872. **d** Miami, FL (USA), 1933. **Casa Bienvenita**, Montecito, CA (USA), c1920s.

Mollet Claude

Fontainebleau

This 'portrait' of the park of the Château of Fontainebleau, drawn by Claude Mollet, shows the garden at the end of Henri IV's reign. Arguably the most 'historic' of all of France's great royal gardens, its present form is mostly due to Le Nôtre. Originally Fontainebleau was transformed from royal hunting ground to palace by François I, who commissioned the best Italian artists of the time to work there: Primatice, Serlio and Vignola all made grand designs, sculptures and grottoes. The italianate tone was further enhanced by Catherine de' Medici's contribution. Drawing on a more specifically French genius, Henry IV commissioned Alexandre Francini to design the 'Tibre' parterre in four parts and, in 1595, Claude Mollet for the small 'island' garden on the great pool. A great designer who worked mostly at Saint-Germain-en-Laye and Versailles, Mollet was also an influential writer. His delightful *Theatre of plans and gardening* was his most important work.

☞ **Francini, L'Orme, Mercogliano, Poitiers, Serlio**

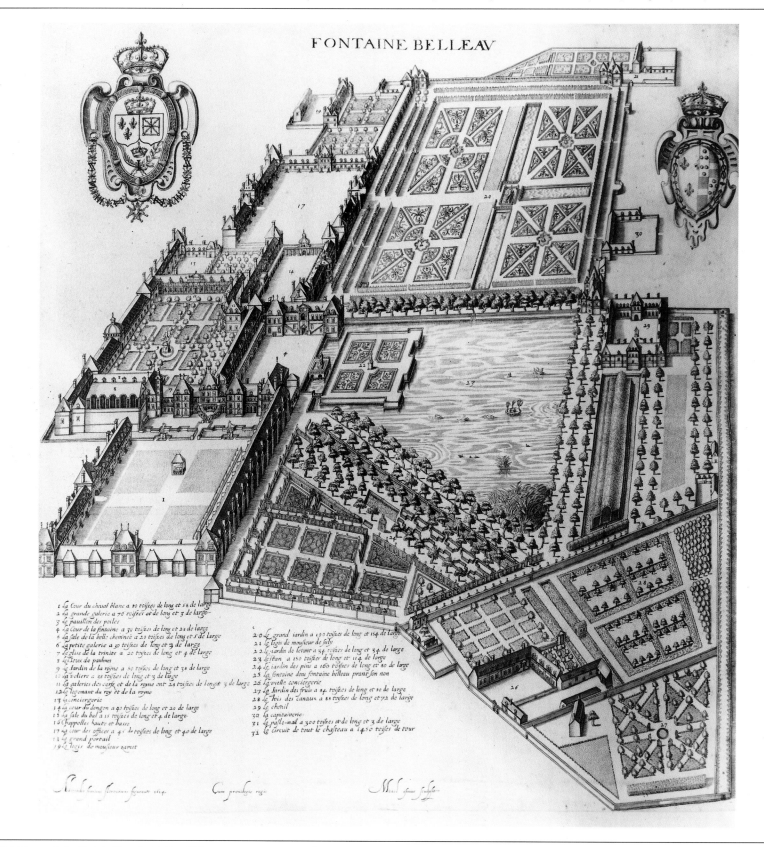

FONTAINE BELLEAV

Claude Mollet. b 1550. **d** 1603. **Fontainebleau**, Fontainbleau (FR), c1595.

Monasterio de San Lorenzo Monastery Cloister

Ancient and uniquely overgrown box hedges shaped by gardeners over centuries to form a dense maze-like pattern fill the cloister garden of the monastery of San Lorenzo de Trasouto in Santiago de Compostela. Established as a monastery in the thirteenth century, it came into the ownership of the counts of Altamira in the fifteenth century, who ceded it to the Franciscans. The box hedges are said to be some 400 years old and are one of the strangest sights in garden history. Among the many religious symbols shaped in the box hedges is that of the pilgrim's shell (a scallop) of St James, a badge still worn by modern pilgrims to Santiago. In one of the quadrants of the cloister garden is a moss-encrusted fountain and sunken pool surrounded by ferns. The lower gallery of the arcaded cloisters that enclose the box hedges is laced with ancient wisteria vines, that perfume the air in spring.

☞ Baron Ash, Blandy, Franco, Rochford, Salisbury, Wirtz

Monasterio de San Lorenzo de Trasouto. Established thirteenth century. **Monastery Cloister**, San Lorenzo de Trasouto, Santiago de Compostela (SP), established c17th century.

Monet Claude

Giverny

This is perhaps the most famous garden view of the twentieth century, familiar to an international audience as a result of the celebrated series of paintings of water-lilies executed by Claude Monet in his garden at Giverny between 1901 and 1925. There are two gardens at Giverny: the flower garden by the house, with about seventy separate flowerbeds, a lawn and a long rose-arch tunnel; and the water garden, on land bought by Monet in 1893, situated across a road. For the water garden, Monet created the large oriental pond with peonies, clumps of bamboos and a Japanese bridge, which he painted green instead of the customary red. In the flower garden, long rectangular beds were planted with one variety to create blocks of colour, an idea inspired by a visit to the Dutch bulb fields. Monet was an enthusiastic and original gardener: for example, he allowed poppies and verbascum to self-seed and spread. An abundance of wild flowers makes Giverny a sensuous, romantic, light-filled garden, which Monet used as a source of solace and relief from his work.

☞ Heron, Hornel, Larsson, Morris, Steele

Claude Monet. b Paris (FR), 1840. d Giverny (FR), 1926. **Giverny**, Normandy (FR), 1893–1901.

Monteiro Antonio & Manini Luigi   Quinta de Regaleira

'Money Bags' Monteiro was an eccentric nineteenth-century Portuguese heir to a Brazilian coffee and gemstone fortune. With virtually unlimited financial resources, he commissioned an Italian architect and set designer from La Scala, named Manini, to build a magnificent allegorical garden and villa in the 1870s. This dreamscape was sited on his estate just outside Sintra, near the Serra mountains, not far from Lisbon. Manini designed both the house and the garden in an eclectic blend of styles in accordance with many of his patron's whims – which drew inspiration from classical mythology as well as fantasy. One of the main attractions is the nine-storey well that descends 20 m (60 ft) into a rock promontory on the estate to a light pointed star. The well was used for initiation ceremonies by the Knights of the Templar. This is a garden of an obsessive, one man's dream transformed into a garden reality.

☛ Bomarzo, Chambers, Cheval, Dashwood, James, Lane, Monville

Antonio Augusto Carvalho Monteiro. b 1848. d 1920. **Luigi Manini.** b 1848. d 1936. **Quinta de Regaleira**, Sintra (POR), 1870s.

Montpellier Charles-Alexis de   Château d'Annevoie

For over 200 years, water has gushed from the fountains and glided over the cascades at Les Jardins d'Annevoie in the wooded hills above the Meuse Valley. The natural pressure of water collected from four springs which rise in the gardens operates imposing jets of water over 7 m (20 ft) high or creates silver fans, as here, that arch like peacock's tails. Charles-Alexis de Montpellier came from a family of ironmasters and was ennobled only in 1743. He laid out the gardens between 1758 and 1778, incorporating the ideas from Italy, France and England that he had observed on his Grand Tour. He created a garden of contrast, of enclosure and openness, of light and shade, of still reflective water and water that moves in a variety of ways, of trimmed hedges and clipped grass side by side with woodland of chestnuts and smooth-trunked beeches. Annevoie is a composition that is magnificent during every season of the year.

☞ Bingley, Duchêne, Le Nôtre, Wirtz

Charles-Alexis de Montpellier. d 1778. **Château d'Annevoie**, Annevoie-Rouillon (BEL), 1758–78.

Monville Baron de   Désert de Retz

In the melancholy landscape of the Désert de Retz, the monumental Ruined Column rises like a ghostly apparition. The creator of this visionary garden, Baron de Monville, an extravagant libertine, is said to have spent many sleepless nights in this fantastic construction. A rare surviving example of French visionary architecture of the late eighteenth century as inspired by Ledoux and Boullée, it is symbolically charged – as are all the other follies throughout this large and mainly wild park. They speak of man's access to the beauties of the world, of the dense culture to which he is heir and of the need to consider nature's precious messages. A wooden Chinese house, a temple to Pan, Egyptian pyramids and obelisks constituted an eclectic landscape which soon became a well-known attraction in the very last years of the French monarchy. The Désert, abandoned during the Revolution, fell into centuries of neglect and disrepair, but since 1986 it has been carefully brought back to life.

☛   Bélanger & Blaikie, Girardin, Laborde, Robert

Baron de Monville. b Normandy (FR), 1734. **d** Paris (FR), 1797. **Désert de Retz**, Ile de France (FR), 1774–89.

Moore Henry

Perry Green

Now so familiar as to be almost commonplace, the sight of monumental, smooth bronze sculptures lying in a field was once a daring innovation. If today the relationship between the modern, three-dimensional object of art and a natural fold of the landscape seems an obvious one, it is partly due to the influence of Henry Moore. When in 1940 he and his wife Irina left London and their house in Hampstead, which had been damaged in a bombing, they headed for the small village of Perry Green in Hertfordshire. There they lived until the end of their lives, progressively adding buildings and land to the original cottage and sheep field. Irina was particularly active in transforming the grounds. She created a series of gardens and less formal settings where the sculptures could be displayed in a flexible and open manner. Moore himself sited some large pieces, while other displays were meant to be temporary.

☛ Heron, Hepworth, Jellicoe, Miró, Monet, Tunnard

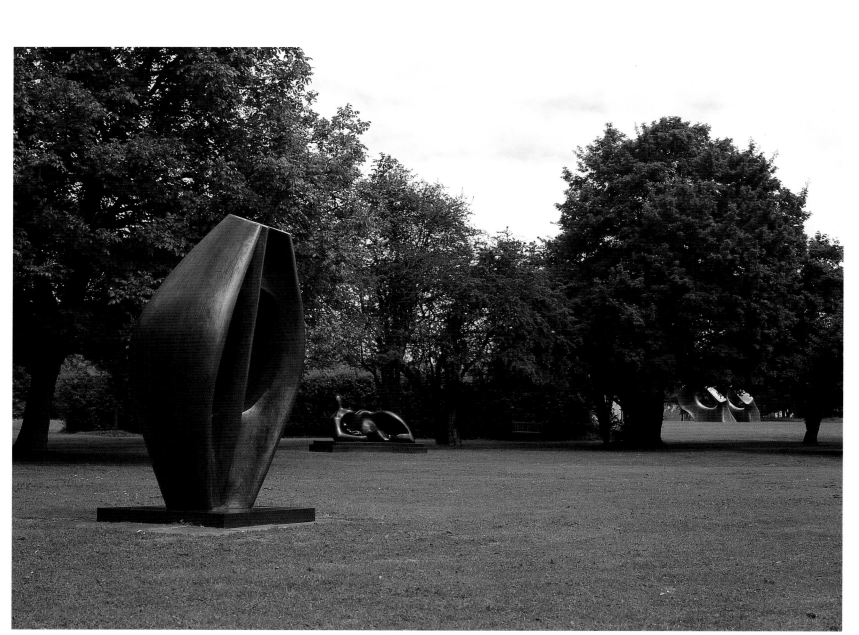

Henry Moore. b Yorkshire (UK), 1898. d Perry Green, Hertfordshire (UK), 1986. Perry Green, Hertfordshire (UK), 1940.

Moorish Governors   Alfabia

Mature ornamental trees and box-lined beds are the eighteenth-century additions to this most evocative of Spanish island gardens. Four centuries of Moorish rule made an indelible mark on Majorcan architecture and landscaping and this legacy is particularly strong at Alfabia, said to be the seat of successive Moorish governors. Although parts of the garden were remodelled during the eighteenth century, the most impressive feature in it is the long walk beside the arched water tank. This walkway, lined with pebble mosaic and brick, is covered with vines and climbers such as wisteria. The arched iron pergola on which they luxuriate is supported by octagonal stone columns. Water jets play across the pathway from the stone capitals, cooling the air and offering respite from the heat. Beyond the vine-clad, cool pathway is a notable collection of trees, shrubs and bamboo groves, all linked by water channels, pools and fountains.

☛ Abd al-Rahman, Muhammad V, Nazarite

Moorish Governors. Reigned Majorca (SP), between 1075 and 1229. **Alfabia**, Majorca (SP), established eleventh century.

More Sir Thomas — Moorhouse

This is one of the clearest illustrations of a Tudor garden in existence. It forms the background to a miniature portrait of Sir Thomas More and his family, painted by Rowland Lockey in the 1590s, a version of the Holbein original. Brick walls form a square enclosure incorporating on one side a covered gallery and what was possibly a chapel. A low clipped hedge surrounds an asymmetrical series of clipped hedges that form little squares, with several trees planted among them. Little care appears to have been taken to make the design geometrically rigorous, and there are none of the heraldic beasts on gilded poles illustrated in contemporary pictures of the royal gardens of Henry VIII. Yet this is an example of an early – and modest – knot garden. A gateway gives on to the fields of Chelsea and, presumably, the Thames. It is not known whether More had a hand in the garden's design, but this portion of his estate was gifted to a daughter and son-in-law at his death.

☞ Jones, Lennox-Boyd, Orsini, Salisbury, Verey

Sir Thomas More. **b** London (UK), 1478. **d** London (UK), 1535. **Moorhouse**, Chelsea, London (UK), 1520–35, as depicted by Rowland Lockey, c1593–4.

Moroni Andrea

Orto Botanico

This early print shows that the Botanic Garden at Padua has changed little since it was first laid out. The main paths still traverse their original axes, exactly aligned north-south and west-east. The four quarters have been reordered from time to time, and the circular wall which encloses them was rebuilt in the eighteenth century, but it is still recognizably the garden which the Bergamesque architect Moroni built for the Anatomy Department at Padua University as an aid to teaching medicine in 1545. It was originally planted only with herbs of pharmacological importance, but the collections were later extended to include useful food plants: when the potato was first introduced to Europe from South America in the 1570s, it was grown in this very garden.

Later came pure ornamentals, which explains why Padua's Botanic Garden is not only the earliest but also one of the most beautiful of its kind.

☛ **Chambers, Clusius, Palladio, Sloane**

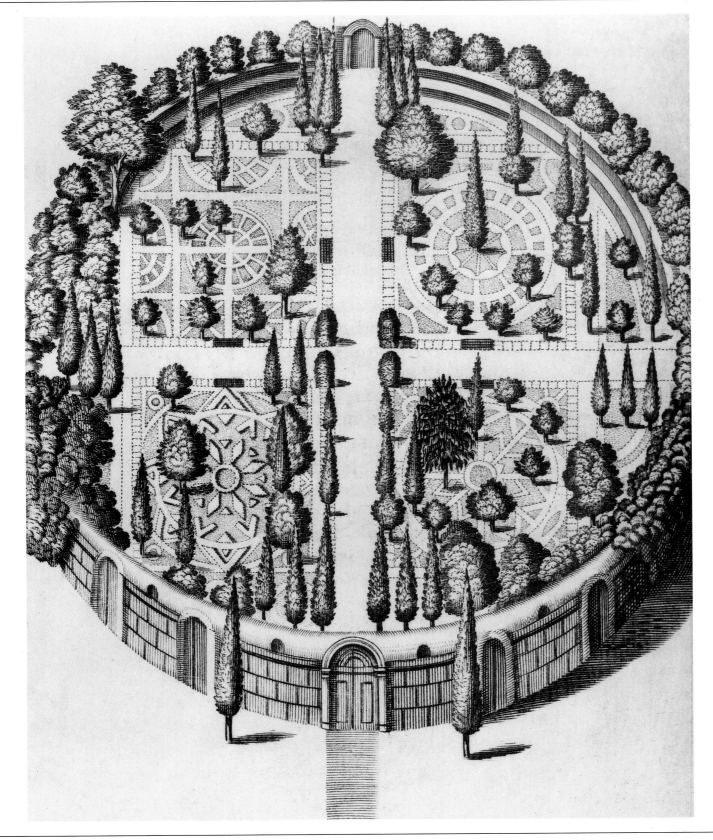

Andrea Moroni. b Bergamo (IT). Active in first half of sixteenth century. **Orto Botanico**, Padua (IT), 1545.

Morris William

Kelmscott Manor

A row of standard roses flanks the path that approaches the front door of this lovely Cotswold house. There is such a strong sense of place that both house and garden feel as if they have simply grown out of the ground, rather than been designed. This setting provided William Morris, famous for his textile designs and writings that promoted the revival of the craftsman, with the perfect setting in which he could apply his own dictum that every workman or artist should have an environment in which he or she could lead a creative and satisfying life. Morris, one of the founders and the leading light of the Arts and Crafts Movement, thought gardens should have straight paths, ordered rows of vegetables and straight borders from which erupted a riot of flowers that spilled over the edges. He found the Cotswolds perfectly suited to his approach, as his comment on another cottage he saw in the village of Broadway in 1876 illustrates – it was 'a work of art and a piece of nature – no less'.

☛ Barnsley, Greene & Greene, Lutyens, Mawson, Parsons

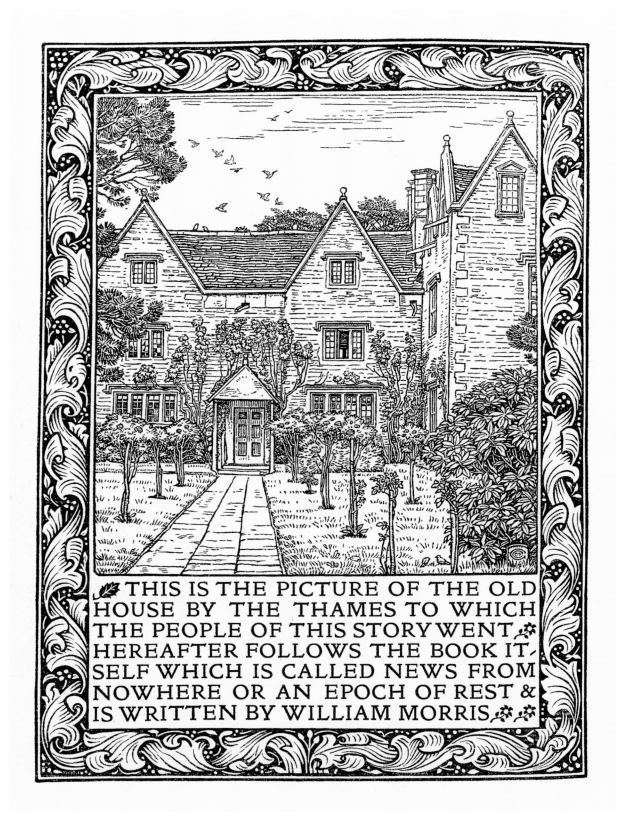

William Morris. b London (UK), 1834. **d** London (UK), 1896. **Kelmscott Manor**, Gloucestershire (UK), 1871.

Mozzoni Ascanio

Villa Cicogna Mozzoni

The sunken, enclosed courtyard garden at the Villa Cicogna Mozzoni comprises two square box parterres and two square cisterns with fountains. The walls are clad with large pieces of tufa, classical statues in niches and a small nymphaeum (centre). An elaborate system of water tricks has recently been restored to working order and the far end of the sunken garden features a small grotto with a secret door. This garden perfectly complements the Renaissance villa, remodelled in the 1550s by the Campi brothers of Cremona under the direction of Conte Ascanio Mozzoni. It is not clear who designed the rest of the garden. From the first floor of the house overlooking the sunken garden, the sight lines are carefully arranged so that each window provides a completely different view. It has a spatial felicity that distinguishes it as a rare surviving example of a High Renaissance garden. A dramatic water staircase leads steeply up from the principal saloon on the mountain side of the villa.

☛ **Borghese, Bramante, Garzoni, Vignola**

Conte Ascanio Mozzoni. d (IT), 1593. **Villa Cicogna Mozzoni**, Varese, Lombardy (IT), 1550s.

Muhammad V

Court of the Lions, the Alhambra

A forest of slender alabaster columns and elaborate stucco carved into plant motifs help to fuse indoors and outdoors in this Moorish jewel of a courtyard at the Alhambra, begun in 1377 by the Nasrid sultan Muhammad V. Holding the design together are four water channels flowing outwards from the kiosks and surrounding chambers to meet beneath a central basin held aloft by twelve dribbling stone lions, symbol of sovereignty and power. Now largely gravelled, the courtyard was once planted with orange trees, and sunken flowerbeds that formed a floral carpet.
The Alhambra was already a citadel by the ninth century and it flourished as a city palace under the Nasrid sultans from the mid-thirteenth century until Granada surrendered to Ferdinand and Isabella of Spain in 1492. Linked to a summer pleasance (the Generalife) across the hill, it fired the romantic imagination and kept alive the memory of Islamic paradise gardens that appeal to the senses and to the spirit.

☞ **Allah, Moorish Governors, Nazarite, Tortella**

Muhammad V. Reigned 1354–59 and 1362–91. **Court of the Lions, the Alhambra**, Alhambra, Granada (SP), 1377.

Musgrave (Governor of Kerman)   Bagh-e-Shahzadeh

Solitary as a desert oasis, this Persian garden, at the foot of a jagged and barren mountain range, stands in opposition to its setting. Holding to tradition, Bagh-e-Shahzadeh is walled, highly ordered and symmetrical in layout, and set with stone walks, water channels and pools. It offers escape and solitude. It encompasses airy pavilions, shady paths, cascading waterchutes and cypress and poplar avenues. Eight parterres that lie to either side of the central waterway add to the balance and inherent ease of this exquisite space. As the oasis promised life to the weary desert traveller, and the Qur'anic similitude of heaven promised the faithful life everlasting in an abundant paradise, the terrestrial Persian garden is where life was and is fully lived. It is from the idea of the garden that the arts, language, and religions of Persia draw much of their inspiration.

☞   Allah, Assurbanipal, Ineni, Moorish Governors, Nazarite

Musgrave (Governor of Kerman). **Bagh-e-Shahzadeh**, Mahann, Persia (IR), nineteenth century.

Nash John

Royal Pavilion

The building, conceived as a seaside villa for the Prince Regent, was built in 1787, but the remodelling in the Indian-influenced 'Hindu' style which the Prince had admired at Sezincote was undertaken by Nash in 1808. Nash had been recommended to the prince by Humphry Repton as the architect for a conservatory – part of the new gardens that Repton had added to the villa in 1797.

However, when it came to the remodelling, Nash – who benefitted from thirty years of royal patronage – acted in an underhand way. He did not keep his part of the agreement with Repton, and even excluded Repton's plans for the remodelling of the villa that were drawn up in 1806. However, Nash's approach to garden and landscape design was strongly influenced by Repton, and in the

limited space of the Pavilion gardens Nash responded to the growing passion for floriculture, designing a series of flowerbeds which were filled with exotic plants by W T Aiton, the superintendent of the Royal Botanic Gardens at Kew.

☛ **Chambers, Cockerell, Repton, Shah Jahan**

John Nash. **b** London (UK), 1752. **d** E Cowes, Isle of Wight (UK), 1835. **Royal Pavilion**, Brighton (UK), 1808.

Nasoni Niccolo

Villa Mateus

The turreted buildings of Mateus, like the original gardens, are said to be the work of Tuscan painter and architect Niccolo Nasoni for Antonio Jose Botelho Mourao. A mirror pool reflects the Baroque silhouette of the house. A quirky twentieth-century sculpture by Joao Cutileiro is slightly at odds with the formality of the garden areas beyond. There are four box-lined parterre gardens on the terraces in front of the house. Swirling curlicues at ground level and breath-taking buttresses reaching 2.4 m (8 ft) are among a variety of designs in box. At the centre of the terraces is a massive tunnel, 34.5 m (115 ft) long and 7.5 m (25 ft) high, of closely clipped cypress. Dark, woody and cool on the inside, tunnels similar to this were once common in northern Portuguese gardens. Cypress hedges, trained into arches at intervals, enclose a series of orchard gardens on the upper level of the grounds.

☛ Fronteira, Mardel, Oliveira & Robillon, Porcinai

Niccolo (Nicolau) Nasoni. b San Giovanni (IT), 1691. **d** Oporto (POR), 1773. **Villa Mateus**, Vila Real (POR), after 1725.

Nazarite court architect

Jennat al-Arif (Generalife)

This garden palace is set dramatically high upon the hillside overlooking the Alhambra palace grounds and the city of Granada in the valley below. It comprises a series of terraced gardens, one of which (pictured here) is the main courtyard known as the Patio de la Acequia. The salubriousness of this inner court lies in its long, deep-green axial watercourse. Jets of cooling water trickle and glimmer as they fall into the central pool. The gentle sound of falling water enraptures and immediately calms this exquisitely private interior space. The rooms surrounding the court draw in the cool courtyard air. This inner garden space captures the fragrant spectacle of the flowers and plants within it; the overall effect is one of simplicity, elegance and ease. The expansive views afforded by the site reveal the skilful manipulation of environment which the Islamic rulers achieved in Andalusian garden palace architecture.

☞ Ligorio, Moorish Governors, Muhammad V, Sangram Singh

Nazarite court architect. Active (SP), fourteenth century. **Jennat al-Arif (Generalife)**, Patio de la Acequia, Granada (SP), 1319.

Nesfield William Andrews   Holkham Hall

Delicate tracery, laid out in an intricate Louis XIV pattern of box and flower beds against a background of coloured gravels, distinguishes this parterre of the great formal terrace at Holkham. A pool surrounding the statue of St George and the Dragon, by R C Smith, can just be seen in front of the sunken panels of this southerly terrace. A further terrace by Nesfield to the north integrates the initials of the owners into the parterre. Nesfield led a revival of interest in this elaborate seventeenth century art form, creating parterres for country houses. He is also well known for the series of gardens he created for the Royal Botanic Gardens at Kew from 1844–8. His work at Holkham (1849–72) forms part of a long and distinguished tradition of invention; the vast parkland has been transformed by William Kent, Capability Brown and John Webb, since the creation of the estate in 1720.

☞ Barry, Blomfield, Brown, Marot & Roman, Sophia

William Andrews Nesfield. b 1793. d 1881. Holkham Hall, Thakenham, Norfolk (UK), 1849–72.

Neutra Richard

Loring Residence

The bright sunshine reflected by the blue swimming-pool, the city in the distance, the clear-cut Modernist lines of a comfortable living space: all the ingredients of the 1950s American dream are here. With sliding panels opening on to huge glass walls, the low-level house is an extension of this sun-worshipping poolside environment. Even the carpets were matched to the exterior paving. This idyllic and idiosyncratic southern-Californian vision is the work of Richard Neutra, who specialized in planar residential buildings which he gave an industrial feel and set into carefully arranged landscapes. He often worked in beautiful and remote areas, as in the Kaufmann Desert Home, which accentuated the contrast between modern living and the natural, wild environment. Though he had an acute understanding of American culture and vernacular architecture, Neutra was born in Vienna, where he studied with Adolf Loos and Otto Wagner. He only moved to the USA in 1923.

☛ Halprin, Hargreaves, Herman, Loos

328

Richard Neutra. b Vienna (AUS), 1892. **d** Wuppertal (GER), 1970. **Loring Residence**, Los Angeles, CA (USA), 1950s.

Niven Ninian

Glasnevin

This garden's eclectic plant collection is dramatized by the Palm House's translucent roof. Ninian Niven, who became director of the Glasnevin Botanic Gardens in 1834, was the principal garden designer in Ireland during the Victorian age, having created his own idiom in which the informal English style and the formal French approach were 'judiciously blended'. In 1836, he published the first known popular guide to a botanic garden. He also proposed a number of inventive design ideas, including a rockery which, by the choice and arrangement of its rocks, would represent the geological strata of Ireland, and a garden of exotic and native plants laid out along a serpentine walk, the former being planted to the left and the latter to the right, the different botanical families separated by archways over the paths. As well as being a prodigious garden designer, Niven ran a nursery and horticulture school, published religious tracts and a volume of verse.

☛ **Burton & Turner, Fowler, Loudon, Paxton, Veitch**

Ninian Niven. b Glasgow (UK), 1799. **d** Dublin (IRE), 1879. **Glasnevin**, National Botanic Gardens, Dublin (IRE), 1834–8.

Noailles Charles & Marie-Laure de   Villa Noailles

Thriving on the hillside near Grasse, a surprisingly varied collection of plants is scattered throughout the various parts of this bright and lush southern French garden. Water is present throughout the grounds, flowing from the nympheaum to a succession of fountains. Carefully arranged vistas open onto particularly attractive sights in the nearby countryside, which has unfortunately suffered slightly from over-development in recent years. Here and there passing reference is made, through an enclosure of box or a chain of fountains, to famous gardens, such as those of Sissinghurst and the Villa d'Este. These allusions were viscount Charles de Noailles's way of crediting the inspirations collected on his extensive travels and garden visits.

The plants take center stage: a multitude of naturalized bulbs, collections of magnolias, tree peonies and viburnum.

☞ Guevrékian, Ligorio, Mallet-Stevens, Peto, Sackville-West, Vesian

Viscomte Charles & Marie-Laure de Noailles. Active early twentieth century. **Villa Noailles**, Grasse (FR), 1947–81.

Noel Anthony

Fulham Garden

This view seems to draw the visitor out of the house and into Anthony Noel's own London town garden. Romantic white lilies and petunias in pots contrast with the formality of clipped box, and variegated ivy 'papers' the wall. Ex-actor Anthony Noel combines a penchant for theatricality and glamour with a sure handling of space, particularly on a small scale. His original ideas, such as a beach-hut shed or rows of jauntily striped, painted terracotta pots planted with tiny lollipop box trees, have been copied many times over in recent years. Noel's spatial confidence means he uses large-scale urns, plants or trellised supports in a small space, but always with the same sure elegance. His gardens are carefully lit because his urban, London clientele use their gardens as much at night as in the day. Noel is also unusual in that he has worked almost exclusively on a small scale.

☛ Le Nôtre, Page, Sackville-West

Anthony Noel. **Fulham Garden**, London (UK), 1990s.

Noguchi Isamu

UNESCO Foundation Sculpture Garden

Near a pool, a stone arrangement in the motif of Horai stands below a gently undulating ridge planted with pines and maples. The garden, encircled by Marcel Breuer's modernistic architecture, acts as a sea of perfect quietude. When commissioned in 1956 to make a garden for the UNESCO headquarters in Paris, Isamu Noguchi was at the height of his popularity as a sculptor. He

viewed this both as a challenge to embrace the art of garden making, and as an opportunity to fuse his own modernistic design style with the ancient principles of Japanese garden art which so fascinated him. To re-energize his bonds with that tradition, he twice went to Japan. There he met the great designer Mirei Shigemori who took him to the island of Shikoku to select and

extract stones to be shipped to Paris. Though considered 'the pre-eminent American sculptor' of his time by Robert Hughes, Noguchi really belonged to both cultures, taking on the best of each.

☞ Ando, Brancusi, Enshu, Johnston, Neutra, Shigemori, Suzuki

Isamu Noguchi. **b** Los Angeles, CA (USA), 1904. **d** New York, NY (USA), 1988. **UNESCO Foundation Sculpture Garden**, Paris (FR), 1956.

Nordfjell Ulf

Stockholm Residence

Massed plantings of sedums offset the uncompromising Modernist monolith of a house at this private residence near Stockholm. Since the birth of Modernism, garden designers have struggled to find a design vocabulary that complements this style of architecture. Ulf Nordfjell's wider planting design at this property typifies the approach advocated in recent years of massed, informal plantings of perennials and grasses that sway in the wind and contrast with the smooth, immutable planes of the architecture. In Nordfjell's work craggy boulders, slabs of stone and gravel are carefully placed to echo the natural landscape of Sweden, and this harshness is offset by sophisticated planting schemes incorporating herbaceous perennials that will survive the winters. Nordfjell is also an accomplished ceramicist, and a high standard of decoration characterizes his work.

☛ Greene, Gill, Oehme & Van Sweden, Oudolf, Tunnard

Ulf Nordfjell. Stockholm Residence, Stockholm (SWE), 1990s.

Oehme Wolfgang & Van Sweden James   Meyer Garden

A path winds through bold masses of grasses and bright perennials. Swaying in the wind, the plants seem to owe nothing to human hand and look as if they had always grown right there on each side of this natural looking path. This seamless planting and deceptively simple design are the trade mark of James van Sweden and Wolfgang Oehme, who in the early 1990s were credited with the invention of the 'New American Garden'. This now-familiar image of a loose and free garden planted with simple, often native, perennials and most importantly, grasses, was a novelty in 1990. Unlike many of his contemporaries, van Sweden didn't believe in remodelling the landscape, preferring to go along with the existing topography. He also rejected the use of lawns, which he calls 'green concrete', and clipped evergreens. Instead, with the help of his botanist partner Oehme, he wanted to put the focus back on plants that change according to the seasons, harmonizing and composing natural schemes.

☞ Clément & Provost, Jekyll, Jensen, Kingsbury, Oudolf

Wolfgang Oehme. b Chemnitz (GER), 1930. **James van Sweden. b** Grand Rapids, MI (USA), 1935. **Meyer Garden**, Harbert, MI (USA), 1989.

Ogawa Jigei

Murin-an Villa

With a few large flat rocks, a meandering path encounters and crosses over a gently flowing stream. This leads on into a shrubbery and a woodland, with distant mountains forming a perfect backdrop to this naturalistic scene. This stroll garden is carefully composed around two streams and two shallow ponds. Here the stone arrangements have a distinctly naturalistic flavour, the azaleas are carefully trimmed and the alternating of trees and clearing is precisely orchestrated. The grounds of the Murin-an Villa are a prime example of Meiji era gardens, a period when such spaces were expected to be truthful 'copies' in what amounted to a tribute to nature, using nature's tools. The gesture of the designer was meant to remain hidden, leaving no space for symbolism or abstraction. Some gardens of this time are strangely lacking in personality but the Murin-an Villa is an exception. It is the work of Jigei Ogawa who was commissioned in 1896 by elder statesman Aritomo Yamagata to landscape the grounds of his luxurious villa.

☛ Hepworth, Mandokora, Shigemori, Soami

Jigei Ogawa. b (JAP), 1860. d (JAP), 1932. **Murin-an Villa**, Kyoto (JAP), 1896.

Oliveira Mateus Vicente de & Robillon Jean-Baptiste   Palace of Queluz

The rococo style of the palace buildings of Queluz is screened by the mature trees and wide avenues of the park. Each walkway leads to statuary or to a water feature. Cool and shaded, these woodland areas are in sharp contrast to the open formality of the parterre gardens that dominate the are in front of the palace buildings. The architect Mateus Vicente de Oliveira built Queluz for the future king Dom Pedro III, then Infante Dom Pedro, transforming it from a hunting lodge into a royal summer residence. The second phase of building work, including the layout of the two large-scale parterre gardens, the Malta Garden and the Pensile Garden, was the work of the French architect Jean-Baptiste Robillon. The gardens were designed to supplement the interior ceremonial rooms and were the centre of the royal family's summer entertainments. Music, fireworks and boating on the extravagantly tiled canal were among the outdoor pursuits enjoyed by the royal family and their guests.

☞ **Fronteira, Mardel, Monteiro & Manini, Pinsent**

Mateus Vicente de Oliveira. b Barcarena (POR), 1706. d 1785. **Jean-Baptiste Robillon**. b Paris (FR). d Queluz, Estemadura (POR), 1782. **Palace of Queluz** (POR), 1785.

Olmsted Frederick Law   Central Park

The curved walkways and roads of Olmsted's 1858 design for Central Park in New York are a triumph of landscape design and city planning, notable for their disruption of the city's grid street pattern. In collaboration with Calvert Vaux, Olmsted envisaged a park composed of various picturesque elements to complement the natural landscape: rocky and wooded to the south, gently sloping to the north. Olmsted had to incorporate transverse roads into his park design, and to counter this intrusion he sunk the roads below the natural level of the land. Central Park has been much altered, and the advent of skyscrapers means that the city can now be seen from most areas of the park, but Olmsted's original vision of successive surprises, a plethora of discrete areas, and planned contrasts between open spaces and woodland, has largely survived. Olmsted was the USA's foremost nineteenth-century landscape architect, known chiefly for his large-scale public schemes in New York and Boston.

☛ Downing & Vaux, Hardouin-Mansart, Le Nôtre, Vanderbilt

Frederick Law Olmsted. b Hartford, CT (USA), 1822. d Waverley, MA (USA), 1903. **Central Park**, New York, NY (USA), 1858.

Ongley Lord   Swiss Garden

The Swiss chalet, with its rustic wood, thatched roof and surrounding carpet of yellow daffodils in spring, is the garden's central feature and graces a number of specially arranged vistas. Created by Lord Ongley in the 1820s, the 1.6-hectare (4-acre) garden is made up of a series of intimate, flowery glades. It is Britain's finest example of the Swiss Picturesque. Just as Chinese gardens and features had been popular in Europe since the eighteenth century, so Switzerland came to be something of a cult – particularly following the publication of romantic travel fiction about the Alps. The rustic chalet is thought to be the work of John Bounarotti Papworth and the garden also includes a thatched tree shelter, cast-iron humped bridges that cross the stream, a grotto-fernery, floral arcades supported on large iron hoops, and a picture-postcard village in which formerly the women inhabitants were required to wear red cloaks and tall hats.

☛ Bateman & Cooke, Greene & Greene, Wordsworth

Lord Ongley. Active early nineteenth century. **Swiss Garden**, Bedfordshire (UK), 1820s.

Orrery John, 5th Earl of   The Bone House, Caledon

Among the whimsical creations of the 5th Earl of Orrery was a bone house, its ruins surviving to this day. Sometimes called 'The Ivory Palace' because of its bleached white colour, it is entirely covered with the femurs of deer and oxen. The knuckles face outwards so that the mortar joints between the bones lie hidden. Orrery was a friend of the writers Alexander Pope and Jonathan Swift, and the

Bone House was part of the most important rococo garden in Ireland. Other whimsical creations included the hermitage, entirely constructed of grotesquely shaped tree roots, as well as rustic cascades amid fir-tree groves. In the groves, Orrery erected classical statues with appropriate Latin inscriptions on their pedestals. Caledon was adorned c1807 by John Sutherland, the principal

landscape gardener in Ireland working in the Capability Brown style. Terraces around the house were added in 1829 by William Sawrey Gilpin, champion of the Picturesque.

☛   Brown, Gilpin, Hamilton, Robins

John, 5th Earl of Orrery   The Bone House, Caledon

John, 5th Earl of Orrery. b London (UK), c1706. d 1762. The Bone House, Caledon, Co Tyrone (UK), 1747.

Orsini Ottavia

Castello Ruspoli

The parterre at Castello Ruspoli (formerly Vignanello), reputedly the oldest in Italy, was created by Ottavia Orsini, daughter of the creator of Bomarzo. She began working on the garden in 1574. Twelve rectangular box parterres, each of a different pattern, combine to form a large rectangular garden which has a perfectly scaled, scalloped-edge fountain pool at its centre. The outer hedges, punctuated by lemons in pots, are a mix of bay and laurel, and evergreen oaks cast shadows at the corners. The parterres would originally have contained flowers – particularly bulbs – and herbs were perhaps used instead of box. For the central parterres, Ottavia incorporated her own initials and those of her two sons, Sforza and Galeazzo, and this tradition has been continued.

Ottavia was modernizing an ancient site whose history can be traced back through documents to 853 AD, when Benedictine monks erected a citadel there.

☛ Bomarzo, Lennox-Boyd, More, Salisbury, Verey

340

Ottavia Orsini. Active (IT), late sixteenth century. **Castello Ruspoli**, Viterbo (IT), 1574.

Otruba Ivar

University Botanic Gardens

The Botanical Garden of the University of Brno is one of the most significant twentieth-century gardens in central Europe. Its designer, Ivar Otruba, derives his inspiration not from any previous or contemporary garden style, but from his own unique imagination. His style is based on a set of natural features – prairies, mountain torrents and a mountainside – the latter forming an appropriate location for the garden's collection of alpine plants. In this, vertical dividers of concrete or sheet metal separate natural rock compositions representing different mountain formations and their plants. In another area, lumps of tufa rock raised to eye-level on metal poles support miniature alpine gardens. Otruba's creation is highly unusual – if not unique – as a large botanic garden that is characterized by an original and consistent design style. William Chambers' original plan for Kew fitted this description, but little of it remains.

☛ Blanc, Chambers, Hardtmuth, Loos, Moroni, Sloane

341

Ivar Otruba. b 1933. University Botanic Garden, Brno (CZ), late twentieth century.

Oudolf Piet

Hummelo

This view of 'new perennial' plantings in Piet Oudolf's own garden demonstrates exactly why he is such an influential garden designer and nurseryman. Historically he may be seen as reconciling the German traditions of large-scale natural planting promoted by Karl Förster with the traditional herbaceous borders of the English school, represented by Gertrude Jekyll. In so doing, he enables the owners of small private gardens to combine maximum effect with minimum maintenance. He is a master of mood: he believes light, movement, harmony, control, the sublime and the mystical are all attainable within the garden. His designs combine forms and colours, repetition and rhythm, shrubs and herbaceous plants. Those plants may be structural or infills, natural or contrived: many are grasses and umbellifers, since his plantings give value to form and leaves as much as colour. And he is strongly aware of the changing seasons, and the need for a garden to give pleasure year-round.

☛ Förster, Kingsbury, Lloyd, A Parsons, Peto

342

Piet Oudolf (Kwekerij Piet Oudolf). Hummelo, Arnhem (NL).

Page Russell

La Mortella

The composer Sir William Walton invited Russell Page to give his opinion on the potential of a garden on the site of the house that he was building on a steep scree slope on the island of Ischia in the Bay of Naples. Page – a master of simple yet sound design principles – counselled crisis management. He suggested making the most of what he called 'the beautiful weathered chunks of lava' littering the site, the views both of the majestic volcano Mount Nepomeo and out to sea, and the native vegetation of rosemary, cistus, spurges, broom and, as the house-name indicates, myrtles. He also devised a simple L-shaped axis for the garden and suggested a series of formal pools and fountains. In the care of Sir William and his wife Susana, the garden flourished. Page was a very successful twentieth-century garden designer, with a select international practice. Notable works include the courtyard garden at the Frick Collection in New York, and designs for Battersea Park to celebrate the Festival of Britain in 1951.

☛ Hanbury, Manrique, Shipman, Washington Smith

Russell Page. b (UK), 1906. **d** 1985. **La Mortella**, Ischia (IT), 1956–85.

Palladio Andrea

Villa Barbaro

The Villa Barbaro at Maser proved to be so influential that the US Capitol is one among many buildings based upon its outlines. This is the famous semicircular exedra in the so-called *giardino segreto* or 'secret garden' which faces the house across a circular pool. The central archway and the two ends of the exedra are supported by giants, while the niches in the curving wall are filled with life-sized statues. All the beautiful embellishments are based on classical precedents and tricked out in plasterwork. Palladio sought not only to recreate the nobility and dignity of the architecture of ancient Rome, but also to develop a style of decoration which fitted the sixteenth-century taste for ornament. The details of this composition were the work of sculptor Alessandro Vittoria from Trento in northern Italy. The integration of architecture and landscape in Palladio's villa designs, notably the Villa Rotonda in the Veneto, has influenced subsequent generations of architects.

☞ Bramante, Burlington, Cameron, Fontana, Hoare, Kent, Sulla

Andrea Palladio. b Padua (IT), 1518. **d** Vicenza (IT), 1580. **Villa Barbaro**, Maser (IT), 1550s.

Pan En

Yu Yuan

The huge rock, intended to evoke an artificial mountain, somewhat dwarfs the constructions in the courtyard around it. This is possibly the stone named 'Exquisitely Carved Jade', which the Emperor Hui'tsung of the Sung dynasty had once coveted for his own garden. Pan En certainly saw it as a treasured possession and he records placing it carefully at the southern end of his garden. As he says, the garden did not come easily: 'For twenty years I sat a sit – I thought a thought – I rested a rest – it was still not very good – but in [1577] ... I gave my entire heart to the affair.' And he goes on to give a painstaking description of his design efforts. The Chinese word for garden-making literally translates as 'piling rocks and digging ponds', thus illustrating the basic Yin and Yang principles. Pan En went on to create numerous beautifully crafted structures. His garden at Yu Yuan is still exquisite, with well-placed stones, ponds running towards buildings and roofs curling into trees.

☞ Crisp, Kang Xi, Pulham, Qian Long, Tien Mu, Wang Xiang Chen

Pan En. Active (CHN), sixteenth century. **Yu Yuan**, Shanghai (CHN), 1577.

Parsons Alfred

Wightwick Manor

Sizable groupings of vibrant herbaceous colour complement the high yew walls and Arts-and-Crafts architecture at Wightwick Manor. Alfred Parsons, a noted watercolourist who provided the illustrations for Ellen Willmott's *The Genus Rosa*, was engaged to design a garden with W Partridge. He made a self-consciously Old-English garden of formal enclosures of yew, embellished with topiary peacocks, flower borders and climbing roses. His scheme included a long yew walk and a rose garden that was later adorned with a grand circular pergola. Parsons' scheme at Wightwick epitomizes Arts-and-Crafts gardening, in which careful harmonies and contrasts of flower colour are presented against red-brick architecture and high hedges, and the garden is further dignified by the work of Thomas Mawson, who later added terraces, steps and other architectural detailing.

☞ **Jekyll, Lutyens, Mawson, Morris, Willmott**

Alfred Parsons. Wightwick Manor, Wolverhampton (UK), 1887.

Parsons Chris

Dew Garden

The early morning light illuminates an extraordinary abstract pattern in the dew on a bowling green in Aylesbury, Buckinghamshire, England. The pattern is the creation of Chris Parsons, a young groundsman who rises before dawn and repeatedly sweeps a large rag brush over the close-cropped lawn. Parsons discovered the technique by accident one morning in 1991, and he has now made a wide variety of patterns, which he photographs from a nearby tree. The patterns last between three and five hours. 'Dew looks its best in the sun because it glitters,' Parsons says. 'From the moment the sun goes down, the dew starts to come down. You can feel the moistness in the air.' Parsons is also interested in the more conventional technique of creating patterns in lawns through different mowing regimes, and expresses an interest in land art and contemporary sculptors including Andy Goldsworthy. He also sees in his work a natural affinity with the Op-Art style of Bridget Riley.

☛ Bye, Goldsworthy, Hall, Jencks, Smit, Toll

Chris Parsons. **b** Kampala (UG), 1967. **Dew Garden**, Aylesbury, Buckinghamshire (UK), 1991–.

Pawson John & Silvestrin Claudio   Neuendorf House

A long-lap pool stretches towards a monolithic wall where the horizontal lines are repeated in the benches, the window and the roof, etched sharply against the clear Majorcan sky. The stark geometry of the composition is relieved only by the warm ochre of the walls and the organic forms of the olive trees. Created by John Pawson and Claudio Silvestrin in 1989, the Neuendorf House is one of the most striking examples of minimalist design, indoors and out. The house is a cube set within high walls, with a partly shaded courtyard for outdoor dining. House and grounds were planned to be an integral part of the landscape: the wall colour was created by mixing render with the local soil and the long, shallow flight of steps that approaches the house is made of local limestone.

Pawson's minimalism has clear links with the work of Modernists such as Le Corbusier and Luis Barragán, but he is also inspired by the simplicity of functional vernacular architecture. As he says, reducing a design to its essentials offers space for contemplation.

☞ Barragán, Gill, Hargreaves, Majorelle, Walker, Yturbe

348

John Pawson. b Halifax (UK), 1949. Claudio Sylvestrin. b (IT), 1954. Neuendorf House, near Santanyi, Majorca (SP), 1989.

Paxton Sir Joseph

Chatsworth

The Conservative Wall, designed by James Paine and completed in 1763, is one part of previous garden incarnations which Paxton – working closely with his employer, the 6th Duke of Devonshire – incorporated into a programme of garden works that began in 1826. Prior to the wall being glazed in 1848, he had begun planting the Arboretum (1835), built the Great Conservatory (1836), erected the huge rockwork (1842) and reconstructed the Weeping Willow fountain, dating from 1693. The Emperor Fountain (1843) was built for the impending visit of Tsar Nicholas. The gardens at Chatsworth, along with those at Biddulph Grange, had an enormous impact on Victorian suburban villa garden design. Paxton was one of the most energetic polymaths of the nineteenth century – he was a pioneer of public-park design, an architect, author, engineer and politician. But he is undoubtedly most famous as designer of the Crystal Palace for the 1851 Great Exhibition.

☞ Balat, Bateman, Burton & Turner, Dupont, Fowler

Sir Joseph Paxton. b (UK), 1803. d (UK), 1865. **Chatsworth**, Derbyshire (UK), 1826–58.

Pearson Dan

Millennium Dome Landscape

The 171-m (190-yd) long Living Wall leads straight from the Millennium Dome towards the Thames. The wall itself is painted in blocks of muted greys, and repeated groups of silver birch and cut willow create a rhythmic quality that is increased at night when the lighting effects come into play. At the climax of the wall, where it is bisected by the Greenwich Meridian Line, the greys give way to mirrors. Pearson created other effects at the Dome, notably a hanging garden hiding a large ventilation duct at the entrance. Established in the 1980s as a leading designer in a contemporary style, Pearson takes his inspiration from native plant communities worldwide and says his intention is always to garden with nature, not against it. His other major commission of recent years has been the landscaping of Althorp House, Northamptonshire, including the memorial island for Diana, Princess of Wales, which echoes Rousseau's tomb at Ermenonville.

☞ Bradley-Hole, Brookes, Girardin, Oudolf, Smyth

Dan Pearson. **Millennium Dome Landscape**, London (UK), 1999.

Pearson Frank Loughborough & Cheal Joseph   Hever Castle

Terminating the corridor of yew hedge, which leads from the Pergola Garden, the classical archway frames the statue set in front of the Pompeiian Wall. To avoid incongruity, Frank Pearson wisely separated the Italian Garden, with its pair of lawns divided by a sunken garden and grandiose loggia looking out over a large lake, from the thirteenth-century castle and old English garden, with its hedged compartments full of flowers. Although it does not have the spirit of a true Italian Renaissance garden, the Italian Garden was a perfect display area for the millionaire William Waldorf Astor's extensive collection of classical and Renaissance antiquities, and is symptomatic of the Edwardian rediscovery of the nature of the Italian garden, rather than the Victorian stylized notion of the Italianate – a hotchpotch of English, Italian, Dutch and French features. The garden was constructed between 1904 and 1908 by Joseph Cheal & Son, who employed more than 1,000 men, including 800 to dig out the artificial lake.

☛ Duchêne, Gallard, Hardouin-Mansart, Pembroke

Frank Loughborough Pearson. b London (UK), 1864. **d** (UK), 1947. **Joseph Cheal**. Active end of nineteenth century. **Hever Castle**, Kent (UK), 1904–8.

Pembroke Philip Herbert, 4th Earl of   Wilton House

This engraving of 1645 depicts the garden at Wilton House. Built between 1632 and 1635 around a central axis, it featured terraces, elaborate parterres, a wilderness, water features, statuary, a grotto and galleries. It became famous across Europe as a symbol of the civilization and eclecticism of the Caroline court in the years before the Civil War. The garden was designed by Philip Herbert, 4th Earl of Pembroke, with help from Isaac de Caus working with the architect Inigo Jones. The layout was strongly influenced by the villa gardens of the Venetian countryside, which were built on similarly flat sites. It also draws on other European Renaissance gardens, notably the Palais du Luxembourg in France which the Earl had seen when he escorted Henrietta Maria (wife of Charles I) back to England in 1625. Wilton was particularly important, for it inspired other mid-seventeenth century English Renaissance gardens such as Dawley, Haigh and Staunton Harold.

☞ Boyceau, I Caus, Jones, Palladio, Pearson & Cheal

Philip Herbert, 4th Earl of Pembroke. b (UK), 1584. d (UK), 1649 or 1650. Wilton House, Wiltshire (UK), 1632–5.

Pepper Beverly

Sol y Ombra

Growing on the wide paths of this giantic spiral, an army of small trees provides shelter from the blazing Barcelona summer heat. This is the *Ombra* (shade) element of the Sol y Ombra park, which is situated near the main railway station in Barcelona. The *Sol* (sun) element is a grassy bank fronted by blue tiles which, rising from the ground like a giant wave, acts as a platform to catch any winter sunshine. And so, dipping and surging, curving and scrolling, the earth is itself sculpted. This carved landscape was commissioned by the City of Barcelona, which invited artists, architecs and civil engineers to work throughout the city on the occasion of the 1992 Olympic Games. American-born Beverley Pepper, who submitted Sol y Ombra, trained as a painter with Fernand Léger in Paris, but turned to sculpture in the 1960. She became interested in working with the environment a decade later. Pepper lives and works mostly in Umbria, Italy, and much of her environmental work has been done in Europe.

☞ Clément & Provost, Herman, Gustafson, Lutsko, Tschumi

Beverley Pepper. b New York, NY (USA), 1922. **Sol y Ombra**, Barcelona (SP), 1992.

Peter II Tsar of Russia

The Summer Garden

More than 200 classical statues were bought by Peter the Great in Italy for the Summer Garden, and ninety of them survive. They were placed against clipped hedges, but these have since been allowed to grow naturally into trees, giving the garden a less formal appearance. In a labyrinth, many fountains were installed for Peter incorporating gilded sculptural groups illustrating Aesop's fables, each accompanied by a card with explanatory text. These were destroyed in a flood in 1777. Peter's aim with the statues and the fountains was to introduce Russians to the culture of western Europe. The gardeners Matveev and Roosen and the architect Zemtsov worked in the garden, while Trezzini was the architect of Peter's small palace there. The Summer Garden is still the favourite open space in St Petersburg, but early in spring, after the thaw, the ground is too soft to admit the public.

☞ Catherine II, Hardouin-Mansart, Le Nôtre, Rinaldi

354

Tsar Peter II of Russia (Peter the Great). b Moscow (RUS), 1672. **d** St Petersburg (RUS), 1725. **The Summer Garden**, St Petersburg (RUS), 1703.

Peto Harold

Iford Manor

On the far side of the main terrace lies the Casita, with pink marble columns and a Graeco-Roman nymph set into a niche. Clipped box hedges, topiary in lemon pots and a marble figure of a youth fill the foreground. This is not the Italian *campagna* but Iford Manor in Wiltshire, where the English love of the Italian Renaissance garden finds its most personal – and arguably most successful – expression.

Harold Peto gave up his architectural practice (where Lutyens had trained in the early 1890s) to concentrate on garden design. He bought the house in 1899 and set the garden into the steep, wooded Frome valley with great skill, building a series of terraces with retaining walls of local stone, and incorporating colonnades, loggias and a remarkable collection of sculptures. Architectural elements are balanced with evergreens, climbers and plants grown between paving. Through a sensitivity to landscape and integration of planting with architecture, he reversed the trend for the grandiose and overly formal Italianate gardens of the Victorians.

☛ Fairhaven, Lutyens, Mansi, M Rothschild, Verey

Harold Ainsworth Peto. b Somerleyton, nr Lowestoft, Suffolk (UK), 1854. d Bradford-on-Avon, Wiltshire (UK), 1933. Iford Manor, nr Bradford-on-Avon, Wiltshire (UK), 1899.

Pfeiffer Andrew

Linda Taubman Garden

A highly geometric modern take on the historic knot garden, by London- and Sydney-based designer Andrew Pfeiffer. Tudor knot gardens were usually made up of complex interwoven patterns, never rigid triangular shapes as in this design, which is perhaps more reminiscent of the French Modernist tradition of the 1920s. Linda Taubman's Michigan garden is set on terraces within woodland, thus creating an automatic tension between wilderness and manmade formality. This elegant space, the lower vegetable garden, is dignified by sleek brick paving and also the contrast between the horizontals of lawn and extremely low hedges, and the informal verticals of the surrounding woodland. This is further accentuated by the visitor's descending entrance. Pfeiffer describes himself as a landscape designer who creates 'idealized, informal landscapes based on natural habitats, within which there will be formal elements'. In all his work, he combines traditional local architecture styles and materials with indigenous plants.

☞ Beaumont, Johnston, Lainé, More, Page, H Phillips, Salisbury

Andrew Pfeiffer. b Kings Cross, Sydney (ASL), 1944. **Linda Taubman Garden**, Bloomfield Hills, MI (USA).

Phelips Sir Edward Montacute House

This exquisitely beautiful building was part of the original design for the gardens of Montacute House, created for Sir Edward Phelips during the 1590s. The pavilion, or banqueting house, was one of a pair of garden buildings where guests repaired for desserts and refreshments after dining in the main house. The strong Elizabethan ground plan remains, but within it are flower borders dating from the nineteenth century which were designed by Mrs Phyllis Reiss, who lived at nearby Tintinhull House and also created the gardens there. The clear, strong colours and large groups of foliage plants provide interest throughout the year. The borders are packed with clematis, vines, roses, delphiniums and lupins during the summer. The north garden was relaid by Graham Thomas, inspired by Vita Sackville-West, in 1945. The west drive has an avenue of clipped Irish yews, Lebanon cedars and beeches, leading to the new front entrance of the house.

☛ Egerton-Warburton, Farrand, Johnston, Sackville-West, G S Thomas

Sir Edward Phelips. Active (UK), sixteenth century. **Montacute House**, Somerset (UK), c1590s.

Philip II

Aranjuez

A small parterre is all that remains of Philip II's impressive garden schemes at the palace of Aranjuez. Philip employed many Dutch and Flemish gardeners and sent his head gardener, Jeronimo Algora, on garden visits to France, England and Flanders. The enclosed parterre style that was prevalent suited his own preference for formality. At Aranjuez he commissioned the creation of the Island Garden, reached by a short bridge across the Tagus river. The plans for it were drawn up by Juan Bautista de Toledo and the island was laid out in a number of small rectangular and square compartments. Simple fountains and statuary were part of the design. Philip II, a keen plantsman, ordered willows, reeds, acacias, lime trees, hazel and walnuts, many from sources in Flanders. His Island Garden was completely remodelled by the architect Herrera Barnuevo, working for Philip IV, and remains much the same today.

☛ Bullant, Fronteira, Lotti, Philip V

Philip II, King of Spain. **b** Vallodolid (SP), 1527. **d** Madrid (SP), 1598. **Aranjuez**, Aranjuez (SP), depicted by Antonio Joli in c1562.

Philip V King

La Granja

Most impressive of the twenty-six fountains and water features at La Granja is the New Cascade, a flight of marble stairs, down which water descends to a pool in front of a parterre garden that typifies the formal gardens near to the palace. Statuary and fountains are the hallmarks of the 145-hectare (360-acre) garden created by Philip V in homage to Le Nôtre's Versailles, which he had known as a child. Dramatic groups such as the horses traversing a series of pools – *The Route of the Horses* – are the work of French sculptors Réne Fremin and Jean Thierry, commissioned by Queen Isabella. The palace and its pleasure grounds were built on the site of a former hunting lodge. Philip V embarked on the grandiose project in 1720, but it was not until 1740 that the garden could be deemed complete. Less formal plantings, albeit to a geometric plan, are lined with avenues of horse chestnuts, Scots pine and Pyrennean oaks.

☛ Le Nôtre, Philip II, Seinsheim, Vanvitelli

Philip V, King of Spain. **b** Versailles (FR), 1684. **d** Madrid (SP), 1746. **La Granja**, Segovia (SP), 1720–40.

Phillips Henry Alexander   Irwin Gardens

At the end of the nineteenth and the beginning of the twentieth century, a classical revival of Ancient Greek, Roman and Italian Renaissance art and architecture was sweeping across America and shaping the way American designers were designing gardens. The Irwin Gardens, designed and built by Henry Alexander Phillips in 1910 for the prosperous banker William G Irwin, are no exception. Phillips was heavily influenced by Charles A Platt, an American landscape architect who wrote and illustrated a book entitled *Italian Gardens* (1894). Sunken parterres, pergolas, blind-arched niches, busts of Greek philosophers, classical columns, and tri-arched pavilions are used effectively to create this New World Ancient Roman garden, a headily romantic, antiquarian mix. Pictured here is an intimate courtyard with sunken beds and a Roman carved central stone well.

☞ Bosworth, Harrild, Kiley, London, Lennox-Boyd, Pfeiffer, Rose

Henry Alexander Phillips. **b** Springfield, MA (USA), 1875. **d** (USA), 1950. **Irwin Gardens**, Columbus, IN (USA), 1910.

Phillips Lady Florence | Vergelegen

The brick entrance path is the main axis in the octagonal garden at Vergelegen near Cape Town. The grand house, gabled in typical Cape Dutch style, was built in 1700 by Willem Adriaan van der Stel, an early and controversial governor of Cape Town. He laid out radial avenues of almonds, oaks and chestnuts, and reinterpreted the traditional corral in front of the house – designed to keep wild animals out – as a huge, octagonal, walled orange garden. This was replanted in 1921 by Lady Florence Phillips and her gardener, who had previously been employed at her estate at Tylney in Hampshire. Typically English twin herbaceous borders line the path, but the encircling bougainvillea pergola, jacaranda trees and looming mountains are reminders that this garden is a long way away from the English Home Counties. 'Florrie' Phillips, a native South African whose husband was a diamond-mine magnate, was a significant patron of the arts and she created another noted garden, Arcadia in Johannesburg.

☞ Barlow, Farrand, Jakobsen, Walling

Lady Florence Phillips. b Cape Town (SA), 1863. **d** Vergelegen, Cape Province (SA), 1940. **Vergelegen**, Cape Province (SA), 1921–.

Pinsent Cecil

Villa I Tatti

At Villa I Tatti the strong lines of the hedges, parterres, stairs and paths create an effective green architecture which seems to dictate rather than follow the existing vistas and levels. Although all the ingredients of the Tuscan Renaissance garden can still be tasted, the boldness of the design has a distinctly modern feel to it. In the 1920s and 1930s the expatriate English designer Cecil Pinsent had made it

his speciality to rework and rethink the Renaissance style for his many Anglo-American clients who had bought dilapidated villas in and around Florence at the turn of the century. Aided by Geoffrey Scott, he created more than twenty such gardens and restored a number of historical gardens throughout Tuscany and Rome. He was only twenty-six years old when he was commissioned to work at

I Tatti by Bernard Berenson, the great American art historian responsible for the rediscovery of fifteenth-century Italian painting. Berenson had bought the considerably run-down villa in 1905 and when he died in 1957 he bequeathed it to Harvard University.

☞ **Acton, Bacciocchi, Boy, Mansi, Porcinai, Rochford, Trezza**

Cecil Pinsent. b 1884. **d** 1964. **Villa I Tatti**, Fiesole (IT), 1910.

Piper Fredrik

Haga

In 1785 King Gustavus III commissioned the Swedish architect Fredrik Piper, who had just returned from England, to landscape the area surrounding his resort home in Stockholm. Gustavus had just returned from a trip to the Désert de Retz in 1784. The royal park Haga, near the Baltic coast, is one of Sweden's first gardens designed in the English landscape tradition. Lawn and field, and groups of trees form broad rolling vistas. The Maison de Plaisance, pictured here elegantly reflected in the lower lake, was designed later by Olof Templeman. Piper originally made plans for a number of garden structures at Haga, but his overall design for the park was never completed, and only his Turkish kiosk was built. A palace in the neo-classical style was designed for Haga by the French architect Louis Duprez, but never completed. Later in the nineteenth century a Chinese pavilion and copperclad tents were designed and built for Haga by the Swedish architect C C Gjorwell.

☛ Brown, Emes, Goethe, Hirschfeld, Monville, Repton, Tessin

Fredrik Magnus Piper. b 1746. **d** 1824. **Haga**, Stockholm (SWE), 1785.

Plato

The Academy

By the columns of a portico in the shade of the surrounding trees, the students gathered around their teacher were at their most receptive. On occasion, master and pupils would set off on walks and discuss plants and wildlife, mathematics and politics. Plato founded this extraordinary school, a model for centuries to come, in 387 BC, after he returned from his extensive travels in Egypt,

Italy and Sicily. It was situated in a magnificent shady park in the most beautiful suburb of Athens. Dedicated to the Attic hero Akademos, the sacred precinct was also a burial ground. In addition to his public teachings in the Akademos park, it is believed that Plato also had a private garden nearby, in which he taught. A philosophical and scientific research centre, the

Academy, as it came to be known, also led the way in jurisprudence and mathematics. Plato considered it his lifetime's achievement – greater than any of his writings.

☞ **Darwin, Michelozzi, Palladio, Raphael, Ruskin**

364

Plato. b Athens (GR), 428. **d** Athens (GR), 348 BC. **The Academy**, a scene from the school of Plato from the house of T Siminius, Pompeii, 1st century BC.

Pliny the Younger Tuscan Villa

This early eighteenth-century plan for a reconstruction of Pliny the Younger's favourite summer villa in remote Tuscany says more about England's emerging landscape style than about its Roman original. Ostensibly based on Pliny's letters of c100 AD, the plan shows three different garden styles: parkland with fishponds on either side; formal gardens laid out by 'the Rule and Line'; and a third style (in the top roundels) of meadow and imitation country, where rocks, water, trees and buildings were thrown into natural disorder 'like so many beautiful Landskips'. Pliny designed his villas to unite house and garden, painting leafy bird frescoes inside and creating delightful outdoor pavilions. Robert Castell published the plan in *The Villas of the Ancients Illustrated* (1728), dedicated to Lord Burlington. Crucially, it gave an antique pedigree to the 'new' landscape style emerging at Chiswick and elsewhere, but few copies were produced and Castell died soon afterwards in debtors' prison.

☞ **Burlington, Hadrian, Switzer, Sulla, Tibernitus**

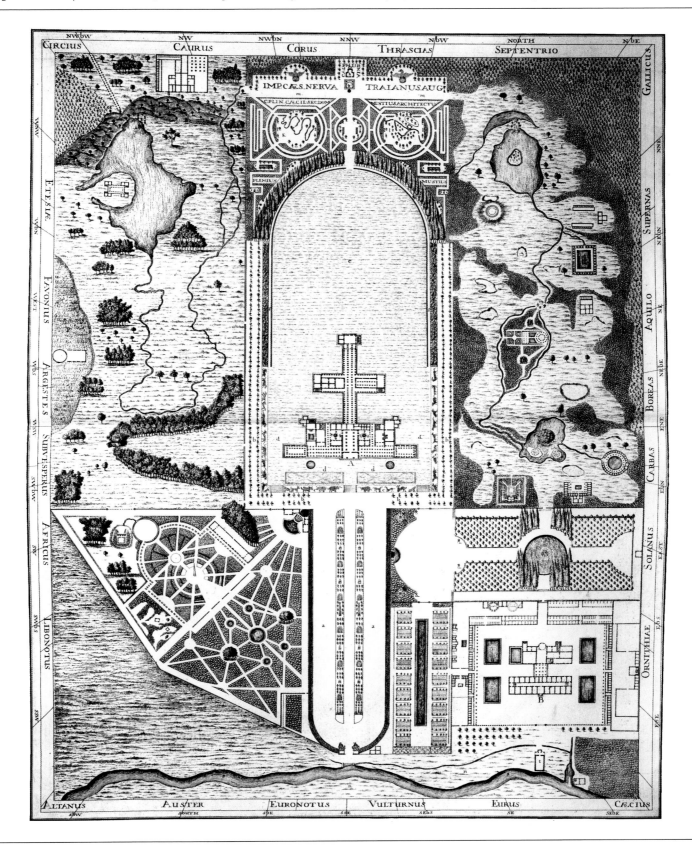

Pliny the Younger (Gaius Plinius Caecilius Secundus). b Novum Comum (IT), c61 AD. **d** Bithynia or Rome, 113 AD. **Tuscan Villa**, Città di Castello, Tuscany (IT), c100 AD.

Poitiers Diane de   Château de Chenonceau

The *broderie* of santolinas forms an elegant parterre, dedicated to Diane de Poitiers, on a raised terrace above the River Cher, flanking one of the most marvellous châteaux in France. Though in a different form, this garden was famous in the sixteenth century when Diane de Poitiers, the notorious and powerful mistress of Henri II, created it. She had received Chenonceau in 1551 as a gift from the king on his accession. She ordered the formal parterres to be planted with rare fruit trees, some vegetables and her favourite flowers: roses, lilies and thousands of violets which were transplanted from the nearby woodland. Diane held court as virtual queen of France during Henri II's lifetime, but on his death Catherine di Medici, the actual queen, confiscated most of Diane's possessions, including Chenonceau. Catherine took up residence there and created her own Italianate gardens. Modern interpretations of the gardens of both ladies still stand on either side of the castle, vying with each other for supremacy.

☛ Du Cerceau, L'Orme, Mercogliano, Mollet, Serlio

Diane de Poitiers (Duchesse de Valentinois). b Poitiers (FR), 1499. d Anet (FR), 1566. Château de Chenonceau, nr Tours (FR), 1551.

Pope Alexander

Twickenham Garden

The open shellwork temple was a highlight of Pope's garden, a rectangular 2-hectare (4.8-acre) plot where the poet experimented with painterly techniques of light and shade in his plantings of trees and shrubs, and ornamented the straight *allées*, serpentine paths and glades with classical urns and statuary. Variety was key, and the whole scene could be surveyed from a mount. The garden could only be reached from the house via a tunnel under the road, and this Pope converted into a grotto clad with minerals, shells, glass and stalactites shot down in Wookey Hole. From here a camera obscura view of the Thames, back past the house, could be enjoyed; it is just visible in the doorway behind the temple in this drawing by Kent, which shows Kent, Pope and Pope's dog in the garden, as well as fanciful additions such as the sculptural group on the left.

☞ Bridgeman, Grenville-Temple, Kent, Orrery, Switzer, Vanbrugh

Alexander Pope. b London (UK), 1688. d Twickenham, London (UK), 1744. **Twickenham Garden**, London (UK), 1718–44.

Porcinai Pietro

Villa Il Roseto

A graceful modern parterre gently slopes away from the house towards the city of Erector. Beneath it, a room of imposing proportions, bathed in dappled daylight, serves as the main entrance to the property and underground car park. With concrete columns and cupolas, geometrically decorated floor and walls, it is a modern reinterpretation of the underground grottoes of the sixteenth and seventeenth centuries. This design innovation is typical of Pietro Porcinai's capacity to find workable solutions to modern situations and denotes his striking ability to translate the essential characteristics of the Italian tradition into contemporary aesthetics. He applied these qualities to many private gardens in Europe, the Middle East, North and South America, but also on larger projects such as the Brenner motorway. The fact that he was brought up at the Tuscan villa of La Gamberaia, where his father was head gardener, helps explain his fluency and the confidence of his instincts.

☛ **Capponi, Nasoni, Pinsent, Scarpa, Trezza**

368

Pietro Porcinai. b Florence (IT), 1910. **d** 1986. **Villa Il Roseto**, nr Arcetri, Tuscany (IT).

Post Pieter

Huis ten Bosch

This intimate and engaging portrait of the garden at Huis ten Bosch illustrates Pieter Post's use of uncluttered symmetry and classical statuary, inspired by Italian Renaissance models. Together with Jacob van Campen, Constantijn Huygens and Johan Maurits van Nassau – all of them members of a group that came to be known as the Hague Circle – Post developed a characteristically Dutch formal garden style. Huis ten Bosch is a small and intimate garden, bounded by straight canals and rows of trees. The square outline was divided into simple compartments. In the middle stood four stone statues and beside them were two flights of steps leading on each side to a plant-covered pavilion. Post designed the garden of Huis Ten Bosch ('House in the Wood') near the Hague, between 1645–52 for Amalia van Solms, the wife of Frederik Hendrik, Stadholder and Prince of Orange. The parterres were monogrammed with the initials of F H and A v S. Later it became the summer retreat of William and Mary, who acquired it in 1686.

☛ **Colchester, Frederik Hendrik, Huygens, Van Campen**

Pieter Post. b Haarlem (NL), 1608. **d** The Hague (NL), 1669. **Huis ten Bosch**, Haagse Bos, The Hague (NL), 1645–52.

Potter Beatrix

Hill Top

Lurking behind the onions and carrots of a tousled kitchen garden are the old-fashioned spade, sieve and galvanized watering can familiar to children around the world reared on *Peter Rabbit* and other tales by Beatrix Potter. Just behind this viewpoint is Hill Top, the working Lakeland farm Potter bought in 1905 where she wrote many of her stories, illustrating them herself in watercolour, pen and ink. In later years, her compulsion to draw gave way to sheep-breeding (of the native Herdwick sheep) and gardening. No horticultural innovator, she favoured the traditional cottage garden plants that bordered the path to her front door: azaleas, phlox, roses, saxifrages, hollyhocks, lilies, rock plants and fruit trees, casually interspersed with vegetables. Her influence endures through her carefully observed illustrations imprinted on the visual memory of each new generation. After her death, she willed more than 1,500 hectares (4,000 acres) of Lake District land along with a number of working farms and cottages to the National Trust.

☞ **Burnett, Landsberg, Shurcliff, Vogue**

Beatrix Potter (Helen Beatrix Potter). **b** London (UK), 1866. **d** Cumbria (UK), 1943. **Hill Top**, nr Sawrey, Ambleside, Cumbria (UK), 1905.

Powerscourt 7th Viscount

The 7th Viscount Powerscourt inherited a partially completed Italianate garden, designed by Daniel Robertson. In 1858 he invited six different architects and garden designers to draw up plans for the completion of the layout. The family then selected elements from the designs offered by Daniel Robertson, William Brodrick Thomas, James Howe, Sir George Hodson, Edward Milner and Francis Penrose. The result, a superb example of the hybrid taste of the late nineteenth century, was overlaid with a prodigal display of architectural and sculptural detail; the copies of classical statues are of the highest quality. The architectural framework of the garden is complimented by an eclectic collection of conifers, extensive forestry plantations and a view of the Sugar Loaf Mountain, the last illustrating the dictum of the Italian Renaissance architect, Alberti, that 'Familiar mountains' should be seen 'beyond the delicacy of gardens'.

☛ Bomarzo, Goldney, Hill, Lane, Wilhelmina

371

7th Viscount Powerscourt. b 1836. d 1904. Powerscourt, County Wicklow (IRE), 1858.

Pückler-Muskau Prince Hermann Schloss Branitz

This conical mound (Prince Pückler called it a pyramid) was built on an island in one of the lakes on his estate at Branitz and finished in 1856: it contains the graves of Prince Pückler and his wife and is topped by a quotation from the Qu'ran which reads 'Graves are the mountain-peaks of a distant new world'. The pyramid bursts into flame in early autumn when the Virginian creeper which covers it turns to scarlet and crimson. The swashbuckling Prince Pückler was the greatest amateur landscaper in nineteenth-century Germany. He landscaped on a splendid scale: his main estate at Muskau has a home park of 550 hectares (1,358 acres) – partly in Germany and partly in Poland. His initial inspiration came from journeys to England and contact with Humphry Repton. Later on, he introduced ornamental bedding schemes inspired by those of Victorian England. Through his travel writings and practical advice to landowners, Pückler was an effective promoter of the English landscape style.

☞ Asplund, Girardin, Medinaceli, Repton, Scarpa

Prince Hermann Pückler-Muskau. b Muskau (GER), 1785. d Branitz (GER), 1871. Schloss Branitz, nr Cottbus (GER), c1850.

Pulham James

Higham Court

At first glance this garden room seems to be a natural scene made with real rock outcrops, home to that most Victorian of obsessions, a collection of conifer trees. Dating from 1849, it is, however, the first rockery made by James Pulham (son of James Sr, a pioneer in the manufacture of Portland cement) from a mixture of natural stone and 'Pulhamite'. Pulhamite was an artificial rock made by pouring a special mix of Portland cement over a rough structure made of brick and clinker and sculpting it into natural-looking strata. Pulham became so skilful at imitating real rock that it is very difficult to distinguish the reproduction from the genuine article. Pulham's work had a huge impact on the Victorian fashion for creating rock gardens that imitated natural scenes, and other famous examples of his work include Sandringham Park in Norfolk and Battersea Park in London. Sadly, the secret recipe for Pulhamite went to the grave with James' son.

☛ I Caus, Crisp, Isham, Lainé, Lane, Pope

James Pulham. b (UK), c1820. d (UK), 1898. **Higham Court**, Gloucestershire (UK), 1849.

Qian Long Emperor of China   Yuan Ming Yuan

This eighteenth-century watercolour shows the landscape of the Yuan Ming Yuan, the gardens of the Old Summer Palace, part of the Garden of Perfect Brightness just outside Beijing. Yuan Ming Yuan was begun in the early eighteenth century and significantly developed by Emperor Qian Long between 1736 and 1795. Yuan Ming Yuan was famous for the many and varied scenes created within it, inspired by specific inscriptions. By the end of Chien Lung's reign, some forty scenes had been created, but by the mid-nineteenth century there were 150. Many of the scenes were inspired by natural vistas celebrated in China, but built architecture played an important part. There were shopping streets, theatres and temples built in the garden, and Qian Long even commissioned Père Giuseppe Castiglione to make a series of marble buildings in a Western style – at the same time as William Chambers was celebrating Eastern style with his pagoda at Kew.

🐦 **Chambers, Kang Xi, Pan En, Wang Xian Chen**

374

Qian Long, Emperor of China. b (CHN), 1711. **d** (CHN), 1799. **Yuan Ming Yuan**, near Beijing (CHN), 1736–95.

Radziwill Princess Helena Arkadia

The Roman Aqueduct with a Cascade is one of many 'new' classical ruins created as garden features and focal points in this 15-hectare (36-acre) garden on the Radziwill estate, 80 km (48 miles) from Warsaw. The site was designed in 1778 by Szymon Bogumil Zug, the most fervent supporter of the English Picturesque Movement in Poland at that time. Princess Helena Radziwill commissioned the gardens and they were built between 1778 and 1785. The name Arkadia was inspired by the Arcadian myth, and this is the prominent theme, one that is focused by the Latin inscription *Et in Arcadia ego* ('And I also am in Arcady') on a tombstone in the garden. Like Rousseau's Memorial at Ermenonville in France, the tomb is on an island in the lake that has been planted with poplar trees. The inscription is a reminder that death exists alongside love and happiness, even in the ideal environment of Arcady. Arkadia is the best-preserved eighteenth-century garden layout in Poland, and it is now being gradually restored.

☛ **Boy, Czartoryska, Girardin, Hamilton, Palladio, Stanislas II, Zug**

Princess Helena Radziwill (née Czartoryska). d (POL), c1802. **Arkadia**, Lowicz (POL), 1778–85.

Raffles Sir Stamford

Singapore Botanic Gardens

These beautiful orchids are part of the Orchid Garden in Singapore's Botanic Gardens. They were established in the early 1980s in honour of the pioneering work conducted by R E Holttum into the hybridizing of orchids (work that has made Singapore one of the world's leading orchid-producing countries). The Botanic Gardens, located on Government Hill and now a public park as well as an experimental station, were founded by Sir Stamford Raffles in 1822 as a place in which to grow plants that had an important economic role to play in the colonies of the ever-expanding British Empire. The gardens closed in 1829 and were re-established some thirty years later by the Agri-Horticultural Society who, in 1866, added a further 10 hectares (24 acres) to the gardens. The garden also played a significant role in the development of the Malayan rubber industry in the late nineteenth century, when H N Ridley, the director, successfully extracted latex from para rubber trees sent out to the gardens from Kew.

☛ Bawa, Cook, Moroni, Otruba, Rhodes, Thwaites, van Riebeeck

Sir Stamford Raffles. b nr Jamaica, 1781. d Singapore, 1826. **Singapore Botanic Gardens**, Singapore, 1822.

Raphael

Villa Madama

As this plan shows, Cardinal Giulio di Medici's great Renaissance villa looking east towards Rome was designed as a series of formal landscapes radiating from a central open court. Guests entered the first courtyard by a monumental stairway (far left of plan). Other features included an amphitheatre dug into the hillside; a northern loggia opening on to formal terraces and the private garden (*giardino segreto*); and the villa's main facade with spectacular views across the River Tiber. Begun in 1516, the villa and its gardens are usually attributed to the artist Raphael with help from his pupil Giulio Romano, Antonio Sangallo the Younger and Giovanni da Udine. Before it could be completed, the villa was burnt during the Sack of Rome in 1527 and now takes its name from a later owner, Margaret of Austria. Outshone in terms of influence on Italian gardens only by Bramante's Belvedere Court, the Villa Madama dissolved the boundaries between house and garden.

☞ Bramante, Michelozzi, Moroni, Orsini, Palladio

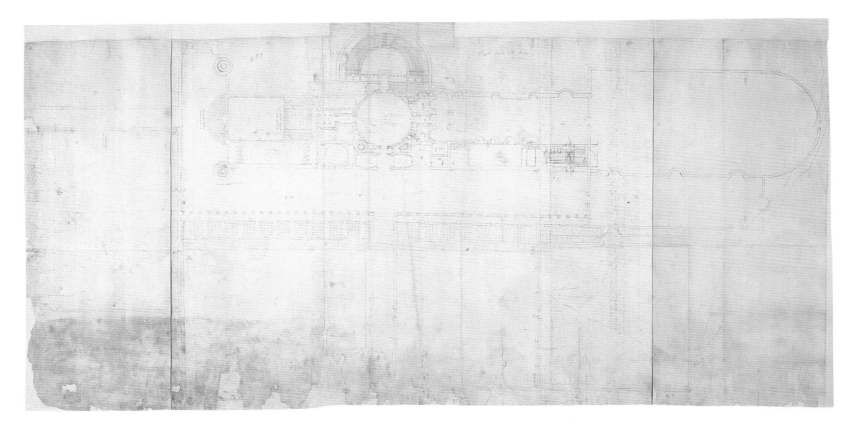

Raphael (Raffaello Sanzio or Santi). b Urbino (IT), 1483. d Rome (IT), 1520. **Villa Madama**, Rome (IT), 1516.

Raven Peter

Missouri Botanical Garden

Missouri Botanical Garden aims to represent local as well as international garden themes. The tall grasses of this garden planted around a pavilion of traditional log-cabin construction remind us that Missouri is located in the tall grass prairie of the American Midwest. Opened to the public in 1853 by its founder, Henry Shaw, the garden has become, under the present director Peter Raven and the designer Geoffrey Rausch of Marshall Tyler Rausch, a model of a modern, large-scale botanic garden. As well as the usual facilities for botanists, it features many themed display gardens for public education. The Climatron, a greenhouse in the form of a geodesic dome, houses tropical and other plants under the Integrated Pest Management System, using predaceous insects instead of chemical insecticides. The garden's herbarium of 3.5 million items, horticultural library of 110,000 volumes and tropical field research programmes (employing seventy people) are all among the best in the world.

☞ Burley Griffin, McNab, Moroni, Rhodes, Sloane

Peter Raven. b (CHN), 1936. **Missouri Botanical Garden**, St Louis, MS (USA), late twentieth century.

Repton Humphry

Sheringham Park

Humphry Repton designed both house and garden at Sheringham Park, set in a wooded valley within sight of the sea. After the death of Capability Brown, Repton saw a career opening and successfully took on the mantle of England's foremost landscape designer. In many ways he also inherited Brown's style (on a smaller scale), creating skilful compositions that exploited the natural topography to form romantic visions of pastoral ease. Repton's main innovation was to reintroduce areas of formality by the house (Brown had pasture right up to the walls): terraces, shrubberies, steps, balustrades and enclosed flower gardens (as at Sheringham). Like Brown, Repton also had a shrewd commercial eye, and his Red Books – before-and-after views of potential clients' estates, complete with flip-over sections that added lakes or clumps of trees – were an early appeal to the 'makeover' mentality.

☛ Brown, Crowe, Nash, Pückler-Muskau, Southcote

Humphry Repton. b Bury St Edmonds (UK), 1752. **d** Romford (UK), 1818. **Sheringham Park**, Norfolk (UK), 1812–19.

Rhodes Cecil

Kirstenbosch National Botanical Garden

Everywhere you look at Kirstenbosch, you see wild flowers with the soaring slopes of Table Mountain as a background. These are like all the plants in the National Botanical Garden, they are natives of Cape Province. South Africa has one of the richest and most fragile flora in the world and we owe its survival to Cecil Rhodes. Rhodes acquired Kirstenbosch in 1895 and planted avenues of Moreton Bay figs and camphor trees. He then bequeathed it to the people of South Africa, as part of his Groote Schuur estate, to preserve it for posterity. The idea of a garden dedicated to 'the preservation of our vegetation' dates back to 1915. Now Kirstenbosch is home to 7,000 different species of yew, all natives of the Cape. They are preserved in a naturally designed garden of 36 hectares (86 acres), surrounded by nearly 500 hectares (1,200 acres) of wild *fynbos* and forest.

☞ **Barlow, Chambers, F Phillips, Raffles, Thwaites**

Sir Cecil Rhodes. b Bishop's Stortford (UK), 1853. **d** Cape Town (SA), 1902. **Kirstenbosch National Botanical Garden** (SA), 1895.

Rikkyu Sen no   Omote Senke School

A modest path covered in rough stones and moss snakes through an undergrowth of indistinct shrubs. Leading to a rustic arbour via various gates and shelters, this is the *roji* or 'dewy path' which in Japanese signifies a tea garden. The short journey to the tea garden is a rite in itself, during which one leaves worldly distractions behind to enter a state of simplicity and harmony. Modest in essence, with no distinctive stones, ponds or elaborate buildings, no *roji* have survived in their original form. Tea drinking was established as a complex ceremony almost as soon as tea was brought over from China by Buddhist monks. Over the centuries its ritual and spirit underwent minor but significant transformations depending on the influence of successive 'tea masters'. These masters were at first scholarly Zen monks, then lay men in search of spiritual enlightement.

☛   Enshu, Gyokuen, Kokushi, Mandokora, Ogawa, Toshihito

Sen no Rikkyu. b Sakei, nr Osaka (JAP), 1522. **d** Kyoto (JAP), 1591. **Omote Senke School**, Kyoto (JAP), sixteenth century.

Rinaldi Antonio

Oranienbaum Palace

This is a nineteenth-century view of the east wing of the Oranienbaum Palace from the Lower Pool. The Lower Pool was formed by damming the River Karost when the palace was built for Prince Menshikov by the architects Fontana and Schädel between 1710 and 1725. At that time, a flotilla of small boats was a diversion for guests. On a terrace in front of the palace overlooking the sea the architects added formal gardens embellished with fountains and sculpture. But the most important design contribution at Oranienbaum was that of Antonio Rinaldi. For Peter III, who was interested only in military pursuits, he designed between 1757 and 1762 a small palace, barracks, a guard-room, houses for officers, an arsenal and a powder-cellar. For his wife, Catherine, he built the so-called Chinese Palace. He also laid out formal gardens and made some early attempts at landscaping. The finest building in the park is his Sliding Hill Pavilion, which was the starting-point and viewing-place for an impressive early rollercoaster.

☛ **Cameron, Catherine II, Chambers, Fontana, Peter II**

382

Antonio Rinaldi. b (IT), 1709. **d** Rome (IT), 1794. **Oranienbaum Palace**, St Petersburg (RUS), 1710–25, from a painting by Yegor Maier (1822–67).

Robert Hubert   Rambouillet Dairy

A white marble nymph and her goat emerge from the rugged boulders of a fantasy cave in the elegant pavilion known as the Queen's Dairy. This neo-classical building by Thévenin and the surrounding 'fold' were commissioned by Louis XVI in the hope of pleasing Marie-Antoinette, and persuading her to stay in Rambouillet, a château she disliked. The queen enjoyed playing at milkmaids and the great landscape painter Hubert Robert was partly responsible for giving life to her whims as he had been appointed Designer of the King's Gardens in 1778. A follower of Claude and close friend of Fragonard, Robert spent ten years in Italy before returning to France where he became greatly interested in landscape design. Robert was ready to make the leap from landscape painting to designing in a romantic style derived from English precedents. Although no gardens exist that can be directly and firmly attributed to him, he inspired and contributed to places like Ermenonville, Méréville, Compiègne or Trianon.

☞ **Bélanger & Blaikie, Carmontelle, Girardin, Laborde**

Hubert Robert. b Paris (FR), 1773. **d** Paris (FR), 1808. **Rambouillet Dairy**, Château de Rambouillet (FR), after 1778.

Robeson Graham & Gray Alan   Old Vicarage

The sunken garden at the Old Vicarage is part of a recently built Arts-and-Crafts garden worthy of Lutyens and the Edwardian era. The owners began their garden in the late 1980s and have energetically expanded it ever since. It is a typical English mix of formal architecture softened by luxuriant and imaginative planting: the brick walls, garden buildings and gates are of the highest quality, but they are nevertheless upstaged by the planting. As well as classic herbaceous borders (enlivened by grasses), box parterres and high yew hedges, the garden is packed with rare and tender plants and boasts a Mediterranean garden and a tropical border influenced by Christopher Lloyd. High yew hedges afford shelter from strong winds off the sea, which is only 3.2 km (2 miles) away. Gaps in the yew frame vistas over agricultural fields towards two church towers which serve as dynamic eyecatchers. The energy of the owners means the Old Vicarage is set to become a twenty-first century Sissinghurst or Hidcote.

☞ Farrand, Jekyll, Johnston, Lloyd, Lutyens, Sackville-West

Graham Robeson. Alan Gray. Old Vicarage, East Ruston, Norfolk (UK), late 1980s.

Robins Thomas

Painswick Rococo Garden

The elaborate rococo border of foliage and shells gives a hint of the unusual attractions of the garden this painting depicts. A figure of Pan greets visitors as they enter the garden; there are long straight vistas and serpentine paths leading around a strange and idiosyncratic collection of buildings, to reveal sudden glimpses of the house and valley below. Robins' painting shares a pictorial convention with the rococo style of garden design, which exploits the tension between realism and extreme artifice. The garden lies in a valley hidden behind the house, but here the plane of the painting has been tilted in order to give a clear and detailed view. It is thought that Robins, a painter of houses and gardens in the mid eighteenth century, may also have designed Painswick for owner Benjamin Hyett. It remains the finest and fullest example of a rococo garden in the country and boasts an exceptional snowdrop display.

☞ Bushell, I Caus, Lane, Orrery, Pope

Robinson William Gravetye Manor

The formal architecture of the Elizabethan manor is all but hidden by a riot of mixed native and exotic perennials. This triumph of informality over architecture is a perfect cameo of William Robinson's views on garden-making. A prolific author, advocate of woodland gardening, hardy plants and champion of the natural approach, where plants were positioned to best display their individual beauties, Robinson vehemently disliked the High Victorian style of formal flowerbeds. He vitriolically attacked parterres and geometric beds cut into lawns, describing them as 'broken brick' and 'pastry cook' gardening. Robinson also argued that garden design was the realm of gardeners, a stance that brought him into conflict with architects, notably Sir Reginald Blomfield. Blomfield favoured the formal Renaissance style, and saw garden design as a matter for the architect. The matter was resolved when Jekyll and Lutyens demonstrated that both gardener and architect could design the garden together.

☞ **Blomfield, Jekyll, Lutyens, MacDonald-Buchanan, A Parsons**

William Robinson. b (IRE), 1838. **d** West Sussex (UK), 1935. **Gravetye Manor**, East Grinstead, West Sussex (UK), 1885.

Rochford Earl of

Powis Castle

Like billowing eiderdowns, the yews at Powis Castle appear to cascade lazily over the walls. Today the gardens are renowned for this feature and, although it is hard to believe that the yews were once neat topiaries set at regularly spaced intervals, with each slender tree trimmed into three plate-like tiers, an engraving from 1742 shows that this was so. The pink-stone castle stands on a C-shaped hill commanding dramatic views of Offa's Dyke and the England–Wales border. Its estate belonged to the princes and (later) earls of Powis from around 1200 until the mid-twentieth century, but the fine gardens were made by the Earl of Rochford during his brief tenure, between 1696 and 1708. Its three Italianate terraces, around 152 m (500 ft) long, drop in steep, southeast-facing steps from the castle to the lawned valley floor. Rochford's lavish arrangement of statues, topiaries and water basins has long since gone, but the gardens are celebrated today for the sumptuously planted borders on the terraces.

☞ **Barron, Beaumont, Boy, Salisbury, Verey, Wirtz**

Willem van Nassau, **Earl of Rochford. d** Zuylenstein (NL), 1708. **Powis Castle**, Powys (UK), 1696–1722.

Roper Lanning

Glenveagh Castle

In full bloom and high colour, Glenveagh's gardens were designed to be at their best during the summer months. The American architect Lanning Roper, who lived and worked in England, designed this wonderful kitchen garden for the American-based Henry MacIlhenny of Rittenhouse Square, Philadelphia. The garden was part of MacIlhenny's *demesne* at Glenveagh Castle, his summer retreat in Ireland. The conservatory and greenhouse were filled with fruit for the table and exotic plants for the house. The glasshouses and the gardens were designed to be admired by visitors on their way to the shore of the lough and the Irish Sea beyond. Roper had a genius for understanding clients' needs and the gardens at Glenveagh brilliantly reflected an opulent lifestyle with the necessary staff to ensure that the summer show was always perfect. Roper was a leading mid-century proponent of the romantic English style of herbaceous planting.

☞ Carvallo, Jefferson, La Quintinie, Vanderbilt, Washington

Lanning Roper. b (USA), 1912. d (UK), 1983. **Glenveagh Castle**, Glenveagh National Park, Co Donegal (IRE), 1920s.

Rose James

The James Rose Center

Beautifully finished, raised natural wooden floors and *shoji* screens are but two of the Japanese influences on the designs made by James Rose in 1954 for his own house and garden in Ridgewood, New Jersey. This style was inspired by time spent in the Pacific during World War II. Rose's garden spaces are seen as interlinked volumes, often divided by transparent screens. Woven wooden fencing allows glimpses into adjacent spaces. Rose called the garden 'the gateless gate of Zen Buddhism'. His designs depended on the changing character and fleeting nature of the effects of light, shadow, sound, space and texture. The tradition of the Orient allied to the modernity of Bauhaus espoused at Harvard in the late 1930s, where Rose, Garrett Eckbo and Dan Kiley rebelled against the Beaux Arts fashion, radically changed professional landscape design philosophies both in the United States and in a wider, international context.

☞ Ashikaga Takauji, Eckbo, Egerton-Warburton, Enshu, Hornel, Kiley

James C Rose. **b** PA (USA). **d** Ridgewood, NJ (USA), 1991. **The James Rose Center**, Ridgewood, NJ (USA), 1954.

Rothschild Beatrix de   Villa Ephrussi-Rothschild

The Temple of Love at the focal point of this classic view of the Villa Ephrussi-Rothschild is much closer than it seems: Béatrix Ephrussi insisted that the lines which lead up to it should converge to create an optical illusion of great distance. Palms, cycads, dracaenas and bold bedding plants all add to the sense of the exotic in this extravagant and opulent garden near Nice, laid out in the first decade of the twentieth century by Aaron Messiah, who was the French partner of Harold Peto. Off to the right of this view is a sequence of enclosed gardens in Japanese, Spanish, English, Moorish and Italian styles, as well as an atmospheric cactus garden and a sumptuous collection of exotic plants. Every feature was intended to delight, impress and educate the visitor – and to leave them in no doubt as to the power and the wealth of the Rothschilds. But the overall impression is of a light-hearted holiday from reality rather than unpalatable pretentiousness.

☛ **Barry, Joséphine, Lainé, Peto, Walska**

Mme Maurice Ephrussi (née Baronne Charlotte Béatrix de Rothschild). b 1864. d 1934. **Villa Ephrussi-Rothschild**, Saint-Jean-Cap-Ferrat (FR), 1905.

Rothschild Miriam de   Ashton Wold

Miriam de Rothschild planted clematis, wisteria, ivy, brambles and roses to cover her house. They are allowed to grow as they wish, almost obliterating windows and doors. The Rothschild family has lived at Ashton Wold for almost one hundred years. In the 1970s Miriam started to create a wild-flower meadow around the house, sweeping away the original herbaceous borders. The seeds for the meadows were collected from deserted airfields nearby. Subsequently, Miriam de Rothschild invented the popular seed mix called Farmer's Nightmare. It consists of corn daisy, feverfew, cornflower, corn marigold, corn cockle and two species of poppy. At the right time of year the meadow, which covers almost 60 hectares (150 acres), looks entirely natural, but to create such a look needs a great deal of energy and much care, so that the individual wild flowers bloom and seed profusely.

☞ Brookes, Harrison, Kingsbury, Linden, Oudolf, Peto, Toll

Miriam de Rothschild. b 1908. **Ashton Wold**, Peterborough, Cambridgeshire (UK), 1970s.

Ruskin John   Brantwood

Ruskin's local slate seat (specially made by a friend's gardener) turns to face the Lakeland stream rather than Coniston's grander scenery. By closely observing the stream's leaps and pools, Ruskin declared that he could learn as much about the underlying laws of nature as from Niagara's vulgar cataracts. The great Victorian thinker's purchase of Brantwood in 1871 gave him a 'living laboratory' in which to explore his ideas on social welfare, aesthetics and practical land-management. Until the onset of mania, he developed the simple house and 8.4 hectares (21 acres) of craggy rock and coppiced woodland into a cottage villa where he could achieve a sense of rightness and peace. Happiness would come, he believed, 'not by the enlargement of the possessions, but of the heart'. As artist, scientist, philosopher, writer, political radical and pre-eminent art critic, Ruskin straddled the Victorian age, prefiguring especially the rise of environmentalism. His garden is now being sympathetically restored.

☞ Larssen, Lutyens, Morris, Ruskin, Wordsworth

392

John Ruskin. b London (UK), 1819. **d** Brantwood, Coniston, Cumbria (UK), 1900. **Brantwood**, Coniston, Cumbria (UK), 1871.

Ruys Mien

Mien Ruys Tuinen

Mien Ruys began her career by designing borders for the landscaping section of her father's nursery business at Moerheimstraat, Dedemsvaart. She began to lay out small model gardens there in 1925, beginning with the Wild Garden and the old Experimental Garden with the pebbled concrete slabs that she designed and which are now commonplace. By 1929 Mien Ruys was studying garden architecture seriously and later joined a group of progressive architects who believed in functionalism. This was followed by a period of teaching landscape architecture. It was twenty-five years before she again began to add to the gardens at Dedemsvaart, with the Water Garden in 1954, pictured here, and the Herb Garden in 1957. In the 1960s the number of gardens multiplied as a result of Mien Ruys' growing practice as a garden designer, increasing in number until the 1990s. The Mien Ruys Tuinen are a permanent record of her design ideas as they developed over a lifetime.

☛ Brookes, Childs, Linden, Oudolf, D Pearson, M Rothschild

Mien Ruys. b (NL), 1904. **Mien Ruys Tuinen**, Overijssel (NL), 1925–1990.

Saarinen Eliel

Cranbrook Academy of Art

The mist swirling around the simple lines of the Modernist building at the end of the pool enhances the romantic imagery of the grounds of Cranbrook Academy. Cranbrook was planned and conceived as a community for nurturing artists and their work so they would be capable of producing a pleasing and harmonious contemporary world. The buildings are of a modern style, yet the materials and surfaces echo traditional local architecture. The Finnish architect Eliel Saarinen, who was president of the Cranbrook Academy between 1932 and 1948, was one of the leading architects of his generation in Finland before he emigrated to the USA in 1923. At Cranbrook he drew on work he had done for urban planning competitions in Finland, mostly unrealized, to create 'his aesthetic and intellectual masterwork', an exemplary urban design incorporating landscape and architectural elements. He wrote about his work at the Academy in *The Cranbrook Development*, 1931.

☛ **Brancusi, Fairhaven, Halprin, Kiley, Neutra, Palladio, Scarpa**

Eliel Saarinen (Gottlieb Eliel Saarinen). b Rantasalmir (FIN), 1873. **d** Bloomfield Hills, MI (USA), 1950. **Cranbrook Academy of Art**, Bloomfield Hills, MI (USA), 1928–41.

Sackville-West Vita   Sissinghurst Castle Garden

White roses, clematis and honeysuckle combine to create a striking white colour-scheme, which is harmoniously balanced by a background of green. The White Garden at Sissinghurst, Kent, is one of the most influential 12 sq m (42 sq ft) plots of land in recent garden history. Planted in 1948, some twelve years after Vita Sackville-West and her diplomat husband Harold Nicolson arrived at the derelict Jacobean estate, the White Garden started a cult in gardening taste that can still be discerned in gardens from Cape Town to Sydney. The White Garden is a small part of the overall layout, which is based on a series of 'garden rooms' – formal in shape but informally planted. This was another influential concept, although not one pioneered at this garden. Sackville-West had an enormous influence on gardening taste in the second half of the twentieth century, principally through Sissinghurst and her gardening column in the *Observer* newspaper.

☛ **Barron, Hoare, Messel, Noel, Seinsheim**

Vita (Victoria) Sackville-West. b Knole, Kent (UK), 1892. **d** Sissinghurst, Kent (UK), 1962. **Sissinghurst Castle Garden**, Sissinghurst, Kent (UK), 1948.

Saint-Phalle Niki de The Tarot Garden

Glistening in the Tuscan sun on top of a hill near the Argentario coast, the huge sculptures of the Tarot Garden can be seen for miles around. Covered in bright mosaics, coloured glass or pieces of mirror, they depict various figures in the deck of the 'Sacred Game', forming a mythical and esoteric landscape. The sculptor Niki de Saint-Phalle describes a dream she had: while walking in an enchanted garden, she met a multitude of benevolent and magical figures, gigantic and covered in precious stones. Years later she brought her dream to life, giving birth to this highly personal garden of the mind. The widow of Swiss sculptor Jean Tinguely, she scandalized the art world in the 1970s with her giant 'Nanas', her monumental sculptures of women whose brightly coloured bodies could be entered through a door between their spread legs. She has been working on the Tarot Garden for the past forty years and lives inside the enormous *Empress* sculpture.

☛ Arakawa & Gins, Chand Saini, Gaudí, James, Miró, Orsini

Niki de Saint-Phalle. b Neuilly-Sur-Seine (FR), 1930. **The Tarot Garden**, Capalbio, Tuscany (IT), 1960.

Salisbury Marchioness of   Hatfield House

Avenues of evergreen oaks grown on 2-m (6.4-ft) stems and clipped like lollipops comprise the edges of the East Garden at Hatfield House. The formal beds are box-edged squares, each with a taller box topiary in the middle. The plantings are mixed and random: it is the formal design which holds the garden together. Hatfield House was built for Robert Cecil in 1607. The planting of the original garden was supervised by John Tradescant the Elder. Hatfield now has the most ambitious neo-Jacobean gardens ever made. So successful have Lady Salisbury's designs proved that it comes as a surprise to learn that she did not start work on the East Garden until 1977. Lady Salisbury has written: 'I have tried in the last years to re-make the gardens as they might have been, and bring them back into sympathy with the great unchanging house. It is my dream that one day they will become again a place of fancies and conceits, where not only pleasure and peace can be found but a measure of surprise and mystery.'

☞ Johnston, Kennedy, Strong & Oman, Wirtz, Wise

Molly Gascoigne-Cecil, Marchioness of Salisbury. b 1922. East Garden, Hatfield House, Hatfield, Hertfordshire (UK), 1977–.

Sanchez & Maddux

Meister Garden

All too often the clichés of the English Arts-and-Crafts garden – mixed borders of old-fashioned herbaceous plants, the restrained use of colour (typically white climbing roses such as 'Iceberg'), box hedges, white gardens, pergolas or arches covered in wisteria or laburnum – are imported wholesale into gardens on the other side of the world. Here, however, Jorge Sanchez has artfully interwoven the native flora of Florida into this classic look and given it a wholly new meaning. In this context, the ficus tree and its complex network of branches and roots is an astonishing and delightful interpolation, a defiantly exotic counterpoint to the classical urns and hedge-backed twin herbaceous borders on either side of the lawn. While the manicured lawn seems bizarrely out of place in this climate, the traditional borders have been given an exotic twist through the inclusion of native plants.

☛ Bannochie, Barlow, Johnston, Rhodes, Silva, Suarez, Thwaites

Sanchez & Maddux. Philip M Maddux. b Hopkinsville, KY (USA), 1942. Jorge A Sanchez de Ortigosa. b Havana (CU), 1948. Meister Garden, Palm Beach, FL (USA), 1996.

Sangram Singh Maharana of Uidapur — Saheliyon Ki Bari or 'Maids of Honour Garden'

The Maids of Honour Garden at Udaipur gracefully blends European and high Mughal garden-design features to create the distinctive late-Mughal style. As early as the seventeenth century, European traders were building their country mansions in India and naturally incorporated their national tastes into their architecture and garden design. The English brought the Brownian landscape with its rolling lawns and clumps of trees; the French preferred their formal display of geometrical flowerbeds and fountains. The gardens of the Indian princes, such as Maharana Sangram Singh, tended to copy many European fashions. Spacious lawns and large specimen trees are used in this garden to create a formal manmade landscape. Throughout the garden the play of water is dazzling – a broad chevron-patterned paved walk lined with water jets and channels (as pictured here), the use of falling water from the eves of a central circular Mughal-style pavilion, and a freestanding three-tiered fountain are a few of the dominant features.

☛ André, Babur, Brown, Jahangir, Forestier

399

Maharana Sangram Singh of Uidapur. Active (IN), eighteenth century. **Saheliyon Ki Bari or 'Maids of Honour Garden'**, Fateh Sagar Lake, Udaipur (IN), 1734.

Sargent Charles Sprague   Arnold Arboretum

This wooded glade is part of the 160-hectare (384-acre) site left to Harvard University by Benjamin Bussey in 1842 for use as a school of horticulture and agriculture. It was in 1872 that the eminent botanist Asa Gray, with the aid of a bequest from Hames Arnold, was able to transform the rolling farmland into an arboretum. Sargent, a former member of the Union Army and pupil of Gray's, was appointed professor and was able to persuade the landscape architect Frederick Law Olmsted to help in laying out the grounds, which formed a part of his 'emerald necklace' of municipal parks that encircled Boston. Sargent was clearly a persuasive man, for he also 'headhunted' the famous plant hunter Ernest Wilson from the Veitch Nursery in England in 1906. Wilson, who explored China and Japan (Sargent had visited Japan in 1892) on the arboretum's behalf, succeeded Sargent as the second professor or, as he titled himself, the 'Keeper'.

☛ Holford, Olmsted, Raffles, Veitch, Vilmorin, Williams

Charles Sprague Sargent. **b** Boston, MA (USA), 1841. **d** Boston, MA (USA), 1927. **Arnold Arboretum**, Boston, MA (USA), 1872.

Saunders Douglas   Amanzimnyama

Massed groupings of native plants create a bold abstract design at Amanzimnyama near Durban, South Africa. The garden was developed from the 1930s in the grounds of the Saunders' sugar-cane plantation house atop a hill. Douglas Saunders' grandmother, Katharine Saunders, was a noted orchidist and botanical artist, and he inherited her eye for colour and love of plants. The painter Gwelo Goodman also provided design advice. The idiosyncratic design style at Amanzimnyama incorporates massed groups of exotic plants such as cannas, brunfelsias, aloes and bougainvilleas, amid sweeping lawns, trees and a range of ponds, streams and cascades (Amanzimnyama is a Zulu word meaning 'black water'). There is a swamp garden, a Japanese garden, an orchid house, a finely planted main drive and a series of modern formal courtyards round the new house, headquarters of the sugar company, whose motto is 'Beauty Leads to Right Action'.

☛ Burle Marx, Cook, Jungles, Walling

Douglas Saunders. Amanzimnyama, Durban (SA), 1935–63.

Savill Eric

Savill Garden

Heathers, rhododendrons, azaleas, camellias and other acid-loving plants thrive at the 14-hectare (35-acre) Savill Garden, a plantsman's garden that also works as an informal landscape designed to show off the plants in a natural way. Eric Savill was deputy ranger of Windsor Great Park when, in 1932, he began to make a colourful woodland garden under the canopy of fine old oaks, beeches and pines. Today the Savill Garden is one of the best woodland gardens anywhere, with a vast range of species, including a large number of bog plants (ferns, primulas, lysichitons) by the stream which runs through the garden, and a famed narcissus display. The fine dry garden was the first of its kind to be made on this scale in the UK. The adjacent Valley Garden, begun by Savill in 1947, covers a much larger area, and has as its showpiece an azalea display, as well as notable collections of magnolias and rhododendrons.

☞ Chatto, Cook, McNab, Robinson

402

Sir Eric Savill. b (UK), 1895. d (UK), 1980. Savill Garden, Surrey (UK), 1932.

Scarpa Carlo

Garden of Rest, Brion-Vega Tomb

This uncompromisingly modern Garden of Rest is enclosed in a sharp, clearly delineated environment, although one can distinguish an underlying narrative and poetical approach which steers it away from arid functionalism. When he designed this private family tomb in the Cemetery of San Vito d'Ativole in 1970, the Italian architect Carlo Scarpa said he was trying 'to further what meaning there was in death, in the ephemerality of life'. Scarpa is perhaps better known for his many important historical restorations. Being Venetian born and bred may have predisposed him to think in terms of the historic fabric inherent to a place. He had an instinctive gift for combining the existing historic elements of a site with newly invented ones. He applied this approach successfully in a number of private gardens, as in the courtyard of the Castelvecchio museum in Verona. The Brion-Vega tomb was, however, most important to Scarpa, and he asked to be buried there. As he himself liked to say: 'The place for the dead is the garden.'

☛ Asplund, Brongniart, Girardin, Le Corbusier, Pückler-Muskau

Carlo Scarpa. b Venice (IT), 1906. **d** Sendai (JAP), 1978. **Garden of Rest, Brion-Vega Tomb**, Cemetery of San Vito d'Ativole, Treviso (IT), 1969–78.

Schaal Hans Dieter   Villa Moser-Liebfried

Wooden walkways lead to an inviting barrel-shaped arch, but the latticed structure, reminiscent of a grotto or an arbour, only opens on to a partial view of the overgrown garden. Further on, a circular belvedere reached via a footbridge is punctured by dozens of small apertures, allowing only restricted views. The elegant and – literally – superficial wooden structure goes on in this manner throughout the wilderness of the former gardens of the Liebfried-Moser Villa which were largely destroyed during World War II. Artist, architect and landscape designer Hans Dieter Schaal meant to leave this intriguing but essentially unremarkable place untouched, while carefully directing the visitor's gaze and leading us on a contemplative journey. To Schaal this illustrates one of 'only two ways in approaching the world and the landscape: actively or comtemplatively'. He illustrated the other choice with an intensely architectural and narratively loaded urnfield in the Singen cemetery.

☞ **Asplund, Dow, Geuze, Lassus, Tschumi**

Hans Dieter Schaal. b Ulm (GER), 1943. **Villa Moser-Liebfried**, Stuttgart (GER), 1993.

Schwartz Martha

Dickenson Garden

The entrance courtyard at the Dickenson Garden in Santa Fe, New Mexico, is a modern update of the geometric Islamic tradition. Four raised brick plinths containing small fountains are connected by brightly coloured, tiled runnels. Nine flowering crab-apple trees embedded in large chunks of white Colorado marble complete the grid-like effect, which is especially effective at night. On the other side of the modern adobe house, views over wide-open desert spaces open up from a terrace. 'It's kind of like a Frank Lloyd Wright thing,' Schwartz explains. 'You create a pressurized space, then you are released by the wider landscape.' Schwartz is one of the most consistently innovative and iconoclastic landscape artists working today. Recent works include New York's Jacob Javits Plaza and the Marina Linear Park in San Diego, but her most famous work is probably the 1979 Bagel Garden, for which Schwartz adorned her own tiny Boston front yard with real varnished bagels.

☞ Barragán, Cao, Delaney, Muhammad V, Nazarite, F L Wright

Martha Schwartz. b (USA). **Dickenson Garden**, Santa Fe, NM (USA), 1982.

Sckell Friedrich Ludwig von   Englischer Garten

The Monopteros, the white Ionic temple which crowns a steep artificial mound in Munich's Englischer Garten, was given by King Ludwig I of Bavaria in 1837. It is the most harmonious of the architectural features in the 370-hectare (888-acre) civic park which begins in the centre of Munich and stretches for some 5 km (3 miles) up the valley of the River Isar. The park was laid out from 1789 onwards by Friedrich Ludwig von Sckell, a disciple of Capability Brown and an admirer of neo-classicism. Since it was intended purely for public recreation, the Englischer Garten may be regarded as the oldest public park in Germany. It is not attached to a palace or public building: the landscaping provides its own momentum and direction. It is beautifully shaped in the English style with clumps of trees, mainly beech, extending the whole way up the wide valley. Ever since it was built, the park has been well used by the people of Munich.

☞ Brown, Chambers, Grenville-Temple, Hirschfeld

Friedrich Ludwig von Sckell. b Weilburg (GER), 1750. **d** Munich (GER), 1823. **Englischer Garten**, Munich (GER), 1789–.

Seinsheim Adam Friedrich von Veitshöchheim Hofgarten

Several layers of Baroque gardening are represented in this view of the Pegasus fountain in the Grosser See at the Bishops' Garden at Veitshöchheim. The formal lake was laid out in 1703. Beyond is a complex design of high hornbeam hedges and alleys of bleached limes, first planted in the 1720s. The huge winged horse of Pegasus rears up to fly heavenwards and is surrounded by statues of Apollo. The sculptures and the nine Muses on Mount Parnassus, which were added in 1765, were the work of Ferdinand Dietz, whose studios produced some 300 statues for the garden, infinitely inventive and entertaining. Dietz worked in collaboration with the head gardener Johann Prokop Mayer, but most of the credit for turning Veitshöchheim into the most enchanting and famous rococo garden in Germany should go to Prince-Bishop Adam Friedrich von Seinsheim, who commissioned the work.

☛ Le Blond, Peter II, Robins, Sackville-West, Sophia

Adam Friedrich von Seinsheim (Prince-Bishop of Würzburg). b Regensburg (GER), 1708. d (GER), 1779. Veitshöchheim Hofgarten, nr Würzburg, Bavaria (GER), mostly created during 1703–65.

Sennacherib

Hanging Gardens of Babylon

Recent research has indicated that it was Sennacherib of Assyria rather than Nebuchadnezzar II of Babylon who built the Hanging Gardens of Babylon, at his palace at Nineveh in ancient Mesopotamia (now northern Iraq). This watercolour view is a romantic evocation of descriptions of the gardens by Roman eyewitness writers, including Strabo and Diodorus Siculus. All these descriptions mention the impressive trees, and several the mechanical irrigation system which called for a series of artifical terraces to allow the water to flow down in runnels. It is now believed that the gardens were sited at the edge of the city overlooking the Khosr River. Sennacherib installed the sophisticated watering mechanism, planted exotic trees brought back from conquests, dedicated the gardens to his wife and described them as 'a wonder for all peoples'.

☛ Allah, Assurbanipal, Judeo-Christian God, Tibernitus

Serlio Sebastiano

Ancy-le-Franc

The design and layout of Ancy-le-Franc were considered innovative in their day because, for the first time in France, the house and its garden had been designed as a whole. It is clear from this bird's-eye view that both house and garden were axially aligned along the same central perspective. It was this unity and symmetry which distinguished Ancy-le-Franc. The example was, however, much copied throughout Europe, largely through the influence of Serlio's eight-volume treatise on classical architecture, *Tutte l'opere d'architettura*, which was reprinted several times and translated into all the major European languages. In it, Serlio expounded the principles of Vitruvius and set out detailed specifications for both buildings and gardens. Serlio was first summoned from Italy by Francis I in about 1540, but he started on Ancy-le-Franc in 1546 for Antoine de Clermont, the brother-in-law of Henri II's mistress, Diane de Poitiers. His parterre designs were widely copied well into the seventeenth century.

☞ Bramante, Carvallo, Gallard, L'Orme, Wise

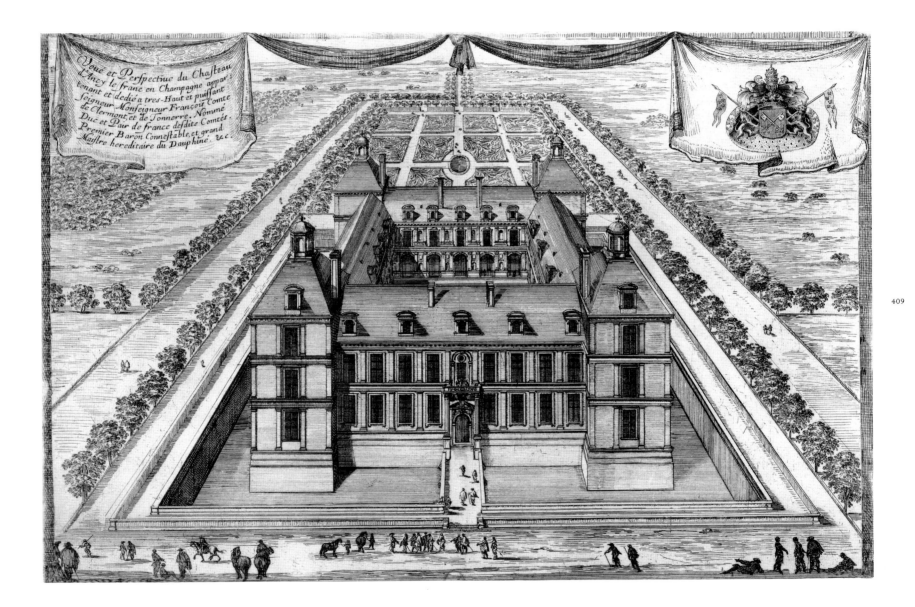

Sebastiano Serlio. b Bologna (IT), 1475. **d** Fontainebleau (FR), 1554. **Ancy-le-Franc**, Tonnerre (FR), seventeenth century, engraving by Israel Sylvestre, c1650.

Shah Jahan

Taj Mahal

Mumtaz Mahal's tomb reflected in the still waters of the courtyard pool has been described as a spiritually transporting, ethereal vision. Beneath the main central arch an Arabic inscription carved in black marble reads: 'Only the pure of heart are invited to enter this Garden of Paradise.' Yet beyond the enchantment of her tomb, it is important to note that the grounds surrounding it as well as the outer buildings combine to form a complex and highly symbolic design. The overall plan is simple: it is a Babur-inspired *chahar-bagh*. What distinguishes the Taj from all other famous Mughal tombs is the placement of the beautifully raised white marble tank in the centre of the four-fold parterre. Previously, funerary gardens featured the tomb building in the centre of the parterre. It is believed that Shah Jahan may have drawn his ideas from Hindu influences, inherited from his Rajputani mother. Using the banks of the Jumna River as the perch for this pearly paradisaical site, a spectacle is made of Lord Vishnu's lotus lilies in the reflecting pools.

☞ Almohad, Babur, Girardin, Jahangir, Scarpa

Shah Jahan. b Agra (IN), 1592. d Agra (IN), 1666. **Taj Mahal**, Agra (IN), 1632–54.

Shenstone William The Leasowes

This watercolour view by the poet and landowner William Shenstone is of the hermitage in his garden, The Leasowes, Halesowen. The figure in the foreground appears to be the hermit himself, a fanciful addition that chimes with the whimsical atmosphere of the place. Shenstone built the garden, on modest means, to ornament the working fields surrounding his farmhouse between 1740 and his death in 1763. It consisted of a varied, circular walk along two wooded combes, relieved by open pastureland, seats and small buildings. It was a solid realization of Shenstone's fanciful verse, evocative of a classical pastoral idyll. Shenstone posted his own verses, written on pine boards, at strategic points along the garden route. The largest building, the Ruined Priory, was demolished in 1965. For its originality (and the owner's known eccentricity), The Leasowes became one of the most famous and much-visited gardens of the time. The Leasowes is currently undergoing complete restoration by the local council.

☞ Girardin, Hamilton Finlay, Hoare, Lotti, Southcote

William Shenstone. b (UK), 1714. **d** Halerowen (UK), 1763. **The Leasowes**, Halesowen, West Midlands (UK), 1745.

Shigemori Mirei   Tofuku-ji

A field of white sand, finely raked in a criss-cross pattern, fills a transitional space in the Tofuku-ji gardens. Of the four modern gardens redesigned in 1940, after a fire ruined the Zen monastery, the most famous is the South Garden. There, on the patterned white gravel, four groups of large rocks form a striking vertical/horizontal composition, while five low mossy mounds crouch in the opposite corner. Though the classical syntax of Japanese gardens is followed almost to the letter, a profound sense of modernity and individuality reigns is this masterpiece by Mirei Shigemori. His immense influence was compounded by his authority as a historian and theoretician. Shigemori argued that, after centuries of inspired and supreme mastery, Japanese garden design fell into decline when it became the attribute of professional designers. To counteract the subsequent dryness and emptiness, Shigemori returned the garden to its original status as an integral and specific work of art, never to be repeated or copied.

☞ Enshu, Mandokora, Noguchi, Ogawa, Rikkyu, Soami

412

Mirei Shigemori. Active (JAP), twentieth century. Tofuku-ji, Kyoto (JAP), 1940.

Shipman Ellen Biddle   Longue Vue House

The long *allée* from the house culminates in a circular pool which is part of a water garden inspired by the Generalife in Granada. The clipped yew borders on either side of the *allée* are planted with perennials, including roses. Longue Vue House was built in 1941 by Mrs Stern as an adaptation of a late eighteenth-century English country house. The gardens designed by Ellen Biddle Shipman were started in the mid-1920s, on Mrs Stern's arrival, and represented a mixture of European styles creating a contrast with the native swamplands of New Orleans. All the gardens are influenced by the European tradition. The wild garden, for example, is a reference to the Italian *bosco*. Leading on from it is a French potager, or formal vegetable garden. Ellen Shipman was aware of Mrs Stern's passion for things European and the walk around the 2.8 hectares (7 acres) of the Longue Vue gardens is carefully considered to reflect this.

☞ **Emma, Manning, Nazarite, Steele, Vignola, Washington-Smith**

413

Ellen Biddle Shipman. b 1869. **d** 1950. **Longue Vue House**, New Orleans, LA (USA), mid-1920s.

Shoden-ji Sensai of

A path bordered by maples and pines leads off to a distant pavilion, the entrance to the Shoden-ji garden. Inside the walls, near the *hojo* or abbot's quarters, lies the dry Zen temple garden, or sensai. It is often linked to the famous Ryoan-ji as it, too, contains a mere fifteen objects placed on a rectangle of white gravel and designed to be seen from a fixed vantage point. In the Shoden-ji, however, the objects in the composition are not stones but mounds of clipped azalea shrubs, a feature known as *karokomi*. They give this relatively small garden (343 sq yards) a particularly sensuous character. Set off by the whiteness of the end wall, the contrasting heights and shapes of the shrubs form a rhythmic counterpoint to the powerful image of Mount Hiei which can be seen clearly in the distance, beyond the treetops. A high expression of *shakkei*, Shoden-ji cannot be linked to any particular designer but, like the nearby Entsu-ji, it almost certainly belongs to the early Edo era, around 1680.

☛ **Egerton, Enshu, Hornel, Ogawa, Rikkyu, Toshihito**

414

Sensai of Shoden-ji. Active (JAP), seventeenth century. **Shoden-ji**, Kyoto (JAP), c1680.

Shurcliff Arthur A

Colonial Williamsburg

The individual gardens of Williamsburg, with their box-edged beds and narrow brick paths, as well as their mixture of topiary, flowers, vegetables and fruit, were an inspiration for small-scale twentieth-century garden design. The restoration of the eighteenth-century colonial capital of Virginia, funded by John D Rockefeller Jnr, encompassed approximately ninety individual gardens as well as the planting of entire streets, squares and public parks in what was one of the major garden restorations of the twentieth century. Begun in 1930, it pioneered the use of garden archaeology and historically derived planting schemes. Although the results were far from authentic, the immaculate townscape is nevertheless successful on its own terms. The restoration's landscape architect, Arthur Shurcliff, was working for the City of Boston when he was engaged in 1928. He was succeeded in the 1940s by Alden Hopkins.

☛ Hosack, Jefferson, Landsberg, Post, Sloane, Washington

Arthur A Shurcliff (Shurtleff). b Boston (USA), 1870. d 1957. **Colonial Williamsburg**, Williamsburg, VA (USA), 1930.

Silva Roberto

Forsters Garden

This London garden was Brazilian designer Roberto Silva's first major commission. A sinuous drystone wall snakes round a cherry tree and fountain in a painterly arc before encircling a timber deck. The orange-yellow gravel contrasts with the green lawn, and Silva's planting consists mainly of shrubs and trees chosen for their foliage effects – eucalyptus, maples, tree ferns. The slate wall and fountain of three boulder stacks were inspired by the work of sculptor Andy Goldsworthy. Randomly arranged in the gravel is a collection of flat stone slabs, and hidden beyond the deck is amplification equipment – the garden is a venue for family concerts. Silva trained in Brazil, where he was naturally influenced by the work of Roberto Burle Marx, and then worked on public park restoration in São Paolo. He came to train in London in 1992, where he has mainly 'English gardened', as he puts it, for metropolitan clients.

☛ Burle Marx, Church, Goldsworthy, Jensen, Oehme & Van Sweden

Roberto Silva. b Recife (BR), 1964. **Forsters Garden**, London (UK), 1999.

Sitta Vladimir

Smith Residence

Black bamboo (*Phyllostachys nigra*) and tufts of mondo grass border a simple rectangular pool that culminates in a relief sculpture. At this private Sydney garden, Vladimir Sitta has created a formal space with a strong Japanese tone. The Czechoslovakian-born designer has emerged over the last decade as one of the leading avant-garde designers currently working in Australia. His work often incorporates geologically inspired elements, such as fissures cracking through otherwise pristine stone, artificial mist and monolithic slabs. In the Smith Residence garden, two jagged spears of stone bisect the the reflections of the pool and lend it an elemental quality that compromises what would otherwise be an example of pristine Modernism. In the best Japanese tradition, Sitta explores this tension between order and untamed nature. Sitta's garden designs will be amongst the most closely followed of the next decade.

☞ Herman, Latz, Lutsko, Toll

Vladimir Sitta. b (CZ). **Smith Residence**, Sydney (ASL), 1991.

Sitwell Sir George   Renishaw Hall

Renishaw's gardens teach us that structure is more important than flowers: indeed, the flowers here are not part of Sir George Sitwell's original design. Sitwell was a distinguished scholar and connoisseur, whose essay, 'The Making of Gardens' (1909) was written in emulation of Francis Bacon's essay 'Of Gardens' (1625). His knowledge of Italian gardens was unrivalled – he visited over 200 in the course of his researches – so it is not surprising that Sitwell employed the Italian style when he remade the gardens of his ancestral seat at Renishaw in the 1890s. Sitwell believed that 'the formal garden in England falls short of the great examples of the Italian Renaissance; it is seldom related as it should be to the surrounding scenery; it is often wanting in repose and nearly always in imagination'. He stressed the importance of wonder and surprise, harmony and contrast, the refreshing presence of water: all are wonderfully acknowledged at Renishaw.

☞ Acton, Blomfield, Peto, Pinsent, Tilden

Sir George Sitwell. b Renishaw, Derbyshire (UK), 1860. **d** Locarno, Ticino (IT), 1943. **Renishaw Hall**, Derbyshire (UK), 1890s.

Sloane Sir Hans

Chelsea Physic Garden

This plan shows an attractive arrangement of rectangular beds, which would have held collections of plants gathered together by their medicinal use, or as part of a pre-Linnean (Latin) classification system. The garden was established in 1673 by the Society of Apothecaries for the purpose of teaching students the pharmacological uses of different plants, hence the name 'Physic'.

In 1722 the garden was rescued from its financial difficulties by the generous patronage of Sir Hans Sloane, physician to George I and plant collector, who had bought the Manor of Chelsea from Lord Cheyne in 1712. Sloane also installed as curator Philip Miller, whose dedication ensured that it became the most richly stocked botanic garden in the world. One plant in the garden, *Sophora*

microphylla, is a direct descendant of the original introduction grown from seed brought back from New Zealand by Sir Joseph Banks, another great patron of the garden. The current layout dates from the late nineteenth century.

☞ **Carvallo, Landsberg, La Quintinie, Moroni, Roper**

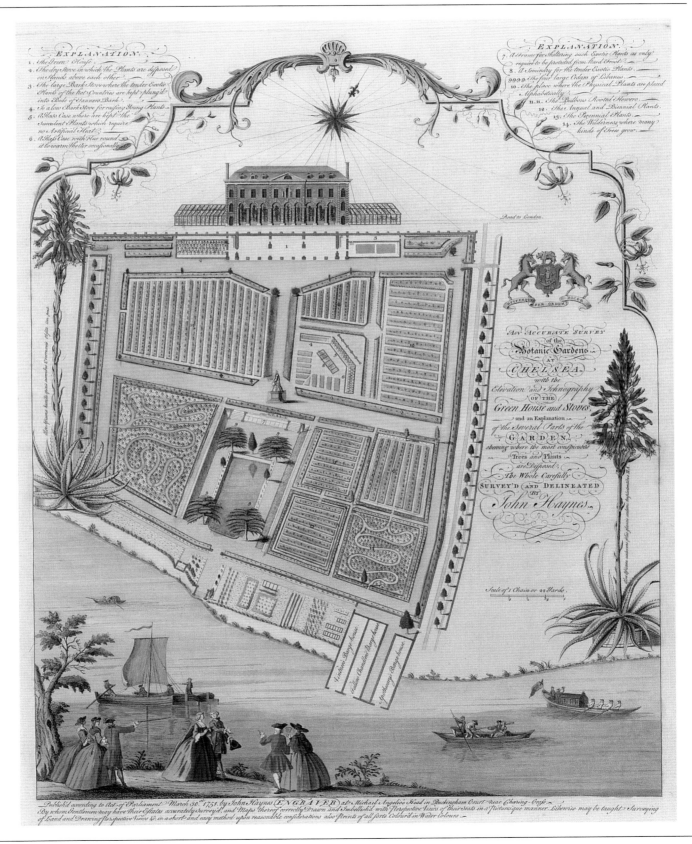

Sir Hans Sloane. b (IRE), 1660. **d** (UK), 1753. **Chelsea Physic Garden**, London (UK), established 1673, restored 1722.

Smit Tim

The Lost Gardens of Heligan

Fallen tree trunks evoke a sense of prehistory in the Jungle Garden, a lush subtropical landscape of giant bamboos, primaeval tree ferns and mysterious pools. Heligan, in Cornwall, is a time-capsule garden. Laid out during the eighteenth and nineteenth centuries by the Tremayne family, it was neglected for much of the last century. Then, in 1990, archaeologist-turned-record-producer Tim Smit cut through the 5 m (15 ft) high brambles with a machete and began uncovering a garden that had lain unchanged for almost a hundred years. Smit and his team have turned Heligan into one of the most visited private gardens in Britain, partly by shrewd marketing and partly by cleverly preserving something of the garden's feeling of being 'lost'. The 32-hectare (80-acre) site includes a vertiginous ravine, a charming Italian Garden, a grotto and some magnificent rhododendrons. The working areas include a walled vegetable garden with a pineapple pit heated by manure.

☛ Dunmore, Grimshaw, McKenzie, Sturdza, Williams

420

Tim Smit. b (NL), 1954. **The Lost Gardens of Heligan**, Pentewan, Cornwall (UK), 1990.

Smith Augustus

Tresco Abbey Gardens

Sheltered from Atlantic gales behind a belt of trees, the vast collection of rare, exotic and tender plants imbues the garden with an air of subtropical luxuriance. Augustus Smith, who began the gardens in 1834, terraced the steeply sloping site and introduced paths that wind along the natural contours or plunge steeply downwards. Plants from the Southern Hemisphere, especially Australasia, are particularly well represented amongst the collection, which looks very much at home covering the rocky slopes. In many ways, Smith's collector's mentality was typical of the Victorian era, when floral mania gripped the well-to-do, as plant hunters introduced thousands of new species from all around the world. And while Smith gathered plants that thrived in the mild microclimate of Tresco, others collected plants from a particular geographic location, or specific botanical groups – favourites included rhododendrons, conifers, ferns and orchids. Smith died in 1872 and the family continues to care for the garden to this day.

☛ Burley Griffin, Mackenzie, Middleton, Williams

Augustus Smith. d 1872. **Tresco Abbey Gardens**, Isles of Scilly (UK), 1834.

Smithers Peter   Villa Smithers

New magnolia hybrids flower in the garden at Vico Morcote, which has a spectacular setting on a precipitous slope overlooking Lake Lugano. A contemporary Japanese-style house has been designed as two wings linked by a bridge spanning a mountain torrent. In addition to growing new magnolia hybrids, Sir Peter has pioneered the introduction of many other plants to Europe. Chief among these are new plants from contemporary Asia, especially Japan – extraordinary paeonies, wisterias, hostas and irises. Sir Peter has himself bred many new varieties of nerine. The use of new plant varieties, with their new forms, colours and textures, allows a gardener to compose 'pictures' with a new and exciting palette quite different from the garden 'pictures' composed with the familiar palette of traditional plants. The principles of the garden's management are described in Sir Peter's book *The Adventures of a Gardener*.

☞ **Hanbury, Middleton, Miller, Savill**

Sir Peter Smithers. b 1913. **Villa Smithers**, Vico Morcote, Lugano (SW).

Smyth Ted

Sanders Garden

A swimming pool with jagged geometric edges, focused on a stainless steel tubular sculpture, complements a pure white 1980s Modernist house in this New Zealand garden. The smooth, elegant curve of the retaining wall beyond, hemming in a range of subtropical plants (cycads, aloes, dragon trees) produces a satisfying contrast in what is a wide, shallow garden. The designer,

Ted Smyth, is little known outside New Zealand, and professes no interest in the design scene. He has created a tranquil space using stainless steel, marble, stone and large-leaved plants. 'I like the anonymity and modernity of materials,' Smyth explains. 'They shouldn't be too animated like terracotta, brass or gold, which are like busy, noisy animals. In order to create serenity and spatial

quality you have to reduce the personality of the materials.' At night the garden is lit in eerie blue light, creating reflections in the still pool.

☞ Bradley-Hole, Le Corbusier, Noguchi, Pearson, Sitta, Watson

Ted Smyth. Sanders Garden, Auckland (NZ), 1996.

Soami

Ryoan-ji

Fifteen stones, 332 sq m (400 sq yds) of raked sand and a brown wall: perhaps the most perfect of all dry landscape gardens, the Ryoan-ji, remains untouched and retains its mystery after more than five centuries. No plants, no water and no contours distract from its rigorous simplicity. Are we seeing islands on a symbolic sea, wild animals crossing a stretch of water? Or should we just suspend thought and let ourselves be transported by the unique beauty of this garden? Assembled in five groups, the stones are placed and balanced with ultimate precision. Supreme awareness and deep meditation are palpable even to the lay visitor, unfamiliar with the mysteries of Zen. Established in 1473 by the powerful Lord Hosokawa Masamoto, the temple garden was built by a crew of 'river men', the *kawara-mono* craftsmen who would eventually become Japan's professional garden designers. Tradition has it that the landscape painter Soami found there the ultimate canvas for his art, but other scholars believe an unknown zen master was responsible.

☞ **Enshu, Kokushi, Ogawa, Shigemori, Tadayoshi**

424

Song Zenhuang

Wang Shi Yuan

Around the rocky edge of this tiny lake a wealth of buildings, bridges and courtyards seem to beckon, enticing the visitor to cross the seemingly short distance. But the Master of the Fishing Nets' Garden is a tangle of zigzagging walkways, hidden bamboo groves and secret courtyards. The visitor is led along, slightly disorientated, to discover unexpected vistas. One of the most elaborate and subtle gardens in Suzhou, the Wang Shi Yuan has a complicated history. It was built in 1140 by a scholar official to house his huge private library of more than 10,000 scrolls. At his death the garden seems to have been abandoned and only came back to life when, in 1760, Song Zenhuang a vice-director of Imperial Entertainment at the court of Qian Long, decided to rebuild it to his own design. A second era of neglect after Song's death was followed by successive waves of rebuilding and improvement by a long series of owners, but always to harmonious effect.

☞ Wang Xian Chen, Xu Shi-tai, Yi Song Gye, Zhang Yue

Song Zenhuang. Active (CHN), eighteenth century. Wang Shi Yuan, Suzhou (CHN), 1760.

Sophia Electress of Hanover   Herrenhausen

This is part of the Grand Parterre at Herrenhausen, designed and laid out in the 1680s by Electress Sophia of Hannover, the mother of George I of England. The elaborate vases and sculptures represent gods, seasons, virtues and continents: all are painted bright white to protect the soft sandstone from a north-German winter – it also makes them stand out brilliantly against the parterres. The beds are richly planted in the modern style, with seasonal bedding. The Grand Parterre at Herrenhausen is some 200 sq m (238 sq yds). Indeed, the whole garden is conceived on an enormous scale as a statement of power by the wife of Germany's most military prince. Sophia described the gardens at Herrenhausen as her life's work. She died there, of a sudden heart attack, in June 1714. Had she survived two more months, she would have become queen of England.

☞ Friedrich I, Heinrich, Lotti, Marot & Roman, Peter II, Wise

Princess Sophia of the Palatinate (Electress of Hanover). b The Hague (NL), 1630. d Herrenhausen (GER), 1714. **Herrenhausen**, Hanover (GER), 1680s.

Sørensen Carl Theodor · University of Aarhus

This amphitheatre was Sørensen's design solution to a change in level on the site at the University of Aarhus, Denmark. The screen between the amphitheatre and the university buildings is of oak trees. Sørensen's vision was to create a university set in an oak grove. Over the course of his career, Sørensen designed six green amphitheatres in Denmark, each of them slightly different.

Concentric circles were among many geometric forms that he used repeatedly in a career spanning over 2,000 commissions. As well as public sites like this campus, he designed many smaller gardens. His broad range as a designer, and his work as a teacher and author, earnt him a reputation as the father of modern landscape architecture in Denmark and an influence throughout Scandinavia.

He is also credited with the invention of the adventure playground, which he explored in his book *Park Politics in Parish and Borough*, written in 1931.

☛ Cane, Jakobsen, Jencks, Larsson, Wilkie

Carl Theodor Sørensen. b (GER), 1893. **d** 1979. **University of Aarhus**, Aarhus (DK), 1960s.

Southcote Philip

Woburn Farm

In 1712 Joseph Addison had enjoined landowners to embellish their estates, so 'a Man might make a pretty landskip of his own Possessions', and in the 1730s Philip Southcote was in a position to follow the advice literally. The happy intermixing of practical farming and landscape gardening was an essential tenet of the early landscape movement. At Southcote's influential *ferme ornée* he made a circuit walk of his estate, lined with a flowerbed, 'for convenience as well as pleasure: for from the garden I could see what was doing in the grounds'. He diverted a stream to create a winding waterway and added small garden structures, including a grotto (seen on the right). Southcote's example caused several gentleman farmers (notably Shenstone) to decorate their estates similarly, though in more modest fashion. By the late eighteenth century, the *ferme ornée* idea had waned: the only aspects of a working farm Capability Brown allowed in the designed landscape were grazing livestock on decorous pasture.

☛ Bridgeman, Burlington, Caruncho, Kent, Pope, Shenstone

Philip Southcote. b (UK), 1698. **d** (UK), 1758. **Woburn Farm**, Surrey (UK), 1735.

Stanislas II King of Poland Lazienki Park

The palace at Lazienki was developed on an island, and two formal stretches of water north and south of the site became large irregular pools when Poniatowski transformed the Ujazdów hunting-ground into an outstanding pleasure park. From the amphitheatre, adorned with fine sculpture, by the side of the pool, an audience of a thousand could view the stage on the small island across a narrow strip of water. Among the romantic buildings in the park, the simple wooden Turkish House surprised visitors with its palatial interior. There were two pavilions for the king's mistresses, while another served as a *seraglio* for his guests. The gardener Jan Chrystian Schuch and the architects Jan Chrystian Kamsetzer and Dominik Merlini helped create Lazienki in what became known as the Stanislas Augustus style. Even after his exile to St Petersburg in 1796, Poniatowski continued to send directions for work at Lazienki.

☛ **Brandt, Hirschfeld, Joséphine, Radziwill, Tyers**

King Stanislas II of Poland (Stanislas Augustus Poniatowski). b Woteyn (POL), 1732. **d** St Petersburg (RUS), 1798. **Lazienki Park**, outskirts of Warsaw (POL), *Palace and Lake in Lazienki Park*, watercolour, by Zygmunt Vogel, 1796.

Mabel Choate's request for some simple steps to help her climb the slope to her vegetable garden at Naumkeag, Massachusetts, produced an icon of twentieth-century garden design. In the Blue Steps, created in the 1920s, Fletcher Steele interpreted a classic Renaissance form in a strikingly modern way. A series of blue-painted concrete arches, flanked by double flights of stairs and sweeping Art-Deco-style railings, climb between the gleaming white trunks of silver birches. The birches contrast beautifully with the symmetry of the architecture. Water cascades through the arches as in an Italian water staircase. Steele had a classical Beaux-arts training but admired the contemporary French garden designers Vera, Legrain and Guevrékian. He worked at Naumkeag (an Indian word meaning 'Haven of Peace') from 1925 until the late 1950s, adding an eclectic range of features, including a Chinese pagoda and moon gate, a green garden, and a rose garden of scalloped beds.

☞ **Gaudí, Guevrékian, Legrain, Vera, Vignola**

Fletcher Steele. b (USA), 1885. **d** (USA), 1971. **Naumkeag**, Stockbridge, MA (USA), 1925.

Steven Christian

Nikitsky Botanic Garden

A distinctive pavilion, surrounded by yuccas and cacti, sits in the shade of an Aleppo pine with a cypress avenue beyond. Situated by the Black Sea with a near-Mediterranean climate, the Nikitsky Botanic Garden is both an important scientific institution and a garden of great beauty with a wide range of plants. Cypresses, sequoias, North American pines and cedars stand out among the trees, and there are some 2,000 species and varieties of rose. Ornamental water features include pools of water-lilies and a water staircase. The Swedish botanist Christian Steven laid the foundations of the garden between 1812 and 1827, when he was succeeded as director by N A Hartvis who continued its development until his death in 1860. The garden was a vital source of plants for the great parks which were then being developed in the Crimea – Alupka, Livadia, Massandra and Gurzuf among them.

☛ Chambers, Kebach, Moroni, Otruba

Christian Steven. b (SWE). **d** Yalta (RUS), 1827. **Nikitsky Botanic Garden**, nr Yalta (RUS), 1812–27.

Strong Sir Roy & Oman Dr Julia Trevelyan   The Laskett

A gold-antlered stag is one of many surprises in the intensely personal, autobiographical garden of Sir Roy Strong and his wife, the theatre designer Dr Julia Trevelyan Oman. The 1.8 hectare (4.5-acre) garden is a series of thirty-two rooms, corridors and ante-chambers, contained by high yew, leylandii and beech hedges which effectively cut out the rest of the world. The garden has

been built up gradually, section by section, since the 1960s. Punctuating it are monuments commemorating aspects of the couple's life – a temple is a reminder of Sir Roy's directorship of the Victoria & Albert Museum, for example. A knot garden just behind the house is testament to Sir Roy's pioneering work in garden history and championing of formality in small spaces

during the 1980s. The biographical elements enhance rather than compromise the garden's design strengths, which are the evocation of atmosphere and the manipulation of perspective. The garden is further enriched by an organic kitchen garden.

☞ Carter, Hamilton Finlay, Lloyd

Sir Roy Strong. b London (UK), 1935. Dr Julia Trevelyan Oman. The Laskett, Hertfordshire (UK), c1960–.

Sturdza Princess Greta   La Vasterival

A plant paradise where thousands of species thrive in a benevolent atmosphere, the garden of Vasterival near the shores of the Atlantic in Normandy is a world apart. It is blessed with a very mild climate, owing to the shelter of gentle hills and dense, fertile woodland. Each season brings ever-changing richness to the balanced and remarkable combinations of perennials throughout the 7-hectare (16.8-acre) garden. It is hard to say whether the plants dictate the design or whether the design skilfully follows their lead. The soul of this plant paradise is Norwegian-born Princess Sturdza who, since 1957, has dedicated her life to this project. The only way to visit and experience Vasterival is on one of the tours she personally leads through her realm. With her passion and extensive knowledge, she touches the lives of many garden-lovers, and has become quite a renowned figure, both in France and abroad.

☛ Bawa, Copeland & Lighty, Mallet, Wolkonsky

433

Princess Greta Sturdza. b (NOR). **La Vasterival**, nr Dieppe (FR), 1957–.

Suarez Diego

Vizcaya

The Italian Renaissance style had an overriding influence on the flamboyant villa and grounds made for the industrialist James Deering in Miami. Four men – Deering as owner, Diego Suarez as landscape architect, Paul Chalfin as interior designer, Francis Burrall Hoffman Jr as architect – shared a passion for the period and for the houses and gardens of Italy, and together they created a successfully unified if utterly incongruous design. Originally the site covered over 72.8 hectares (180 acres) but its current area is around 12.1 hectares (30 acres). A large fan-shaped formal garden extends from the south of the house, with low clipped hedges and walled terraces. A water stairway, shell-lined grottoes, sculptures, urns and pools create a pastiche of an Italian-Renaissance garden. The planting of the garden, however, includes tropical species native to the USA. Suarez had worked alongside Arthur Acton during the restoration of the Villa La Pietra in Florence.

☞ Acton, Ligorio, Mizner, Pfeiffer, Vignola, Washington-Smith

434

Diego Suarez. b 1888. **d** 1974. **Vizcaya**, Miami, FL (USA), 1914–21.

Sulla

Praeneste

On the hillside site of a pre-Roman temple dated to the seventh or eighth century, the Roman architect Sulla developed the Praeneste, the gardens and temple of Fortuna Virilis in 82 BC. This measured drawing and reconstruction of the site by Andrea Palladio in the 1560s illustrates the grand scale of the temple and its ten terraces. These phenomenal terraces – the lowest of which was 400 m (1,312 ft) long – were linked by ramps and staircases reaching the summit of the temple at 160 m (525 ft). The use of expansive porticos, and the architectonic order that the terracing placed on the hillside site, served as great inspirations to later Italian garden designers, most notably Hadrian in his Villa at Tivoli, and later Roman Renaissance proponents such as Bramante at his Belvedere Court. Little remains of the structure, and the planting scheme can only be speculated upon. In keeping with other ancient Roman gardens, such as those found at Pompeii, the terrace porticos were probably decorated with wall frescoes, reliefs, mosaics and classical statuary.

☛ Bramante, Hadrian, Kent, Palladio, Raphael, Tibernitus

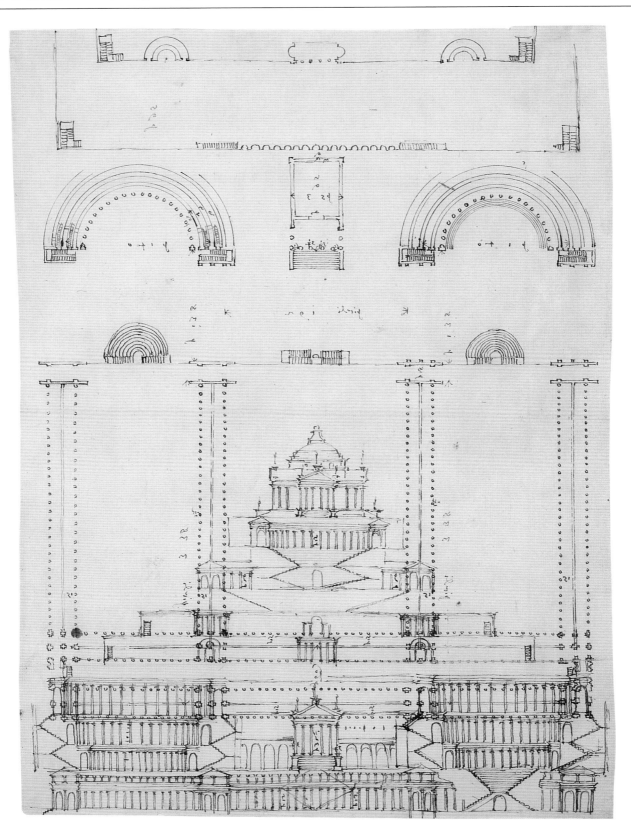

Sulla. b (IT), 138 BC. d (IT), 78 BC. Praeneste (now Palestrina), Lazio (IT), 82 BC.

Suraj Mal Raja of Bharatpur   The Moonlight Gardens and Palace at Dig

The main palace at Dig, Agra, shows its broad terrace overlooking a vast four-part parterre and a sunken water tank studded with elegantly carved fountain heads. Following the decline of the Mughals, the great Hindu palace builders of the seventeenth and eighteenth centuries revived the tradition of Indian garden-making. Foremost among these builders was Suraj Mal, Maharaja of Bharatpur, who began construction of his garden palace at Dig in 1725. Built on a level site, he adopted the Mughal *chahar-bagh* courtyard layout and fanciful water-garden features such as fountains and swimming pools. Many of the decorative marble garden features were looted from earlier Mughal palaces, including the lovely white-marble arched swing. The Moonlight Gardens were designed to be enjoyed after dark. The rooftop terraces were used for evening promenades and courtly ladies enjoyed the cool evening air in their pavilions or swam in the pools beneath the trees.

☞ Almohad, Akbar, Jahangir, Sangram Singh

Suraj Mal, Raja of Bharatpur. d 1768. **The Moonlight Gardens and Palace at Dig** (IN), c1725.

Su Zimei

Cang Lang Ting

An elegant *lou chuang* window opens on to an interior corridor of the Surging Wave Pavilion Gardens. Such windows were important framing devices in Chinese gardens. The Cang Lang Ting is one of the oldest gardens in Suzhou and has been so miraculously preserved that it still resembles the drawing its creator, the scholar and poet Su Zimei, made when he designed the garden in 1044.

Carved on to a black stone, which still stands at the entrance to the garden, the plan shows a bird's-eye view of a sprawling network of walls, buildings and corridors at the centre of which is a large artificial mountain. Here, as in most Suzhou gardens, the characteristic stones come from nearby Lake Taihu. These rocks are naturally moulded in the most extraordinary shapes and perforated by a plethora of holes, combining qualities of airiness and transparency with solidity and strength. Cang Lang Ting has no surrounding wall but is bordered by a canal which is borrowed in the design.

☞ Wang Xian Chen, Xu Shi-tai, Yi Song Gye, Zhang Shi

Su Zimei. Active (CHN), early eleventh century. **Cang Lang Ting**, Suzhou (CHN), 1044.

Suzuki Shodo

Private Garden, Chichibu

Asymmetrical and rectilinear, this stone stream occupies most of the space in the garden of a private residence in Chichibu. This assured and superbly simple design plays on almost imperceptible but dramatic changes of levels, with the strong horizontals emphasized further by the flat-topped stones. In this perfectly balanced composition, the placement and treatment of the stones denotes a superior understanding of the material. Combined with water and a few well-chosen plants, they provide the complete, age-old tools of the traditional Japanese garden designer and Shodo Suzuki doesn't feel the need to expand on it in this small garden. Inside these parameters, however, Suzuki conjures up radically new designs, and a whole new language. Widely influential, he designed many public spaces in Japan, sometimes using unexpected materials, but always espousing the same simple techniques and basic aesthetic precepts.

☞ Ando, Enshu, Lutsko, Noguchi, Shigemori

438

Sventenius Eric   Jardin Canario

Jardin Canario is a contemporary native-plant garden enlivened by statuary, in which a variety of plant habitats are created to mimic in miniature the natural habitats of the Canary Islands so that a representative collection of the region's unique flora can be grown for conservation and educational purposes. Modern conservation theory requires both on-site and off-site conservation, the latter usually taking the form of a living-plant collection in a garden. Should the population of a plant be extinguished in the wild, the location can be repopulated from off-site locations. However, a living-plant collection does not on its own make a garden. The collection, like that of Jardin Canario, must be arranged so that it has aesthetic impact. The garden was conceived by the Swedish botanist Eric Sventenius and is currently directed by the English botanist David Bramwell.

☛ Gildemeister, Hepworth, Manrique, Raffles

Eric Sventenius. b (SWE), 1910. d 1973. **Jardin Canario**, Las Palmas de Gran Canaria (CI), 1952.

Switzer Stephen

Illustration from *Ichnographia Rustica*

This illustration from Switzer's book *Ichnographia Rustica* (1718) clearly demonstrates the author's commitment to creating a relationship between the garden and the surrounding landscape, as well as his respect for the classical tradition of design. He gave this approach the title of 'Rural Gardening'. Switzer did not believe in garden walls, he thought that 'all the adjacent country should be laid open to view'. Clearly visible on the plan is the main axis, on which lies the house – an Italian-Renaissance idea – and a long canal – an idea drawn from the French Renaissance tradition. The cross-axis also centres on the canal. Switzer saw the use of such long axes as imperative in linking the house to the garden. Crucially, however, the straight *allées* devolve to become serpentine walks in the outer reaches of the design. Switzer was apprenticed to George London and Henry Wise, and worked alongside Charles Bridgeman as a superintendent at Blenheim.

☞ **Bridgeman, London, Loudon, William III, Wise**

Stephen Switzer. b (UK), 1682. **d** (UK), 1745. **Illustration from** *Ichnographia Rustica*, Somerset (UK).

Taverna Marchesa Lavinia   Giardino della Landriana

Descending towards the lake, the Viale Bianco (White Avenue) is a wide path of local tufa steps, bordered by a combination of white-flowering and silver-leaved plants. Arranged on different levels, this garden is a successful blend of formal Italian characteristics and luxuriant English-style planting. The 4 hectares (10 acres) have an iris-skirted lake, rose gardens and numerous paths winding through shrubs and trees. When Lavinia Taverna decided to create a Mediterranean garden at her estate on the Adrea plain near Rome in 1956, the odds were against her: the soil was clay and the air charged with salt from the nearby sea. Persevering, she experimented with hundreds of plants. In 1968 she called on Russell Page, then working in the vicinity, to help her organize the garden. He provided the underlying grid, which has been used as a guide. Since 1985, the marchesa has introduced many Australian plants. These complement the Mediterranean species.

☞ Gildemeister, Johnston, McEarcharn, Page

Marchesa Lavinia Taverna. Giardino della Landriana, 1956–.

Tessin Nicodemus, the Younger Drottningholm

Water parterres are rare: this extensive example at Drottningholm in Sweden is among the most northerly in Europe and is particularly remarkable here for the way in which it reflects the Baltic sky in early autumn. Drottningholm is often called 'the Versailles of the North' and, despite its setting on a watery island in Lake Mälar near Stockholm, it exhibits the same quality of Baroque splendour as Louis XIV's palace. Queen Hedvig Eleanora, mother of Charles XI of Sweden, is the queen ('Drottning') after whom it was named: she commissioned Nicodemus Tessin the Elder to design the palace in the 1680s. His son, Nicodemus Tessin the Younger, laid out the gardens, including the water parterres, in the 1720s. The series of flat pools and slender fountains was based on the famous gardens of Chantilly and was embellished with fine statues. The gardens were remade in the 1960s and offer a splendid opportunity to see a Baroque water garden still in its prime.

☛ Bouché, Clément & Provost, Esterházy, Jekyll, Oudolf, Piper

Nicodemus Tessin the Younger. b Nyköping (SWE), 1654. d Stockholm (SWE), 1728. Drottningholm, Stockholm (SWE), 1720s.

Thays Charles

Buenos Aires Municipal Parks

The creation of the public-park system of Buenos Aires between 1891 and 1914 was the responsibility of Charles Thays, a French student of Jean-Charles Alphand and Edouard André, the designers who renovated Paris' public parks and gardens in the second half of the nineteenth century. The Paris public-park system became a model for the creation and redesign of public parks worldwide. The style used was an aggregation of elements from the French formal style of garden design and the English informal approach. Thays' principal achievement was the design of the Buenos Aires Municipal Botanic Garden which opened in 1908. He was employed to create public parks in other Argentinian cities and to make gardens on many large private *estancias* or estates. His influence spread throughout South America as he also undertook commissions in Chile, Uruguay and Brazil.

☞ André, Clément & Provost, London, Switzer

Charles Thays. **b** Paris (FR), 1849. **d** Buenos Aires (ARG), 1934. **Buenos Aires Municipal Parks**, Buenos Aires (ARG), 1891–1914, watercolour perspective shows May Square (Major Plaza) and Colón Park.

Thijsse Jacob P

Thijsse Park

Flowers and trees in the J P Thijsse Park, situated on a narrow strip of land between the Amsterdam Bos and suburban houses. The park was made in 1940 by J P Thijsse. It is a *heemtuin* or 'home garden'. Paths, each named after a different wild flower, wind through the site. Although some of them follow a parallel course, they are hidden from each other, making the park seem far larger than its 2 hectares (4.8 acres). The planting is conceived with the ecological skill that Thijsse first explored when he created a natural garden in Blomendaal in 1925, working in collaboration with Leonard Springer. Thijsse saw development destroying the natural environment of the Netherlands, and he made a study of the new sciences of botanical geography and plant ecology. In the Thijsse Park the planting is done with both ecological skill and artistry. The paths are lined with swathes of tiny wild flowers under a light canopy of trees. An area of oaks and alders is planted with ferns and aquilegias.

☞ Bijhouwer, Harrison, Oehme & Van Sweden, Oudolf, Ruys

444

Jacob P Thijsse. **b** 1865. **d** 1945. **Thijsse Park**, Amstelveen (NL), 1940.

Thomas Graham Stuart   Mottisfont Abbey

Entering the brick-walled garden, the senses are assailed by the heady colours and fragrances of over 300 varieties of old roses and magnificent herbaceous borders. Here, in the fertile soil of the old kitchen garden, Thomas houses his unique collection of old roses, now the National Rose Collection, many acquired from the Empress Joséphine's late eighteenth-century garden at Malmaison.

The garden's tranquility is heightened by the sound of a splashing fountain and ancient trees, oaks, sweet chestnuts and cedars, recalling days when monks walked the green lawns. The garden, created in 1972, comprises four symmetrical lawns surrounded by spacious beds, spilling on to two intercepting main paths or contained by box hedges, entwined with gallica and moss roses.

Earlier interesting features at Mottisfont include a Victorian-style bower and Jellicoe's pleached lime alley. Graham Stuart Thomas was for many years the National Trust's highly influential gardens adviser.

☛ André, Forestier, Jellicoe, Joséphine, Lindsay

Graham Stuart Thomas. b (UK), 1909. **Mottisfont Abbey**, Mottisfont, nr Romsey, Hampshire (UK), 1971.

Thomas Inigo

Athelhampton Manor

This view of the Great Court garden at Athelhampton, a Victorian reconstruction, is redolent of an imagined Old English gardening style. The tall pyramids of clipped yew enclose an Italianate fountain and are themselves echoed by the shape of the pinnacles on the terrace garden beyond. What it does not tell us is that the entire area around the pool was originally laid out with parterres that were filled with bright bedding in summer and autumn. Inigo Thomas was the architect of the garden and he designed it with such regard for authenticity that it is often mistaken for a seventeenth-century garden rather than a product of the 1890s. Thomas was a proponent of the formal garden, and illustrated Sir Reginald Blomfield's *The Formal Garden in England* (1892).

Both helped to create a demand for period gardens to go with Jacobean houses.

☞ Barnsley, Blomfield, Mawson, Pinsent, Sitwell

Inigo Thomas. **b** Yorkshire (UK), 1865. **d** London (UK), 1950. **Athelhampton Manor**, Dorset (UK), 1890s.

Thutmosis III King Karnak 'Botanical Court'

Enlivening the walls of the secret 'garden' chambers or sun rooms built in c1440 BC as part of the Festival Temple, this relief shows plants, animals and birds collected by Thutmosis III on his expeditions. Texts clarify the foreign imports this early plant hunter brought back to Egypt as: 'Plants which His Majesty found in the Land of Retenu (Syria). All plants that grow, all flowers that are in God's Land.' These rooms were only accessible through a small window portal, and in a sense served as an eternal 'botanical garden' dedicated to the god Amun. Here offerings were left and it is also believed the rooms may have had open ceilings, which would indicate that live plants were also grown. The once-vibrant colours have disappeared and the scale of the plants and fruits depicted in the carvings is unclear, making positive identification difficult. This 'garden' interior, whether actual or purely decorative, may be a forerunner to the sunken gardens of the palace of Tel El-Amarna.

☛ **Cyrus the Great, Darius the Great, Ineni, Sennacherib**

King Thutmosis III. b Karnak (EG), 1501 BC. **d** (EG), 1448 BC. **Karnak 'Botanical Court'**, Karnak (EG), 1440 BC.

Thwaites G H K

Peradeniya Botanic Garden

Tropical fig trees symbolize the burgeoning growth which is distinctive of a tropical climate. Peradeniya Botanic Garden, according to Thistleton Dyer, a director of the Royal Botanic Gardens at Kew, is 'the most beautiful tropical garden in the world'. It was one of the four great colonial botanic gardens of the British Empire, part of an integrated imperial network centred on the Royal Botanic Gardens at Kew and with exchange of information and plants to other botanic gardens throughout the world. Although Peradeniya was begun in 1821, its layout dates from 1849 when its director, G H K Thwaites based his design on the transposition of the English landscape garden to a tropical part of the world. However, one part of the garden was created by Thwaites to have a jungle effect – trees were left unpruned and fallen trees were not removed – and this concept of a tame wilderness has a late twentieth-century echo to it.

☞ **Chambers, Clusius, Moroni, Raffles, Rhodes**

448

G H K Thwaites. b 1812. **d** Sri Lanka (IN), 1882. **Peradeniya Botanic Garden**, Sri Lanka (IN), 1821–49.

Tibernitus Loreius · House of Loreius Tibernitus

The remains of this garden which was buried in ash in the 79 AD eruption of Vesuvius have been preserved and authentically restored. Enclosed by walls is a rectangular garden space called the *peristyle*. Rather than a small, central water feature surrounded by beds, this garden is wholly shaded by a series of wooden pergolas clad with vines (archaeologists found vine roots *in situ* near the post holes). Between the posts are panels of trellis, a popular adornment in Roman gardens. Running along the sides of the path with its verdant roof, are a series of water features. Although attractive, these are of the simple style called *eripus*, and range from a series of small interconnected rectangular pools to a long, narrow canal-like tank, complete with little bridges. The Romans were very fond of fountains and often designed intricate systems to power them using gravity.

☞ Bosworth, Hadrian, Nazarite, Pliny the Younger, Sennacherib, Sulla

Loreius Tibernitus. b unknown. **d** c79 AD. **House of Loreius Tibernitus**, Pompeii (IT), before 79 AD.

Tien Mu

Shi Zi Lin

A plum door affords a glimpse of a contorted stone which seems to dance in the courtyard. This carefully composed view is typical of the gardens of Suzhou, where apertures and doors play a great role. Always placed with great precision, they symbolize entrances for the Breath of Life and act as a divide between Nature (the garden) and Shelter (habitation). Dating back to the Yuan dynasty,

Shi Zi Lin is famous for its spectacular stones, around which the garden is centred, the *pièce de résistance* being the huge rock that rises out of the central pond. Shi Zi Lin was originally commissioned by the Buddhist monk Tien Mu in 1336 and designed by possibly as many as ten different artists and designers. One of them, the great painter Ni Tsan, celebrated it in a well-

known scroll dating from 1380, but he depicts a much more rigorous and simple garden than the extravagant showpiece seen today. Many additions have been made to the garden over the centuries, not all of them appropriate.

☞ Su Zimei, Wang Xian Chen, Xu Shi-tai, Yi Song Gye, Zhang Shi

Tien Mu. Active (CHN), fourteenth century. **Shi Zi Lin** (the Lion Grove Garden), Suzhou (CHN), 1336.

Tilden Philip Armstrong

Port Lympne

The Great Stair, constructed from Cumberland stone, rises in 125 steps from the water garden to the parkland above. Despite austerities following World War I, Sir Philip Sassoon commissioned Tilden to design the house and garden as a holiday home – he was only in residence in August – between 1918 and 1921. Described as 'a triumph of beautiful bad taste and Babylonian luxury' the garden comprised a series of terraces and a collection of garden compartments that was almost Victorian in its diversity, including a Striped Garden, Chess Garden, Mogul Court and Pool Lawn. However, it is the nearest England has to an Italian villa garden in purely aesthetic, rather than spiritual terms, and helps demonstrate just how influential the Italian Renaissance garden was between 1900 and 1939. Tilden, who could turn his hand to most styles, became a society architect and garden designer in the 1920s working for, amongst others, Winston Churchill, David Lloyd George and Lady Warwick.

☛ Acton, Johnston, Peto, Pinsent, Sitwell, Williams-Ellis

Philip Armstrong Tilden. b (UK), 1887. d (UK), 1956. **Port Lympne**, Kent (UK), 1918–21.

Toll Julie

Puffing Mosses

Moss-covered boulders in a pond belch out white mist to create a slightly disturbing, sci-fi ambience in a Stockholm show garden. Artificial mist has become popular among landscape architects, but usually in a Modernist setting. Toll is unusual in that she brings a modern sensibility to ecological or naturalistic gardening (she dislikes the word 'wild' because it implies a lack of control), here

in collaboration with two young Swedish artists, Thomas Nordström and Annika Oskarsson, who constructed the balls of chickenwire, compost and moss, linked by pipes to a mist machine. Toll admits that her work is sometimes more habitat reclamation than design. The native flora is always used as a basis. Working from a base in East Anglia, Toll leads the way in

wildflower meadow gardening, a significant contemporary trend. However, unlike contemporaries in the new perennials movement (Oudolf and Kingsbury for example), Toll's aim is to produce apparently artless designs taken straight from nature.

☞ Jensen, Latz, Robinson, M Rothschild, Sitta

452

Julie Toll. b Worcestershire (UK), 1953. **Show Garden**, Stockholm (SWE), 1998.

Tortella Benvenuto

Casa de Pilatos

The delight of the gardens at the Casa de Pilatos, the sixteenth-century palace of the dukes of Medinacelli in the centre of Seville, lies in the way in which they blend effortlessly with the architecture. The palace and gardens represent a fusion of Renaissance ideas with Islamic tradition. Here, narrow classical columns are set against bright and complex tilework in a covered arcade, neither inside nor outside, that gives on to the palace's large garden, laid out by Benvenuto Tortella in about 1640. Several orange trees, a lemon tree and a giant *Magnolia grandiflora* survive from that period. This design was overlaid in the nineteenth century with a scheme of eleven box-edged sections, with a fountain and glorietta in the centre. Three sides of the garden feature two-storey loggias filled with antique Roman sculpture, and a pleasing perspective of the whole can be obtained from an alcove halfway up the wide main staircase inside the palace.

☛ Allah, Medinaceli, Nazarite, Tien Mu

Benvenuto Tortella, sixteenth century (SP). **Casa de Pilatos**, Seville (SP), c1640.

Toshihito Prince

Katsura Detached Palace

Stylized pebble beaches and a profuse vegetation of maples, pines and ferns adorn the intricate shoreline of the lake at the Katsura Palace. Despite the abundance of its features (four tea arbours, three shoin dwellings, sixteen bridges, twenty-three lanterns, a 0.8-hectare (2-acre) lake with numerous islands) and its extensive 44-hectare (11-acre) grounds, this garden is considered primarily a tea garden. It was inspired by the cult of the tea ceremony and the teachings of the master Sen-no-Rikkyu, who preached the virtues of simplicity (*wabi*), rusticity (*sabi*) and solitude (*yugien*). Originally a tea garden was meant to consist of a semi-derelict tea house or hovel surrounded by wild vegetation and a short 'dewy path', but Prince Toshihito translated these values on a grand scale when he designed the grounds of his country residence in 1620. Surrounding himself with writers and artists, among them the famous garden designer Kobori Enshu, Toshihito was considered a refined and pious man.

☛ **Enshu, Gomizunoö, Kokushi, Rikkyu, Soami**

454

Prince Hacho no Mya Toshihito. b Katsura (JAP), 1579. **d** Katsura (JAP), 1629. **Katsura Detached Palace**, Katsura (JAP), 1620.

Trezza Luigi   Giardini Giusti

Against the mellow ochres of the *palazzo*'s facade, the parterre of box and grass forms a deep green swell. The vertical lines of the cypresses are echoed by the graceful statues standing amongst the box scrolls. In this lower, flat part, the garden is bisected by a magnificent cypress *allée* and further divided into a number of square green rooms by smaller paths. To the north, the visitor encounters a steep cliff where an enormous grimacing face is carved out of the rock. Climbing up the slope, a spiral staircase leads to a grotto which was once magnificently decorated to evoke the elements, with corals for the fire, mother-of-pearl and shells for the water and tiny painted alpine flowers for the air. Mirrors were placed to create optical illusions and the impression of harmony and balance so typical of Tuscan Renaissance gardens resonates here in Luigi Trezza's design, even though the Giardino Giusti is strictly a garden of the Veneto.

☞ **Bomarzo, Monasterio de San Lorenzo, Mozzoni, Orsini, Pinsent**

Luigi Trezza. b Verona (IT), 1725. **d** 1823. **Giardini Giusti**, Verona (IT), 1565–80.

Tribolo Niccolò

Boboli Gardens

The Boboli Gardens, situated behind the Pitti Palace in Florence, is a complex aglomeration of distinct features by many different designers. This view of a dolphin and shell fountain adorning the edge of a splendid semi-circular canal is the work of Giovanni da Bologna, part of an elaborate waterworks system to complement the Ocean Fountain, visible in the background. Vying with this as the garden's most celebrated single feature is Bernardo Buontalenti's extraordinary grotto – really three grottoes in one. The garden's basic overall design, however – so often eclipsed by these later marvels – was completed in 1549 by Niccolò Tribolo for Cosimo I de' Medici, who acquired the unfinished palace and surrounding land. The groundplan is similar to Tribolo's earlier design for the Villa Medici at Castello: an upward-sloping series of green garden compartments set in symmetrical harmony on either side of a strong central axis. Tribolo's skill lay in exploiting the site's natural amphitheatre shape without adorning his design with too much decoration or incident.

☞ Bramante, Buontalenti, Garzoni, Ligorio, Mardel, Vignola

456

Niccolò Tribolo (Niccolò di Raffaello de' Pericoli detto Tribolo). **b** c1500. **d** 1550. **Boboli Gardens**, Pitti Palace, Florence (IT), 1549.

Tschumi Bernard

Parc de la Villette

One of twenty-five 'follies' in La Villette's vast urban park, this bright red metal structure is, like the other constructions, based on the systematic 'deconstruction' and rearrangement of a 10-m (33-ft) cube. Dotted around the multi-function park in an exact grid at 120-m (384-ft) intervals, they represent the points in a point-lines-surface organization where walkways and covered avenues are lines, while lawns and bare earth are surfaces. Swiss-born architect Bernard Tschumi devised this radical scheme for the revamping of the site of the huge old slaughterhouses east of Paris in the early 1980s. It was chosen after a lengthy and controversial competition and fuelled a very public but constructive debate on the state of public architecture, urbanism and landscape. Its incorporation of Jacques Derrida's concept of deconstruction in the physical and functional dimensions was revolutionary. One of the first radically Postmodern projects ever realized, it also uncompromisingly addressed the idea of a 'cultured' Nature.

☛ Arakawa & Gins, Clément & Provost, Geuze, Jencks, Pepper

Bernard Tschumi. b Lausanne (SW), 1944. **Parc de la Villette**, Paris (FR), early 1980s.

Tunnard Christopher   Bentley Wood, Sussex

This garden at Halland in Sussex was one of a small handful of commissions that Christopher Tunnard, the torch bearer for the Modernist garden in Britain, received in the 1930s. In his 1938 manifesto, *Gardens in the Modern Landscape*, he railed at informal gardens of herbaceous colour: 'The present day garden, with the sixpenny novelette, is a last stronghold of romanticism.' Halland featured a large paved terrace all round the Modernist house by Serge Chermayeff, which is on the south side (below) boldly extended via a straight, narrow path that leads to another terrace with a rectangular grid framing the landscape. It was here, on the platform to the right of the steps, that Tunnard envisaged the placement of a sculpture by Henry Moore. Indeed, Moore's *Recumbent Figure* was briefly installed. Tunnard's example was largely ignored in practical terms, and in the 1940s he moved to the USA to teach at Harvard and Yale, where he continued to publish work on the Modernist Movement.

☞ Bradley-Hole, Crowe, Le Corbusier, Guevrékian, Mies van der Rohe

Christopher Tunnard. b (CAN), 1910. d (USA), 1979. **Bentley Wood**, Halland, Sussex (UK), c1938.

Tyers Jonathon

Vauxhall Pleasure Gardens

This stage was built at the centre of the New Spring Gardens in Vauxhall, London. It was used by visitors to the pleasure gardens as a place to drink, feast and watch the crowds walking up and down the *allées*. The gardens were designed and built in the early to mid-seventeenth century and their principal feature was a series of grand walks and smaller *allées* which cut through a wood of elm and sycamore, intersecting at right angles. This thickly wooded wilderness, where people could choose to be seen or hidden, was the Pleasure Gardens' main appeal to the public. From the central set visitors could watch moonlight concerts, al-fresco banquets, masquerades, fireworks and spectacles of every conceivable kind. Pleasure gardens continued to exist in England until the end of the nineteenth century but none have survived intact. The Tivoli Gardens in Copenhagen were influenced by Vauxhall.

☞ Catherine II, Brandt, Hirschfeld, Piper, Stanislas II

Jonathon Tyers. **b** (UK), 1702. **d** (UK), 1767. **Vauxhall Pleasure Gardens**, London (UK), c1661–1859.

Tyrwhitt Jacqueline   Sparoza

Jacqueline Tyrwhitt started to create the Greek garden of Sparoza in 1962, designing it to look as though it might have been made over many centuries by a family of Attican farmers. The garden's terraces were made to look like traditional olive and vine plantations. The planting is of olives, cypress and Mediterranean oaks, trees traditional to the surrounding countryside. Native herbs, rhizomes and bulbs set the theme for the underplanting, although many appropriate exotic plants have also been introduced. This style of garden design and planting, known as the neo-vernacular style, that is indigenous or native to a particular locality, is common today, particularly in the Mediterranean world. Sparoza is the headquarters of The Mediterranean Garden Society, which unites gardeners from all the Mediterranean climates of the world – California, South Africa and Australia as well as the entire seaboard of the Mediterranean itself.

☞ Gildemeister, Hanbury, Manrique, van Riebeeck

460

Jacqueline Tyrwhitt. b (SA), 1905. d Sparoza, Attica (GR), 1983. **Sparoza**, Attica (GR), 1965.

Vanbrugh Sir John   Castle Howard

Vanbrugh's Temple of the Four Winds (completed after his death) slips heroically into the wild, romantic Yorkshire landscape, offering a distant prospect of Nicholas Hawksmoor's mausoleum and the later 'Roman bridge'. Inspired by Andrea Palladio's Villa Capra near Vicenza, the Temple creates harmony by combining the circle and the square. Vanbrugh came to Castle Howard in 1699, fresh from success as a playwright (and earlier imprisonment in the Bastille on suspicion of spying). Working closely with his patron and friend the 3rd Earl of Carlisle, and assisted by Hawksmoor, Vanbrugh added drama to the landscape with his striking buildings that included mock-medieval curtain walls strung with towers and bastions, obelisks and pyramids. Though he never designed gardens himself, Vanbrugh's great talent was for 'composing' his buildings in the landscape like a painter, stimulating the imagination of owners and landscape gardeners like Viscount Cobham at Stowe and Charles Bridgeman at Claremont.

☛ Bridgeman, Brown, Hoare, Kent, Palladio

Sir John Vanbrugh. b London (UK), 1664. **d** London (UK), 1726. **Castle Howard**, nr York, Yorkshire (UK), 1699–1726.

Van Campen Jacob   Kleve

Designed between 1647 and 1678, the Kleve project was a radically innovative civic experiment for its time. Johan Maurits was the mastermind behind the development. He envisioned a civic landscape incorporating parks, formal gardens, pedestrian walks and boulevards, which were all to be linked to the city of Nassau-Siegen by a network of avenues. The landscape is divided into five sections: one of which is the Springenberg Amphitheatre designed by Jacob van Campen (pictured here). Van Campen was an exponent of the Dutch classical garden style and drew much of his inspiration from the classical world and Italianate schools. His hillside amphitheatre in the New Deer Park is crowned by a Palladian styled semi-circular gallery from which cascades lead down a series of terraced ponds studded with fountain jets and classical sculpture. At the base of the terraced amphitheatre, a long canal flanked (in the foreground) by two rectangular island parterres stretches into the distance.

☞ **Colchester, Huygens, Marot & Roman, Olmsted, Palladio, Post**

Jacob Van Campen. b Haarlem (NL), 1595. **d** Randenbroek (NL), 1657. **Kleve** (Cleves), North-RhineWestphalia (GER), 1647–78.

Vanderbilt George W Biltmore House

This beautiful orchid house stands in a 1-hectare (2.4-acre) walled garden at Biltmore House. It is surrounded by rose parterres and to one side is an English walled garden filled with espaliered trees. On the other side are reflecting pools with an elaborate Italianate trellis arbour planted with evergreen shrubs. Frederick Law Olmsted, the designer of Central Park and the leading American landscape architect, worked at Biltmore from 1891 to 1895 for George Vanderbilt, one of the richest Americans at that time. Biltmore mansion is surrounded by 4,100 hectares (9,840 acres) of spectacular Appalachian mountain scenery. Olmsted was originally employed by Vanderbilt to assist in the acquisition of the estate. In addition to designing the gardens, he became most interested in Vanderbilt's experiments in the new science of forestry at Biltmore.

☞ Downing & Vaux, Farrand, Hearst, Olmsted, Roper, Washington

463

George W Vanderbilt. b New Dorp, Staten Island, NY (USA), 1862. d Washington, DC (USA), 1914. Biltmore House, NC (USA), 1895.

Van Hoey Smith Family   Arboretum Trompenburg

'The place where the élite of the world's trees meet.' Developed by the Van Hoey Smith family since 1859, Arboretum Trompenburg, situated in the centre of Rotterdam, is an outstanding museum of living plants chosen with discrimination, placed with taste and expertly curated. Some of the most popular ornamental trees of today's gardening world were bred or distributed from here. For example the golden and purple forms of the Dawyck beech originated here, and the prostrate Siberian conifer, *Microbiota decussata*, was introduced to Trompenburg in 1968, distributed and is now widely used in contemporary landscaping. The collection is particularly strong in oaks, maples, hollies and cedars. The garden's layout was partly conceived c1870 by J D Zocher, a member of the Dutch family of garden architects, who adapted the English garden style to a dyke-bound Dutch site 4 m (12 ft) below sea level.

☛ de Belder, Holford, Mackenzie, Veitch, Vilmorin

Van Hoey Smith Family. Between 1859 and present day. **Arboretum Trompenburg**, Rotterdam (NL), 1859.

Van Riebeeck Jan   Company's Gardens

When Jan van Riebeeck of the Dutch East India Company landed at the southern tip of Africa in 1652, one of his first priorities was to establish a vegetable garden to sustain the new settlers and all the ships which stopped there on their way east. For the new orchard and vegetable plot, he chose a spot serviced by a stream and dramatically sited below Table Mountain. Crops were grown in rectangular beds and protected from the wind by hedges. In 1679, Governor Simon van der Stel reconstituted the garden as an ornamental repository for all the botanical riches flooding into Cape Town from the Antipodes and the East. The formal garden layout was retained, enhanced by pools, groves and an oak avenue running along Government Avenue, the main walkway and spine of the garden. Today, the shady groves of Company's Gardens offer a delightful respite from the heat of the city, with tree ferns and towering tree aloes as their most dramatic feature.

☞ Phillips, Raffles, Rhodes, Sargent, Smit

Jan van Riebeeck. b Culemborg (NL), 1619. **d** Batana (now Vakorta, Indonesia), 1677. **Company's Gardens**, Cape Town (SA), 1652.

Vanvitelli Carlo   La Reggia di Caserta

It is the sheer scale of the formal garden at the royal palace at Caserta which most impresses us – as indeed it was intended to. The palace itself is also enormous, as may be deduced from its size some 3 km (1.8 miles) down the length of the three central canals and water-staircases. The whole estate proclaims the power of the kingdom of Naples and its Bourbon rulers, Charles III and Ferdinand II. Carlo Vanvitelli started work on the canals in 1777. Their sides are plain, but fountains and statues representing scenes from Ovid's *Metamorphoses* embellish their ends. Water is the dominant element, a symbol of abundance in the hot, dry summer of Campania. Up the hillside beyond the canals is yet another cascade, steep and straight, fed by water brought by aqueduct from mountains 30 km (18 miles) away. As so often at that time, the gardens also functioned as statements of engineering prowess and military might.

☞ Gallard, Le Blond, Ligne, Tessin, Vignola

Carlo Vanvitelli. b Naples (IT), 1770. d Caserto (IT), 1773. **La Reggia di Caserta**, nth of Naples (IT), 1777.

Veitch Sir Harry   Ascott

Intricate bedding schemes surround an ornate fountain and bring colour to the sheltered Madeira Walk, part of the garden designed for Lionel de Rothschild by Sir Harry Veitch, head of the famous dynasty of nurserymen, in 1874. From about 1840 until 1914 Veitch Nursery was Britain's most famous nursery company, responsible for sending out twenty-two plant hunters to all corners of the globe. The company also bred the first orchid hybrid in 1856. The Rothschilds generally stayed at Ascott in winter, so Veitch used predominantly evergreen plants, and by the 1890s it had an unrivalled collection of figurative topiary 'animals and birds of almost every kind, with tables, chairs, churches, and other objects' cut in golden yew. The *pièce de resistance* was a large sundial in clipped box. Juxtaposed with the formal geometric gardens was the naturalistic landscape, in which Veitch planted many examples of shrubs and trees with coloured and variegated foliage.

☛   **Lainé, Nesfield, Paxton, B Rothschild, Vilmorin**

467

Sir Harry Veitch. b (UK), 1840. **d** (UK), 1924. **Ascott**, Buckinghamshire (UK), 1874.

Vera André and Paul

La Thébaïdë

The box-edged flower garden designed by the brothers Vera for their country retreat at Saint-Germain-en-Laye is perhaps the most honest reconciliation ever made in garden design between classicism and modernity. André Vera subscribed to the seventeenth-century view that a garden should be 'a refined version of nature ... nature shaped into intelligible forms'. But he argued

for a modernized version of this formal approach that allowed for painterly use of bright colours and modern materials, such as concrete. This was also a patriotic celebration of the optimism of post-war France – Vera suggested the use of native French plants instead of exotic imports. In their designs – a public garden at Honfleur, or the modern parterre garden at the de Noailles' Paris

house – the Veras sought to honour the French gardening tradition while making it relevant to modern circumstances.

☞ Blomfield, Duchêne, Guevrékian, Legrain, Le Nôtre, Noailles

André Vera. b 1881. d 1971. Paul Vera. b 1882. d 1957. La Thébaïdë, Saint-Germain-en-Laye (FR), c1920.

Verey Rosemary

Barnsley House

A modern knot garden of interwoven box hedges is a delightful feature of the grounds at Barnsley House, the Cotswolds home of Rosemary Verey, leading exponent of the classic English Arts-and-Crafts country garden in the last decades of the twentieth century. In its 1.6 hectares (4 acres), this immaculate garden epitomizes the style, with exuberant mixed borders, a formal potager, a small classical temple, shrubby wilderness, laburnum tunnel, yew topiary and well-judged, unostentatious vistas. The house, dating from 1697, stands in the middle. Verey has lectured all over the world and her books have been widely translated. Even in post-colonial times, 'English' gardens continue to be made in all corners of the globe, regardless of climate, native flora or local vernacular. Mrs Verey has advised HRH the Prince of Wales on the design of a part of his garden at Highgrove, which is quite close to Barnsley House.

☞ Fish, Johnston, Peto, Sackville-West, Salisbury

469

Rosemary Verey. b Gloucestershire (UK), 1918. **Barnsley House,** Gloucestershire (UK), 1951–.

Vesian Nicole de

Bonnieux Garden

Trimmed balls of box contrast with the wild exuberance of unclipped lavender and the stately verticals of four cypresses beyond. This is Nicole de Vesian's garden in the Lubéron in the South of France. Such sculptural compositions are repeated throughout the garden, which de Vesian, who was head of fashion at Hermès for many years, started when she was seventy years old.

The clipped evergreen shapes are offset by gnarled stone balls, slabs and boulders, and rustic fragments such as millstones, slates and a simple fountain. These shapes echo the natural topography of the landscape beyond the garden, and there are further echoes in the choice of plant material, principally indigenous aromatic herbs – lavender, thyme, rosemary, santolina, box, sage – which can

survive the stony soil and harsh climate. The colour palette is generally restricted to greens, from vibrant to silvery in tone, with the occasional splash of colour from cistus or roses.

☛ Baron Ash, Gildemeister, L'Orme, Page, Tyrwhitt

Nicole de Vesian. Bonnieux Garden, Le Lubéron (FR), late twentieth century.

Vignola Giacomo Barozzi da Villa Lante

Hedges enclose this famous water staircase or chain at Villa Lante. This is one of the most perfect and seductive gardens of the Italian Renaissance, where water is the ultimate philosophical instrument, used to retell the story of Man's ascent from the Golden Age to the Age of Civilization, as recounted by Ovid in the *Metamorphoses*. From the primaeval grotto covered in moss and fern at the summit of the garden, the waters flow through a series of extraordinary fountains, rills and pools into the openness of the grand lower parterre. This masterpiece is the work of the architect Vignola who, while working on nearby Villa Caprarola in 1568, was commissioned by the wealthy and refined young cardinal, Gambara. The villa itself is rather inconveniently split into two separate buildings for the sole purpose of accommodating the design, an eloquent affirmation of the commitment of both architect and cardinal to the Renaissance garden ideal.

☞ Buontalenti, Ligorio, Mardel, Shipman, Steele

Giacomo Barozzi da Vignola. b Vignola (IT), 1507. **d** (IT), 1573. **Villa Lante**, Bagnaia (IT), 1568.

Vilmorin Family   Arboretum des Barres

Arguably the most beautiful ensemble of trees in France, the Arboretum des Barres consists of a magnificently landscaped park of 34 hectares (86 acres). Over 8,500 plants grow in the dells and hillsides, representing 2,700 genera. Now the property of the French State, the arboretum was created by Philippe André de Vilmorin in 1804. His father, a great plantsman and horticulturist, was the business partner of Louis XVI's botanist and together they founded a commercial nursery. But Philippe-André's preference was for trees, particularly pines, which he started to collect and plant out in his newly acquired des Barres estate. A large part of the arboretum was sold to the state in the nineteenth century and a forestry school was founded, but the Vilmorin family remained closely connected to des Barres until 1935. Maurice de Vilmorin greatly augmented the collection in the 1850s, thanks to his relationship with French missionaries in the Far East and particularly China.

☞   Holford, Spath, Thwaites, Veitch, van Hoey Smith

Vilmorin Family. Between 1804 and 1935. **Arboretum des Barres** (FR), 1804.

Vogue Comte & Comtesse de Miromesnil

The Comte and Comtesse de Vogue bought Miromesnil in 1938. Shortly afterwards, the Comtesse started the kitchen garden. Although the idea was born from the necessity of feeding her family, she always combined flowers with the vegetables, in the French manner. Today, Miromesnil, where Guy de Maupassant was born, is famous for its classic potager, where old fruit trees, luxuriant clumps of peonies, vivid dahlias and stately delphiniums grow alongside a great range of fruit and vegetables nurtured in traditional ways. Geometric beds are separated by basketwork brick paths. French beans, peas and carrots grow in immaculate rows. One row is dedicated to aromatic herbs, but old-fashioned single hollyhocks are not far away. This kitchen garden, surrounded by extensive woods and massive beech trees. is enclosed by 640 m (700 yds) of old brick wall, a perfect backdrop for the mass of flowers, particularly clematis, and fruit that grows against it.

☞ Blanc, Carvallo, Jefferson, Landsberg, La Quintinie, Shurcliff

Comte & Comtesse de Vogue. Miromesnil, nr Dieppe, Normandy (FR), 1938.

Waldner Baronne de   Jas Crema

A classic combination of soft flower colour and silver foliage softens the geometric plan of the garden. The Provençale garden was the first of many regional garden styles to develop. Its originator, Baronne de Waldner, was the first to use the native herbs and other scented or aromatic plants of Provence as the basis of a garden's planting design. Lavender, sage and santolina parterres, rosemary hedges, iris fields, formal cherry orchards, cypress alleys and olive groves festooned with climbing roses have featured prominently in the garden of Jas Crema, begun in 1979 and much emulated since. Although the creative energy of the owner is such that this garden is constantly being re-invented, her consistently decorative use of both native plants as well as those such as lavenders and cherries, which are grown as crops by her neighbouring farmers, has meant that the garden and its surrounding landscape have always combined in visual unity.

☛ Hanbury, Sturdza, Vesian, Wolkonsky

Lulu, Baronne de Waldner. b 1914. **Jas Crema** (FR), 1979.

Walker Peter

IBM Solana

An *allée* of poplars encloses a dead-straight canal at one of Peter Walker's biggest commissions, an IBM office complex, hotel and 'village' in Texas. Walker is the leading contemporary proponent of large-scale formalism and, like Le Nôtre before him, he sculpts with space as if it were a physical entity. A variety of formal, modern effects embellishes IBM Solana: *allées* of trees, parterres, viewing benches, sculptural features such as a vast circular stone mound emanating mist and, within the complex, intimate formal courtyard gardens. The furthest reaches of the 340-hectare (850-acre) site have been planted with prairie, wild-flower meadows and new-oak woodland. Walker's use of repeated or subtly varied motifs on a large scale, and his ability to create startling new features as a focus, have improved public spaces in the USA and Japan, notably the Center for Advanced Science and Technology in Hyogo, the Toyota Municipal Museum of Art, Japan, and the plaza at Costa Mesa, California.

☞ Barragán, Colchester, Le Nôtre, Schwartz, Wirtz

Peter Walker. b 1932. **IBM Solana**, Solana, TX (USA), 1984–93.

Walling Edna

Cruden Farm

This romantic composition of herbaceous perennials ornaments the garden at Cruden Farm, an early work by British-born Edna Walling, Australia's leading twentieth-century garden designer. This garden is typical of Walling's work in a distinctive Arts-and-Crafts style – always based on a strong architectural structure but more rustic and forested than the designs of Gertrude Jekyll, the source of her inspiration. Even at this early stage of her career, Walling was using native Australian plants (in this case, lemon-scented eucalyptus along the driveway) in order to reconcile house, garden and landscape. This preoccupation was to grow stronger, until in the 1950s Walling was designing gardens constituted entirely of native plants grouped naturalistically. Based in Melbourne, Walling fulfilled hundreds of commissions throughout Australia, from grand country gardens to small town spaces.

☞ Farrand, Jekyll, Jellicoe, Robinson, Shipman

Edna Walling. b Yorkshire (UK), 1895. **d** Queensland (ASL), 1973. **Cruden Farm**, Victoria (ASL), 1931.

Walpole Horace   Strawberry Hill

In 1747 Horace Walpole bought a small villa at Strawberry Hill in Twickenham, just outside London; in subsequent years he transformed it into a Gothic castle. He was initially attracted to the house because he saw the potential for a spectacular view down to the Thames and the 'borrowed' landscape beyond. This picture shows how successful he was in incorporating the house into the 'natural' landscape that he created. As part of this process he planted trees in clumps of four or five in the meadows. The land was protected from the property of neighbouring villas by a series of ha-has. There was also a wide paved terrace around the house and many plants in pots. Walpole grew these in his own nursery which was also in the grounds. His essay *On Modern Gardening*, written between 1750 and 1770, hails William Kent as the founder of the English Picturesque tradition, citing Claude Lorrain as his inspiration. However, Walpole differed from Kent in preferring to retain avenues and some formality near the house.

☞ **Gilpin, Kent, Nash, Repton**

Horace Walpole. b London (UK), 1717. **d** London (UK), 1797. **Strawberry Hill**, Twickenham, London (UK), 1753–76.

Walska Ganna

Lotusland

Giant South Pacific clam shells ornament the Abalone Shell Pond, a converted swimming pool at Lotusland in California. The estate was transformed in 1941, when it was acquired by the eccentric Polish-born opera star Ganna Walska. The existing design, which mixes Italianate and Spanish styles, was overlaid by exuberant collections of cacti planted right up to the house, as well as cycads, bromeliads, aloes and a rich variety of botanical rarities. Madame Walska hired a succession of designers and botanists, and energetically set about creating a succession of highly individual, theatrical set-piece designs, ranging from a garden theatre peopled with antique stone grotesques, to a floral clock surrounded by topiary animals. During her forty-three-year tenure at Lotusland, Madame Walska presided over celebrated fancy dress parties and concerts in the gardens, which are now celebrated as much for their botanical interest as for their outlandish design.

☞ Bushell, Hertrich, Manrique, Washington-Smith

Ganna Walska. b (POL), 1887. d Santa Barbara, CA (USA), 1984. Lotusland, Santa Barbara, CA (USA), 1941–84.

Wang Xian Chen

Zhou Zheng Yuan

Seen through an open stained-glass window, a small garden pavilion, shrouded in bamboos and maples, stands above the still waters of a tiny inlet. This extensive Ming-dynasty garden contains many such elaborate views along a complex network of twisting paths, hidden courtyards and elegant buildings. Composed of as much water as land, the garden sometimes feels like an aquatic maze: islands are connected by covered bridges or pavilions on stilts, inlets run out of sight and lakes seem to go on forever. Wang Xian Chen had this garden built between 1506 and 1521 after he had been put out of office, using wealth accumulated while he was high-court administrator. He invited the great painter and poet Wen Cheng-ming to stay, following the Chinese tradition that a garden's merit is as much dependent on the quality of its visitors as its beauty. When he died, his son gambled and lost the entire garden in one night. It was then divided, resold and generally much altered over the centuries, but is now well restored.

☛ Kang Xi, Pan En, Qian Long, Tien Mu, Xu Shi-tai

Wang Xian Chen. Active (CHN), sixteenth century. **Zhou Zheng Yuan** (The Humble Politician's Garden or Chuo Yeng Yuan), Dong Bei Jie (CHN), 1506–21.

Washington George   Mount Vernon

The vegetable garden, with its neat gravel paths and box-edged beds somewhat indiscriminately planted with vegetables, herbs and flowers, was restored in 1936 using the diaries that Washington had kept between 1748 and 1799, other correspondence and books from his library. Washington had a passion for fruit trees, which tied in with his interest in agronomy. He scoured the countryside in search of new native trees and shrubs, bringing them back to plant in the garden. Mount Vernon also has a bowling green and bowls was as popular in America as it had been in Elizabethan England, until the American Civil War. It is sobering to remember that included on the estate were quarters for slaves. Washington was a master gardener, as was Thomas Jefferson at nearby Monticello, and taken together, their writings provide the fullest and best information on post-revolutionary gardening in the southern United States.

☛ Jefferson, Landsberg, La Quintinie, Shurcliff, Vogue

George Washington. b Westmoreland County, VA (USA), 1732. d Vernon, VA (USA), 1799. Mount Vernon, VA (USA), 1761.

Washington Smith George   Casa del Herrero

Designed in the Spanish Revival style and heavily influenced by the Moorish palace gardens of Granada in Andalusia, Casa del Herrero (House of the Blacksmith) typifies the Country Place era in the United States. From the 1880s through the 1920s American tycoons spent fortunes on their estates and gardens, often drawing their inspiration from European and Mediterranean garden traditions.

Similar to that of Andalusia, Southern California's climate and terrain inspired Washington Smith to use Islamic-style design features, such as the *chahar-bagh* (quartered garden), centralized courtyard fountains, and plants which typify the Moorish garden – most notably date palms and myrtle hedges. Original elements of the design are his use of rugged and informal stone paving, as

shown here, in a highly symmetrical formal courtyard and terrace, and his use of inventive fountain heads and basin shapes. The flowing plantings, borders and walks also depart from strict Islamic symmetry.

☛ Gill, Mizner, Muhammad V, Nazarite, Peto, Vanderbilt, Walska

George Washington Smith. Active Santa Barbara, CA (USA), early twentieth century. **Casa Del Herrero**, Los Angeles, CA (USA), 1922–5.

Massive boulders of burnt-orange granite, sourced locally, define the garden designed by Patrick Watson in a suburb of Johannesburg. The client had an interest in Japanese garden design, hence the koi carp, bamboos, still water and the careful placement of rocks to create a meditative atmosphere. Water surrounds the house, following the contours of the land, and even travels beneath it, through a grotto-like tunnel. The rock fig (*Ficus ingens*) and the small evergreen *Euclea crispa* scramble across the rocks of the terraces that descend from the house. Like other forward-looking designers, Watson avoids the obvious Sissinghurst pastiche traditionally favoured in English-speaking countries, and uses instead the native flora to dramatic effect. In this case his planting includes indigenous bulbs, such as zephyranthes, schizostylis and crinum lilies.

☞ **Church, Gildemeister, Jungles, Smyth**

Patrick Watson. Private Residence, Sandhurst, Johannesburg (SA), 1980s.

Wilhelm of Hessen-Kassel Prince Wilhelmsbad

Pyramids give a strange, exotic flavour to a garden, but they were originally political statements too – symbols of rationalism and free-thinking. This is one of the first, squatting on a green island in a landscaped lake at one of the earliest English-style parks in Germany. Wilhelm of Hessen-Kassel started to lay out Wilhelmsbad as a spa in 1777 by excavating a lake and building a Gothic castle in the middle: the ruined exterior concealed comfortable living quarters for the prince. Nearby is a fortified gatehouse – actually the kitchens – but also built as a ruin. A programme of earthworks resulted in interesting contours in the wider landscape park. Prince Wilhelm did no further work on Wilhelmsbad after he succeeded his father as Landgraf Wilhelm IX and moved to Kassel in 1785: it therefore remains a uniquely homogeneous example of the more progressive landscape theories of the period.

☞ W Aislabie, Carmontelle, Girardin, Pückler-Muskau, Vanbrugh

Prince Wilhelm of Hessen-Kassel. Succeeded as Landgraf Wilhelm IX in 1785 and as the Elector Wilhelm I in 1803. Reigned 1785–1803. **Wilhelmsbad**, Hanau (GER), 1777–85.

Wilhelmina of Bayreuth Margravine — Sanspareil

These rocky gates mark the entrance to the remarkable garden of Sanspareil, which lies high in the Franken Schweiz. Sometimes considered a prototype of the German Romantic movement, Sanspareil actually owes more to literary allusions: the design is based on references to Fénelon's *Les Aventures de Télémaque*, which tells the story of what happened when the young Télémaque and his tutor Mentor were shipwrecked on Calypso's Isle. The natural rock outcrops and boulders at Sanspareil take on such names as the Grotto of Calypso, Pan's Seat, the Temple of Aeolius and Vulcan's Cave; small plaques encourage contemplation. The rocks are otherwise quite unembellished and unadorned, just as they were found. Wilhelmina's path leads you to the most appropriate place to appreciate the story. 'Nature herself was the builder', Wilhelmina wrote to her brother, Frederick the Great of Prussia, in 1745. There is no underplanting, just the wild plants of old beech woods – ivy, dog's mercury and wild strawberry.

☛ Bomarzo, Friedrich II, Goethe, Powerscourt, Pückler-Muskau

Princess Wilhelmina of Prussia, Margravine of Bayreuth. Reigned 1735–63. **Sanspareil**, nr Bayreuth (GER), c1745.

Wilkie Kim

Heveningham Hall

Turf terraces create an informal green amphitheatre behind Heveningham Hall mansion, where the estate was landscaped by Capability Brown in the eighteenth century. Kim Wilkie was allocated the task of accurately restoring the large-scale Brownian landscape, but he was given a free rein when it came to the formal Victorian garden which lay behind the house, the site of which is shown here. Wilkie's new scheme contains sympathetic echoes of eighteenth-century precedents – such as the turf amphitheatre by Charles Bridgeman at Claremont – but it is nevertheless unmistakably contemporary. Wilkie specializes in fusing modern design and practical needs with historic landscapes. These aims are shown in his current projects, which include the long-term regeneration plan for the Thames Path and the redesign of the outdoor spaces in Beirut's old port area.

☞ Bridgeman, Brown, Gustafson, Hall, Jencks, Kent

Kim Wilkie. b 1955. **Heveningham Hall,** Suffolk (UK), 1999–2000 (ongoing).

William III

Hampton Court Palace Privy Garden

Walking through the Privy Garden, recently restored to Baroque splendour from the obscurity of overgrown Victorian thickets, visitors will be enthralled by the elegance of William and Mary's creation. Raised walks with pyramid yews give views over grass quarters, *plates-bandes* with topiary trees, shrubs and bulbs, and *fleur-de-lis* designs cut in grass. The backdrop is formed by Wren's State Apartments, a fountain, white-marble statues, Queen Mary's bower and ornate Tijou screens. The reconstruction is the most recent of several incarnations for this garden space, notably the Tudor design, when it was decorated with gilded heraldic beasts on poles, and its role as a public garden in the Victorian era. Although the design of the Privy Garden is in the style of Daniel Marot, creator of William III's garden at Het Loo, the work may be attributable to Henry Wise in collaboration with George London, who together laid out many great country houses of the time.

☞ London, Marot & Roman, Sophia, Wise

William III. b 1650. d 1702. Hampton Court Palace Privy Garden, East Molesey, Surrey (UK), c1689.

Williams John Charles   Caerhays Castle

Hidden away from the prevailing south-westerly winds that batter the south Cornish coast, the sheltered gardens not only enjoy a spectacular view, but are also home to an enormous collection of rare trees and shrubs, with a particular emphasis on rhododendrons, magnolias and camellias. The garden was begun in the 1890s, and throughout the early part of the twentieth century Williams was a member of various syndicates which sponsored plant hunters such as George Forrest to explore remote parts of China and bring back new plants. Williams also had close ties with the Veitch Nursery at Exeter, and the gardens boast many early introductions from Veitch's plant hunter, Ernest Wilson. However, the gardens are most famous as the birthplace of the *Williamsii* hybrid camellias, created in 1925 when *C. japonica* was crossed with *C. saluenensis*, which had been brought to Britain by Forrest the previous year. The *Williamsii* are probably the camellias best suited to general planting in Britain.

☞   **Mackenzie, Middleton, Veitch**

487

John Charles Williams. b (UK), 1861. **d** (UK), 1939. **Caerhays Castle**, Cornwall (UK), 1890s.

Williams-Ellis Clough Plas Brondanw

The beautiful pair of gates set between walls of Welsh slate perfectly frames the glowering peaks of the mountains of Snowdonia, which provide a spectacular backdrop to Williams-Ellis's hillside garden. A life's work begun in 1908, the garden is made up of a cluster of formal garden compartments, defined by tall yew hedges, and is full of conspicuous topiary and statuary.

The blue colour of these gates is repeated throughout the garden. However, its major theme is the carefully contrived vistas out over the 'borrowed' landscape. Together with its English counterpart, Harold Peto's Iford Manor, Plas Brondanw is the most successful Edwardian attempt to marry the British landscape and love of plants with the spirit of sixteenth-century Italy. A self-declared

'Architect Errant', Williams-Ellis was an ardent environmental activist who, in the 1920s and 1930s, campaigned hard to preserve the countryside. However, he is most famous for the architectural fantasy village of Portmeirion.

☞ Acton, Hamilton Finlay, Peto, Sitwell, Strong & Oman

Sir Clough Williams-Ellis. b (UK), 1883. d (UK), 1978. **Plas Brondanw**, Gwynedd, North Wales (UK), 1908.

Willmott Ellen Ann

Warley Place

The delightfully informal display of foxgloves and Solomon's seal are part of the huge designed collection of common, rare and exotic plants that filled Warley Place. A skilled gardener – many a cultivar or species is named 'Willmott' or 'Warley' – in 1897 Miss Willmott, along with Gertrude Jekyll, became the first recipient of the Royal Horticultural Society's Victoria Medal of Honour. She was also a patron of several plant hunters, including Ernest Wilson, and one of the 'levers' Charles Sargent used in order to persuade Wilson to join him at the Arnold Arboretum. If her *magnus opus* was *The Genus Rosa* (1910), she is perhaps better remembered for her popular *Warley Gardens in Spring and Summer* (1909). She was one of the first women elected to the Linnean Society in 1904 and 'Miss Willmott's Ghost', a common name for *Eryngium giganteum*, refers either to her habit of surreptitiously sprinkling its seed in gardens she visited, or to her somewhat prickly character.

☛ Jekyll, Parsons, Robinson, Sargent

Ellen Ann Willmott. b (UK), 1858. d (UK), 1934. **Warley Place**, nr Brentwood, Essex (UK), c1900.

Wilton Job & Cockayne Leonard · Otari New Zealand Botanical Gardens

Otari's tropical and subtropical fernery is a small part of the largest single collection of native plants and flora in New Zealand. Otari was founded on an area of land formerly owned by Job Wilton, an early settler who had preserved a large area of native bushland, which had become public domain after his death. In the 1920s, the noted New Zealand botanist Dr Leonard Cockayne developed the Otari Plant Museum in Wellington, on the North Island of New Zealand. His aim was to create a new type of botanic garden that focused on the collection, propagation and cultivation of native plants. The Otari site already contained much of the indigenous vegetation of the bush forest when Dr Cockayne began to develop the collection. Most notable sections of the collection are the rock garden, the tropical and sub-tropical fernery, and the small alpine garden. A spectacular look-out point affords views over the main bushland area and wilderness garden.

☞ Burley Griffin, Manrique, Rhodes

Job Wilton. Active end of nineteenth century. **Dr Leonard Cockayne**. Active (NZ), twentieth century. **Otari New Zealand Botanical Gardens**, Wilton, Wellington (NZ), formally established c1920.

Winkler Tori

Private Garden

All gardens are temporary, or at least constantly changing. Some garden spaces, such as this extraordinary vision by Tori Winkler exploit this quality to the full, and are expressly made as temporary outdoor installations that survive principally as photographs of one specially constructed moment. Richard Long's sculptures and Chris Parson's dew gardens work in a similar way, as did, for

example, the diversions within the bosquets at Versailles during Louis XIV nocturnal *fêtes champêtre*. Here, paint has converted plants into living sculpture and the introduction of the white horse lifts the scene to a surreal plane. The *allée* of coloured plants is a prelude to the gateway that takes the visitor from what is clearly a manmade display into the beauties of naturally planted woodlands.

Fallen leaves make an ephemeral pathway artfully links both aspects of this design. The use of gaudy colours and unusual forms brings a sense of the contemporary to what appears to be an established landscape.

☞ Delaney, Goldsworthy, Hardouin-Mansart, C Parsons, Schwartz

Tori Winkler. Private Garden, VA (USA), late 1990s.

Wirtz Jacques

Schoten Garden

A cloud hedge, an idea derived from Japanese garden design, forms an abstract, undulating relief of boxwood at Jacques Wirtz's own garden in Belgium. With his sons, Peter and Martin, Wirtz creates gardens underpinned by an organic formalism, in which large numbers of suitable plants, such as beech, hornbeam, yew and box, are clipped and shaped to create walls and buttresses to complement sculpture, smooth greensward and reflective expanses of water. In this garden, Wirtz has allowed the established evergreen framework to grow almost unchecked – hence its pleasingly random appearance. Wirtz is also a dedicated horticulturist, and luxuriant borders of perennials and plantations of fruit trees recur in his schemes. In 1998 the Duchess of Northumberland commissioned the Wirtzes to produce designs for a formal water garden in the old walled garden at Alnwick Castle.

☞ Bradley-Hole, Jellicoe, Monasterio de San Lorenzo, Rochford

Jacques Wirtz. b (BEL). **Schoten Garden** (BEL), 1970–.

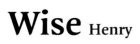

Wise Henry

Hampton Court

This view shows Hampton Court Palace as it was soon after Henry Wise, as royal gardener to King William III, took charge in 1699. The Great Fountain Garden in the foreground, with thirteen fountains and complex parterres de broderie, had been laid out by Daniel Marot, and the Privy Garden at top left had just been finished, possibly with design input from Wise and George London, his partner at the Brompton Road Nursery. Wise made several improvements at Hampton Court, including the famous maze, but the most radical changes followed the accession, in 1702, of Queen Anne, who ordered the removal of the box hedges, parterres and most of the fountains. Wise was the leading designer in England in the late seventeenth century, responsible for major works at Blenheim, Castle Howard and Longleat. Almost all his gardens were erased when the mid-eighteenth century fashion for landscapes in the style popularized by Capability Brown dictated expanses of smooth pasture rather than formal parterres.

☛ **Brown, London, Marot & Roman, William III**

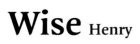

Henry Wise. b Oxford (UK), 1653. **d** Warwick (UK), 1738. **Hampton Court**, Middlesex (UK), 1699–1728.

Wolkonsky Prince Peter   Kerdalo

Conspicuous juxtapositions of rare plants are possible if the site for a garden is well chosen. Most gardens are made where the maker happens to live. In the case of Kerdalo the opposite is the case – Prince Peter Wolkonsky chose to live where he believed a good garden could be made. The naturally beautiful, well-watered site of Kerdalo enjoys the mild oceanic climate of Brittany and from 1965 it became the location of an archetypal late twentieth-century Post-modernist garden with architectural 'quotations' from many different historical styles and planting schemes characteristic of many of the world's temperate vegetations and climates. The result is not, however, a simple accretion of these diverse elements. They are instead woven into an apparently seamless unity by the artistry of their designer, Prince Peter Wolkonsky.

☛ **Fairhaven, Gibberd, Sturdza, Tyrwhitt**

Prince Peter Wolkonsky. b St Petersburg (RUS). d Kerdalo, Brittany (FR), 1997. **Kerdalo**, Brittany (FR), 1965.

Wordsworth William Rydal Mount

Built in local slate with interior rustic panelling, Wordsworth's summer-house opens to a surprise view of Rydal Water and marks his extension of the narrow terraces that suited his active style of composing poetry. After the minute effects of Dove Cottage, where William and sister Dorothy planted native flowers and mosses, his last home gave Wordsworth scope to indulge his passion for making gardens that blended with the landscape. From 1813 onwards he brought the old kitchen garden into his overall design, and linked the house to its Lakeland setting through terraces, lawns, shrubberies, fields and woodland, planting many evergreens, including a newly-introduced Japanese red cedar (*Cryptomeria japonica*) near the house. An early conservationist, Wordsworth lamented the mass plantations of 'foreign' larch and fir and praised humble cottage gardens. His romantic, largely vernacular gardening looked forward to William Morris, John Ruskin and William Robinson.

☞ **Morris, Robinson, Ruskin**

William Wordsworth. b Cockermouth (UK), 1770. **d** Cowmere (UK), 1850. **Rydal Mount**, Cumbria (UK), 1813–50.

Wright Frank Lloyd — Falling Water

Deep in the Pennsylvania forest, hovering above the bed of a mighty waterfall, the house seems to emanate from the landscape like a natural outcrop. Falling Water is perhaps one of the best-known modern private houses in the world and is undoubtedly one of Frank Lloyd Wright's best works. This 1935 commission for a weekend retreat by the Philadelphia department-store owner, E J

Kaufman, marked a turning point in Wright's career and stretched his art beyond even his previous work, the influential 'prairie house'. Here the house is so at one with the elements and the landscape that it doesn't actually allow the mental perception of physical space that defines a garden. In its groundbreaking newness Falling Water is a primaeval reference to the essence of

both man and nature. It refers back to a time when the cultural space of the garden made no sense, where no transition was needed between human habitation and the wilderness. The wilderness itself was man's garden.

☛ Aalto, Barragán, Beck & Collins, Burley Griffin, Le Corbusier

Frank Lloyd Wright. b Richland Center, WI (USA), 1867. d Phoenix, AZ (USA), 1959. Falling Water, Bear Run, PA (USA), 1935.

Wright Thomas

Shugborough

On a very English river bank, the remains of a druid in artificial Coade stone perches on a rubble crag, at least partly attributed to eccentric astronomer, fantastical architect and landscape gardener, Thomas Wright of Derby. Erected c1750, the ruins supposedly contained fragments from a bishop's palace and originally extended into a Gothic pigeon house. Thomas Anson's rococo landscape at Shugborough survives as a scattering of neo-classical buildings and a Chinese house built to contain the porcelain collection made by his younger brother. Also attributed to Wright are two mysterious monuments, to a cat and a shepherd; the latter's rustic stonework recalls his pattern-book of arbour designs, published in 1755 and quickly followed by more designs for grottoes. A true individualist, Wright designed mathematical flower and rose gardens against the prevailing fashion and became an unlikely celebrity. His taste for the primitive can still be seen in his root house for the Duke of Beaufort at Badminton.

☞ **Bushell, Goldney, Hamilton, Robins**

Thomas Wright. b Byers Green, nr Bishop Auckland, Durham (UK), 1711. **d** 1786. **Shugborough**, Milford, Stafford, Staffordshire (UK), c1750.

Xu Shi-tai

Liu Yuan

The delicate latticework of the *lou chuang* window offers the visitor a glimpse of greenery in a tiny open space. There are dozens of such windows – each absolutely unique – in the Lingering Garden. One discovers these exquisite views while walking through halls and courtyards and along the 700 m (763 yds) of open-sided corridors that lead to a central pool. The garden unfolds like a precious scroll painting. It is so complex that the mere 0.8 hectares (2 acres) seem infinitely larger. It was originally built in the Ming dynasty by Xu Shi-tai, a retired official. Like many other gardens in fashionable Suzhou, Liu Yuan also contains a collection of calligraphy tablets with poems from famous visitors. The prosperous city of Suzhou, in the beautiful and fertile region of Jiangsu west of Shanghai, had since the Song dynasty attracted nobles and retired officials who, according to Confucius' teachings, aspired only to make beautiful gardens and dedicate themselves to 'recreation through the arts'.

☛ **Pan En, Su Zimei, Tien Mu**

Xu Shi-tai. Liu Yuan, Suzhou (CHN), established during Ming Dynasty (1368–1644).

Yi Song Gye

Secret Garden of Changdokkung

Under the dense cover of the native trees is one of the many pavilions in the Huwon, the secret or back garden of the great royal palace of Changdokkung in Seoul. This vast park of 32 hectares (79 acres) contains all the hallmarks of the traditional Korean garden: canals and waterfalls, bridges and stairs, stone arrangements and lotus ponds. But the overall design and abundant features remain subservient to the natural environment of this densely wooded site, exemplifying the principle of harmony with nature which typifies most Korean gardens. First constructed in 1405 by King Ta Jong, the Palace of Changdokkung and the Secret Garden were destroyed during the Japanese invasion led by the great shogun Hideyoshi, builder of the Sambo-in, in 1592. King Song Gye splendidly rebuilt the main structures and revived the gardens. Despite political turmoil and fires, Changdokkung remained the residence of the Yi kings until 1989 when the last surviving menber of the royal family died there.

☞ Egerton, Hideyoshi, Wang Xian Chen

Yi Song Gye. b (S KOR), 1567. d (S KOR), 1608. **Secret Garden of Changdokkung**, Seoul (S KOR), 1590s.

Yturbe José de

Miguel Gomez Residence

The bright walls of this spectacular courtyard, in which slots in the walls act as windows, defining the view out over the tropical hills beyond and letting in natural sunlight, are in contrast with the striking patio of recinto (black volcanic rock chips) and marble, and the fountain made out of carved volcanic rock. This is typical of de Yturbe's work, in which he reinterprets Mexican vernacular architecture. He has also been strongly influenced by the work of the Mexican architect Luis Barragán, and his courtyards, where he tries to establish the notion of dwelling rather than building by allowing plants to invade the architecture, clearly expose both inspiration sources. His designs show an intimacy, privacy and serenity, which is enhanced by the acoustic capabilities of moving water. The use of water reflects the strong Islamic influences in the Iberian peninsula, a legacy of the Moorish conquest. De Yturbe's use of strong colour also has echoes of the work of the painter Jesus Reyes Ferreria.

☞ Barragán, Herman, Pawson & Silvestrin, Schwarts, Suzuki

500

José de Yturbe. Miguel Gomez Residence, San José (CR), 1990s.

Zhang Shi

Ji Chang Yuan

Through a round *lou chang* window, a fragment of a rockery can be seen in a courtyard at the Garden for Easing the Mind, sometimes known as the Garden of Ecstasy. The distinctive wavy-topped wall is also visible. Though relatively small, the garden is famous for the use of *chie ching*, which consists of 'borrowing' a feature in the landscape, or even a distant architectural landmark. Here the Tin Hill and the Dragon Light Pagoda are brought into the design: both are reflected in the garden's pond. Fascinating rock arrangements also distinguish the garden's design. Emperor Qian Long, the great garden builder, is said to have visited it seven times. Piled high so as to resemble a natural rocky needle near the pond or carefully chosen for their outstanding forms, rocks – such as the one called (and resembling) The Lady Combing Her Hair – were the speciality of the garden's creator, Zhang Shi.

☛ Qian Long, Tien Mu, Xu Shi-tai

Zhang Shi. Active (CHN), sixteenth century. **Ji Chang Yuan**, Wuxi (CHN), 1506–20, rebuilt 1860.

Zuccalli Enrico

Schloss Lustheim

Schloss Lustheim is surrounded by water. Under the bridges shown on either side of this late eighteenth-century print is a broad canal which entirely encircles the palace, so that it seems to be built on an island. It was begun in 1684 by the Elector Maximilian-Emanuel of Bavaria, who also laid out the formal gardens at Nymphenburg. Enrico Zuccalli was the architect and built the canal in the fashionable Dutch style, though Dominique Girard was also partly responsible for the design of the garden. The broad canal in the foreground runs back to the somewhat larger Schloss Schleissheim, built in 1701: the two princely gardens face each other over nearly 1 km (0.6 mile) of formal gardens. Schleissheim and Lustheim share the most important early Baroque garden in southern Germany, contemporary with Herrenhausen in the north.

☛ Girard, Marot & Roman, Philip II, Sophia

Enrico Zuccalli. b Roveredo (IT), 1642. **d** Munich (GER), 1724. **Schloss Lustheim**, Park Schloss Schleissheim, Oberscheissheim, Bavaria (GER), 1684–.

Zug Szymon Bogumil

Nieborów

Zug's plan of 1775 for Michal Hieronim Radziwill, who had commissioned the distinguished architect to supervise the rebuilding of the palace and the re-fashioning of the earlier garden, was inspired by the French tradition, with *allées* and intricate geometrical parterres, divided by a tree-lined avenue leading to the house. The first garden, laid out in the seventeenth century by Tylman van Gameren, had reflected the architect's Dutch origin. Beyond the L-shaped canal to the right of the formal garden, Zug created a landscape park with meandering streams and a large irregular pool with an island. There was also a kitchen garden and an orangery. Gerard Ciolek restored the garden between 1948 and 1951. Not far from Nieborów, Radziwill's wife Helena commissioned Zug to create the celebrated landscape park at Arkadia.

☛ **Girardin, Le Nôtre, Radziwill, Switzer**

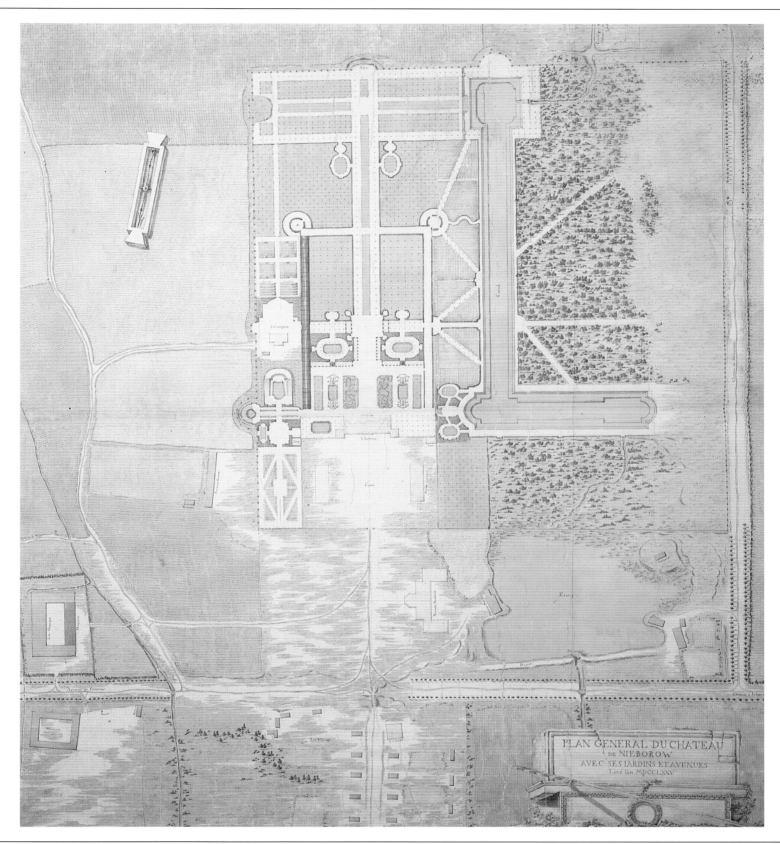

PLAN GENERAL DU CHATEAU DE NIEBOROW AVEC SES IARDINS ET AVENUES Levé l'an MDCCLXXV

Szymon Bogumil Zug. b Merseburg, Saxony, 1733. **d** 1807. **Nieborów**, nr Lowicz (POL).

Glossary of garden terms and styles

Agdal

A Moroccan term for a country garden estate. Also called an arsa, the agdal was a series of terraced gardens, laid out in square plots for easy irrigation. Typically the traditional agdal estates were principally for pleasure. However, in addition to supplying the households with fruit and vegetables, excess crops were sold.

Allée

Straight walk, path or ride bordered by trees or clipped hedges. A series of straight *allées* will often form an ordered geometric pattern.

Alpines *see* Winter garden

Annuals

Plants (usually, in a garden context, brightly coloured flowers) that live for a single year. They germinate from seed in the spring, are then planted out to flower in summer, then set seed and die as winter approaches. Annuals are the plants most often used in formal carpet-bedding displays.

Arboretum

A botanical garden for the display of trees and shrubs – often rare native species in danger of being lost or star exotic introductions.

Arts and Crafts Movement

Late nineteenth-century British movement, promoted by William Morris, John Ruskin and others, that extolled a return to the perceived values of medieval craftsmanship as a reaction to increasing industrialization. In a garden context, Arts and Crafts style often refers specifically to the work of Jekyll and Lutyens and their followers working in the first two decades of the twentieth century. The dominant approach in twentieth-century garden design worldwide, challenged only in the final decades of the century as the native-plant movement gained influence in the USA, Australia, South Africa, the Middle East and elsewhere.

Azulejo

Glazed ceramic tile, often painted in blues and yellows, common in Spanish and Portuguese gardens.

504

Baroque

Seventeenth- and eighteenth-century European style making exuberant use of ornamentation. In a garden context, Baroque features include richly carved fountains, nymphaeums, water tricks, grottoes and statuary.

Bassin

A formal pool, often stone-edged and/or with a fountain at its centre, and usually part of a formal plan.

Belvedere

Ornamental building on an outcrop or raised area that commands an extensive view of its surroundings.

Bosco

A grove of trees or a wood, natural or manmade, often incorporated into the design of an Italian Renaissance garden. Wilder in aspect than a bosquet [see below] and frequently sited on a mount.

Bosquet

A small clump of trees, or a decorative glade with statuary, enclosed by a hedge or fence, usually a part of a seventeenth- or eighteenth-century French formal landscape.

Carpet bedding

Nineteenth-century practice of planting out young seedlings of annual plants *en masse* to create abstract effects based on masses of colours. A technique still used widely in municipal parks worldwide. See mosaiculture.

Chadar (Chaddar)

A Persian word meaning shawl or sheet, used to describe stepped or decorative water chutes in Persian and Mughal Indian gardens. Chadars are masonry slabs set at 45 degree angles to conduct waterflow from one garden terrace to another. Water may cascade down the chadar in one unbroken sheet, or a textured, ripple effect may be achieved by raising the surface of the chute, adding sparkle and sound to the garden. This feature may be found in Achabal and Shalamar Garden at Lahore, and most spectacularly at Nishat Bagh, Kashmir.

Chahar-Bagh

Term meaning 'four-part garden'. The word bagh, or garden, came into common usage in Central Asia, under the Turkish speaking rulers in the area of Samarkand and Bukhara in the thirteenth-fourteenth centuries. The etymology of bagh is unclear, but it appears in mid-Persian text and is thought to be an ancient Persian word known to the Achaemenians and Sassanians. The prefix chahar means four in Persian. Chahar-bagh commonly refers to the quartered enclosed gardens divided by four water channels. This layout is found throughout the Muslim world in gardens designed in the Persian tradition.

Chinoiserie

Chinese-style decoration as imagined by European designers from the seventeenth century onwards. It was based mainly on travellers' descriptions – although the architect William Chambers championed the style in the eighteenth century – and was influential throughout Europe, particularly in Germany.

Contextual

Designed to relate to or imitate its context or setting.

English Landscape Style

Garden design style formulated during the first years of the eighteenth century, first as an artform analogous to literature, with complex symbolic and political meanings expressed as buildings and landscape features. Later, it became a purely visual or painterly medium, evocative of a pastoral idyll – as with the work of Capability Brown. A style reproduced throughout Europe in the eighteenth and nineteenth centuries.

Eyecatcher

Structure in the wider landscape designed to draw the eye and provide a focus in a broad vista. Eyecatchers are usually buildings, often towers, with a romantic aspect.

Ferme Ornée

Precursor of the English landscape style: a working farm ornamented by seats, temples, viewpoints and walks. Ferme ornées were generally of modest size and relatively cheap to create. William Shenstone and Philip Southcote created the most celebrated examples.

Fête champêtre

A large-scale open-air party, often requiring guests to wear fancy dress or masks, and usually in the grounds of a large country house with a variety of diversions for the party-goers. Louis XIV's *fêtes champêtre* at Versailles were probably the most sumptuous events ever seen.

Folly

A built structure whose principal purpose is decorative or whimsical rather than practical; occasionally a utility building made to look like a historic, ruined or fantastical structure. For example, the Pineapple House at Dunmore Park in Scotland.

Garden cemeteries

Landscape style developed in the nineteenth century, in which cemeteries were designed with as much care as rustic parks. Later, in the USA and elsewhere, the forest cemetery was developed.

Gazon coupé

Grass with shapes cut out of turf and filled with coloured earths or gravels. Used principally in England in the seventeenth century for formal parterre designs.

Giardino segreto

Literally, a secret garden, often concealed by being sunken below ground level. It was a feature found in most Italian gardens.

Grotto

A cave-like room usually man made, decorated with shells, minerals and fossils. Italian Renaissance grottoes were semi-open structures set in the open garden. Later, in eighteenth-century England, grottoes began to be made as discrete buildings – sometimes underground – lined with shells and minerals.

Ha-ha

A sunken 'fence', resembling a dry ditch or moat with one vertical stone side. This meant that livestock could graze on pasture quite close to the house, furthering the illusion of pastoral ease in eighteenth century landscape gardens.

Heempark, Heemtuin

Dutch park or garden planted with native flora; dates from the 1920s.

Herbaceous border

Areas that consist entirely of perennial plants that die back to an underground root every winter, then regrow in spring. In practice, most 'herbaceous' borders are in fact mixed borders: ie they also contain evergreens, bulbs and annuals.

Hortus Conclusus

An enclosed medieval garden, generally consisting of low hedges, flowers and herbs.

Ivan (also called a liwan or iwan)

A Persian term for an often high barrel-vaulted space or hallway open at one end. This feature is widely used in mosque, palace and garden pavilion architecture throughout the world of Islam. In ancient Persia, the cave grottoes at Taq-e Bostan illustrate one of the earliest forms of the Sasanian ivan.

Jardin Anglais, Giardino Inglese

Terms used in France and Italy to describe a garden or landscape (nineteenth-century in most cases) made in a naturalistic style, ie undulating parkland with wooded glades, lakes and little that is apparently manmade.

Knot garden

An enclosed garden, based on Tudor precedents, comprising low evergreen hedges, usually box, yew, or thyme, planted to create an intricate and pleasing symmetrical pattern, sometimes with infills of brightly coloured flowers or gravel.

Landscape Style *see* English Landscape Style

Latin

The two-word plant-naming system was devised by Swedish botanist Linnaeus in the eighteenth century. The first word is the genus, the second is the species. The system is useful as it is precise, accurate and international. However, it means that plant names can be hard to pronounce and difficult to remember.

Modernism

Style formulated in the 1920s, characterized by architecture that could be mass produced and the use of modern materials such as concrete. The 'white-cube' building is an archetypal Modernist style. A variety of garden styles have been used in an attempt to complement the building style.

Mosaiculture

Sophisticated French or Italian version of British carpet bedding, with heavier reliance on recognizable figurative motifs.

Mughal gardens

A hybridized style of Indo-Persian garden design spanning sixteenth to nineteenth century India. The Persian garden tradition was first brought to India from Kabul with Emperor Babur's conquest of northern India in 1526. Enclosed symmetrical and axial parterre layouts, or the chahar-bagh – a typical Islamic garden architectural design – combined with features such as stone terracing, geometric and foliate shaped basins and fountains, water chutes and channels, and open air pavilions, typify the Mughal style.

Native plants

Plants that naturally occur in the wild in a given area. In nineteenth century horticulture the emphasis was on recently introduced exotic plants, but from the late twentieth century there has been increasing interest in native flora and this has impacted on design.

Nymphaeum

Semicircular structure, often semi-open, containing statuary on the theme of rustic nymphs and water.

Objet trouvé

From the French 'found object'. The integration into the garden's design of objects of daily use such as mirrors or crockery and natural shells or stones goes back to the Renaissance and flourished in Baroque and rococo gardens. In more recent times however it became the hallmark of the fantastic environments and gardens created by self taught eccentrics or 'outsider' artists.

Pairidaeza

Old Persian word for 'walled space'. Xenophon, the Greek historian and essayist, first heard this word in 401 BC during his travels in Persia where he fought with Greek mercenaries. In his Socratic Discourse, the Oeconomicus, Socrates notes: 'In whatever countries the king resides…he is concerned that there be gardens, the so-called pleasure gardens, filled with all the fine and good things that the earth wishes to bring forth, and in these he himself spends most of his time, when the season of the year does not preclude it.' The word paradise isa translation of the Greek word *paradeisos* that Xenophon used to describe the Persian garden.

Pallissade

A clipped hedge, often hornbeam, constituting a green wall to line an *allée*.

Parterre

Formal terrace decorated in one of a variety of styles, from simple patterns of cut turf and gravel (*gazon coupé*) to intricate designs made of hedges, grass, gravel, turf and flowers (*parterre de broderie*).

Patio

Traditionally, a small, paved Spanish courtyard surrounded by an arcade, often filled with potted plants.

Perennials *see* Herbaceous Border

Pergola

Wooden and/or stone structure that forms a covered walkway, often covered with climbing plants such as roses, vines or wisteria.

Piano nobile

Principal floor of a large house; usually the raised floor above a basement or ground floor.

Picturesque

Late-eighteenth-century landscape style (almost exclusively English) that celebrates the power of untamed nature, frequently in a setting of extreme terrain. Loosely used to describe the English landscape style in Europe. The term comes from the idea of making landscapes in the manner of pictures.

Potager

French-style decorative kitchen garden, edged with box and incorporating vegetables grown partly for their appearance. One of the principal examples of such a garden is Villandry in France.

Putti

The plural form of *putto* in Italian, meaning boy, lad, stripling, male child. They are found in fifteenth to nineteenth century European (especially Italian) art and architectural works. Putti adorn garden ornaments such as urns, carved wall and fountain reliefs, and are featured in classical floor mosaics and as free standing garden statuary. Also referred to as cherubs or cherubim.

Qanat

An irrigation canal system developed in ancient Persia that depends on subterranean water sources. A master shaft is driven to reach the water source. Then a tunnel is dug to wherever to water is needed and emerges to the surface. In order to propel the water forward, the tunnel is slightly inclined using gravity to create a pressure system. Every 18 to 20 m (50 to 60 ft), the tunnel is interrupted by shafts from the surface which permit the removal of excavated dirt, allow access for maintenance, and air to the workers. Ceramic rings are used to line the tunnel. The Iranian desert is lined with these water systems and they still supply much of Iran's water today.

Rehant (or Persian Wheel)

A pre-Mughal Indian method of watering and irrigating a garden, also known as an arghatt. A rehant was used to draw water from rivers and lakes for use in palaces and large estates. It works by means of a geared wheel with a rope-chain fitted with water pots and operated by livestock. The jugs pour the water into an aqueduct that would then fill garden tanks, watercourses, and pools. The water flows from a higher point downwards thus enabling the system to produce the head of water necessary to work fountains. The Emperor Babur found this system in use in Lahore, India, in the 1530s and noted it in his personal memoirs, the Baburnama.

Rill

With their origins in early Persian gardens, a rill is a narrow, shallow manmade stream or rivulet, usually lined with stone, and used on a gentle gradient to convey water from one area of the garden to another. Rills can be serpentine – a famous example is William Kent's rill at Rousham – or linear, as used in the Islamic chahar bagh, and by Sir Edwin Luyens and Gertrude Jekyll in their Arts and Crafts gardens.

Rococo

Exuberant eighteenth-century decorative style derived from *rocaille*, the Italian word for shell. In rococo gardens, decoration is at least as important as form.

Romantic style

Refers to the landscaping style evolved from the English landscape movement and corresponding with the European literary and philosophical romantic movement. Usually involving sweeping lawns, wooded groves, ponds or lakes and follies, it became widespread in Europe throughout the nineteenth century often at the expense of older formal gardens.

Saut de loup

A deep trench dug at the further end of an *allée* to prevent trespassing.

Serpentine paths

Curving or twisting paths running through areas of shrub and tree planting. Serpentine paths frequently lend a note of informality to otherwise symmetrical schemes.

Shakkei/Chie ching

In both Japanese (*shakkei*) and Chinese garden (*chie ching*) design traditions, a technique which consists of 'borrowing' a particular landscape or part of a landscape into the garden composition. An application of scroll painting techniques, the 'borrowing' is achieved by playing on the various parts or 'layers' of a view (foreground, middle ground and background). It is different from the Western use of vistas or surrounding landscape in the same way as a landscape painting is unlike a Japanese or Chinese landscape scroll.

Stroll garden

A Japanese style of garden, popular from the thirteenth century, which is designed to be viewed while walking following a particular path. The garden is then revealed gradually in a sequence of views, ambience and perspectives. It is reminiscent of the act of looking at a long Oriental scroll landscape painting. It usually involves a circuit around a lake with various tea arbours, bridges and islands.

Tapis vert

Literally, a green carpet: a close cropped expanse of grass – usually part of a formal scheme.

Topiary

The art of clipping evergreen plants, such as box and yew, into abstract or figurative shapes.

Trompe-l'oeil

From the French 'deceive the eye' An effect designed to alter normal perception. Often used in gardens to increase distances and change perspectives. It can take the form of out-of-scale plantings, trellises, mirrors or even painted surfaces.

Tudor garden

Gardens made in Britain during the Tudor Period (1485–1603). Knot gardens were a principal motif of the gardens of this type.

Wilderness

Enclosed, informal areas in a landscape garden, planted with trees and shrubs and featuring serpentine walks.

Winter garden

Alpine or rock garden, or an indoor heated conservatory for display of exotic plants.

Directory of gardens

Ancient Egypt

Karnak 'botanical court'
Karnak
Open to the public
Thutmosis III, King

Queen Hatshepsut's Funerary Temple
Dier el-Bahari
Open to the public
Ineni

The academy
Garden vanished
Plato

Argentina

Public Gardens
Buenos Aires
Open to the public
Thays, Charles

Australia

Australian National Botanic Garden
Clunies Ross Street
Black Mountain
Canberra, ACT 2601
Open Jan & Feb, 9am to 8pm daily. Mar to Dec, 9am to 5pm daily
Burley Griffin, Walter

Cruden Farm
Victoria
Private, not open to the public
Walling, Edna

Nooro, Mount Wilson
Blue Mountains
NSW 2786, nr Richmond
Open mid-Sept to early Nov & mid-Apr to early May
Hay, William

Smith Residence
Sydney
Private, not open to the public
Sitta, Vladimir

The Chinese Garden of Friendship
Darling Harbour, Sydney NSW
Open daily, 9.30am to 6.30pm (4.30pm in winter)
Guangdong, Gardeners of

Austria

Belvedere Palaces
Prinz Eugenstrasse, Vienna
Open Apr to Sept (not Mon), 10am to 6pm & 5pm in winter
Hildebrandt, Johann Lukas von

Prater Park
Prater, Vienna
Open to the public
Hirschfeld, CCL

Schönbrunn
Schönbrunn Garten, Vienna
Open to the public
Fischer von Erlach, Johann Bernhardt

Barbados

Andromeda Gardens
Bathsheba, St Joseph
Open daily, 9am to 5pm
Bannochie, Iris

Belgium

Chateau d'Annevoie
Rue des Jardins, Annevoie
Open Apr to Nov daily, 9.30am to 6.30pm
Montpellier, Charles-Alexis de

Chateau de Beloeil
Beloeil
Open Easter to Sept daily & weekends in Oct, 10am to 6pm
Ligne, Prince Claude Lamoral II de

Enghien
Chateau d'Enghien, Place Pierre Delannoy, Enghien
Open to the public
Arenberg, Philippe d'

Kalmthout Arboretum
Kalmthout
Open to the public
de Belder Family

Serres Royales du Chateau de Laeken
Avenue du Parc Royal, Brussels
Open one week every year to the public. Enquire at the Belgian tourist office
Balat, Auguste

Mariemont
Musee Royal de Mariemont
Morlanwelz, Hainault
Open to the public
Albert & Isabella

Wirtz Garden
Private, not open to the public
Wirtz, Jacques & Peter

Brazil

Fernandez Residence
Correias
Private, not open to the public
Burle Marx, Roberto

Canada

Les Quatre Vents
Quebec
Open to the public by appointment
Cabot, Francis

Canary Islands

Jardin Canario
Las Palmas De Gran Canaria
Open daily 9am to 6pm. Closed 25 Dec & 1 Jan
Sventenius, Eric

Jardín du Cactus
Guatiza, Lanzarote
Open daily from 10am to 6pm
Manrique, Cesar

Quinta da Palheiro
Madeira
Open Mon to Fri, 9.30am to 12.30pm. Closed 25 Dec, 1 Jan, 1 May & Easter
Blandy Family

China

Canglangting
Green Wave Pavilion, Suzhou
Open to the public
Su Zimei

Ji Chang Yuan
Wuxi
Open to the public
Zhang Shi

Liu Yuan
Suzhou
Open to the public
Xu Shi-tai

River Summer Palace (Bi Shu Shan Zhuang)
Chengde, Hebei Province
Open to the public
Kang Xi, Emperor

Shizi Lin
Suzhou
Open to the public
Tien Ru

Summer Palace (Ye He Huan)
Beijing
Open to the public
Qian Long, Emperor

Wang Shi Yuan
Suzhou
Open to the public
Song Zenhuang

Yu Yuan
Shanghai
Open to the public
Pan En

Yuan Ming Yuan
Beijing
Open to the public
Qian Long

Zhuo Zheng Yuan (The Humble Administrators Garden)
Dong Bei Jie
Open to the public
Wang Xian Chen

Costa Rica

Manuel Gomez Residence
San Jose
Private, not open to the public
Yturbe, Jose de

Czech Republic

Botanic Gardens and Arboretum
Mendel University of Agriculture & Forestry. Zem d lská, Brno
Open Mon to Fri, 7am to 3pm
Otruba, Ivor

Buchlovice
Buchlovice, Zamek
Open Tues to Sun, 8am to 4pm. Closed 1 Nov to 31 Mar
Martinelli, Domenico

Lednice Valtice Park
South Moravia, Brno
Open daily (not Mon). Apr to Aug 8am to 6pm. Sept to Oct 9am to 4pm
Hardtmuth, Joseph

Lysice
Blansko, nr Brno
Open May, Jun & Sept, 9am to 5pm. Jul & Aug, 8am to 6pm. Closed 12pm to 1pm
Dubsky, Emanuel

Villa Müller
Prague 6, Stresovice

Open to the public
Loos, Adolf

Denmark

University of Aarhus
Aarhus
Grounds open to the public
Sørenson, Carl Theodor

Foresters House
Sherston
Private, not open to the public
Jakobsen, Preben

Fredensborg
Hellerød, Zealand
Open Jul daily, 9am to 5pm
Krieger, Johann Cornelius

Tivoli Gardens
Copenhagen
Open late Apr to mid-Sept, Sun to Wed, 11am to midnight, Thurs to Sat, 11am to 1am
Brandt, G N

Ecuador

Tulcan Gardens
Tulcan
Open to the public
Franco Guerrero, Jose

Finland

Villa Mairea
Noormarkku
Private, not open to the public
Aalto, Alvar

France

Ancy-le-Franc
Burgundy
Open Apr to mid-Nov daily
Serlio

Arboretum National des Barres
Nogent-sur-Vernisson
Open mid-Mar to mid-Nov daily, 10am to 12pm, 2pm to 6pm. Groups by appointment
Vilmorin, Pierre-Philippe André de

Bagatelle
Bois de Boulogne, Paris
Open daily, 8.30am to 8pm (9am to 5.30pm winter)
Bélanger, Francois Joseph & Blaikie, Thomas and Forestier, J C N

Blois
Loire Valley, Loir-et-Cher
Open daily (not 25 Dec & 1 Jan)
Mercogliano, Pacello de

Chateau d'Anet
nr Dreux, Ile de France
Open selected days throughout the year
L'Orme, Philibert de

Château de Brécy
Saint-Gabriel-Brécy, Caens
Open Easter to Oct, Tues, Thurs & Sun, 2.30pm to 6.30pm. Other times by appointment
Le Bas, Jacques

Château de Chantilly
Chantilly, Cédex
Open Mar to Oct daily, 10am to 6pm (closes on Tues from 12.45pm to 2pm). Nov to Feb daily, 10.30am to 12.45pm & 2pm to 5pm
Bullant, Jean

Château de Chaumont, vegetable wall, mist installation
Loire Valley, Chaumont
Open daily, not 1 Jan
Blanc, Patrick and Latz, Peter

Château de Chenonceau
Chenonceau
Open mid-Mar to mid-Sept, 9am to 7pm & mid-Sept to mid-Mar, 9am to 4.30pm
Poitiers, Diane de

Château de Courances
Courances, Ile-de-France
Open Apr to Oct, Sat, Sun & public holidays, 2pm to 6.30pm. Groups by appointment on weekdays
Gaillard, Claude

Château de Fontainebleau
Fontainebleau, Ile-de-France
Open spring & summer daily, 8am to 7.45pm. Autumn & winter daily, 9am to 4.45pm
Mollet, Claude

Château de Malmaison
Avenue du Château, Rueil-Malmaison, Hauts de Seine
Open weekdays (not Tues), 9.30am to 12pm & 1.30pm to 5.30pm. Apr to Sept, Sat & Sun 10am to 6.30pm. Oct to Mar , Sat & Sun, 10am to 6pm
Joséphine, Empress

Château de Méréville
Méréville
Open Easter to Oct on Sun, Mon, public holidays & Ascension day, 2pm to 7pm. Groups all year by appointment
Laborde, Marquise de

Château de Miromesnil
Tourville-sur-Arques
Open May to mid-Oct daily (not Tues), 2pm to 6pm
Vogue, Comte & Comtesse de

Château de Rambouillet dairy
Rambouillet
Open daily. Opening & closing times vary throughout the year
Robert, Hubert

Château de Versailles
Versailles
Open May to Sept daily (not Mon), 9am to 6.30pm. Oct to Apr, 9am to 5.30pm
Le Nôtre, André

Château de Villandry
Villandry
Open daily. Opening & closing times vary throughout the year
Carvallo, Dr Joachim

Cimetière du Père Lachaise
Paris
Open Mar to Nov daily, 7.30am to 6pm. Dec to Feb daily, 8am to 5.30pm. Opens 8.30am weekends & public holidays
Brongniart, Alexandre-Theodore

Les Colombières
Menton
Open by appointment only
Bac, Ferdinand

Concrete Trees
Paris
Garden vanished
Mallet-Stevens, Robert

Désert de Retz
Allée Frédéric Passy, Chambourcy
Open Mar to Oct, tours on the fourth Sat of the month, at 2.30pm & 4pm. Groups by appointment at other times
Monville, Baron de

Domaine de Marly
Marly-le-Roi
Open daily, sunrise to sunset
Hardouin-Mansart, Jules

Giverny, Musée Claude Monet
Fondation Claude Monet
Giverny, Haute-Normandie
Open Apr to Oct daily (not Mon), 10am to 6pm
Monet, Claude

Jas Crema
Private, not open to the public
Waldner, Baronne de

Kerdalo
Trédarzec
Open Mar to Nov, on the first Sat of each month, 2pm to 6pm, otherwise by appointment
Wolkonsky, Prince Peter

Labyrinth
Saint-Paul de Vence
Open Oct to June, 10am to 12.30pm & 2.30pm to 6pm. Jul to Sept, 10am to 7pm
Miró, Joan

La Roseraie der Val-de-Marne
l'Haÿ-les-Roses
Open mid-May to Sept daily, 10am to 8.30pm
André, Edouard

Le Vasterival
Sainte-Marguerite
Open by appointment only
Sturdza, Princess

Les Bois des Moutiers
Varengeville-sur-Mer, nr Dieppe,
Open daily, mid-Mar to mid-Nov, 10am to 7.30pm
Mallet family

Les Buissons Optiques
Garden vanished
Lassus, Bernard

Luxembourg Gardens
Boulevard St Michel, Paris
Open daily, 7am to one hour before sunset. (8am in winter)
Boyceau, Jacques

Own garden
Bonnieux
Private, not open to the public
Vesian, Nicole de

Palais Idéal du Facteur Cheval
Hauterives
Open Apr to Sept daily, 9am to

7pm; Oct to Nov daily, 9.30am to 5.30pm; Dec to Jan daily, 10am to 4.30pm; Feb to Mar daily, 9.30am to 5.30pm
Cheval, Facteur

Parc André Citroën
Paris
Open daily
Clément, Gilles and Provost, Alain

Parc de la Villette
Paris
Open daily
Tschumi, Bernard

Parc des Buttes-Chaumont
Rue Manin, Paris
Open daily, 9am to sunset
Barillet-Deschamps, Jean-Pierre

Parc Jean-Jacques Rousseau
Ermenonville
Open daily (not Tues), 2pm to 6.15pm. Closed from 20 Dec to 10 Jan
Girardin, René-Louis, Marquis de

Parc Monceau
Boulevard de Courcelles, Paris
Open daily, 9am to sunset
Carmontelle (Louis Carrogis)

Potager du Roi
4 rue Hardy, Versailles
Open to the public
La Quintinie, Jean-Baptiste de

St Germain-en-Laye
Rue Maurice Denis
St Germain-en-Laye
Open Wed to Sun, 10am to 5.30pm
Francini, Tomasso & Alessandro

Tachard Garden
Garden vanished
Legrain, Pierre-Emile

Terrasson Park
Place du Fiorail
Terrasson-Lavilledieu
Open Apr, May, June, Sept till mid-Oct daily (not Tues), 9.50am to 11.20am & 1.50pm to 5.20pm. Jul & Aug, 6pm closing
Gustafson, Kathryn

UNESCO Foundation Sculpture Garden
Place de Fontenoy, Paris
Open Mon to Fri, 9.30am to 12.30pm & 2.30pm to 6pm. Closed public holidays
Noguchi, Isamu

Vera Garden
Garden vanished
Vera, Andre & Paul

Verneuil
Garden vanished
Du Cerceau, Jacques Androuet

Villa Bomsel
Garden vanished
Lurçat, Andre

Villa Ephrussi de Rothschild
Avenue E de Rothschild
Saint-Jean-Cap-Ferrat, Nice
Open Feb to Nov, 10am to 6pm. Nov to Feb, weekends & public holidays, 10am to 6pm &

weekdays, 2pm to 6pm
Rothschild, Beatrix de

Villa Noailles
Avenue Guy de Maupassant, Grasse
Open in spring by appointment. Contact Grasse tourist office
de Noailles, Charles

Villa Noailles
Hyères
Open daily, 8am to 6pm
Guevrékian, Gabriel

Villa Savoye
rue de Villiers, Poissy
Open daily (not Tues), Apr to Oct, 9.30am to 12.30pm & 1.30pm to 6pm. Nov to Mar, 9.30am to 12.30pm & 1.30pm to 4.30pm. Closed on 1 Jan, 1 May, 1 & 11 Nov & 25 Dec
Le Corbusier

Germany

Branitz
Cottbus-Branitz
Open to the public
Pückler-Muskau, Hermann

ETA Hoffman Garden
The Jewish Museum
Lindenstrasse, Berlin
Open daily, 10am to 6pm
Libeskind, Daniel

Englischer Garten
Englischergarten, Munich
Open daily
Sckell, Friedrich Ludwig

Future Garden
Bonn Kunstmuseum
Rheinaue, Bonn
Open daily
Mayer, Helen & Newton, Harrison

Gross-Sedlitz
Barockpark Gross-Sedlitz
Open Apr to Sept daily, 7am to 8pm. Oct to Mar daily, 8am to 6pm
Augustus the Strong

Herrenhausen (Grosser Garten)
Herrenhausen, Hanover
Open daily, 8am to 8pm. Closes at 4pm in winter
Sophia, Duchess of Hanover

Hortus Palatinus
Heidelberg
Open to the public
Caus, Salomon de

Karlsruhe Schlossgarten and Botanic Garden
Hans-Thoma-Strasse, Karlsruhe
Open daily, dawn to dusk
Baden-Durlach, Carl-Wilhelm von

Mainau
Insel Mainau, Mainau
Open daily, 7am to 8pm. Mid-Oct to mid-Mar, 9am to 5pm
Friedrich I, Grand Duke of Baden

Nymphenburg
Nymphenburg, Munich
Open daily, 8am to dusk
Girard, Dominique

Own garden
nr Bornim
Open to the public
Förster, Karl

Park an der Ilm
Ilm Goethes Gartenhaus, Weimar
Open daily, dawn to dusk
Goethe, Johann Wolfgang von

Pfaueninsel
Berlin
Open May to Aug, 8am to 8pm. Apr & Sept, 8am to 6pm. Mar to Oct, 9am to 5pm. Nov to Feb, 10am to 4pm
Lenné, Peter Josef

Pillnitz
Schloss Pillnitz, Dresden
Open daily, dawn to dusk
Bouché

Rheinsberg Schlosspark
Rheinsberg
Open daily (not Mon), 9.30am to 5pm
Heinrich of Prussia, Prince

Sanspareil
Wonsees
Open daily, dawn to dusk
Wilhelmina of Bayreuth, Margravine

Sanssouci
Potsdam
Open daily, dawn to dusk
Friedrich II, King of Prussia

Schleissheim
Oberschleissheim, Munich
Open daily, dawn to dusk
Zucalli, Enrico

Schwetzingen Schlossgarten
Schwetzingen
Open daily, 8am to 8pm, or dusk
Carl Theodor of Neuburgh-Sulzbach, Elector Palatine

Veitshöchheim Hofgarten
Veitshöchheim
Open daily, dawn to dusk
Seinsheim, Adam Freidrich von

Villa Moser-Liebfried
Stuttgart
Open daily
Schaal, Hans Dieter

Wilhelmsbad
Hannau
Open daily, dawn to dusk
Wilhelm of Hessen-Kassel, Prince

Wilhelmshöhe
Kassel
Open daily, dawn to dusk
Guerniero, Gianfrancesco

Wörlitz
Dessau
Open daily, dawn to dusk
Anhalt-Dessau, Leopold Friedrich Franz von

Greece

Sparoza
Attica
Open to the public
Tyrwhitt, Jacqueline

Hungary

Esterháza
Fertöd, Eisenstadt
Open to the public
Esterházy, Prince Nikolaus

India

Amber Palace
Jaipur
Open 9am to 5.30pm
Bai, Jodh

Dig
Agra
Open sunrise to sunset
Suraj Mal, Raja of Bharatpur

Fatehpur Sikri
nr Agra
Open to the public
Akbar, Emperor

Nishat Bagh
Srinagar
Open to the public
Asaf Khan IV

Ram Bagh
Agra
Open 10am to 4.30pm
Babur, Emperor

Saheliyon ki Bari, or Gardens of the Maids of Honour
Open daily, 9am to 6pm
Singh, Maharana Sangram

Taj Mahal gardens
Agra
Open daily (not Mon), 6am to 7pm
Shah Jahan

The Rock Garden
Chandigarh
Open daily (not Thurs & official holidays), 10am to 7pm
Chand Saini, Nek

Iran (Persia)

Bagh-e Takht
Shiraz
Open to the public
Atabak Qaracheh, Shah

Frieze at Nineveh Palace
Open to the public
Assurbanipal, King

Apadana Palace
Persepolis
Open to the public
Darius The Great

Bagh-e-Shahzadeh
Mahann
Open to the public
Musgrave (Governor of Kerman)

Golestan Palace
Tehran
Open to the public
Fath Ali Shah

Pasargadae Palace
Open to the public
Cyrus the Younger

Taq-e-Bustan Grottoes
Kermanshah
Open to the public
Khosrow II Parvis

Ireland

Carton House Gardens
Co Kildare
Private, not open to the public
Leinster, 1st Duke & Duchess of Ireland

Castle Coole
Co Fermanagh
Open daily (not Thurs), 1pm to 6pm
Fraser, James

Glasnevin
National Botanic Gardens
Glasnevin, Dublin
Open daily (not 25 Dec), 9am to 6pm in summer & 10am to 4.30pm in winter. Opens 11am on Sun
Niven, Ninian

Glenveagh Castle Garden
Churchill, Letterkenny, Co Donegal
Open mid-Apr to Nov daily, 10am to 6.30pm
Roper, Lanning

Kilruddery Gardens
Bray, Co Wicklow
Open Apr to Sept daily, 1pm to 5pm
Meath, 11th Earl of

Powerscourt
Enniskerry, Co Wicklow
Open daily (not 25 & 26 Dec), 9.30am to 5.30pm or dusk
Powerscourt, 7th Viscount

Italy

Belvedere Court
Vatican Gardens, Vatican City, Rome
Open by appointment only
Bramante, Donato

Boboli Gardens
Pitti Palace, Florence
Open daily (not the first & last Mon of month), 9am. Closing depends on season
Tribolo, Niccolò

Bomarzo
Parco dei Mostri, Bomarzo
Open daily
Bomarzo, Orsini, Duke of

Botanic Gardens
Via Orto Botanico, Padua
Open Apr to Oct daily, 8.30am to sunset
Moroni, Andrea

Brion Cemetery
Brion
Open to the public
Scarpa, Carlo

Capalbio sculpture garden
Pescia Fiorentina, Capalbio
Groups may visit the garden on the first Sat of each month by appointment only.
Saint Phalle, Nicky de

Caserta, Palazzo Reale and the English Garden
Caserta, Naples
Open daily (not 25 Dec, 1 Jan & 1

Mar), 9am to dusk
Vanvitelli, Luigi

Castello Ruspoli
Vignanello
Open Sun, 10am to 2pm
Orsini, Ottavia

Giardini Guisti
Via Guisti 2, Verona
Open daily, 8am to 8pm in summer, to sunset in winter
Trezza, Luigi

Giardino e Rovine di Ninfa
Rome
Open Apr to Nov, first Sat & Sun of the month. Apr to June, the third Sun of every month. 1 May, guided visits only
Caetani Family

Hadrian's Villa
Tivoli
Open daily, 9am to 6.30pm
Hadrian, Emperor

Isola Bella
Lake Maggiore
Open Mar to Sept daily, 9am to 12pm & 1.30pm to 5pm. Oct daily, 1.30pm to 5pm
Borromeo, Count Carlo

La Mortella
Via Calise, Fofia, Isola d'Ischia
Open Apr to Oct, Tues, Thurs, Sat & Sun, 9am to 7pm
Page, Russell

La Mortola (Giardini Botanici Hanbury)
C.so Montecarlo, Latte, loc La Mortola
Open Nov to Mar daily (not Wed), 10am to 4pm. Apr to mid Jun & Oct, 10am to 5pm. Mid Jun to Sept, 9am to 6pm
Hanbury, Sir Thomas

La Pietra
Via Bolognese, Florence
Open by appointment only
Acton, Harold

Laurentian villa
Ancient Rome
Garden vanished
Pliny the Younger

Praeneste
Garden vanished
Sulla

Villa Aldobrandini
Via G. Massaia, Tivoli, Lazio
Open by appointment only, Mon to Sat, not public holidays, 9am to 1pm
Maderno, Carlo

Villa Barbaro
Village of Maser
Treviso District
Open Mar to Sept, Tues, Sat & Sun, 3pm to 6pm. Oct to Feb, 2.30pm to 5pm
Palladio, Andrea

Villa Borghese
Rome
Open daily (not the secret gardens), dawn to dusk
Borghese, Cardinal Scipione

Villa Chigi Cetinale
Sovicille, Siena
Open by appointment only
Fontana, Carlo

Villa Cicogna Mozzoni
Lake Como, Piazza Cicogna, Bisuchio
Open end Mar to Sept, Sun & public holidays, 9.30am to 12pm & 2.30pm to 7pm. Aug daily, 2.30pm to 7pm
Mozzoni, Ascanio

Villa Cimbrone
Via Santa Chiara
Ravello
Open daily, 9am to dusk
Mansi, Nicola

Villa d'Este
Piazza Trento, Tivoli
Open daily (not 25 Dec, 1 Jan & 1 May), 9am to 1 hour before sunset
Ligorio, Pirro

Villa Gamberaia
Via del Rossellino, Florence
Open by appointment only
Capponi Family

Villa Garzoni
Via di Castello, Collodi, Tuscany
Open daily, Feb to Nov, 9am to sunset
Garzoni, Romano

Villa i Tatti
nr Florence, Tuscany
Open by appointment only
Pinsent, Cecil

Villa il Roseto
Via Beato Angelico, Fiesole
Open weekdays, 9am to 1pm
Porcinai, Pietro

Villa Lante
Via J. Barozzi, Bagnaia
Open daily (not public holidays), 9am to one hour before sunset
Vignola, Giacomo Barozzi

Villa Madama
Garden vanished
Raphael

Villa Medici
Via Mantellini, Fiesole, Florence
Open by appointment only
Michelozzi, Michelozzo

Villa Pisani
The Veneto, Padua
Open daily (not Mon)
Frigimelica, Girolamo

Villa Pratolino
Parco Demidoff, Via Bolognese, Florence
Open Sun only
Buontalenti, Bernardo

Villa Reale
Via Villa Reale, Marlia, Lucca
Open Mar to Nov daily (not Mon)
Bacciocchi , Elisa

Villa Taranto
Lake Maggiore, Via Nazionale del Sempione Sud, Stresa
Open mid-Mar to end Oct daily,

9am to 6pm
McEarcharn, Neil

Villa Tibermitus
Pompeii
Open to the public
Tibernitus

Japan

Chichibu Residence
Tokyo
Private, not open to the public
Suzuki, Shodo

Entsuji
Kyoto
Gyokuen

Garden of Fine Arts
Kyoto National Museum
Open daily 9am to 4.30pm.
Closed Mon & between 26 Dec & 3 Jan
Ando, Tadao

Garden of reversible destiny
Kyoto
Open 9am to 5pm. Closed Mon, 25 Dec & 1 Jan
Arakawa + Gins

Kinkaku-ji (Golden Pavilion)
Kyoto
Open Apr to Sept, 8.30am to 5.30pm, Oct to Mar 8.30am to 5pm
Ashikaga Yoshimitsu

Joju-en Park
Kumamoto
Open 9am to 5pm. Closed Mon
Hosogawa, Tadayoshi

Katsura Detached Palace
Kyoto
Advance reservation only
Toshihito, Prince

Kodai-ji
Kyoto
Open Dec to Mar, 9am to 4pm.
Apr to Nov 9am to 4.30pm
Mandokora, Kita no

Murin-an Villa
Kyoto
Ogawa, Jigei

Nanzen-Ji
Kyoto
Open Dec to Feb, 8.40am to 4.30pm. Mar to Nov, 8.40am to 5pm
Enshu, Kobori

Omote Senke Tea Headquarters
Kyoto
Advance reservation only
Rikkyu, Sen no

Ryoan-ji
Kyoto
Open Dec to Feb, 8.30am to 4.30pm. Mar to Nov 8.40am to 5pm
Soami

Saiho-ji
Kyoto
Open, visits require advance permission from the temple
Kokushi, Muso

Sambo-in
Fushimi (nr Kyoto)
Open Mar to Oct, 9am to 5pm.
Closes one hour earlier other months
Hideyoshi, Toyotomi

Shoden-ji
Kyoto
Open 9.00am to 5pm
Shoden-ji Sensai

Shugaku-in Imperial Villa
Kyoto
Visits require advance permission from the Imperial Household
Gomizunoö, Emperor

Ginkaku-Ji (Silver Pavilion)
Kyoto
Open mid-Mar to end Nov, 8.30am to 5pm. Dec to mid-Mar, 9am to 4.30pm
Ashikaga Yoshimasa

Tenryuji Garden
Kyoto
Open Apr to Oct, 8.30am to 5.30pm. Nov to Mar, 8.30am to 5pm
Ashikaga Takaji

Tofuku-ji
Kyoto
Shigemori, Mirei

Republic of Korea

Secret Garden of Changdokkung
Seoul
Open daily (not Mon), 9.15am to 5.30pm
Yi Song Gye

Chollipo Arboretum
Namdo
Open to members only & academicians and students by appointment
Miller, Ferris

Mexico

Las Pozas
Las Pozas, San Luis Potosí
Open to the public
James, Edward

San Cristobal
Open by appointment
Barragán, Luis

Morocco

Menara Garden
Marrakesh
Open to the public
Almohad empire

La Majorelle
Marrakesh
Open daily
Majorelle, Jacques

Netherlands

Het Loo
Koninklijk Park, Apeldoorn
Open Tues to Sun, 10am to 5pm.
East & Westwing, 1pm. Closed on Mon & on 1 Jan
Marot, Daniel & Roman, Jacob

Hofwijck
Garden vanished
Huygens, Constantijn

Honselaarsdijk
Garden vanished
Frederik Hendrik, Prince

Huis ten Bosch
Garden vanished
Post, Pieter

Kleve
Garden vanished
Van Campen, Jacob

Kröller-Müller Museum Park Hoge Veluwe
Houtkampweg, Otterlo
Open daily (not Mon), 10am to 4.30pm
Bijhouwer, Jan

Kwekerij Piet Oudolf
Arnhem
Private, not open to the public
Oudolf, Piet

Leiden Botanical Garden
Leiden University
Open to the public
Clusius, Carolus (Charles de L'Ecluse)

Mien Ruys Tuinen
Dememsvaart
Open Apr to Oct, Mon to Sat, 10am to 5pm, Sun, 1pm to 5pm
Ruys, Mien

Thijsse Park
Amstelveen
Open to the public
Thijsse, Jacob P

Arboretum Trompenberg
Rotterdam
Open Apr to Sept, Mon to Fri, 9am to 5pm. Oct to Mar, as above but closed Sun
van Hoey Smith Family

Tuinen Ton ter Linden
Achterma, Ruinen
Open to the public
Ton Ter Linden

VSB Bank
Utrecht
Open to the public
Geuze, Adriaan

New Zealand

Otari
New Zealand Botanic Garden
Wellington
Information Centre open 9am-4pm weekdays, 10am-4pm weekends.
Wilton, Job & Cockayne, Dr Leonard

Pukeiti Rhododendron Garden
Carrington Road
New Plymouth, Taranaki
Open daily
Cook, Douglas

Sanders' Garden
Auckland
Private, not open to the public
Smyth, Ted

Pakistan

Shalimar Bagh
Lahore
Open to the public
Jahanigir

Poland

Arkadia
Nieborow
Open to the public
Radziwill, Helena, Princess

Lancut
Lancut Village
Open to the public
Czartoryska, Duchess Izabela

Lazienki Park
Warsaw
Open to the public
Stanislas II Poniatowski, King of Poland

Nièberow
Satelite of National Museum of Warsaw
Open to the public
Zug, Szymon Bogumil

Wilanów
Warsaw
Open daily 9am to dusk
Boy, Adolf & Ciolek, Gerard

Portugal

Palace of Pombal
Oeiras, Lisbon
Open to the public
Mardel, Carlos

Palace of Queluz
Queluz, Lisbon
Open daily (not Tues & public holidays). May to Oct, 10am to 6.30pm. Nov to Apr, 10am to 5pm
Oliveira, Mateus Vicente de & Robillon, Jean-Baptiste

Palacio dos marquises de Frontera
Lisbon
Open daily (not Sun & public holidays)
Fronteira, Marquis of

Quinta da Regaleira
Fundação Cultursintra, Sintra
Open daily. Closed Feb
Monteiro, António Carvalho & Manini, Luigi

Quinta de Aveleda
Penafiel
Open daily, 9am to 5.30pm
Guedes, Manoel Pedro

Villa Mateus
Vila Real
Open daily, 9am to 7pm in summer, 10am to 5pm in winter
Nasoni, Niccolo

Romania

Tirgu Jiu sculpture Park
Open to the public
Brancusi, Constantin

Russia

Alupka
Yalta
Open to the public
Kebach, Karl

Nikitsky Botanic Garden
nr Yalta
Open to the public
Steven, Christian

Oranienbaum
Yalta
Private, not open to the public
Rinaldi, Antonio

Pavlovsk
nr St Petersburg
Open daily, 2pm to 6pm. Closed Fri
Cameron, Charles

Peterhof
nr St Petersburg
Open 10.30am to 5pm. Closed Tues
Le Blond, Jean-Baptiste

Summer Garden
St Petersburg
Open 10.30am to 5pm. Closed Tues
Peter II

Tsarskoye Selo
Pushkin, nr St Petersburg
Open daily (not Tues & the last Mon of the month), 10am to 5pm
Catherine II

Singapore

Singapore Botanic Garden
Holland and Cluny Roads
Open daily, 5am until midnight
Raffles, Sir Stamford

South Africa

Amanzimnyana
Private, not open to the public
Saunders, Douglas

Company Gardens
Government Avenue, Cape Town
Open to the public
van Riebeeck, Jan

Kirstenbosch Botanic Garden
Rhodes Drive, Newlands
Open Sept to Mar, 8am to 7pm & Apr to Aug, 8am to 6pm
Rhodes, Cecil

Private Garden
Sandhurst, Johannesburg
Private, not open to the public
Watson, Patrick

Rustenberg Farm Gardens
Stellenbosch
Open to the public
Barlow, Pamela

Vergelegen
Lourensford Road, Somerset West
Open daily, 9.30am to 4pm
Phillips, Lady Florence

Spain

Alfabia
Majorca

Open Sept to May, 9.30am to
5.30pm. June to Aug, 9.30am to
6.30pm. Sat, 9.30am to 1pm.
Closed Sun
Moorish Governors

Buen Retiro
Paseo del Prado, Madrid
Open Tues to Sat, 9am to 7pm,
Sun & holidays, 9am to 2pm.
Closed Mon
Lotti, Cosimo

Casa de Pilatos
Plaza de Pilatos, Seville
Open, ground floor, 9am to 8pm.
First floor, 10am to 2pm & 4pm
to 6pm
Tortella, Benevenuto

Generalife (Jennat-al-Arif)
Granada
Open daily, 9am to 8pm.
Summer, 9am to 6pm in winter
Nazarite

Jardin del Palacio de Aranjuez
Aranjuez
Open to the public
Philip II, King of Spain

La Granja
Segovia
Open Tues to Sun, 10am to 7pm
in summer, 10am to 6.30pm in
winter
Philip V, King of Spain

Medina Azahara
Córdoba
Open Tues to Sun
*Abd al-Rahman III, Caliph of
Cordoba*

**Monasterio de San Lorenzo de
Trassouto**
Santiago de Compostela
Open Mon & Thurs, 11am to 1pm
& 4.30pm to 6.30pm
*Monasterio de San Lorenzo de
Trassonto*

Neuendorf House
Majorca
Private, not open to the public
Pawson, John & Silvestrin, Claudio

Own Garden
Majorca
Private, not open to the public
Gildemeister, Heidi

Parc Güell
Carrer d'Lot, Barcelona
Open daily, May to Aug, 10am to
9pm. Closing time varies in
other months
Gaudí, Antoni

Patio of the lions
Alhambra Palace, Granada
Open Mar to Oct daily, 8.30am to
8pm. Nov to Feb daily (not 25
Dec & 1 Jan), 8.30am to 6pm.
Night visits also possible
Muhammad V

Pazo de Oca
Santiago da Compostela
Open daily, 9am to 1pm & 4pm
to 8pm summer
Medinaceli Family

Barcelona Pavillion
Montjuïc, Barcelona
Open daily, 10am to 8pm
Mies van der Rohe

Sol I Ombra
Barcelona
Open to the public
Pepper, Beverly

Wheat Garden
Palma, Majorca
Private, not open to the public
Caruncho, Fernando

Sri Lanka

Lunuganga
nr Bentota
Private, not open to the public
Bawa, Geoffrey

Peradeniya Botanical Garden
Kandy
Open to the public
Thwaites, G H K

Sweden

Drottningholm Palace
Lake Mälaren, Stockholm
Open May to Sept, 11am to
4.30pm. Closed 20 June
Nicodemus Tessin the Younger

Haga
Haga Norra, Stockholm
Open Apr to Sept, Tues to Fri,
10am to 4pm, Sat & Sun, 11am to
5.30pm. Oct to Mar, Tues to Fri,
10am to 3pm. Sat & Sun, 11am
to 4pm
Piper, F M

Stockholm Residence
Private, not open to the public
Nordfjell, Ulf

Sundborn
Carl Larsson-gården
Open May to Sept daily, 10am to
5pm
Larsson, Carl

Puffing Mosses
Temporary installation
Toll, Julie

Woodland Cemetery
Stockholm
Open to the public
Asplund, Gunnar

Switzerland

Uetliberg Gardens
Zürich
Open to the public
Kienast, Dieter

Villa Smithers
Vico Morcote
Visits by appointment only
Smithers, Sir Peter

Turkey

Kiraç Villa
Tarabya
Private, not open to the public
Eldem, Sedad

Topkapi Palace
Ankara
Open all year daily (not Tues),

9.30am to 5pm
Mehmed II

United Kingdom

48 Storey's Way
Cambridge
Private, not open to the public
Baillie Scott, M H

Alton Towers
Alton, Staffordshire
Open daily, 9.30am to 6pm
Allason, Thomas & Abraham, Robert

Anglesey Abbey
Lode, Cambridgeshire
Open Mar to Jul, Wed to Sun &
bank holidays; Jul to Sept daily,
11am to 5.30pm
Fairhaven, Lord

Arley Hall & Gardens
nr Northwich, Cheshire
Open Apr to Oct, Tues to Sun &
bank holidays, 11am to 5pm
Egerton-Warburton, R-G

Arundel House
London
Garden vanished
Jones, Inigo

Ascott Residence
Leighton Buzzard,
Buckinghamshire
Private, not open to the public
Lennox-Boyd, Arabella

Ascott
Ascott, Wing, Leighton Buzzard
Buckinghamshire
Open May to Aug, Wednesdays
& the last Sun of the month. Apr
& Sept daily (not Mon), 2pm to
6pm
Veitch, Sir Harry

Ashton Wold
Ashton, Northants
Private, not open to the public
Rothschild, Miriam

Athelhampton House Gardens
Athelhampton, Dorset
Open Mar to Oct daily (not Sat).
Nov to Feb, Sun, 10.30am to 5pm
Thomas, Inigo

Barnsley House Garden
Barnsley, Gloucestershire
Open Feb to mid-Dec, Mon, Wed,
Thurs & Sat, 10am to 5.30pm
Verey, Rosemary

Bayleaf Farmhouse
Weald & Downland Open Air
Museum
Singleton, Chichester, Sussex
Open Mar to Oct daily, 10.30am
to 6pm. Nov to Feb on Wed, Sat &
Sun, 10.30am to 4pm. Dec 26 to 1
Jan daily, 10.30am to 4pm
Landsberg, Sylvia

Beckford's Ride
Lansdowne Cemetery, nr Bath
Garden vanished
Beckford, William

Belsay Hall
Belsay, nr Ponteland,
Northumberland
Open daily (not 24 to 26 Dec & 1

Jan), 10am to 6pm or dusk
Middleton, Sir Arthur

Bentley Wood
Sussex
Private, not open to the public
Tunnard, Christopher

Biddulph Grange
Biddulph, Staffordshire
Open 25 Mar to 29 Oct, Wed,
Thurs & Fri, 12 noon to 6pm; Sat,
Sun & bank holidays, 11am to
6pm. Closed 21 Apr
Bateman, James & Cooke, Edward

Blenheim Palace
Woodstock, Oxfordshire
Park open daily (not 25 Dec), 9am
to dusk
*Brown, Lancelot 'Capability',
Duchêne, Achille*

Bodnant Garden
Gwynedd, Wales
Open mid-Mar to Oct daily,
10am to 5pm
Aberconway, 2nd Baron

Bramham Park
Wetherby, West Yorkshire
Open Feb to Sept daily, 10.30am
to 5.30pm
Bingley, Robert Benson, Lord

Brantwood
Coniston, Cumbria
Open mid-Mar to mid-Nov daily,
11am to 5.30pm
Ruskin, John

Broughton House
Kirkcudbright, Dumfries &
Galloway
Open daily, Apr to Oct, 1pm to
5.30pm. Jul & Aug open from
11am
Hornel, E A

Caerhays Castle Garden
St Austell, Cornwall
Open Mar to May, Mon to Fri,
11am to 4pm
Williams, J C

Caledon
Co Tyrone
Private, not open to the public
Orrey, John 5th Earl of

Castle Howard
York, North Yorkshire
Open mid-Mar to Oct daily,
10am to 4.30pm
Vanbrugh, Sir Charles

Castle Tor
Devon
Private, not open to the public
Harrild, Frederick

Chatsworth
Bakewell, Derbyshire
Open mid-Mar to Oct daily, 11am
to 5pm
Paxton, Joseph

Beth Chatto Gardens
Colchester, Essex
Open Mar to Oct, Mon to Sat,
9am to 5pm
Chatto, Beth

Chelsea Flower Show Garden
Temporary garden
Bradley-Hole, Christopher

Chelsea Physic Garden
Royal Hospital Road, London
Open Apr to Oct, Wed, 12pm to
5pm. Sun, 2pm to 6pm
Sloane, Sir Hans

Chiswick House
Chiswick, London
Open daily, 8.30am to dusk
Burlington, Richard Boyle, Lord

Claremont Landscape Garden
Esher, Surrey
Open daily (not Mon), Nov to
May, 10am to 5pm (summer
weekdays 6pm & weekends
7pm)
Bridgeman, Charles

Coleton Fishacre
Kingswear, Dartington, Devon
Open Apr to Oct, Wed, Sun &
bank holidays, 10.30am to
5.30pm. Also open Sun in Mar,
2pm to 5pm
Milne, Oswald

Cottesbrooke
Creaton, Northamptonshire
Open Easter to the end of Sept,
Wed, Thurs, Fri & Bank Holiday
Mon (Sun afternoons in Sept),
2pm to 5.30pm
MacDonald-Buchanan Family

Cowley Manor
Cowley, Gloucestershire
Open May to Oct daily (not Mon,
Fri & bank holidays), 10am to
6pm. Other times by
appointment
Kingsbury, Noel

Cragside Garden & Grounds
Rothbury, Morpeth,
Northumberland
Open Apr to Oct daily (not Mon,
but open bank holidays),
10.30am to 7pm. Nov to Dec,
weekends, 10.30am to 7pm
Armstrong, Lord

Dartington Hall
Dartington, Devon
Open daily, dawn to dusk
Cane, Percy

Denmans
Fontwell, West Sussex
Open Mar to Oct daily, 9am
to 5pm
Brookes, John

Derby Arboretum
Derby, Elvaston, Derbyshire
Open daily
Loudon, John Claudius

Derry & Toms Roof Garden
Kensington High Street, London
Open by appointment daily, 9am
& 5pm
Hancock, Ralph

Dew gardens
Aylesbury, Buckinghamshire
Temporary gardens
Parsons, Chris

Downe House
Downe, Kent
Open Apr to Oct, Wed to Sun,
10am to 6pm; Mar, Nov to Jan,
Wed to Sun, 10am to 4pm
Darwin, Charles

Downton Castle
nr Ludlow, Herefordshire
Private, not open to the public
Knight, Richard Payne

Drummond Castle
Muthill, Perthshire, Scotland
Open May to Oct daily & Easter,
2pm to 6pm
Kennedy, George & Lewis

Eagles' Nest
Zennor, Cornwall
Private, not open to the public
Heron, Patrick

East Lambrook Manor
South Petherton, Somerset
Open Mon to Sat, 10am to 5pm
Fish, Margery

Eden Project
Bodelva, Cornwall
Official opening Easter 2001
Grimshaw, Nicholas, & Partners

**Edinburgh Royal Botanic
Garden**
Inverleith Row, Edinburgh
Open daily (not 25 Dec & 1 Jan)
McNab, James

Elvaston Castle Country Park
Derby, Derbyshire
Open daily
Barron, William

Enstone
Oxfordshire
Garden vanished
Bushell, Thomas

Erddig
Clwyd, Wales
Open Mar to Nov, Sat to Wed,
11am to 6pm or dusk
Emes, William

Folly Farm
Reading, Berkshire
Open occasionally through the
National Gardens Scheme
Lutyens, Sir Edwin Landseer

Forsters Garden
London
Private, not open to the public
Silva, Roberto

Friar Park
Henley on Thames, Oxfordshire
Private, not open to the public
Crisp, Sir Frank

Fulham Garden
London
Private, not open to the public
Noel, Anthony

The Garden in Mind
Stanstead Park, Rowlands
Castle, Derbyshire
Open Mar to Oct, 1pm to 5pm
Hicks, Ivan

Garden of Cosmic Speculation
Portrack, Scotland
Private, not open to the public
Jencks, Charles

Gibberd Garden
Harlow
Open Apr to Sept, Sat & Sun,
2pm to 6pm
Gibberd, Sir Frederick

Golders Green Garden
London
Private, not open to the public
Cooper, Paul

Goldney Hall
Lower Clifton Hill, Bristol
Private, not open to the public
Goldney, Thomas

Gravetye Manor
East Grinstead, West Sussex
Open to hotel guests
Robinson, William

Great Dixter
Northiam, Rye, East Sussex
Open Apr to Oct daily (not Mon,
but open bank holidays), 2pm to
5pm
Lloyd, Christopher

Great Maytham Hall
nr Ashford, Kent
Open May to Sept, Wed & Thurs,
2pm to 5pm
Burnett, Frances Hodgson

Grizedale Forest
Grizedale, Hawkshead
Ambleside, Cumbria
Open daily, sunrise to sunset
Goldsworthy, Andy

Hackfall
Grewelthorp, North Yorkshire
Open daily
Aislabie, William

Hafod
Pwllpeiran, Wales
Open daily
Johnes, Thomas

Hampton Court Palace & Privy Garden
East Mosely, London
Open daily, dawn to dusk
William III and Wise, Henry

Hanbury Hall
Droitwich, Worcestershire
Open mid-Mar to mid-Oct, Sun
to Wed, 2pm to 6pm
London, George

Harewood House
Harewood, Leeds, West
Yorkshire
Open Apr to Oct daily; Nov to
mid-Dec, weekends, 10am to
6pm or dusk
Barry, Sir Charles

Hatfield House
Hatfield, Hertfordshire
Open mid-Mar to mid-Sept daily
(not Mon, but open bank
holidays), 10.30am to 8pm; West
Gardens daily (not Mon & Fri),
11am to 6pm
Salisbury, Marchioness of

510

Hawkstone Park
Shrewsbury, Shropshire
Open Jul to Aug daily; Apr to
June & Sept to Oct, Wed to Sun;
Jan to Mar, weekends, 10.30am
to 6pm or dusk
Hill, Sir Rowland & Sir Richard

Henry Moore Foundation garden
Much Hadham, Hertfordshire
Open by appointment, Apr to
mid-Oct daily, guided tours,
2.30pm
Moore, Henry

Heveningham Hall
Private, not open to the public
Wilkie, Kim

Hever Castle
Edenbridge, Kent
Open Mar to Nov daily, 11am to
6pm
Pearson & Cheal

Hidcote Manor Garden
Chipping Campden,
Gloucestershire
Open Apr to Nov daily (not Tues
& Fri). June & Jul, also open
Tues, 11am to 7pm or dusk
Johnston, Lawrence

Highnam Court
Highnam, Gloucestershire
Open Apr to Oct, on the first Sun
in the month, 11am to 5pm
Pulham, James

Hill Top
Beatrix Potter's garden
nr Sawrey, Ambleside
Open daily (not Thurs & Fri) &
Good Fri, 11am to 5pm
Potter, Beatrix

Holkham Hall
Wells-next-the-Sea, Norfolk
Open end May to end Sept daily
(not Fri & Sat), 1pm to 5pm
Nesfield, William Andrews

Iford Manor Garden
Bradford-on-Avon, Wiltshire
Open May to Sept daily (not Mon
but open on bank holidays), Apr
& Oct, Sun, 2pm to 5pm
Peto, Harold

Inverewe
Inverewe Garden
Poolewe, Ross & Cromarty
Open daily
Mackenzie, Osgood

Kellie Castle
Pittenweem, Fife, Scotland
Open daily
Lorimer, Sir Robert

Kelmscott Manor
Kelmscott, Gloucestershire
Open Apr to Sept, Wed & third
Sat of each month, 11am to 1pm
& 2pm to 5pm
Morris, William

Kew Palm House & Royal Botanic Gardens
Kew, Richmond, London
Open daily (not 25 Dec & 1 Jan),
9.30am to 7.30pm or dusk. Palm

house open at different times
throughout the year
*Burton, Decimus & Richard Turner;
Chambers, William*

Lamport Hall & Gardens
Lamport, Northamptonshire
Open Easter to Oct, Sun & bank
holidays, 2.15pm to 5.15pm
Isham, Sir Charles

Levens Hall
Kendal, Cumbria
Open Apr to Oct daily (not Fri &
Sat), 10am to 5pm
Beaumont, Guillaume

Little Peacocks (Filkins)
Filkins, Lechlade,
Gloucestershire
Open occasionally under the
National Gardens Scheme
Colvin, Brenda

Little Sparta
Lanarkshire, Scotland
Closed to the public
Hamilton Finlay, Ian

Mellerstain House
Gordon, Berwickshire, Scotland
Open Apr to Sept daily (not Sat);
& Easter, 12.30pm to 5pm
Blomfield, Reginald

Millennium Dome
North Greenwich, London
Open daily, 9am to 8pm in 2000
Pearson, Dan

Montacute House
Montacute, Yeovil, Somerset
Open Apr to Oct daily (not Tues),
11am to 5.30pm; Nov to Mar,
Wed to Sun, 11.30am to 4pm or
dusk
Phelips, Sir Edward

Moonhill
Garden vanished
Mawson, Thomas

Moorhouse
London
Garden vanished
More, Thomas

Mottisfont Abbey Garden
Mottisfont, Hampshire
Open mid-Mar to Oct, Sat to
Wed, 12pm to 6pm or dusk
Thomas, Graham Stuart

Mount Stewart
Newtownards, Co Down
Open Apr to Sept daily; Mar, Sun;
Oct, Sat & Sun, 11am to 6pm
Londonderry, Marchioness of

Munstead Wood
Godalming, Surrey
Open on selected days, 2pm to
6pm
Jekyll, Gertrude

Myddelton House Gardens
Bulls Cross, Enfield, London
Open weekdays, 10am to
4.30pm; also open Apr to Oct,
Sun & bank holidays, 2pm to
5.30pm
Bowles, EA

Nonsuch Palace
Surrey
Garden vanished
Lumley, Lord

Nymans
Handcross, nr Haywards Heath,
West Sussex
Open Mar to Oct, Wed to Sun &
bank holidays; Nov to Feb,
weekends, 11am to 6pm or dusk
Messel, Ludwig & Leonard

Old Vicarage
East Ruston Old Vicarage
nr Stalham, Norfolk
Open end Apr to end Oct, Wed,
Sun & bank holidays, 2pm to
5pm
Robeson & Gray

Packwood House
Solihull, Warwickshire
Open Mar to Oct, Wed to Sun &
bank holidays, 10am to 5.30pm
or dusk
Baron Ash, G

Painshill Landscape Garden
Cobham, Surrey
Open Apr to Oct daily (not Mon,
but open bank holidays),
10.30am to 6pm; Nov to Mar
daily (not Mon & Fri), 11am to
4pm or dusk
Hamilton, Charles and Lane, Joseph

Painswick Rococo Garden
Painswick, Gloucestershire
Open Jan to Nov, Wed to Sun; Jul
to Aug daily, 11am to 5pm
Robins, Thomas

Penicuik
nr Edinburgh, Scotland
Private, not open to the public
Clerk, Sir John

Plas Brondanw
North Wales
Open daily, 9.30am to 5.30pm
Williams-Ellis, Clough

Pope's Grotto
Pope's Villa, Twickenham,
London
Open by appointment only
Pope, Alexander

Port Lympne Gardens
Lympne, nr Hyde, Kent
Open daily
Tilden, Philip

Powis Castle
Powys, Wales
Open Apr to Oct daily not Mon &
Tues (but open bank holidays),
11am to 6pm. Open Tues in Aug
Rochford, Earl of

Prior Park Landscape Garden
Bath, Somerset
Open end Apr to Sept daily (not
Tues), 11am to 5.30pm
Allen, Ralph

Prospect Cottage
Dungeness, Kent
Private, not open to the public
Jarman, Derek

Renishaw Hall
Eckington, Derbyshire

Open Apr to Sept, Fri, Sat, Sun &
bank holidays, 10.30am to
4.30pm
Sitwell, Sir George

Rievaulx Terrace & Temples
Rievaulx, North Yorkshire
Open Apr to Sept daily, 10.30am
to 6pm (or 5pm in Apr & Oct)
Duncombe III, Thomas

Rodmarton Manor
Rodmarton, Gloucestershire
Open May to Aug, Wed, Sat &
bank holidays, 2pm to 5pm
Barnsley, Ernest

Rousham House
Steeple Aston, Oxfordshire
Open daily, 10am to 4.30pm
Kent, William

Royal Pavilion
Brighton, East Sussex
Open daily
Nash, John

Rydal Mount
Ambleside, Cumbria
Open Mar to Oct daily, 9.30am to
4pm. Nov to Feb daily (not
Tues), 10am to 4pm
Wordsworth, William

Savill Garden
Windsor Great Park
Windsor, Berkshire
Open Mar to Oct daily, 10am to
6pm (Nov to Feb, 4pm)
Savill, Eric

Scotney Castle
Lamberhurst, Kent
Open Mar, weekends, 12pm to
4pm; Apr to Oct, Wed, Thurs &
Fri, 11am to 6pm; Sat & Sun,
2pm to 6pm; bank holidays,
12pm to 6pm
Gilpin, William Sawrey

Sezincote
Moreton-in-Marsh,
Gloucestershire
Open Jan to Nov, Thurs, Fri &
bank holidays, 2pm to 6pm or
dusk
Cockerell, Samuel Pepys

Sheringham Park
Upper Sheringham, Norfolk
Open daily, dawn to dusk
Repton, Humphry

Shugborough
Great Haywood, Staffordshire
Open end Mar to Sept daily (not
Mon); Oct, Sun only, 11am to
5pm
Wright, Thomas

Silverstone Farm
Private, not open to the public
Carter, George

Sissinghurst Garden
Sissinghurst, Kent
Open Apr to mid-Oct, Tues to
Fri, 1pm to 6.30pm; weekends,
10am to 5.30pm
Sackville-West, Vita

Barbara Hepworth Museum & Sculpture Garden
Barnoon Hill, St Ives, Cornwall
Open all year, Tues to Sun; Jul &
Aug daily, 10.30am to 5.30pm
Hepworth, Barbara

St Paul's Walden Bury
Whitwell, Hertfordshire
Open on selected days each year,
2pm to 7pm
Bowes-Lyon, David

Stourhead
nr Warminster, Wiltshire
Open daily
Hoare, Henry

Stowe Landscape Garden
Buckingham, Buckinghamshire
Open Apr to Oct, Wed to Sun &
bank holidays
Temple, William

Strawberry Hill
St Mary's University College
Twickenham, London
Open Easter to Oct, Sun
Walpole, Horace

Studley Royal
Ripon, North Yorkshire
Open daily (not 24 Dec, 25 Dec &
Fri, Nov to Jan)
Aislabie, John

Sutton Courtenay
Sutton Park, Sutton-on-the-
Forest, North Yorkshire
Open Apr to Sept, Sun & Wed;
Easter, 1.30pm to 5pm
Lindsay, Norah

Sutton Place
Guildford, Surrey
Open by appointment for pre-
booked parties
Jellicoe, Sir Geoffrey

The Swiss Garden
Old Warden, Bedford,
Bedfordshire
Open Mar to Sept daily
Ongley, Lord

Syon House
Syon Park, Brentford, London
Open daily (not 25 to 26 Dec),
10am to 5.30pm or dusk
Fowler, Charles

Tatton Park
Knutsford, Cheshire
Open Apr to Oct, Tues to Sun &
bank holidays, 10.30am to 6pm
(11am to 4pm in winter)
Egerton, 3rd Baron

The Grove
Oxfordshire
Private, not open to the public
Hicks, David

The Laskett
Hertfordshire
Open by appointment only
Strong, Sir Roy

The Leasowes
Halesowen, Warwickshire
Open daily
Shenstone, William

The Lost Gardens of Heligan
Pentewan, St Austell, Cornwall
Open daily (not 24 & 25 Dec),
10am to 6pm (winter 5pm)
Smit, Tim

The Pineapple at Dunmore Park
North of Airth, Scotland
Open daily, 9.30am to sunset.
Accommodation can be reserved
through the Landmark Trust
Dunmore, Lord

Tresco Abbey Gardens
Isles of Scilly, Cornwall
Open daily, 10am to 4pm
Smith, Augustus

Turn End
Townside, Haddenham,
Buckinghamshire
Open selected days throughout
the year
Aldington, Peter

Vauxhall Pleasure Gardens
Garden vanished
Tyers, Jonathan

Waddesdon Manor
Waddesdon, Buckinghamshire
Open Mar to Dec, Wed, Sun &
bank holidays, 10am to 5pm
Lainé, Elie

Warley Place
Brentwood, Essex
Open once a year by
appointment
Willmott, Ellen

West Wycombe Park
High Wycombe,
Buckinghamshire
Open Apr to May, Sun & Wed;
June to Aug, Sun to Thurs; also
open bank holidays, 2pm to 6pm
Dashwood, Sir Francis

Westbury Court Garden
Westbury-on-Severn,
Gloucestershire
Open Apr to Oct, Wed to Sun &
bank holidays, 11am to 6pm
Colchester, Maynard

Westonbirt Arboretum
sw of Tetbury, Gloucestershire
Open daily
Holford, Robert Stayner

Wexham Springs
Garden vanished
Crowe, Sylvia

Wightwick Manor
Wightwick Bank, Wolverhampton
West Midlands
Open Mar to Dec, Wed, Thurs,
Sat & Bank Holiday Sun & Mon,
2pm to 6pm
Parsons, Alfred

Wilton House
Wilton, Wiltshire
Open Apr to Oct daily, 10.30am
to 5.30pm
Pembroke, Philip Herbert, Earl of

Woburn Abbey
Woburn, Bedfordshire
Open Mar to Sept daily
Caus, Isaac de

Woburn Farm
Surrey
Private, not open to the public
Southcote, Philip

USA

ALCOA Forecast Garden
Los Angeles, CA
Garden vanished
Eckbo, Garrett

Allerton Gardens
National Tropical Botanical
Garden, Kaua'i, Hawaii
Tours available Tues to Sat at
9am, 10am, 1pm & 2pm by
appointment
Emma, Queen

Arnold Arboretum
Boston, MA
Open daily, sunrise to sunset
Sargent, Charles Sprague

Bank of America (Windsocks)
Private, not open to the public
Delaney, Topher

Bartrams Garden (heritage)
Philadelphia, PA
Open daily, 10am to 5pm. Closed
all public holidays
Bartram, John

Biltmore
Asheville, NC
Open daily (not Thanksgiving &
25 Dec), Jan to Mar, 9am to 5pm.
Apr to Dec, 8.30am to 5pm
Vanderbilt, George W

Bloedel Reserve
Bainbridge Island, WA
Open by appointment only
Haag, Richard

The Capitol
Washington, DC
Open daily, Mar to Aug, 9am
until 6pm. Sept to Feb, 9am to
4.30pm
*Downing, Andrew Jackson & Vaux,
Calvert*

Casa Bienvenita
Los Angeles, CA
Private, not open to the public
Mizner, Addison

Casa del Herrero
Santa Barbara, CA
Private, not open to the public
Washington Smith, George

Central Park
New York, NY
Open daily
Olmsted, Frederick Law

Cranbrook
North Woodward Avenue
Bloomfield Hills, MI
Grounds open to the public
Saarinen, Eliel

Dawnridge
Los Angeles, CA
Garden vanished
Duquette, Tony

Dickensen Garden
Santa Fe, NM

Private, not open to the public
Schwartz, Martha

Douglas House
Phoenix, AZ
Private, not open to the public
Martino, Steve

Dumbarton Oaks
Washington, DC
Open daily, Apr to Oct, 2pm to
6pm. Nov to Mar, 2pm to 5pm.
(Closed public holidays)
Farrand, Beatrix

El Novillero
Dewey Donnell Garden, Sonoma
Sonoma County, CA
Church, Thomas

Ellison Residence
San Francisco, CA
Private, not open to the public
Herman, Ron

Falling Water
Bear Run, PA
Tours by appointment
Wright, Frank Lloyd

Forest Lawn Cemetery
Glendale, CA
Open daily
Eaton, Dr Hubert

Garden for J Irwin Miller
Columbus, IA
Private, not open to the public
Kiley, Dan

Glass garden
Los Angeles, CA
Private, not open to the public
Cao, Andy

Grand Isle Residence
Grand Isle, VT
Private, not open to the public
Child, Susan

Hearst Mansion
San Simeon, CA
Tours daily (not Thanksgiving,
25 Dec & 1 Jan). Booking
recommended
Hearst, William Randolph

Huntington Library
San Marino, CA
Open Tues to Fri, 12pm to
4.30pm. Weekends, 10.30am to
4.30pm. (Closed Mon & public
holidays.) June to Aug, 10.30am
to 4.30pm
Hertrich, William

IBM Solana
Solana, TX
Private, not open to the public
Walker, Peter

Innisfree
Tyrell Rd, Millbrook, NY
Open May to Oct, Wed to Fri,
10am to 4pm & weekends, 11am
to 5pm
Beck, Walter & Collins, Lester

Irwin Garden
Columbus, IA
Open Tues to Fri, 9am to 4pm
Phillips, Henry

Kykuit
Pocantico Hills, NY
Tours available daily (not Tues),
end Apr to Oct
Bosworth, William Welles

Laughlin House
Santa Monica, CA
Garden vanished
Gill, Irving

Leitzsch Residence
CT
Private, not open to the public
Bye, A E

Lincoln Memorial Garden
East Lake Drive, Springfield, IL
Open daily (closed public
holidays), sunrise to sunset
Jensen, Jens

Linda Taubman Garden
Bloomfield Hills, MI
Private, not open to the public
Pfeiffer, Andrew

The LongHouse Garden
East Hampton, NY
Open end Apr to Sept, 2pm to
5pm Wed, plus the first & third
Sat of the month
Larsen, Jack Lenor

Longue Vue
New Orleans, LA
Open Mon to Sat, 10am to
4.30pm, Sun, 1pm to 5pm
(closed public holidays)
Shipman, Ellen Biddle

Longwood Gardens
Pennsylvania, PA
Open daily, Nov until
Thanksgiving, 9am to 5pm. June
to Aug, Mon, Wed, Fri & Sun,
9am to 6pm. Apr & May, Sept to
Oct, 9am to 6pm. Thanksgiving
to 1 Jan, 9am to 9pm
Dupont, Pierre S

The Loring House
Los Angeles, CA
Private, not open to the public
Neutra, Richard

Lotusland
Santa Barbara, CA
Tours available by advance
booking. Reservation office
open weekdays, 9am to 12pm
Walska, Ganna

McIntyre Garden
Bay Area, CA
Private, not open to the public
Halprin, Lawrence

Meister Garden
Palm Beach, FL
Private, not open to the public
Sanchez, Jorge

Meyer Garden
Harbert, MI
Private, not open to the public
Oehme, Wolfgang & Van Sweden

Missouri Botanical Garden
Missouri, MO
Open from Memorial Day to
Labor Day, 9am to 8pm daily.
Rest of year, 9am to 5pm daily.
Raven, Peter

MOMA Sculpture Garden
New York, NY
Open Sat, Sun, Mon, Tues &
Thurs, 10.30am to 5.45pm. Fri,
10.30am to 8.15pm. (Closed
Wed, Thanksgiving & 25 Dec)
Johnson, Philip

Monticello
Thomas Jefferson Memorial
Foundation, Charlottesville, VA
Open Mar to Oct from 8am to 5
pm. Nov to Jan from 9am to
4.30pm
Jefferson, Thomas

Mount Auburn Cemetery
Cambridge, MA
Open daily, 8am to 5pm & 8am
to 7pm during summer
Bigelow, Jacob

Mount Vernon
Washington, DC
Open daily, Apr to Aug, 8am to
5pm. Mar, Sept & Oct, 9am to
5pm. Nov to Feb, 9am to 4pm
Washington, George

Naumkeag
Prospect Hill, Stockbridge, MA
Open Memorial Day to
Columbus Day, 10am to 5pm
Steele, Fletcher

Own garden at Mount Cuba
Wilmington, DE
Copeland, Mrs Pamela

Own Garden
Coconut Grove, FL
Private, not open to the public
Jungles, Raymond

Plastic garden
Northampton, MA
Private, not open to the public
Cardasis, Dean

Private Garden
Virginia
Private, not open to the public
Winkler, Tori

Rockefeller Center Roof garden
New York, NY
Private, not open to the public
Hancock, Ralph

The James Rose Center
Ridgewood, NJ
Open to the public
Rose, James

Schnabel House
Brentwood, CA
Private, not open to the public
Gehry, Frank

Show Case House
New York, NY
Garden vanished
Cox, Madison

Stan Hywet Garden
N. Portage Path, Akron, OH
Open end Jan to Mar, Tues to
Sat, 10am to 4pm & Sun 1pm to
4pm. Apr to beg of Jan daily,
9am to 6pm
Manning, Warren H

Stoney Hill Ranch
San Francisco, CA
Private, not open to the public
Lutsko, Ron

The Dow Gardens
Midland, MI
Open daily (not Thanksgiving, 25
Dec & 1 Jan), 10am to sunset
Dow, Alden B

The Gamble House
Westmoreland Place, Pasadena
Tours Thurs to Sun, 12pm to
4pm (last tour 3pm). Closed on
public holidays
Greene & Greene

The J Paul Getty Museum
Malibu, CA
Open Tues & Wed, 11am to 7pm.
Thurs & Fri, 11am to 9pm.
Weekends, 10am to 6pm. Closed
Mon & public holidays
Irwin, Robert

Valentine Garden
Santa Barbara, CA
Private, not open to the public
Greene, Isabelle

Villa Zapu
Napa Valley, CA
Private, not open to the public
Hargreaves, George

Vizcaya
Biscayne Bay, Miami, FL
Open daily, 9.30am to 4.30pm
Suarez, Diego

Waterland
CT
Private, not open to the public
Hall, Janis

Colonial Williamsburg
Williamsburg, VA
Open Jun to Aug
Shurcliff, Arthur

Garden opening times may vary
across the year and access may
be limited during restoration
work. It is advisable to check the
times and dates of opening in
advance of making travel
arrangements.

Acknowledgements

Consultant Editor Tim Richardson
Texts written by Barbara Abbs, David Askham, Iona Baird, Sonya Bjerman, Patrick Bowe, Kathryn Bradley-Hole, Anne de Charmant, Stuart Cooper, Jo Haire, Peter Hayden, Emma Mahony, Aulani Mulford, Toby Musgrave, Jennifer Potter, Charles Quest-Ritson, Tim Richardson, Barbara Segal, Barbara Simms

The publishers would like to thank Tim Richardson for his invaluable advice. Thanks also to Miroslava Benes, Patrick Bowe, Michel Conan, Brent Elliott, David Lambert, Leonard Mirin, Aulani Mulford, Toby Musgrave and Jess Walton for their vital contribution.

And Alan Fletcher for the jacket design.

The decorated letters (on the jacket) are from a collection of twenty-three alphabets engraved on wood c1820 for the London typefounder Louis John Pouchée. They were designed for use on contemporary posters. The original alphabets, published in *Ornamented Types* in 1990, are in the collection of the St Bride Printing Library, London. They are reproduced by permission of the St Bride Printing Library and I M Imprimit.

Photographic Acknowledgements

Barbara Abbs: 464; AKG, London (Bibliotheque nationale de France): 374; AKG, London (Coll Archiv f Kunst & Geschichte, Berlin): 408; AKG, London/Erich Lessing: 305; AKG, London/Erich Lessing (Musee des Beaux-Arts, Dijon): 1; AKG, London/Orsi Battaglini (Museo dell'Opera del Duomo, Florence): 234; Lynn Alstadt: 207; Heather Angel/Natural Visions: 311, 399, 437, 479, 498; Architektur-Bilderservice Kandula, M Krause: 121; The Art Archive: 13, 19, 60, 64, 67, 71, 120, 127, 142, 157, 194, 233, 293, 358, 372, 375, 382, 419, 447, 456; The Art Archive/Musee Condee, Chantilly: 77; The Art Archive/Parker Gallery, London: 459; The Art Archive/State Museum, Munich: 169, 502; Ashmolean Museum, Oxford: 84; David Askham: 82; Paul Barker/Country Life Picture Library: 209; Bastin & Evrard: 21, 37, 104, 107, 162, 265, 275, 314, 322; Bibliothèque nationale de France, Paris: 34, 68, 259, 278, 409; Bildarchiv-Monheim.de/ Florian Monheim: 30, 171, 200, 406, 407, 462, 484; Bildarchiv-Monheim.de/Roman von Goetz: 261; Bitter + Bredt Fotografie: 264; The British Library: 31, 70, 152, 274, 277, 310, 319, 352, 410, 436, 440; © Copyright The British Museum: 28, 128, 301, 367, 428; Luc Boegly/Archipress: 332; Clive Boursnell/Country Life Picture Library: 8, 9, 49, 89, 143, 168, 172, 190, 196, 213, 226, 386, 487, 492; British Architectural Library, RIBA, London: 59, 295, 435; Nicola Browne: 342, 350, 405; Nicola Browne/New Eden/IPC Syndication: 333; Richard Bryant/Arcaid: 12, 48, 344, 348; June Buck/Country Life Picture Library: 263; June Buck/New Eden/IPC Syndication: 416; Jonathan Buckley: 269; A E Bye: 85; Dean Cardasis: 92; Dixi Carrillo: 475; Fernando Caruncho Photo: Laurence Toussaint: 96; Frederick Charles: 389; Martin Charles: 27; Jean-Loup Charmet: 286, 468; Charles Cheshire: 20, 174, 335; Child Associates: 105; Photograph Becky Cohen: 218; © Peter Cook: 496; Joe Cornish/GPL: 371; Courtesy of Chollipo Arboretum: 306; Christie's: 260; Photography by Stephen Robson taken from *Irish Gardens* by Conran Octopus: 298, 329; The Country Life Picture Library: 14, 117, 225, 268, 280, 327, 351, 373, 451, 458, 493; Jerôme Darblay: 138; Karl Dietrich-Buhler/ www.elizabethwhiting.com: 368; Jacques Dirand/Inside/Interior Archive: 491; Ken Druse: 294; Edifice/Darley: 466; Edifice/Mayer: 454; Edifice/Sayer: 129, 366; English Heritage P.L.: 122; English Heritage P.L./(c)Skyscan Balloon Photography: 304; Franck Eustache/Archipress: 39; Photograph Julian Feary: 203; Richard Felber: 116, 235, 398; Helen Fickling/Interior Archive: 482; © Mark Fiennes: 175; Mark Fiennes/Country Life Picture Library: 446; Roger Foley: 400, 415; Courtesy of Fondation Maeght, Photo: Claude Germain: 308; Nigel Francis/GPL: 214; © Scott Frances/Esto: 230; John Frost/Country Life Picture Library: 258; Garden Matters: 132, 191, 106, 430, 480; Garden Matters/Jeremy Hoare: 499, 414; Garrett

Eckbo Collection (1990-1) Environmental Design Archives, University of California, Berkley: 135; Georg Gerster/Network Photographers: 323; Photograph Heidi Gildemeister from *Mediterranean Gardening, A Waterwise Approach*: 166; John Glover: 69; Graphische Sammlung Albertina, Wien: 210; Graphische Sammlung Albertina, Wien: 272; Photograph Antonio Guedes: 180; F Guiziou/Hemispheres: 217; Kathryn Gustafson: 183; Mick Hales: 46, 63, 228, 463, 478; Janis Hall: 187; Lars Hallen/Design Press: 4, 363; Harpur Garden Library/Jerry Harpur: 40, 41, 75, 86, 87, 103, 111, 115, 124, 144, 147, 148, 176, 204, 238, 250, 255, 281, 297, 338, 361, 376, 380, 397, 421, 465, 334, 469, 476; Harpur Garden Library/Marcus Harpur: 165, 402; Photograph David Hastilow: 420; Peter Hayden: 72, 98, 186, 237, 246, 257, 354, 425, 431, 442, 501; The work illustrated on page 316 is reproduced by permission of the Henry Moore Foundation; Photograph Michael Furze: 316; Marijke Heuff: 393; Marijke Heuff/GPL: 267; Juergen Holzenleuchter: 241; Photograph Peter Horn: 404; Anne Hyde/Country Life Picture Library: 45, 248, 346; Imagination Limited: 178; Tim Imrie-Tait/Country Life Picture Library: 461; Irish Architectural Archive; Photograph Patrick Rossmore+H438: 339; Cecilia Innes/Interior Archive: 500; Stephen Jerrom: 90; Andrea Jones/Garden Exposures Photo Library: 79; Photograph Nitin Kevalkar/Images of India/Dinodia Picture Agency: 102; H C Koningen: 444; Balthazar Korab: 125, 242, 288, 356, 360, 394; Courtesy of the Kroller-Muller Museum: 55; Kunsthistoriches Museum, Vienna: 146; Kurpfalzisches Museum, Stadt Heidelberg: 100; Michele Lamontagne: 26, 35, 141, 161, 245, 291, 326, 345, 412, 413, 424; The Landscape Institute/BCA: 118; Courtesy of Bernard Lassus: 254; Andrew Lawson: 10, 33, 42, 76, 97, 110, 173, 205, 206, 212, 243, 262, 273, 282, 285, 292, 302, 324, 331, 355, 357, 391, 417, 423, 432, 445, 467; Andrew Lawson/New Eden/IPC Syndication: 221; Leiden University Library: 216, 155; Jannes Linders: 164; Ron Lutsko, Jr: 279; From *The Persian Garden; Echoes of Paradise* by Mehdi Khansar, M Reza Moghtader and Minouch Yavari © Mage Publishers, Washington, DC: 29, 240; Marianne Majerus: 65, 95, 114, 227, 330, 433; MAP/Mise au Point – A Descat: 52; MAP/Mise au Point – Yann Monel: 74; Mary Evans Picture Library/Institution of Civil Engineers: 477; Mayer/Le Scanff: 32, 284, 457; John McCarthy/GPL: 179; Peter McGowan: 108; Nick Meers/GPL: 189; John Miller/GPL: 192, 151; Courtesy of the Missouri Botanical Garden (Photograph Mary Ann Kressig): 378; OPG Ltd/David Markson, from 'Gardens of Italy', by Penelope Hobhouse, published by Mitchell Beazley: 296, 340, 441, 455; Tony Morrison/South American Pictures: 153; Courtesy of Mount Auburn Cemetery: 54; Museo Archeologico, Naples/Roger-Viollet, Paris/Bridgeman Art Library: 364; *Téhéran de Jadis* (Geneva: edition Nagel, 1971): 145; © National Gallery, London: 369; The National Library of Wales: 229; The National Museum of Fine Art, Stockholm: 247, 253; National Museum in Warsaw: 429, 503; National Portrait Gallery, London: 232; NT/Wendy Aldiss+H488: 73; NT/Matthew Antrobus: 154; NT/Andrew Butler: 387, 177; NT/Neil Campbell-Sharp: 307; NT/Vera Collingwood: 123; NT/Eric Crichton: 395; NT/Chris Gallagher: 6; NT/Andrea Jones: 130; NT/Marianne Majerus: 22; NT/Nick Meers: 211; NT/David Noton: 15; NT/Stephen Robson: 270, 370; NT/Rupert Truman: 139; NT/Steven Wooster: 271; NTBG Photo: 140; NTPL: 379; Clive Nichols: 136, 156, 384, 390, 439; Clive Nichols (Designer: César Manrique): 289; Clive Nichols (Designer: Julie Toll): 452; Gunter Nitschke: 24, 184, 287, 218, 215; Christine Osborne Pictures: 16; Ivar Otruba: 341; Hugh Palmer: 5, 7, 42, 83, 91, 93, 112, 131, 158, 160, 239, 283, 426, 434, 486; Courtesy of the Parks Service Archive (Photograph Ines Miguens & Angela Copello): 443; Chris Parsons: 347; Michael Paul: 25; © RR Peabody, Architectural Images: 126; Ann & Bury Peerless Picture Library: 119, 220; Photograph Clay Perry (The Mediterranean Garden Society): 460; Beverly Pepper: 353; Roger Phillips: 80, 449, 450, 490; Peter Phipp/GPL: 38; Pukeiti Library: 113; Charles Quest-Ritson: 66, 199, 343, 359, 483; Quinta da Regaleira, Fundacao Cultursintra/Photo: Nuno Antunes, Sintra, Portugal: 313; Alex Ramsay: 62, 266, 290, 303, 362, 471; Alex Ramsay/Country Life Picture Library: 223, 453, 488;

Photograph © Mary Randlett: 185; John Riley/GPL: 497; Gary Rogers: 23, 88, 159, 224, 336, 317, 325; Gary Rogers (Courtesy of Chatsworth Trustees): 349; Gary Rogers/GPL: 58; © Photo RMN – D Arnaudet/G Blot: 193; Lorna Rose/Fotoflora: 198; © Lee Ross, Sky View Pictures: 337; The Royal Collection © 2000, Her Majesty Queen Elizabeth II: 101; Courtesy of The Royal Danish Academy of Fine Arts, School of Architecture: 427; Royal Horticultural Society, Lindley Library: 44, 219, 276, 489; Vivian Russell: 56, 61, 94, 222, 312, 321, 392, 474, 494, 495; Vivian Russell/Country Life Picture Library: 182; Derek St Romaine: 50; San Diego Historical Society Photograph Collection: 167; Scala, Florence: 377; Mark Schwartz: 202; Everett H Scott: 403; Security Pacific Collection/Los Angeles Public Library: 134; William Shaw/New Eden: 57; Shinkenchiku-sha: 17; Shodo Suzuki: 438; Sir Peter Smithers: 422; Staatliche Museen Kassel: 181; Alex Starkey/Country Life Picture Library: 231, 385; Ezra Stoller © Esto: 188; Tim Street-Porter: 43, 133, 163, 309, 328, 448, 481; Curtice Taylor/Conran Octopus: 252; Patrick Taylor: 18, 53, 201, 256, 383, 388, 418, 473; Nigel Temple/GPL: 170; Brigitte Thomas/GPL: 137, 149; The Tongaat-Hulett Group Limited: 401; Travel Ink/Abbie Enock: 236; Travel Ink/Ken Gibson: 208, 300; Photograph Isabelle Van Groeningen: 150; Victoria & Albert Museum, London/Bridgeman Art Library: 244; Courtesy of the V&A Picture Library: 81, 318, 320; Victoria Art Gallery: 51; Deidi von Schaewen: 251, 315, 396, 470, 472; Richard Waite: 195; Weald & Downland Open Air Museum: 249; Weidenfeld & Nicolson Ltd: 365; Photo: Heidrun Weiler: 197; Courtesy of the Wellesley College Library, Special Collections (Photograph Chris Gallagher): 411; Kim Wilkie: 485; Photograph © Woburn Abbey and Jarrold Publishing: 99; Charlotte Wood: 36; May Woods: 78, 109, 299